SCIENTISTS
and their
RESPONSIBILITIES

Scientists
and their
Responsibility

WILLIAM R. SHEA
and
BEAT SITTER
Editors

WP

Watson Publishing International
1989

First published in the United States of America
by Watson Publishing International
Post Office Box 493
Canton, MA 02021

© Watson Publishing International 1989

Library of Congress Cataloging-in-Publication Data

Scientists and their responsibilities / edited by Beat Sitter &
William R. Shea
    p. cm.
    ISBN 0-88135-054-0
    1. Science and ethics. I. Sitter, Beat, 1939- . II. Shea,
William R.
BJ57.S34 1989
174′.96—dc19

                                                        89-5249
                                                            CIP

Designed and Manufactured in the U.S.A.

Contents

Contents

Acknowledgement

The editors wish to thank most warmly the Conference of the Swiss Scientific Academies (Swiss Academy of Sciences, Swiss Academy of Humanities, Swiss Academy of Medical Sciences, Swiss Academy of Engineering Sciences) for providing the intellectual and financial support that made this book possible. They are also grateful to the International Union of History and Philosophy of Science, McGill University, and the Institute for Advanced Study Berlin for their generous assistance.

Foreword

As a nineteenth-century philosopher once said, when man acts on nature to change it, he changes himself in the process. One need not be a Marxist (for it was Karl Marx who made that statement) to agree that man's radical dependence on nature makes it imperative for him to respect the world from which he draws his sustenance and to which he belongs. But whereas, for millenia, man felt threatened by the unpredictability of nature, nature now has to fear the irresponsibility of man.

Bacon, Descartes, and the pioneers of the Scientific Revolution in the seventeenth century dreamt of improving the condition of mankind by harnessing the powers of nature. They saw themselves as the heralds of a new age in which man would be freed from the drudgery of hard work in a hostile environment. What they did not foresee was that the ruthless exploitation of natural resources could one day lead to an even harsher environment.

The march of science has been triumphant, but we run the risk of being crushed by our own Juggernaut. We have captured the energies of nature to the extent of concentrating them in metal cylinders whence, if simultaneously released, they would spell the instantaneous extinction of our species. Knowledge without wisdom, and power without self-discipline worry us more than nature in the raw. The problem, in this sense, is political and involves the whole of society. There is a growing feeling, however, that the class of people that were able to produce the means that led to our present dilemma should shoulder more of the responsibility for getting us out of it. Scientists are increasingly made accountable for the use and misuse of their discoveries. There is perhaps no great novelty in this for there have frequently been protests in the past against the real or imagined woes of scientific innovation (we need only recall the strictures of Blake and the Romantic poets). What is new is the willingness of scientists to question the myth of automatic progress associated with modern science.

The Enlightenment saw science as providing man with the means of controlling his own destiny, instead of leaving the development of the world to Providence. Indeed, man was to play Providence himself. But the script was never written, and man was left to improvise. This is one of the main problems that contributors to this book address from a variety of viewpoints. Attempts are made to analyze man's relation to nature, and to define a new code of ethics that would go beyond Kant's moral imperative and recognize rights that are not strictly human; strategies are deployed to limit the risks of uncon-

trolled research without stifling genuine intellectual curiosity; the role
and significance of technology is reassessed; and the complexity of
moral decision is recognized as well as the fact that no important policy
issue can be merely a technical problem of means.

Nowhere is the network of individual and collective responsibility
so intricate and so vital as in medicine and biology. What may at first
glance look like a strictly personal choice is often found to be embedded in a pervasive social, political, and cultural fabric in which it is
difficult to know where public opinion begins and private judgment
ends. Consider, for instance, a 42-year-old woman who goes to her
doctor because she believes she is pregnant. The physician knows that
such a person runs a risk of about one percent of giving birth to a child
with Down's syndrome. Were such a child to be born, not only would
he make large demands on medical resources, but he might not meet
with the mother's expectations of what constitutes a normal human
being. In our society the physician will recommend that the woman
seek amniocentesis to determine whether the fetus has the syndrome
and should be aborted. But does the state have the right to decrease
the cost of medical welfare by eliminating misfits before birth? What
rights have the parents to control the quality of the children they will
have? Would abortion be justified on the grounds of undesirable traits
such as wrong sex or eye color? Who is to draw the line and where?
Does the fetus have a right to life, and if so, when and under what
circumstances? Who is to determine what rights and obligations mean
in this context?

To raise these questions in a pluralistic society is to have done
little more than provide a forum for discussion, but, as several authors
in this volume show, it, nevertheless, is an essential step in developing
a responsible moral stance. In our moral economy good often conflicts
with good, and right with right. No matter what particular scientific
good or right we may wish to emphasize, it may be overridden in the
light of the possible consequences for other goods or rights. The
particular historical situation in which we find ourselves compels us to
reassess the impact of "good" discoveries on nature and society. The
stimulating essays in this book are an encouraging sign that scientists
are willing to do this, and that they feel increasingly responsible for
their work, its impact on nature, and its wider implications for mankind
as a whole.

Natural and Unnatural History: Biological Diversity and Genetic Engineering

ROBERT K. COLWELL

For more than 3,000 million years before the advent of human culture, the evolution of life on earth was shaped by a complex interplay between opposing forces: between molecular fidelity and genetic mutation; between genetic adaptation to local and immediate circumstances and the adaptive inertia of large populations constrained by development and phylogenetic history; between the origination of new species—of novel patterns of survival—and the extinction of established ones; and between the payoff of individual reproduction and the uncertainty of individual survival in the face of competition, predation, disease, and inimical physical environments. Human culture profoundly altered the scales of time and space within this causal network, through the intentional propagation of desirable genotypes of plants and animals (artificial selection), the indiscriminate shuffling of species of diverse geographical origin, the alteration of landscapes on a geological scale, and, now, the modification of the atmosphere on a global scale.

In Western culture, the traditional mythic view of nature as antagonist cast us always as either victims or heroes. This view still provides the stuff of romance for novels and filmscripts and draws readers to front page stories of the casualties and survivors of natural disasters and the first ascent of Nepalese peaks. But in reality, the current prevailing myth of industrial society is that we have achieved dominion over nature. We have stopped the flow of great rivers, changed the course of molten lava flows, and irrigated deserts. We have learned how to fly and to travel deep beneath the sea. We have found out how to control or even eliminate diseases. Meanwhile, however, we have begun to acknowledge the unintended consequences of human actions—the accumulation of toxic wastes, alteration of the atmosphere, permanent destruction of rain forest soils, extinction of entire faunas and floras. Perhaps in the long term, we may find ourselves the victims, not of nature as we found it, but of nature as we have remade it. In reality the scope of human intervention has placed us in a new role.

1

In this paper I will argue that the power of science and human technology has now completed the transformation of our relationship with nature not from antagonism to dominion, but rather from antagonism into the realm of ethical responsibility. I will explore some of the ethical issues raised by two contemporary confrontations between biological evolution and human technology. The first of these confrontations, between the homogenizing force of technology and the diversifying process of evolution, has produced an alarming acceleration in the loss of biological diversity.

The second, between the relatively slow, organismal processes of Darwinian selection and the powerful potential of genetic engineering to effect rapid genetic alteration by molecular techniques, presents not only immense opportunities but, perhaps, profound pitfalls as well. Finally, I will attempt to explore the scientific, technological, and ethical interactions between the issues of biological diversity and genetic engineering.

Biological Diversity

Biological diversity is hierarchical. Within a species or a local population, genetic diversity may be measured by the number and frequency of genetically different individuals (genotypes), or by the number and frequency of alternative variants (alleles) for a given gene or set of genes. Between populations of the same species, diversity is usually measured as "genetic distance," based on the degree of correspondence between allelic frequencies (Nei 1972; Lewontin 1972). At the level of species, diversity depends on the number and frequency of species within some specified universe, such as a local assemblage, a habitat type, a political unit, a trophic level (carnivores, herbivores, green plants, or decomposers), or a taxonomic unit (a genus, family, or higher taxon).

An extensive literature exists on appropriate means for combining in a single index the number of categories (genotypes, alleles, or species), often called "richness," with a measure of the evenness of their representation (May 1981). Explicitly hierarchical measures of diversity have also been developed (Pielou 1975; Patil and Taillie 1977). Because "diversity" has no precise objective meaning, however, the choice of how to "measure" it has become partly a matter of tradition, partly a function of mathematical or statistical elegance, and partly a matter of taste.

We still do not know how many living species there are (or were, say, 50 or 100 years ago) in most groups of microbes, plants, and animals—well-reasoned estimates for the total range from five to 30 million, of which only about 1.4 million are even described and named (Wilson 1988b). We know even less about genetic variation within species. These challenges, daunting though they are, are at least straightforward conceptually. In addition, however, evolutionary ecologists continue to struggle with questions that appear to have no conceptually easy answers (although many have been suggested) (Colwell 1979; Futuyma 1986; Wilson 1988a): Why did so many different species evolve? Why aren't there more? Why are tropical biotas more diverse than temperate ones? Why does so much genetic diversity exist within species? What controls the level of this genetic variability?

The Structure of Biological Diversity

From the biologist's point of view, the living world is a complex patchwork, a kind of fractal landscape of entities within entities within yet other entities, some distinct and discrete, others vague but no less real. Consider a flagellate protozoan that digests cellulose, living in the gut of a termite in a Central American rain forest. Looking inward from its external structure, we see organelles and membranes, then enzymes, proteins, nucleic acids, and molecular pathways, all organized, all repeated in the next and previous generations.

Looking outward from the body wall of that single protozoan, we find a whole fauna and flora of other coevolved microbial symbionts in the termite's gut. The digestive system of that single termite defines a subpopulation of each symbiont species living within it. The termite, in turn, is a tiny part of a colony, a cog in the machinery of a complicated social machine that turns cellulose into more termites, carbon dioxide, and excrement. Individual colonies of this species of termite in the forest interact in mating flights to define the breeding population. The termites are the principal food of tamanduas (New World anteaters) and are food for a host of other mammals, birds, and other insects. Each of these species has its own population structure, and each differs from the rest. At the level of the forest ecosystem, the carbon cycle would slow to a halt without termites.

In rain forests a few dozen or a few hundred miles away, many of the species composing the termite fauna and the species list for other insects, mammals, birds, and forest trees will differ, yet the story will be much the same. In rain forests of Africa and Asia the pattern is repeated, with intriguing distinctions in each place, arising from different histories, somewhat different selection pressures, and simply from historical accidents.

Speciation, Extinction, and Biological Diversity

Genetic variation is the raw material of evolution within species. Some of the new genetic variants (alleles) that arise continually through mutation are eliminated, and some are "fixed" by selection; some are maintained at an intermediate frequency by geographically and temporally varying selection, and some persist simply because there is strong selection neither for nor against them (Futuyma 1986).

The event of speciation, which we now usually envision as the splitting off of a new population from a parent population through reproductive isolation, permits the preservation of gene combinations adaptive to new circumstances and prevents them from being diluted or swamped by genes that were more appropriate in the ancestral context. Genetically, the incipient species is now free to go its own way under the guidance of natural selection. Although some new species apparently diverge rapidly from the ancestral stock, while others change little over long periods of time, speciation must be viewed as the principal mechanism fostering biological diversity. Because each successive episode of speciation in a lineage produces a new branch that itself may speciate, the process has the potential for producing an exponential increase in genetic diversity over time (Templeton 1981). Here, I speak of the origin of new species by the process biologists call *cladogenesis*—the branching of a lineage. This process is entirely distinct from *anagenesis*—a continuous succession of forms replacing one another without branching, *within* a single line—which many people envision when they hear the word "evolution." Figure 1, see pages 6-7, makes the distinction (along with other points to be discussed later).

The brake on this process, of course, is extinction—a perfectly natural phenomenon that has already removed more species from the face of the earth than the number that now exists, quite apart from any human influence. Superimposed on a long, slow increase, the total number of species has fluctuated over geological time scales—sometimes dramatically, when rare episodes of mass extinction interrupted long-term patterns (Raup and Sepkoski 1982; Raup 1988).

These patterns of *net change* in number of species, however, must be clearly distinguished from species *turnover*—the rate at which existing species are replaced by new ones through the combined effects of speciation (cladogenesis) and extinction. In geological history, turnover has nearly always been far greater than the rate of *net* change in species diversity—with the possible exception of periods of mass extinction. In other words, speciation and extinction rates have been roughly balanced over vast stretches of time (Stanley 1985).

The current alarm over real and potential extinctions caused by human activities must be seen in this context. From an historical point of view, the problem is not that extinctions are occurring, but that the expected *rates* of extinction, for most groups of organisms, are so high that the net change in species diversity, over an exceedingly short period of time, has vastly overwhelmed normal turnover rates (Myers 1979; Ehrlich and Ehrlich 1981; Wilson 1988a).

Economic Value of Species

Why does extinction matter? Human beings, after all, are just as much the product of organic evolution as any other species. If our success means the demise of an extra few million species over the next hundred years, and if extinction—even mass extinction—is a natural phenomenon, then why be concerned? One way of collecting the answers to these questions is to pose another: In what sense do species have value? The many answers that have been given to this question by biologists, philosophers, and economists (e.g., Ehrenfeld 1976; Myers 1979; Caufield 1984; Callicott 1986; Norton 1986, 1987; D. H. Regan 1986; Sober 1986; Randall 1986; Wilson 1988a) may be divided into arguments based on the *instrumental value* of species and their diversity—which I have chosen to subdivide into arguments of *economic value* and of *scientific value*—or on the *intrinsic value* of species. This section treats arguments for the preservation of species based on economic arguments.

Civilization was founded on the adaptive "inventions" of other species. The domestication of food plants simply improved on the existing storage tissues of plants—seed endosperm, roots, tubers. With fiber plants, we simply improved and extracted the support tissues (linen, sisal, hemp, jute) or fibers involved in seed dispersal (cotton, kapok). The effective principles of drug plants, spices, herbs, and natural dyes rely heavily on compounds evolved by plants in protective response to the depredations of insects, mites, and diseases (Simpson and Connor-Ogorzaly 1986). The use of domesticated animals for work or transport simply exploits their existing capacity for locomotion; use of their pelts, hair, or feathers for clothing mimics the role these tissues serve for their original owners; human use of animal milk exploits one of the fundamental evolutionary inventions of the mammals, and our use of honey an analogous invention of bees. "Domesticated" microorganisms make possible alcoholic beverages, leavened bread, cheese, yoghurt, and soy sauce, as well as industrial fermentation processes and many drugs.

In the past century, scientific breeders of plants and animals have reached back into the evolutionary history of domesticated species to recapture useful genetic traits from their wild relatives—sometimes from the true ancestral species, sometimes from evolutionary cousins. Resistance to disease, pests, or stress, nutrient balance, growth form, and fruit shape or quality have been developed in crops through hybridization with wild relatives, followed by complex breeding programs to combine desired traits in a single strain (Goodman, et al.)

Figure 1

A hypothetical phylogenetic tree illustrating modes of evolutionary change and the "conduit effect." *Modes of change:* Species are labeled with lower-case letters. Species *a* is the ancestor of all the others. Because *a* persists to the present unchanged, it would be an example of a "living fossil." Its most ancient descendant, species *b,* on the other hand, changes sufficiently over time through anagenetic evolution that it is eventually recognized as a "new" species *c* (although biologically *b* and *c* are one and the same species). With the further exception of the anagenetic origin of *e* from *d,* all other species in the figure arise by cladogenesis, or branching. In some cases (e.g., the origin of *d* from *a* or *f* from *e*), speciation is abrupt, with little or no gene flow between the new species and its ancestor. In many other cases (shown by stippling), gene flow continues for a long time before finally slowing to zero. Extinct species *x* stands for the multitude of species no longer extant. In a real tree covering a long span of geological time, there would be about as many extinct species as extant ones. *The conduit effect:* species *f* is a domesticated relative of wild ancestor *g.* Like many real domesticates, *f* can still cross with its wild ancestor. Transgenic organism *f′* is created by inserting into *f* a useful gene from species *k,* a member of the group of species (*i, a, k,* and *j*) long isolated genetically from the group to which *f* and *g* belong (*h, e, f,* and *g*). If the transgenic species *f′* is now inadvertently permitted to cross with wild ancestor *g,* the gene from *k* will have followed the biotechnological "conduit," shown by the heavy arrows, between lineages long isolated in nature.

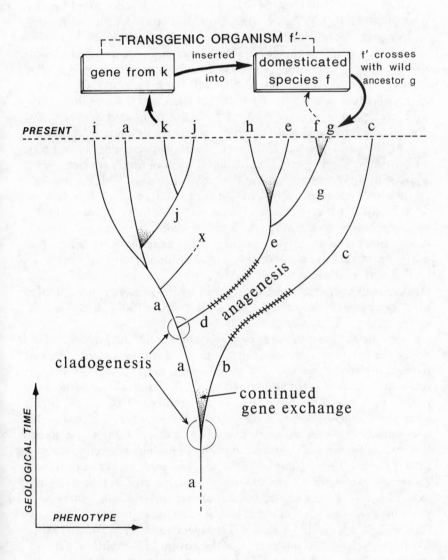

1987; Iltes 1988). Improved breeds of domesticated animals have sometimes been developed in the same way. But crosses between species more distantly related than members of closely related genera were impossible for higher organisms until this decade, when the molecular and cellular techniques of biotechnology became feasible.

The economic argument for the preservation of wild relatives of key domesticated species has always been clear enough: they represent a potential source of commercially useful genetic material—"germplasm" (Witt 1985; Williams 1988). But what about the multitude of wild species—the vast majority of both the plant and animal kingdoms—that have no domesticated or commercially valuable relatives?

At least two general classes of economic arguments have been advanced for the preservation of these "unexploited" species. First, some of these species, in themselves, may prove to be of direct *commodity value* in the human enterprise (Norton 1988), or alternatively may be valued for their potential commercial usefulness at some future time (an aspect of *option value*) (Randall 1988). The second class of economic valuations rests on attempts to estimate the *noncommodity* (or *nonmarket* or *amenity*) value of species, or of biodiversity, as measured by the degree to which people consider the economic value of places, services, or experiences to be increased by the presence or existence of species or by biodiversity (Kellert 1986; Norton 1987, 1988; Randall 1988).

Few would base the argument for the commodity value of currently unexploited species on the prospect that important, totally new food plants are likely to be discovered among wild species—although many known food plant species with excellent nutritional value and promising ecological characteristics are underutilized (NAS 1975; Vietmeyer 1986). Prospects for the discovery of novel biochemical compounds, however, have motivated several well-funded, intensive commercial surveys of pharmacologically or biologically active natural plant products for possible use as drugs, biocides, and industrial biochemicals. Some of these efforts focus on plants used in folk medicine in traditional cultures, whereas others are simply "shotgun" surveys of plant material collected more or less at random, especially in tropical forests (Lewis and Elvin-Lewis 1977; Myers 1983; Farnsworth 1988). There are indications, however, that the advent of computer-designed molecules and the techniques of genetic engineering have already begun to displace these efforts in the pharmaceutical industry (Ehrenfeld 1988).

The latest economic argument for the preservation of as-yet-unexploited species on the basis of their potential commodity value arises from the growing capability to transfer genetic traits among completely unrelated species—both microorganisms and higher organisms—by molecular and cellular techniques in the laboratory. The first genetically engineered plant to be approved for field-testing in the United States (approved in 1985) was a herbicide-tolerant tobacco strain constructed using genetic material from a bacterium (a *Salmonella* species that had become resistant to the herbicide), controlled by additional genetic sequences from a mammal (sheep) and another plant (soybean) unrelated to tobacco, all inserted using a second species of bacterium *(Agrobacterium)* (Comai, et al. 1983).

Gene technologies clearly stand among the ultimate beneficiaries of the vast library of tried-and-true evolutionary inventions of the millions of species in natural ecosystems, and thus have an interest in keeping these libraries in viable condition (Goodman, et al. 1987; Janzen 1987; Witt 1985). The difficulties in transferring any but the simplest traits to an unrelated species are currently formidable, but there is every reason to expect that many difficulties will be overcome in time. Already, traits requiring the coordinated action of more than one gene have been successfully transferred between species (Wong, et al. 1988). Twenty years ago, most biologists would have declared impossible—or at least extraordinarily unlikely—what has already been accomplished today.

Economic arguments for the preservation of species (or of biodiversity or habitat) based on *noncommodity* values rely on measures of the degree to which the value of a place is enhanced by the presence, or decreased by the loss, of particular species (or of a habitat). The value differential may be estimated from actual prices, for example, by comparing the sale price of architecturally equivalent homes at increasing distances from a nature preserve. Alternatively, survey methods may be used to assess how much citizens would, in principle, be willing to pay to keep a species or habitat, or how much they would be willing to accept as compensation for its loss. In theory, such surveys could be used to estimate the value people in one part of the world place on the very *existence* of a particular species or group of species elsewhere, which they may never have seen and will never see, outside photographs or films (for example, the blue whale) (Randall 1988).

Any biologist who has watched people visiting a botanical garden or zoo or who has looked through popular nature magazines will attest to the highly biased and uneven level of public interest in different groups of species. For example, of the most recent 26 photographic covers of the American popular magazine *Natural History* that feature nonhuman animals, 65 percent are of mammals (4,000 species, only 0.04 percent of described animal species), including a disproportionate number of primates and bears. Another 20 percent feature birds (9,040 species, only 0.09 percent of described animal species). In contrast, only two covers (8 percent) are of insects (73 percent of described animal species and a much larger percentage of undescribed species), and one cover (4 percent) shows a noninsect invertebrate (23 percent of described animal species). (Figures for numbers of described species of living organisms are from Wilson 1988a.)

Some of the special appeal of mammals and birds rests on our morphological and sensory affinity with them (Kellert 1986), and some rests on familiarity alone (puffins—*Fratercula*—were unknown to most nonornithologists a decade ago, but are now familiar to the layperson and are doubtless, thus, more highly valued). Some of the appeal even rests on the vagaries of fads and fashion. In the past ten years, penguins, bears, and most recently, cows have become "fad animals" in the United States (and perhaps in Europe as well). While some of these historical shifts in public appreciation of nonhuman species may be evidence of an increasing appreciation of nature and a greater public commitment to conservation (an example of Norton's [1987] "transformational value" of species), they form at best an unsteady platform for public policy.

However important noncommodity valuation may be in particular cases (e.g., Stoll and Johnson 1984), an exclusively species-by-species approach to the noncommodity economic valuation of biodiversity is not only impractical and liable to underestimate consistently the "contributory value" of species to ecosystem function (Norton 1987), but cannot be expected to lead to the even-handed protection of food webs and ecosystems—the key to long-term preservation. The strategy of protecting entire habitats and ecosystems by focusing popular appeals on familiar and evocative species, as exemplified by the campaign to save the giant panda, strikes many biologists as manipulative and somewhat disingenuous—but, nonetheless, most accept it as a means to an end. If the "amenity value" and "existence value" of natural entities can be increased by educational efforts (Randall 1986), then the best program for the promotion of even-handed species preservation from this strictly economic viewpoint calls not only for an attempt to get people to love tapeworms, termites, and toads, but also for a full-scale effort to give biodiversity *itself* the same cachet as pandas and penguins.

Scientific Value of Species

To evolutionary and ecological biologists, the prospect of an accelerating rate of extinction means the increasing loss of the best clues we have to the process and history of organic evolution and its ecological context. In principle, the value of scientific knowledge in ecology and evolutionary biology can be accommodated within the rubric of economic value, as discussed in the previous section. Indeed, significant commodity value may arise in biotechnology from evolutionary studies of various kinds, and the noncommodity (instrumental) value of scientific understanding to scientists and lay naturalists might be evaluated in some way. Because of my sense that economics fails to capture the essence of the scientific value of species and of biodiversity, however, I have chosen to take a separate approach to these topics.

To argue for the preservation of all species on the basis of their scientific value may seem excessive, given the practical impossibility of ever studying all living species, even superficially. Since not all species will become extinct, could not future biologists learn the same principles from the careful study of those that survive? This retort has some merit, but there are strong counterarguments.

First, the species that survive the next 100 years, assuming no increased efforts at preservation, will by no means be a representative sample of what now exists (Vermeij 1986; Norton 1986). We are just beginning the intensive study of species that are naturally and stably rare and of how they are able to persist while remaining rare (Rabinowitz 1981). Yet these rare species are almost always among the first to become extinct when habitat is destroyed or alien species are allowed to invade and take hold. Moreover, certain habitat types, such as temperate prairie and tropical seasonal forest, are especially suited to agriculture; thus, their biotas are even more likely to fall victim to extinction than those of other habitats. Finally, certain categories of species, such as large carnivores, or land birds on oceanic islands, are especially vulnerable to extinction (Diamond and Case 1986; Vitousek 1988).

Second, the study of ongoing evolutionary processes in natural ecosystems, which has become increasingly possible with the development of new molecular and statistical techniques, loses much of its meaning under conditions of rapid habitat alteration or changes in the biota (e.g., Janzen and Martin 1982). A large but unknown proportion of the adaptations of all species are adaptive responses to other species (Futuyma and Slatkin 1983). When the composition of biological communities changes radically, these adaptations are difficult or impossible to interpret in the context of inevitably altered ecological relationships among surviving species.

Realistically, of course, it is already too late to preserve some species already on their way to extinction and even too late to set aside certain rarer kinds of habitat. Biologists of the next century will indeed have to make do with what is left, whatever we do in the meantime. The question then becomes how best to direct our efforts to maximize the long-term scientific return. At present, the consensus favors concentrating funds and efforts on the preservation of tracts or transects of relatively intact representative ecosystems, with minimal loss of species, and in some cases, to attempt restoration of rare habitat types and their associated biotas (Soulé 1986; Allen 1988; Wilson 1988a).

Intrinsic Value of Species

The contention that all species have some entirely noninstrumental *intrinsic value* is at once the most fundamental and most difficult of the three justifications for species preservation that I have chosen to distinguish (Ehrenfeld 1976, 1988; Godfrey-Smith 1980; Callicott 1986; Sober 1986; D. H. Regan 1986; Taylor 1986). Here philosophical, biological, and logical pitfalls lie ready to capture the naive and the sophisticated alike, and I shall doubtless fall into one or another of them—at least by someone's criteria. As a nonphilosopher, I fear to tread where I know neither the subtle connotations of terms, nor the catalogue of accepted wisdom or the lists of acknowledged heresies. Nonetheless, having agreed to provide my "autonomous reflections" as a biologist, I will attempt to make clear a view of intrinsic value that I believe reflects the thinking of many or perhaps most biologists (at least organismal and population biologists) who have considered the matter.

For the purposes of this essay, we shall have to assume that we know what a "species" is and what an "individual organism" is; we will conceive of a species as composed of individual organisms that are genetically very similar due to recent common descent. In fact, scientific disputes abound concerning the proper definition of "species," and additional difficulties arise in defining "individual" for clonal species (Futuyma 1986)—quite apart from philosophical meanings of the term.

In my experience, biologists involved in evolutionary or ecological work consider it self-evident that all species have "scientific value," in the sense that I have used that term. Coming from a biologist, however, the argument that species ought to be preserved for their scientific value may appear narrowly self-serving. In any case, this argument only weakly and unevenly supports the principle that *all* species should be preserved because some are bound to be of more scientific interest than others, even in the long term. Consequently, biologists involved in political and economic struggles over the preservation of species (and their habitats) characteristically overlay their scientific justifications with a heavy veneer of economic arguments—in the broad sense discussed above.

In fact, however, both the scientific and (especially) the economic arguments are often tactical window dressing—a conscious attempt to appeal to the presumed values of the world of politics and business. Biologists certainly believe that scientific and economic arguments are valid and important, but a more fundamental motivation underlies them. When cornered, most organismal and population biologists, and some others as well, will admit to a strongly felt intuition that *every* nonhuman species has value *in itself* (Godfrey-Smith 1980; Callicott 1986; Collar 1986).

This intrinsic value (or "inherent worth" [Sitter 1989]) of a species is independent of whether the species is vital to human welfare, at one extreme, or an imminent threat to human welfare, at the other— although in the latter case (e.g., smallpox or the AIDS virus), we may choose to pursue the extinction of the species *despite* its intrinsic value. In its purest sense, this intuition ascribes intrinsic value even to species that are completely irrelevant to human welfare, of only redundant interest scientifically, and of negligible ecological significance.

Leaving aside theological justifications for the designation or instillation of intrinsic value in earthly entities, the term must inescapably imply human attribution of noninstrumental value. My basic claim here is empirical—that biologists behave, speak (usually off the record), and sometimes write in ways that reveal that they attribute intrinsic value to species. There are good reasons to believe that many nonbiologists, including the peoples of developing countries (Collar 1986), share this appreciation of nonhuman species for their own sake. I will also try to explore the meaning and ramifications of intrinsic value for species and other natural entities, but whether these efforts succeed or fail in philosophical and logical terms, the empirical claim remains.

For a scientist, the real problem arises in attempting to explain—within the supposedly objective, value-free bounds of traditional scientific discourse—the conviction that species have intrinsic value. (Furger [1989] discusses the presuppositions implied by such a conviction.) Philosophers have additional difficulties with the issue (Callicott 1986; Sober 1986; D. H. Regan 1986; Norton 1987), and mainstream economists attempt to avoid it by putting a price on the intrinsic value of species in the form of "existence value" (Randall 1986). Scientists involved in public policy issues tremble at the thought that anyone might accuse them of sentimental—or worse, mystical—motivations, which are easily imputed to anyone claiming that, in principle, an unnamed species of tropical soil mite merits the same protection as the Bald Eagle. Nonetheless, in recent years the argument for species preservation on grounds of intrinsic value has become marginally respectable among biologists (e.g., Ehrlich and Ehrlich 1981), if still considered somewhat defiant of the traditional terms of scientific discourse.

Individual value, individual rights, and appropriate care. In practice, what does it mean to say that something has "intrinsic value"? Although, as we shall see, the argument leads inevitably into conflicts of value, there is no escape from the consideration of human life as a starting point in any such discussion (e.g., Jonas 1984; Callicott 1986). The example leads us into an important detour concerning the value of individuals, en route to a full consideration of the intrinsic value of species. In pursuing this course, I disagree with Norton (1987), who prefers to discard this line of argument because of the conflicts that arise. These difficulties, however, represent issues of genuine substance not only in the philosophy of conservation, but in public policy.

Our prevailing ethical system regards *individual* human beings as having intrinsic value, in the sense that ugly and handsome ones, old and young ones (though the starting point is in dispute), rich and poor ones, good and evil ones *share some irreducible, nonquantitative claim to our respect,* however abstract and grudging granting that respect may sometimes be. The moral claim each human being holds on our respect is usually stated in terms of a short list of "human rights" or "moral rights." (Callicott [1986] discusses the intriguing history of the concept of "rights," in this sense.) The conceptualization of human intrinsic value as conferring rights on individual human beings immediately confronts us with a key question: Does the attribution of intrinsic value to an entity *necessarily* confer some appropriate set of "inalienable rights" upon that entity? I shall argue that the answer is "no."

Certainly modern society has come to acknowledge the intrinsic value of human individuals by recognizing their moral rights. The fact that intrinsic value has been expressed in the language of human "rights" may be a consequence of the recognition, first, of human "wrongs"—through appreciation of the particular forms of injustice suffered by slaves, by children or women in the workplace, by homosexuals, by the disabled, and so on. By analogy, many of those who seek an end to the human exploitation of animals protest it as a violation of the "rights" of higher animals (e.g., T. Regan 1983; Sapontzis 1988); others seek to promote conservation by decrying the uncontested extinction of species or the willful destruction of ecosystems as a violation of the "rights" of species and ecosystems (e.g., Ehrlich and Ehrlich 1981). The power and appeal of rights language as a means to achieve such a variety of ends arises in part because of the connotation that rights are absolute, nonnegotiable, inalienable. The argument then inevitably centers on who or what has such rights, and why. Utilitarian philosophers (e.g., Sapontzis 1988) insist that, in addition to humans, only individual animals capable of pleasure and pain have rights—usually interpreted to mean the higher vertebrate animals, despite the actual impossibility of knowing where to draw the line. (Although few biologists would deny that nonhuman vertebrate animals *do* share sensations homologous with what we call pleasure and pain, equally few would be certain that other animals, including insects and other invertebrates, do *not* feel pleasure and pain.)

What does it mean to say that a nonhuman animal has rights? Consider a domesticated rabbit, raised in a laboratory cage for the production of antibodies. The assertion that the rabbit has the right to wholesome food, shelter, and protection from inhumane treatment is not entirely parallel with the same assertion for a human prisoner in a penitentiary, even if we assume that both are incarcerated for legitimate cause. Where humans are concerned, ethical philosophers consider it a settled issue that reciprocity is not an appropriate criterion for the assignment of rights (e.g., Norton 1987). A severely mentally disabled person or a comatose invalid nonetheless has the same rights as anyone else. Likewise, it is argued, the rabbit in the cage has the same basic rights as a human (food, shelter, freedom from pain and exploitation), even though the rabbit, unlike (in principle) the prisoner, cannot then or ever reciprocate in granting its caretakers the same set rights that they are morally bound to provide. Philosophical heresy or not, the fact that a nonhuman animal cannot, *even in principle,* assume the duties and reciprocate the rights accorded it by its human caretaker casts the rights of animals in a different light from the rights of human beings. To the mentally disabled person and the invalid we may say, "There but for the grace of God, go I"—but it is no accident that none of us was born a rabbit.

Of course, I fully agree that we are morally bound to treat the rabbit humanely. But I suggest that our commitment to its humane treatment should arise not from a recognition of the rabbit's "rights," but from an informed judgment of its capacity for suffering, knowledge of its particular physiological and behavioral needs, and a recognition that our involvement in its current condition (including the domestication of the breed and the birth, confinement, and experimental use of this individual) creates a *responsibility* for proper husbandry and protection from suffering.

Whether or not we choose to express this obligation in terms of rights, at the core of our responsibility to the experimental rabbit lies a recognition (or intuition) of its *intrinsic value as a living being.* If the individual human life represents some kind of paradigm for the concept of intrinsic value, I suggest that individual *non*human lives (of all species) have an analogous claim to intrinsic value, although I shall argue in the next section that the character of moral actions arising from that claim will vary greatly. (I shall also attempt to give a definition of *intrinsic value* without reference to this analogy.) Further, I shall suggest that when we attribute intrinsic value to an entity, we simultaneously create a responsibility, an obligation, to preserve and protect that entity through *appropriate care*—a key idea in this essay.

How do we recognize intrinsic value?.   I think many biologists attribute some intrinsic value to every individual living organism, not through some vitalist esteem for any mystical "life force," but simply because all living things amaze us by their *complexity* and by a quality that might best be called *improbability*—the quality of detail and organization that produces astonishment when one looks into a drop of pond water with a microscope to discover it teeming with exquisitely formed microscopic protists, crustaceans, and algae; that overwhelms the diver on a coral reef; that transfixes the ornithologist watching a weaver bird building a nest, or a bower bird its bower. In Sitter's (1989) words, the intrinsic value of living beings arises in part from their quality as "centers of relations independent of human will." My best stab at a definition of intrinsic value (to meet the challenge of Norton 1987) is thus: "The worth inherent in any complex and improbable natural entity that represents a center of relations independent of human will."

Further, I suggest that the same qualities of complexity and improbability lead us to regard nonbiological individual entities, even, in some cases, "naturalized" human artifacts, as having value in themselves. Two personal anecdotes may help to make this point. I used to be a "caver"—an avid explorer of limestone caves. Serious speliologists, both amateurs and professionals, have a rigid code in regard to the treatment of cave formations. Nothing—not even the smallest and ugliest stalactite in the most inaccessible part of the most obscure cave—may be broken, defaced, or removed from a cave. Any visitor to a cave who violates this code is referred to as a *"vandal,"* which my dictionary (*Random House Unabridged,* second edition) defines as "a person who willfully or ignorantly destroys or mars something beautiful or valuable." Although many cave formations also have positive or negative aesthetic value—arguably a form of instrumental value (Callicott 1986, footnote 15; Norton 1987)—to the caver, all have intrinsic value.

In my second example, a story of actual vandalism makes the point that objects made by human hands may also have intrinsic value. Some years ago, my parents acquired an isolated parcel of land in a remote part of the Rocky Mountains of Colorado. The place was once a thriving gold camp, but by the time they bought it, only a few ramshackle cabins remained, though some were still relatively intact, with decomposing furniture inside. In one of these cabins, was a broken-down player piano—one of those masterpieces of nineteenth-century mechanical invention that played music by itself, guided by perforated paper rolls. The cabinet of the piano had long ago been irretrievably damaged by the elements and the "player" mechanism no longer operated—hauling the piano out of the place would have cost far more than the little it was still worth. But some of the keys still worked, and we used to improvise a few barroom riffs to resurrect the spirits of the gold rush whenever we visited the place.

I shall never forget the day we arrived to find that the cabin—which had not even had a door since we had known it—had been mercilessly vandalized by someone with an ax. The piano had been hacked to pieces, the keyboard smashed, strings severed, legs crippled. Our outrage had little or nothing to do with the loss of whatever small monetary, aesthetic, or even historic value the piano may have had; it was truly an instrument of little instrumental value. Rather, the sight of its intricate workings spilled on the floor—the product of hundreds of hours of care by unknown craftsmen's hands—seemed more like murder and mutilation than simple vandalism. We had valued the piano for itself—for its incongruous complexity in a place of disorder and decay, the improbability of its survival, and its role as a center of relations between physical materials and the intangibility of music, between past and present.

Scales of intrinsic value and appropriate care.   Like cave formations and the player piano, living things—however lowly—are complex products of a complicated process acting improbably through long spaces of time, surviving against great odds, and bearing the marks of their history. Every individual organism is the product of the astonishing capacity of living things to arise, from a handful of molecules, as reflections of their ancestors. Yet there is no escaping the fact that we do not attribute the same level of intrinsic value to all individual organisms, as measured by accepted (or expected) levels of responsibility for individual, nonhuman organisms of different kinds.

Consider again the laboratory rabbit in its cage. I would feel an analogous moral responsibility, though in different measure, for the appropriate care of an experimental colony of ants in a plastic shoebox in my laboratory (food, water, and nesting material) and for a potted palm in the living room of my home (light, water, and nutrients). That we have a moral responsibility to care for each of them reflects their equality as entities of intrinsic value (cf. Sitter 1989). That appropriate care differs for rabbits, ants, and potted palms reflects their biological differences. Moreover, it would certainly be more reprehensible to allow a rabbit to starve to death than to kill a potted palm by negligence—because of the neural capacity of the rabbit for pain.

The intrinsic value of individual organisms must surely scale with biological complexity, sensory capacity, size, age, and generation time, or we are led into absurdities—even the most ardent proponent of animal rights probably swats mosquitoes in the bedroom and surely has no concern for the bacteria he or she kills with the toothbrush or digests with the yoghurt. As a biologist, I feel no ethical responsibility, though I certainly might have some scientific responsibility, for the appropriate care of bacteria growing in a petri dish. At the other extreme, keeping anthropoid apes in captivity—however humanely accomplished—requires in my opinion extremely strong justification and entails a moral responsibility not too distinct from the adoption of children (see Goodall 1987). Even within species, age and size matter. To my mind, the felling of a thousand-year-old, giant redwood tree requires far more justification than the destruction of a seedling of the same species—which is equally an individual.

Replaceability. To argue for an ill-defined "sliding scale" of intrinsic value for individual organisms is not logically or philosophically tidy, but I see no alternative. I believe there may be, however, a unifying rationale, which at last will lead us directly to consideration of the intrinsic value of species. The unifying concept is *replaceability.*

The degree to which we find intrinsic value in individual organisms seems to be a direct function of how quickly and easily they may be replaced—or replace themselves, on a human scale of time and energy. A field mouse, because of its shorter generation time and smaller size, may be considered of less intrinsic value than a black bear, though both are replaceable. To an entomologist, collecting 100 individual (sterile) worker ants requires far less justification than collecting the single queen of a large colony. To a botanist, collecting leaves and flowers of a perennial plant for study is almost always preferred to collecting the entire plant. Although the single redwood seedling and the thousand-year-old mother tree are both genetic individuals of the same species, the seedling is easily replaced, but the tree is not. Likewise, most people would probably mourn the death of a human child more than that of a newborn infant and of a newborn more than a miscarried ten-week embryo.

Intrinsic value and the replaceability of species. By extension of the "human life" paradigm for individual intrinsic value, the human species as a whole presumably has some intrinsic value—at least as the sum of its parts. Intermediate between individuals and the human species at large, I would argue that human cultures have intrinsic value. The degree to which human beings tend to cling to their traditions, even if immersed in a different culture and sometimes at great sacrifice, seems to me to testify to a belief in the intrinsic value of cultural systems, although it would be difficult to separate the instrumental value of cultural conformity. Unfortunately, the idea of reciprocal rights of different cultures is far from established. Despite the often positive instrumental value of Western technological culture (such as sanitation practices and health care), the transformation and destruction of traditional non-Western cultures strikes many of us as akin to vandalism—the "willful or ignorant destruction of something valuable"—and irreplaceable.

A species or biological population, as a group of individuals, is conceptually closer to a cultural group than to an individual (in the usual sense of the word). Is a species—our own included—only as intrinsically valuable as the sum of its intrinsically valuable parts? I think the answer is quite obviously "no," both for *Homo sapiens* and for every other species. I doubt that anyone would argue that our *species* will be twice as valuable when there are twice as many of us as there are now, assuming we get that far. Likewise, if only 1,000 humans survived a nuclear holocaust, the species as a whole would be no less valuable to its members than at present.

A species has intrinsic value because it is essentially irreplaceable. Biologists value species, in themselves, more than any individual organism within a species, for the simple reason that the loss of a species means the loss not only of every living individual member of that species, but of every future member as well—along with any daughter species that might otherwise have arisen. Nonetheless, a sliding scale clearly governs the level of concern and effort that both conservation biologists and the public are willing to expend to discover and save species in danger of extinction (e.g., Kellert 1986; Mittermeier 1988).

Once again, the notion of "replaceability" unites many of the criteria for interpreting the relative intrinsic value of species (apart from any additional scientific or economic value). In the same way that one individual may seem an adequate replacement for another of the same species, despite the actual differences between them, one of two or more extremely similar species will be valued less than a highly distinct species that stands out from the pack—or one of great geological age (D. H. Regan 1986). Thus the single endemic sundew species in a threatened temperate bog may be perceived as having greater intrinsic value than one of three very similar species of moss endemic to the same bog. In terms of replaceability of distinctive genetic information, this approach has some justification.

Population welfare versus individual welfare. In assessing the impact on biological diversity of habitat loss, pollution, scientific collection of organisms, or the introduction of geographically exotic or engineered organisms, biologists are generally concerned not with the survival of individual organisms, but with the welfare of populations (Vermeij 1986). For example, the Juan Fernandez Firecrown, an extremely distinctive and scientifically intriguing species of hummingbird, is found only on a small island (Isla Robinson Crusoe) 660 kilometers off the coast of Chile. Having survived 300 years of deforestation and the introduction to the island of rats, dogs, cats, pigs, sheep, goats, and a host of continental plants, the hummingbird is now severely threatened by the coati—a common, omnivorous, highly intelligent, and charming tropical relative of the raccoon, which was intentionally introduced to the island in the 1930s. To save the Juan Fernandez Firecrown, it will be necessary to control or—preferably—eliminate coatis from the island (Colwell in press).

This example brings clearly into focus the clear potential for conflict between the valuation of individual organisms and the valuation of species (Norton [1987] discusses other examples at length.) No program has yet been mounted to eliminate or control the coatis on Isla Robinson Crusoe, but one may well imagine that the trapping, shooting, or poisoning of the coatis will be difficult to justify to those who place the welfare of individual animals (especially intelligent and beguiling mammals) above that of populations of endangered species.

This inherent conflict in values yields to no easy solution. The principle of replaceability argues for the preservation of species in preference to the preservation of individuals, when those ends are in conflict—but the argument carries weight only if one believes that individuals are more easily replaced than species. People whose chief contact with animals has been with personal pets—who are often unique individuals to us—tend to have great difficulty with the idea of replaceability. The owner of a beloved parakeet may find it impossible to agree with the biologist who argues for the humane sacrifice, required for a carefully planned scientific study, of a hundred chickadees from a wild population of 100,000 (Greene and Losos 1988). It is here that the course of action based on the human rights model for the treatment of individual animals differs most from the alternative view that we are responsible for the appropriate care, not only of individuals, but of species.

Aesthetic value as a form of intrinsic value. Among the lay public, one may guess at the prevailing societal criteria for organismal aesthetics (Kellert 1986) by noting the large amateur following for particular subgroups within higher taxa—chimpanzees, orangutans, and gorillas (but not tree shrews); parrots and hummingbirds (but not flycatchers or swifts); felids, canids, and bears (but not hyenas); mollusk shells (but not their inhabitants and not squid); butterflies and bright-colored moths (but not dull-colored groups of moths); palms, bromeliads, orchids, and "wildflowers" (but not grasses, not spurges). Clearly, bright colors, accessible behavior, and human-like qualities hold great appeal.

The aesthetic value of species is treated by some writers (e.g., Sober 1986) as essentially identical with intrinsic value and by others (e.g., Callicott 1986, footnote 15; Randall 1986; Norton 1987) as a

form of purely instrumental value that can in principle be accommodated in a strictly economic framework. In the case of natural entities, I prefer to view the appreciation of aesthetic value as an imperfect
form of intrinsic valuation.

The trained naturalist's sense of "beauty" grows steadily broader
with intimate understanding of the lives of organisms (Ehrlich and
Ehrlich 1981)—the sense is not different in character, but only in
compass, from the appreciation an orchid fancier has for orchid blossoms. To me, there is no more beauty in the colors and behavior of
a hummingbird than in the structure and natural history of the microscopic mites that feed and breed in hummingbird-pollinated flowers
and ride from plant to plant on the bills of the hummingbirds (Colwell
1985, 1986a, 1986b)—but then, I have studied both mites and hummingbirds for 20 years. I know biologists who find as much beauty in
toads and salamanders, beetles, slugs, snapping-shrimp, spiders,
algae, and roadside weeds as the amateur lepidopterist finds in a blue
morpho butterfly.

In theory, I am comfortable with the idea that, for a given species,
a certain level of aesthetic value overlies a certain level of intrinsic
value. The level of aesthetic value depends on the objective morphological and behavioral attributes of the species in relation to the subjective cultural and intellectual attributes of the observer. The existence of intrinsic value, as discussed previously, arises from the
complexity and improbability of species; the level of intrinsic value
depends on features of the species that can be summarized by the
concept of its replaceability. In practice, I see no way to distinguish
clearly between the broad aesthetic value of a species and its intrinsic
value. The intuition that species have intrinsic value may arise from
aesthetic appreciation—aesthetic value is a means of perceiving intrinsic value, but is not identical with it.

Intrinsic Value of Ecological Systems

In a manner precisely analogous to perception of the intrinsic
value of species, ecologists and evolutionary biologists (and others)
perceive intrinsic value in coevolved ecological systems at many levels.
The levels range from interactions between species, to biological communities and their interdependencies, to local ecosystems and their
involvement with the physical world of material cycling and energy
flow, and, finally, to the global ecosystem itself. Each of the entities in
this vague hierarchy represents a center of relations independent of

human will and partakes of the qualities of complexity and improbability that I have argued are key criteria for intrinsic valuation. Thus, each invites us—I would say, requires us—to assume responsibility for its appropriate care.

And again, the level of effort we are willing to expend in such care will depend on the degree of distinctness—the replaceability of each system. The new Braulio Carrillo National Park in Costa Rica, for example, represents the last elevational transect of undisturbed tropical forest in Mesoamerica connecting lowland rainforest (50 meters elevation) with subalpine cloud forest (2,600 meters) (Pringle 1988). This magnificent mountain landscape faithfully represents the fast-disappearing Central American wet forest, where the descendants of ancient South American and North American biotas were brought together by the most recent appearance of the Isthmus, enriched with additional endemic elements from repeated episodes of isolation when the seas were high (Janzen 1983; Rich and Rich 1983).

Because it is, unfortunately, now unique and thus irreplaceable, Braulio Carrillo requires us to accept responsibility for its appropriate care—in fundamentally the same way that we are called to care for a unique and endangered species, or a captive chimpanzee in a critical program of health research. The appropriate care of Braulio Carrillo requires careful planning for the wise use of its resources in public education and enjoyment, biological tourism, and scientific research; protection from illegal woodcutting, hunting, fishing, mining, and squatters; and a long-term financial endowment to ensure the future of the park.

Just as the intrinsic value of a species is not simply the summation of the intrinsic value of the individuals that constitute it, the intrinsic value of a coevolved system of species interactions (for example) is no simple function of the value of its components. For example, the astonishingly intricate and wondrously varied form and function of flowers and their coevolved pollinators seem to me worthy in themselves of our valuation, quite aside from their economic value in agriculture or their usefulness to biologists in elucidating the process of natural selection. Moreover, some of the most fascinating cases involve such remarkable features as floral odors that mimic rotting flesh to attract pollinating flies, or prosthetic female insect genitalia that induce pseudocopulation (and pollination) by over-eager male insects—hardly the stuff of garden club aesthetics.

It must be admitted that, at the level of ecosystems—especially of the global ecosystem—separating intrinsic value from instrumental value becomes increasingly difficult. One cannot lightly dismiss the economic value of the regenerative capacity of forests, savannas, and the plankton of the ocean, nor the power of living systems to cleanse and balance the components of the atmosphere, running waters, or the soil (Ehrlich and Ehrlich 1981; Norton 1987).

Genetic Engineering

In March 1987, Clara H. Bauer of Pepin County, Wisconsin, wrote to the the U.S. Environmental Protection Agency, which invites public comment on proposed field tests of genetically engineered organisms:

> I am concerned about . . . the Massachusetts Company that is planning to test genetically engineered alfalfa bacteria in . . . Pepin County. . . . I am very much against making little Pepin County a guinea pig so to speak. As you know nuclear power plants were to be safe but now we have had several mishaps. . . . What I want to ask you people is what do you think of this project? Is it all safe? Or are there dangers of contamination? If you think it is safe, I would ask that you draw up a guarantee to that extent . . . and I want all you people of the EPA to sign your names. This may sound stupid but you see I feel that as long as a guarantee is readily issued with our clocks, radios, microwave ovens, cars and most implements manufactured . . . it would be no more than fair for the EPA to render the same guarantee to us the few in Pepin County. . . . I think you people had better do much soul searching before you commit us here in Pepin County to a possible devastation which can not be repaired. I may be an old woman of 74 but I certainly would hate to leave an incorrectable detriment to my children, grand children, and great grandchildren and all future generations. . . .

Mrs. Bauer's letter candidly and poignantly presents some of the key ethical questions raised by any novel technology that affects the environment—in this case, genetic engineering. The questions are not new. They have confronted us before, with chemicals, pollution, and nuclear hazards: What are the moral and social responsibilities of individual scientists, corporate enterprise, and government agencies? What are the rights of individuals, especially those who live near testing or industrial sites? When risks are conjectural, how do we set rational limits on what experiments scientists should be permitted to do? Who should assess the risks? How should potential risks (especially long-term ones) be weighed against potential benefits (especially short-term ones)? What are our responsibilities to unborn generations?

Without minimizing the significance of other aspects of these far-reaching questions, I want to focus on the relationship between biotechnology and biological diversity. (By *biotechnology* or *genetic engineering,* I shall mean molecular and cellular gene technology.) I hope to be able to clarify some of the complex ethical questions that arise from this relationship through the application of ideas developed in the first part of this essay.

Ecological and Evolutionary Risks of Biotechnology

Although virtually no controversy has arisen over the use of genetically engineered microbes in the confinement of industrial settings, biologists continue to disagree about the possible hazards of testing and using genetically engineered microorganisms, plants, and animals in the open environment. Although no one contests the fact that risks are highly case specific and that different kinds of organisms require different levels of oversight, overall assessments still range from confident reassurance to serious concern (Brill 1985a; 1985b; Colwell, et al. 1985, 1987; Davis 1987a; Fiksel and Covello 1988; Sharples 1983, 1987; NAS 1987; Colwell 1988b; Hodgson and Sugden 1988).

In the absence of actual data on engineered organisms in the environment, the diversity of expert opinion reflects a lack of consensus about which historical parallels are most relevant. Ecologists have insisted that there are lessons to be learned from the record of long-term environmental effects of nonnative organisms introduced by humans on every continent and island; the rapid evolution of pests, weeds, and pathogens; and the complex interactions and unexpected consequences of poorly considered environmental decisions in the past (Colwell, et al. 1985; Regal 1986, 1988; Sharples 1987; Colwell 1988a; F. Gould 1988a, 1988b; Simonsen and Levin 1988; Williamson 1988).

Meanwhile, molecular biologists tend to cite the impressive 15-year safety record for recombinant DNA research in the laboratory, the long list of critical contributions to human welfare made by traditional plant and animal breeding, and the safe use of nonengineered microbes in agriculture for many decades (Brill 1985a, 1985b, 1988; Davis 1987a, 1987b). In fact, each of these histories bears on the issue of risk, but to different degrees for different kinds of engineered organisms.

The great majority of genetically engineered organisms will surely prove environmentally innocuous. Some will likely help to solve press-ing ecological problems, such as the cleanup of toxic chemicals (Rob-erts 1987) or the replacement of chemical insecticides with environ-mentally safer microbial ones. The potential for significant risk, however, not only mandates scientific vigilance, but raises ethical problems. As Mrs. Bauer of Pepin County clearly comprehends, the release of an engineered organism (especially a microorganism) that causes some unanticipated harm will likely have effects beyond the point of application in both time and space. However difficult toxic waste dumps may be to clean up, the successful integration of a nox-ious organism, or simply a nuisance organism, into either a managed or natural ecosystem is probably permanent and not likely to respect property lines. As we have learned with toxic wastes, moreover, assign-ing legal liability after the fact is little help—either economically (given bankruptcy protection) or ecologically.

Managed ecosystems.   In managed ecosystems (agriculture, silvicul-ture), many of the potential hazards presented by genetically engi-neered organisms have counterparts in traditional technologies. Among other examples, the risk of crop failure in genetic monocul-tures as a result of the rapid evolution of newly virulent strains of plant pathogens (Doyle 1985) would be neither more nor less for a geneti-cally engineered crop variety than for a variety produced by traditional crop breeding techniques. Likewise, the risk of inadvertently exacer-bating a problem with an insect pest by the application of a pesticide that also eliminates natural enemies of the pest, a common problem with chemical pesticides, is no less likely with broad-spectrum engi-neered microbial pesticides. (In fact, many biotechnology companies are now attempting to broaden the host range of existing microbial pesticides to increase market share [Betz, et al. 1986].)

Other potential risks of engineered organisms in managed ecosys-tems are less familiar. For example, many commercial research groups are beginning to test crop plants that have been engineered to express pesticidal biochemicals in their tissues. The most common and feasible transformation at present involves inserting into the plant genome a toxin gene from the ecologically safe EPA-approved microbial pesti-cide, the bacterium *Bacillus thuringiensis* ("B.t."). To date, insect resist-ance to B.t. has been rare because the bacterium itself does not survive long after application. If expressed continuously by plants, however, especially if widely cultivated, rapid evolution of resistance in pest insects is a virtual certainty. The evolution of resistance would mean the loss of a rare and precious resource: an effective, safe, narrow-spectrum microbial insecticide (Colwell 1988a; F. Gould 1988a, 1988b).

One of the principal concerns, from both ecological and evolutionary viewpoints, is the potential role of engineered organisms as "conduits" for the movement of genes between distantly related or completely unrelated organisms. Although a variety of natural mechanisms are known for the passage of genetic information *between* species, ranging from hybridization (by ordinary sexual reproduction) to much rarer and more arcane mechanisms (Miller 1988), the techniques of genetic engineering permit the routine movement of genes among genera, phyla, and even kingdoms. Once released in the environment, these novel genetic constructions may in some cases move with ease into the gene pools of close relatives of the engineered organism— which thus acts as a "conduit" between lineages previously isolated genetically for eons.

Figure 1 outlines this phenomenon. For example, genes now being inserted in crop genomes confer herbicide-tolerance, resistance to insect pests or plant pathogens, or tolerance for extreme physical factors such a saline soil, drought, or frost. Most crops have closely related, wild, weedy relatives, some of which are serious economic pests in field crops (e.g., wild relatives of rice in rice paddies, Johnson grass in sorghum). If the engineered crop hybridizes with a weedy relative, the weed will likely acquire whatever competitive advantage the crop obtained from the novel genes and become an even more serious pest (Colwell, et al. 1985; Ellstrand 1988). The same scenario applies to engineered animals, such as fish. The ecological effect is likely to be a release of the unintended recipient from one or another regulating factor that previously helped to hold its population in check. The evolutionary effect is the passage of genetic information from one evolutionary lineage to another by human intervention.

Natural ecosystems. In natural ecosystems, the issues of risk and responsibility are more profound. The hazards of greatest long-term concern arise from the "conduit" effect just outlined. Like managed ecosystems, natural ecosystems also support wild relatives of engineered organisms that may be altered (and may profit, to the detriment of other species) through genetic crossing with engineered relatives. Without appropriate oversight now, given the rapidly accelerating pace of research in biotechnology, our descendants may see the present period as the beginning of a massive reshuffling, under human direction, of the "evolutionary inventions" that 3,000 million years of natural selection have produced in the earth's biota.

Perhaps less likely than genetic "conduit" effects, but still possible, is the actual invasion of an unmanaged, relatively intact natural ecosystem by an engineered species itself. Suppose a game fish is genetically engineered to grow 50 percent larger than its ancestors, through the insertion of an extra gene for the production of growth hormone—a project already feasible and underway (*Sports Illustrated,* March 7, 1988; *New York Times,* June 1, 1988, 1). Releasing the fish in waters even where there are no nonengineered wild counterparts still poses serious ecological hazards.

Because larger fish eat larger prey, changes may be expected in the structure and composition of the prey community (through altered patterns of predation), as well as the composition and possibly the stability of the predator fauna (though altered patterns of competition) (Moyle 1986; Moyle, et al. 1986). In addition, ecosystem effects such as changes in aquatic primary productivity can result from such faunal shifts.

Suppose the engineered fish were (foolishly) introduced into a lake that historically had only smaller fish, with the intention of providing a better source of food for local people or simply under pressure from sport anglers. If the result were anything like the story of the (nonengineered) Nile Perch *(Lates niloticus)* in Lake Victoria, the result could be disastrous and far-reaching (Hughes 1986). Since its first introduction into the lake in 1960, as a food source for the local populace, this large, predatory fish has led to the extinction of literally hundreds of endemic fish species in the lake—which once had one of the richest fish faunas in the world. The Nile perch now feeds on small shrimp and its own young.

But the effects of this introduction do not stop at the lakeshore. Fish have always been a staple food of people living near the lake. The Nile perch is edible, but requires a higher cooking temperature than the native fish did to render its fat. The consequent effects of intensified firewood cutting on local forests may eventually prove a greater economic and ecological disaster than the loss of the native fish fauna.

The lesson is that any intentional introductions, whether of engineered or other organisms, must be assessed beforehand with the utmost care. In the case of the perch, for instance, none of the facts that would have been required to have predicted this scenario would have been hard to discover—apparently there simply was no effort to do so. Never previously exposed to any predator as large as the Nile perch, the local fish species were defenseless—a fact easily determined by experiments with captive fish. Likewise, prior determination of the cooking temperature of Nile perch vs. native fish would have been a simple matter.

Alteration of Natural Entities as Devaluation

Logically and historically, to argue in principle against any alteration of the genetics of a species through human intervention is absurd. As discussed earlier, civilization was built on such interventions—intentional and unintentional. Even opposing in principle the crossing of species that never hybridize in nature falls flat as an argument against change from accepted practice—most of the tomatoes and strawberries we buy in the market carry genes for several genetic traits (e.g., disease resistance or texture) from wild relatives continents away from the farmer's field, introduced into crop germ lines by classical plant breeding techniques (Goodman, et al. 1987). Orchid fanciers' prize blossoms are frequently hybrid products of hand pollination—not just between orchid species, but between orchid genera that never cross in nature, because of the rigid fidelity of co-evolved pollinators (van der Pijl and Dodson 1966). And, of course, there are many other examples, from mules to tangelos.

Nonetheless, the spirit of the plea to move slowly—or not at all—with the genetic engineering of organisms is easily heard as an appeal based on the intrinsic value of species (leaving aside, for now, issues of human health, animal welfare, and environmental safety). But here we have a new element to add to the concept of intrinsic value developed earlier—the notion that *the intrinsic value of a species is diminished by its genetic alteration through human intervention.* I strongly suspect that most biologists would agree with this proposition—*but only for human intervention in the genetics of "natural" (wild) species living in reasonably "natural" ecosystems* (S. J. Gould 1985). All the examples cited (tomatoes, strawberries, orchids, mules) apply to domesticated—or at least captive—species under direct human management.

I struggle to define this devaluation in a way that carries it beyond what must appear a sentimental commitment to shielding "natural" species and other natural biological entities from human intervention. It is akin to the idea of "vandalism"—that to mar a thing of (intrinsic) value, especially when it is not even of our own making, is wrong. Certainly, neither I nor other biologists of my acquaintance would intervene in any natural process of change in a natural ecosystem—

except perhaps in a reversible experimental manner. Most of us would even choose not to stop a natural extinction, if we could somehow be certain that human intervention were not at fault—any more than we would try to stop a wolf in a wilderness area from inflicting a painful and terrifying death on a rabbit whose relatives we make great efforts to treat humanely in the laboratory.

In the case of the engineered fish discussed in the previous section, for example, I suspect that few biologists would object at all to the laboratory study of the novel genotype—even if its parents were taken from the wild (assuming their removal did not significantly harm the natural population). It is the release of the fish into a natural ecosystem that would bring on the objections and create the moral dilemma. Together with any resultant genetic, physical, and behavioral changes in the wild fish species itself, there would very likely be indirect effects on the biological community and possibly at the level of the entire aquatic ecosystem, as outlined above. (Any additional indirect effects on human welfare, as with the Nile perch, are separate issues.) These adverse effects amount to a human intervention in the structure, function, and relations between species—an intervention that devalues them.

Natural and Unnatural History

Some have argued that the distinction between domesticated organisms and wild species and between natural and actively managed ecosystems is philosophically vacuous. Sober (1986, italics his), for example, writes:

> . . . to the degree that "natural" means anything biologically, it means very little ethically. And, conversely, to the degree that "natural" is understood as a normative concept, it has very little to do with biology. . . . *If we are part of nature, then everything we do is part of nature, and is natural in that primary sense.* When we domesticate organisms and bring them into a state of dependence on us, this is simply an example of one species exerting a selection pressure on another. If one calls this "unnatural," one might just as well say the same of parasitism or symbiosis. . . .

Sober is right to point out the contradictory and muddled use of the idea of *natural.* Nonetheless, the distinction he finds philosophically untenable is of fundamental importance to conservation biologists and environmentalists and lies at the heart of my ethical concerns about genetic engineering. I believe that a coherent restatement of the distinctions between "natural" and domesticated species and between "natural" and managed ecosystems can be developed that is both biologically and ethically coherent.

Domestication and component communities. Neolithic human groups were still "part of nature" in the same sense that wild primate species, toucans, or leaf-cutter ants are today. A few human tribal societies are still "part of nature" in this sense. In New World rain forests, leaf-cutting ants (*Atta* species) feed on the hyphae of a fungus that they cultivate in underground "gardens" on leaf and flower material harvested and chewed by the ants. The fungus is a highly domesticated species. Just as cultivated maize can no longer reproduce without human assistance, the fungus in the ant nest cannot reproduce without the attention of the leaf-cutting ants (Stevens 1983). Moreover, just as Mayan society depended critically on the cultivation of maize, the ants depend critically on their fungus. On a larger scale, just as Mayan agriculture partially transformed the landscape and ecology of Mesoamerica, the immense nests and kilometers of trails of leaf-cutting ants mold the microtopography of the forest floor. Moreover, their activities are surprisingly significant in the regulation of production and the cycling of nutrients in New World rain forests (Lugo, et al. 1973).

The most important parallel for the present discussion, however, concerns the place of the Maya and the place of the leaf-cutting ants in their relations with other species. One the most consistent characteristics of coevolved assemblages of wild species ("biological communities") is their organization into smaller sets of strongly interacting species, with much weaker or infrequent interactions between these sets. This property has been recognized in empirical studies in the form of "component communities" (Root 1973), ecological "guilds" (Root 1967; Inger and Colwell 1977), "coevolved food-webs" (Gilbert 1977), and "food subwebs" (Pimm 1982). Theoretical work (Gardner and Ashby 1970, May 1981) suggests that such ecologically based "substructuring" of communities permits more species to coexist in dynamic equilibrium, for a given level of stability in the resource supply. The popular "wisdom" that "in nature, everything affects everything" must be qualified by adding a large variance term.

Neolithic human societies, like leaf-cutting ants and other "natural" species, each lived within a "component community" of strong interactions with a relatively few species, weak interactions with many others, but no significant interaction at all with most of the species in the landscapes they inhabited. In the case of the Maya, the strongest interactions were with their domesticates (maize, beans, squash, and some lesser crops), whose welfare they favored, and no doubt with agricultural weeds and crop pests, whose welfare they did not. Weaker interactions included the plant and animal species whose habitat Mayan agriculture usurped or which they hunted or gathered in the wild state.

Likewise, in addition to the strong interaction leaf-cutting ants have with their fungal domesticate, the ants strongly affect certain tree species they favor as substrate for the fungal gardens. The ants also interact strongly with a whole zoo of inquilines and parasites that live with them. Their interactions with the myriad other inhabitants of the rain forest are much weaker or nonexistent. Many, probably most, species in natural communities are far more "insulated" within the causal web of species interactions than are leaf-cutting ants, which I chose intentionally for their key role in New World tropical forests.

Resolution of the ethical dilemma. On the scale of geological time, modern technological/industrial society emerged abruptly from within the component biological communities of Neolithic human cultures—the intervening millennia (in the Old World) or mere centuries (in the New) were but the blink of an eye in evolutionary terms. Yet that emergence has had the effect of transforming thousands upon thousands of weak interactions between human and wild species into strong ones and creating new interactions where none had existed.

It is precisely this proliferation of strong interactions with other species, this explosive expansion of our sphere of ecological influence that is "unnatural" about contemporary human society. Yes, we are part of nature, in that our actions profoundly affect other natural entities; yes, also in the sense that we are governed by the same physico-chemical laws as any other species. But we have come to be unique among the species of the earth in having largely escaped (though perhaps only temporarily) from the governance of forces within our component biological community.

Surely, the conviction that "natural species" and intact habitats and ecosystems ought to be protected from any human intervention that changes their character, relations, or stability arises chiefly from the consequences of that historic escape and the interventions it has made possible. The record of our past interventions can be seen in deforested, degraded, desertified, destabilized, eroded, filled, flooded, paved, and polluted landscapes and waters the world over. On a more abstract scale, I believe it is fair to say that, without exception, the net effect of the human enterprise on the hierarchical patterning of biological diversity has been toward elimination of boundaries, consolidation of levels, and genetic homogenization—in addition to the actual extinction of species and the loss of ecosystems.

In reply to Sober's (1986) critique of the distinction between the "natural" world and the human world, I would begin by acknowledging that the word *natural* is a poor one for the job that I (and many others) have given it—to represent what is left of the pretechnological/preindustrial biological and geological world and its products and workings. *Natural* is a poor word because of the normative baggage it carries, which confounds the clear laying on of reasoned values—*unnatural* is even worse in this regard. Nonetheless, I hope I have made clear in what sense I consider the human position ecologically and evolutionarily "unnatural," and why the characteristics of that position further threaten the "natural" world.

Our moral responsibility for the appropriate care of *individual* organisms in agriculture, zoos, or gardens does not depend on whether they are wild or domesticated in origin, although the nature of that care will, of course, vary greatly from species to species because of biological differences. (We also have the responsibility to find out what those differences are and to design care and use protocols that respect them.)

I contend, however, that the role of domesticated *species* as co-evolved members of our ancestral component community (most domestications began millennia ago) places them in a biologically and ethically distinct class from "wild" species. As with wild species, we have the responsibility to preserve the genetic variation that exists in domesticated species. But unlike wild species, I see no ethical justification for any bar on genetic alteration of domesticates, by whatever technical means. Molecular and cellular techniques permit "wider crosses" and more rapid and precise alterations, but there is no logical distinction between the use of these techniques of "applied evolution" and the techniques of classical plant and animal breeding—by which our domesticates arose in the first place.

The intentional or accidental genetic alteration of wild species, however, represents a devaluation—a degradation of their intrinsic value, as discussed in the first part of this essay. Thus, perhaps, the first, most efficient, and most economical rule for the appropriate care of "natural" (wild) species, of the individuals that compose them, and of "natural" ecosystems is to intervene as little as possible, unless the intervention will help the species or the ecosystem recover from some previous human intervention (Wilson 1988b, Part 8).

At the same time, there is no contradiction in acknowledging that feeding, housing, and clothing the human species depends on simplified and managed ecosystems—in agriculture, forestry, and fisheries. In those environments, we intervene regularly and will need to continue to do so, not only in the genetics of domesticated species, but in ecosystem functions such as nutrient cycling. The challenge is to limit our interventions to the places they are required.

Conclusion

Some have suggested that the tools of biotechnology will actually add to the pool of biological diversity, by creating new genetic combinations not possible or not likely in nature, or even by the addition of completely synthetic genes to the products of evolution. In whatever measure this ambitious prediction comes true, the implication that laboratory art can truly imitate life betrays a narrowly reductionist view of adaptation and evolution. The diversity of organisms in nature arises from the interplay of genetic variation with the exigencies of life in environments teeming with other organisms and buffeted by shifting physical factors. The adaptive "inventions" of natural selection seem far more likely to be of use in creating new products and (I hope) solving serious ecological problems than any biological feature produced *de novo*. After all, nature has a head start on us of many hundreds of millions of years and maintains 100 million natural laboratories operating 24 hours a day.

Although important, an appreciation of the remarkable past record and future economic potential of natural species as a source of adaptive inventions is not enough. The inherent *complexity and improbability* of individual organisms, species, habitats, and ecosystems as *centers of relations independent of human will* merit our recognition of their *intrinsic value* and thus make us responsible for their *appropriate care*. The concept of *replaceability* provides a guide for choosing among alternative actions and for negotiating conflicts between the valuation of entities at different levels of the biological hierarchy.

Of course, we are a product of nature and occasionally still its victims. But the dismal history of our past effects on biological diversity, together with our need to use much of the earth's surface to feed ourselves, argues that the most effective—and probably the most efficient—way to preserve what we can of the diverse products of evolution is truly to set them aside, in as grand and integral a way as we can afford. I believe we must come to see ourselves no longer as equal participants in natural history, but as responsible for its nurture through appropriate care.

Acknowledgments

I am grateful to all the participants in the conference for their comments, their keen interest, and for greatly expanding my own perspective on ethics and science. This work was supported by a grant from the U. S. National Science Foundation (BSR86-04929).

References Cited

Allen, W. H. 1988. Biocultural restoration of a tropical forest. *BioScience* 38:156–161.

Betz, F., M. Levin, and M. Rogul. 1986. Safety aspects of genetically engineered microbial pesticides. *Recombinant DNA Technical Bulletin* 6:135–141.

Brill, W. J. 1985a. Safety concerns and genetic engineering in agriculture. *Science* 227:-381–384.

Brill, W. J. 1985b. Genetic engineering in agriculture. *Science* 229:115–118.

Brill, W. J. 1988. Why engineered organisms are safe. *Issues in Science and Technology*, Spring issue.

Callicott, J. B. 1986. On the intrinsic value of nonhuman species. Pp. 138–172 in Norton, B. G., ed., *The Preservation of Species*. Princeton, Princeton University Press.

Caufield, C. 1984. *In the Rainforest: Report from a Strange, Beautiful, and Imperiled World.* Chicago, University of Chicago Press.

Collar, N. J. 1986. Species are a measure of man's freedom: reflections after writing a Red Data Book on African birds. *Oryx* 20:15–19.

Colwell, R. K. 1979. Toward a unified approach to the study of species diversity. Pp. 75–91 in Grassle, J. F., et al., eds. *Ecological diversity in theory and practice*. Fairland, Maryland, International Cooperative Publishing House.

Colwell, R. K. 1985. Stowaways on the Hummingbird Express. *Natural History* 94(7): 56–63.

Colwell, R. K. 1986a. Community biology and sexual selection: Lessons from hummingbird flower mites. Pp. 406–424 in Case, T. J. and J. Diamond, eds. *Ecological Communities.* Harper and Row.

Colwell, R. K. 1986b. Population structure and sexual selection for host fidelity in the speciation of hummingbird flower mites. Pp. 475–495 in Karlin, S., and E. Nevo, eds. *Evolutionary Processes and Theory.* Academic Press.

Colwell, R. K. 1988a. Ecology and biotechnology: expectations and outliers. Pp. 163–180 in Fiksel, J. and Vincent T. Covello, eds., *Risk Analysis Approaches for Environmental Releases of Genetically Engineered Organisms.* NATO Advanced Research Science Institutes Series, Volume F. Berlin, Springer-Verlag.

Colwell, R. K. 1988b. Academy's gene report: another reading. (Roundtable feature). *Bioscience* 38:421–423.

Colwell, R. K. In press. Hummingbirds of the Juan Fernandez Islands: natural history, evolution and population status. *Ibis.*

Colwell, R. K., et al. 1985. Genetic engineering in agriculture. *Science* 229:111–112.

Colwell, R. K., et al. 1987. Response to the Office of Science and Technology Policy Notice "Coordinated Framework for Regulation of Biotechnology." *Bulletin of the Ecological Society of America* 68:16–23.

Comai, L., et al. 1983. An altered aroA gene product confers resistance to the herbicide glyphosate. *Science* 221:370–371.

Davis, B. D. 1987a. Bacterial domestication: underlying assumptions. *Science* 235:1329–1335.

Davis, B. D. 1987b. Is deliberate introduction ecologically any more threatening than accidental release? *Genetic Engineering News,* October issue.

Diamond, J., and T. J. Case. 1986. Overview: introductions, extinctions, exterminations, and invasions. Pp. 65–79 in Diamond, J., and T. J. Case, eds., *Community Ecology.* New York, Harper and Row.

Doyle, Jack. 1985. *Altered Harvest: Agriculture, Genetics, and the Fate of the World's Food Supply.* New York, Viking.

Ehrenfeld, D. 1976. The conservation of non-resources. *American Scientist* 64.

Ehrenfeld, D. 1988. Why put a value on biodiversity? Pp. 212–216 in Wilson, E. O., ed., *BioDiversity.* Washington, D. C., National Academy Press.

Ehrlich, P. R., and A. Ehrlich. 1981. *Extinction: The Causes and Consequences of the Disappearance of Species.* New York, Random House.

Ellstrand, N. C. 1988. Pollen as a vehicle for the escape of engineered genes? Pp. S30–S32 in Hodgson, J. and A. M. Sugden, eds., *Planned release of Genetically Engineered Organisms (Trends in Biotechnology/Trends in Ecology and Evolution Special Publication).* Cambridge, Elsevier Publications.

Farnsworth, N. R. 1988. Screening plants for new medicines. Pp. 83–97 in Wilson, E. O., ed., *BioDiversity.* Washington, D. C., National Academy Press.

Fiksel, V., and T. Covello, eds. 1988. *Risk Analysis Approaches for Environmental Releases of Genetically Engineered Organisms.* NATO Advanced Research Science Institutes Series, Volume F. Berlin, Springer-Verlag.

Furger, F. 1989. Moral obligation in biological research: a theological perspective. In Shea, W. R. and B. Sitter, eds., *Scientists and Their Responsiblity* Canton, Mass., Watson Publishing International.

Futuyma, D. J. 1986. *Evolutionary Biology,* 2nd ed. Sunderland, Massachusetts, Sinauer Associates.

Futuyma, D. J., and M. Slatkin, eds. 1983. *Coevolution,* 2nd ed. Sunderland, Massachusetts, Sinauer Associates.

Gardner, M. R., and W. R. Ashby. 1970. Connectance of large dynamic (cybernetic) systems: critical values for stability. *Nature* 228:784.

Gilbert, L. E. 1977. The role of insect-plant coevolution in the organization of ecosystems. Pp. 399–413 in Labyrie, V., ed., *Comportment des insectes et milieu trophique.* Paris, C.N.R.S.

Godfrey-Smith, W. 1980. The rights of non-humans and intrinsic values. In Mannison, D., et al. eds., *Environmental Philosophy.* Canberra, Australian National University.

Goodall, J. 1987. A plea for the chimpanzees. *American Scientist* 75:574–577.

Goodman, R. M., et al. 1987. Gene transfer in crop improvement. *Science* 236:48–54.

Gould, F. 1988a. Evolutionary biology and genetically engineered crops. *BioScience* 38:-26–33.

Gould, F. 1988b. Genetic engineering, integrated pest management and the evolution of pests. Pp. S15–S20 *in* Hodgson, J. and A. M. Sugden, eds., *Planned Release of Genetically Engineered Organisms (Trends in Biotechnology/Trends in Ecology and Evolution Special Publication).* Cambridge, Elsevier Publications.

Gould, S. J. 1985. On the origin of specious critics. *Discover,* January issue.

Greene, H. W., and J. B. Losos. 1988. Systematics, natural history, and conservation. *BioScience* 38:458–462.

Hodgson, J. and A. M. Sugden, eds. 1988. *Planned Release of Genetically Engineered Organisms (Trends in Biotechnology/Trends in Ecology and Evolution Special Publication).* Cambridge, Elsevier Publications.

Hughes, N. F. 1986. Changes in the feeding biology of the Nile perch, *Lates niloticus* (L.) (Pisces: Centropomidae), in Lake Victoria, East Africa, since its introduction in 1960, and its impact on the native fish community of the Nyanza Gulf. *Journal of Fisheries Biology* 29:541–548.

Iltes, H. H. 1988. Serendipity in the exploration of biodiversity: what good are weedy tomatoes? Pp. 98–105 in Wilson, E. O., ed., *BioDiversity.* Washington, D. C., National Academy Press.

Inger, R. F., and R. K. Colwell. 1977. Organization of contiguous communities of amphibians and reptiles in Thailand. *Ecological Monographs* 47:229–253.

Janzen, D. H., ed. 1983. *Costa Rican Natural History.* Chicago, University of Chicago Press.

Janzen, D. H. 1987. Conservation and agricultural economics. *Science* 236:1159.

Janzen, D. H., and P. S. Martin. 1982. Neotropical anachronisms: the fruits the gomphotheres ate. *Science* 215:19–27.

Jonas, H. 1984. *The Imperative of Responsibility: In Search of Ethics for the Technological Age.* Chicago, University of Chicago Press.

Kellert, S. R. 1986. Social and perceptual factors in the preservation of animal species. Pp. 50–73 in Norton, B. G., ed., *The Preservation of Species.* Princeton, Princeton University Press.

Lewis, W. H., and M. P. F. Elvin-Lewis. 1977. *Medical Botany.* New York, John Wiley and Sons.

Lewontin, R. C. 1972. The apportionment of human diversity. *Evolutionary Biology* 6:381–398.

Lugo, A. E., et al. 1973. The impact of the leaf-cutter ant *Atta colombica* on the energy flow of a tropical wet forest. *Ecology* 54:1292–1301.

May, R. M., ed. 1981. *Theoretical Ecology,* 2nd ed. Blackwell Scientific Publications, Oxford.

Miller, R. V. 1988. Potential for transfer and establishment of engineered genetic sequences. Pp. S23–S26 *in* Hodgson, J. and A. M. Sugden, eds., *Planned Release of Genetically Engineered Organisms (Trends in Biotechnology/Trends in Ecology and Evolution Special Publication).* Cambridge, Elsevier Publications.

Mittermeier, R. A. 1988. Primate diversity and the tropical forest: case studies from Brazil and Madagascar and the importance of the megadiversity countries. Pp. 145–154 in Wilson, E. O., ed., *BioDiversity.* Washington, D. C., National Academy Press.

Moyle, P. B. 1986. Fish introductions into North America: patterns and ecological impact. Pp. 27–40 in Mooney, H. A., and J. A. Drake, eds., *Ecology of biological invasions of North America and Hawaii.* Ecological Studies 58. New York, Springer-Verlag.

Moyle, P. B., et al. 1986. The Frankenstein Effect: impact of introduced fishes on native fishes in North America. Pp. 415–426 in Strout, R. H., ed., *Fish Culture in Fisheries Management.* Bethesda, Maryland, Fish Culture Section and Fisheries Management Section of the American Fisheries Society.

Myers, N. 1979. *The Sinking Ark.* Oxford, Pergamon Press.

Myers, N. 1983. *A Wealth of Wild Species: Storehouse for Human Welfare.* Boulder, Colorado, Westview Press.

National Academy of Sciences. 1975. *Underexploited Tropical Plants with Promising Economic Value.* Washington, D. C., National Academy of Sciences.

National Academy of Sciences. 1987. *Introduction of Recombinant DNA-Engineered Organisms into the Environment.* Washington, D. C., National Academy Press.

Nei, M. 1972. Genetic distance between populations. *American Naturalist* 106:283–292.

Norton, B. G. 1986. On the inherent danger of undervaluing species. Pp. 110–137 in Norton, B. G., ed., *The Preservation of Species.* Princeton, Princeton University Press.

Norton, B. G. 1987. *Why Preserve Natural Variety?* Princeton, Princeton University Press.

Norton, B. G. 1988. Commodity, amenity, and morality: the limits of quantification in valuing biodiversity. Pp. 200–205 in Wilson, E. O., ed., *BioDiversity.* Washington, D. C., National Academy Press.

Patil, G. P., and C. Taillie. 1977. An overview of diversity. *In* Grassle, J. F., et al., eds. *Ecological diversity in theory and practice.* Fairland, Maryland, International Cooperative Publishing House.

Pielou, E. C. 1975. *Ecological Diversity.* New York, John Wiley and Sons.

Pimm, S. L. 1982. *Food Webs.* London, Chapman and Hall.

Pringle, C. M. 1988. History of conservation efforts and initial exploration of the lower extension of Parque Nacional Braulio Carrillo, Costa Rica. In Almeda, F. and C. M. Pringle, *Tropical Rainforests: Diversity and Conservation.* Pacific Division, American Association for the Advancement of Science, and California Academy of Sciences.

Rabinowitz, D. 1981. Seven forms of rarity. Pp. 205–217 in Synge, H., *The biological aspects of rare plant conservation.* London, John Wiley.

Randall, A. 1986. Human preferences, economics, and the preservation of species. Pp. 79–109 in Norton, B. G., ed., *The Preservation of Species*. Princeton, Princeton University Press.

Randall, A. 1988. What mainstream economists have to say about the value of biodiversity. Pp. 217–223 in Wilson, E. O., ed., *BioDiversity*. Washington, D. C., National Academy Press.

Raup, D. M. 1988. Diversity crises in the geological past. Pp. 51–57 in Wilson, E. O., ed., *BioDiversity*. Washington, D. C., National Academy Press.

Raup, D. M., and J. J. Sepkoski, Jr. 1982. Mass extinctions in the fossil record. *Science* 215:1501–1503.

Regal, P. J. 1986. Models of genetically engineered organisms and their ecological impact. Pp. 111–129 in Mooney, H. A., and J. A. Drake, eds., *Ecology of Biological Invasions of North America and Hawaii*. Ecological Studies 58. New York, Springer-Verlag.

Regal, P. J. 1988. The adaptive potential of genetically engineered organisms in nature. Pp. S36–S38 in Hodgson, J. and A. M. Sugden, eds., *Planned Release of Genetically Engineered Organisms (Trends in Biotechnology/Trends in Ecology and Evolution Special Publication)*. Cambridge, Elsevier Publications.

Regan, D. H. 1986. Duties of preservation. Pp. 195–220 in Norton, B. G., ed., *The Preservation of Species*. Princeton, Princeton University Press.

Regan, T. 1983. *The Case for Animal Rights*. Berkeley, University of California Press.

Rich, P. V., and T. H. Rich. 1983. The Central American dispersal route: biotic history and paleogeography. Pp. 12–34 in Janzen, D. H., ed., *Costa Rican Natural History*. Chicago, University of Chicago Press.

Roberts, L. 1987. Discovering microbes with a taste for PCB's. *Science* 237:975–977.

Root, R. B. 1967. The niche exploitation pattern of the blue-grey gnatcatcher. *Ecological Monographs* 37:317–350.

Root, R. B. 1973. Organization of a plant-arthropod association in simple and diverse habitats: the fauna of collards *(Brassica oleracea)*. *Ecological Monographs* 43:95–124.

Sapontzis, S. F. 1988. On justifying the exploitation of animals in research. *Journal of Medicine and Philosophy* 13:177–196.

Sharples, F. E. 1983. Spread of organisms with novel genotypes: thoughts from an ecological perspective. *Recombinant DNA Technical Bulletin* 6:43–56.

Sharples, F. E. 1987. Regulation of products from biotechnology. *Science* 235:1329–1332.

Simonsen, L. and B. R. Levin. 1988. Evaluating the risk of releasing genetically engineered organisms. Pp. S27–S29 in Hodgson, J. and A. M. Sugden, eds., *Planned Release of Genetically Engineered Organisms (Trends in Biotechnology/Trends in Ecology and Evolution Special Publication)*. Cambridge, Elsevier Publications.

Simpson, B. B., and M. Connor-Ogorzaly. 1986. *Economic Botany: Plants in Our World*. New York, McGraw Hill.

Sitter, B. 1989. In defence of nonanthropocentrism in environmental ethics. In Shea, W. R. and B. Sitter, eds., *Scientists and Their Responsibility* Canton, Mass., Watson Publishing International.

Sober, E. 1986. Philosophical problems for environmentalism. Pp. 173–194 in Norton, B. G., ed., *The Preservation of Species*. Princeton, Princeton University Press.

Soulé, M. E. 1986. *Conservation Biology*. Sunderland, Massachusetts, Sinauer Associates.

Stanley, S. M. 1985. Rates of evolution. *Paleobiology* 11:13–26.

Stevens, G. C. 1983. *Atta cephalotes* (zompopas, leaf-cutting ants). Pp. 688–691 in Janzen, D. H., ed., *Costa Rican Natural History*. Chicago, University of Chicago Press.

Stoll, J., and L. Johnson. 1984. Concepts of value, nonmarket valuation, and the case of the whooping crane. *Transactions of the North American Wildlife Natural Resource Conference* 49:382–393.

Taylor, P. W. 1986. *Respect for Nature*. Princeton, Princeton University Press.

Templeton, A. R. 1981. Mechanisms of speciation: a population genetic approach. *Annual Reviews of Ecology and Systematics* 12:23–48.

van der Pijl, L., and C. H. Dodson. 1966. *Orchid Flowers: Their Pollination and Evolution*. Coral Gables, Florida, Fairchild Tropical Garden and University of Miami Press.

Vermeij, G. J. 1986. The biology of human-caused extinction. Pp. 28–49 in Norton, B. G., ed., *The Preservation of Species*. Princeton, Princeton University Press.

Vietmeyer, N. D. 1986. Lesser-known plants of potential use in agriculture and forestry. *Science* 232:1379–1384.

Vitousek, P. M. 1988. Diversity and biological invasions of oceanic islands. Pp. 181–189 in Wilson, E. O., ed., *BioDiversity*. Washington, D. C., National Academy Press.

Williams, J. T. 1988. Identifying and protecting the origins of our food plants. Pp. 240–247 in Wilson, E. O., ed., *BioDiversity*. Washington, D. C., National Academy Press.

Williamson, M. 1988. Potential effects of recombinant DNA organisms on ecosystems and their components. Pp. S32–S35 in Hodgson, J. and A. M. Sugden, eds., *Planned Release of Genetically Engineered Organisms (Trends in Biotechnology/Trends in Ecology and Evolution Special Publication)*. Cambridge, Elsevier Publications.

Wilson, E. O., ed. 1988a. *BioDiversity*. Washington, D. C., National Academy Press.

Wilson, E. O. 1988b. The current state of biological diversity. Pp. 3–18 in Wilson, E. O., ed., *BioDiversity*. Washington, D. C., National Academy Press.

Witt, S. C. 1985. *Biotechnology and Genetic Diversity*. San Francisco, California Agricultural Lands Project.

Wong, W. K. R., et al. 1988. Wood hydrolysis by *Cellulomonas fimi* endoglucanase and exoglucanase coexpressed as secreted enzymes in *Saccharomyces cerevisiae*. *Bio/Technology* 6:713–719.

Ethics of Nature

JÜRGEN MITTELSTRASS

1.

'Ethics of nature' is an unusual title. What one expects when ethics and nature are being discussed—especially with respect to the modern debate on the ethics of science and on technology assessment and ecology—is ethics of the natural sciences, what one would probably call ecological ethics, but not ethics of nature. In one case the *natural sciences* or an ecological view of things would have an ethics, in the other *nature* would have an ethics. One seems clear, the other does not.

Talk about an ethics of the natural sciences, however, is never as clear as it seems. It can mean, for example, ethics for natural scientists, or it can mean a theory of moral rules or norms that are used in the work done in the natural sciences. The first case involves the ethics of a profession, the second case a standard of (scientific) rationality viewed from a moral point of view. In any event ethical arguments are being addressed in both cases to science or to the work done by the scientist. This is not, literally speaking, the case with an ethics of nature. According to the alternative meanings I have just outlined, ethics of nature could mean: either ethics for nature or ethics as a theory of moral rules that can be applied in the 'life' of nature or which connects, as it were, the moral world of man with that of nature.

Neither of these is meant here. What is meant, instead, is an extension of the concept of responsibility towards nature, but within and not outside of the limits of an *ethics of reason (Vernunftethik)*. All that is involved is another perspective, another view of things—of the same things. One view concerns our work—here the work of the natural scientist; the other concerns the house in which we do this—nature. One could, however, also assume that in the second case we want to see things *from the view point of nature*. 'Ethics of nature' suggests this turn, but, on the other hand, it would not be clear. The question would indeed have to be: Does nature have such a view and can we adopt it? To achieve clarity here, it is necessary, under the title 'ethics of nature,' to deal first with problems of an ethics of science, in particular an ethics of the natural sciences. I want to argue that what we understand by an

41

ethics of nature is only the other side, the other view of an ethics of the natural sciences.[1]

2.

Any discussion of ethical problems in the sciences, particularly in the natural sciences, usually includes the *consequences* of scientific practice as well as the *assessment* of progress as a problem involving practical, and not theoretical or technological, reason. In scientifically advanced *technological cultures*, such as modern industrial society, theoretical or technological reason alone cannot solve the problem of how to justify scientific progress. Neither can it answer the question of an *orientational knowledge (Orientierungswissen)* that goes beyond what we need to know to control or utilize things *(Verfügungswissen)*. This is something that Max Weber already said: "Natural science gives us an answer to the question of what we must do *if* we wish to master life *technically*. It *leaves quite aside,* or assumes for its purposes, *whether* we should or do wish to master life technically and whether it ultimately makes sense to do so."[2]

For Weber, answering this type of question is not a concern of science; this must limit itself to what I call *Verfügungswissen* (knowledge that gives one control over something). With this self-imposed limitation, however, the problems involved in justifying progress or in deciding the role practical reason should play in guiding our actions becomes more acute. Science realizes this, and at the same time deplores the weakness of practical reason. Albert Einstein wrote in 1948: "The tragedy of modern man lies in the following: he has created for himself conditions of existence which he cannot live up to because of his phylogenetic development."[3] This means simply that the stimulus from the brain is stronger than the control through the cerebrum.

The defects of our moral and political development complement the limits of our genetic make-up. While the world of science and technology is moving rapidly into the twenty-first century, the moral and political world mostly clings to the nineteenth century. The scientific and technological mind looks ahead; the moral and political mind glances backwards. Europe in particular is struggling to free its own discovery—the 'project of the modern age' (Habermas) that originated during the Enlightenment—from the mutual blockade between scientific and technological reason on the one hand, and moral and political reason on the other.

In this situation scientific and technological utopias and moral and political conservatism flourish; contingency is on the rise. The technology metaphor ('technological culture') suggests that modern society is comprehensible in all its parts and functions. Yet this conception is deceptive. Societal reality in technological cultures, caught between scientific and technological progress and moral and political stagnation, has become in fact incomprehensible and 'incalculable.' Not only what a technological culture *should be,* but also what it is *capable of,* not least with respect to the consequences of its actions, has been increasingly caught up in an impenetrable process, about the legitimacy of which Prometheus and Cassandra are quarreling. A subject of these actions, a subject of this progress, is no longer identifiable in technological cultures. Scientific and technological progress goes where it wants—and let those lacking in orientation interpret it. Structures of responsibility in technological cultures can also no longer be derived directly from structures of action precisely because of the lack of subjectivity structures in these cultures. In technological cultures the individual has to accept responsibility even for such anonymous processes as 'technological change.'

There is, by the way, a characteristic difference between natural science and social science, which are both dominant aspects of technological cultures. One has (possible) technological, the other (possible) institutional, consequences. In democratic societies institutional consequences have a democratic basis, but not, as a rule, technological consequences. Society makes decisions about institutions usually before they come into existence, and about technologies almost always after they have developed. This is why technological progress in technological cultures is such a dominant force—it even takes place despite the resistance of society—and why institutional change is so slow—existing institutions tend to resist change. With respect to the problem of the justification of these changes, the (social) justification of institutional changes generally preceeds or at least accompanies these changes, whereas the (social) justification of technological changes as a rule follows them. One could even say, in view of the already existing reality, that it almost always comes too late. Technological cultures are cultures with institutionally weak and instrumentally strong wind power.

3.

Strictly speaking, science and technology are *instrumental* in character. Without establishing or justifying ends, they place at our dis-

posal those rationalities responsible for the special nature of technological cultures. Nevertheless, based on what I have mentioned up to
now, they are also subject to moral judgement, though with two important restrictions.

First, in judging the consequences of scientific progress, the scientist is not omniscient. He too is unable to overlook the contingent
nature of future developments or to bring them under control beforehand. Science and technology assessment are an art without masters,
and their future achievements are hardly assessable. This is why even
in this case (as in that of anonymous processes), the responsibility for
the consequences of scientific (and technological) research can only be
assigned according to human standards. Research in the sciences, for
example, in the natural sciences, inevitably has consequences that
neither the scientist nor the nonscientist can overlook. The same is
true for technicians, who, with respect to the development of products,
combine research and development in their work. This, however,
means that moral standards are not the only standards here.

In this context, of course, it is important to answer the question
of what we can and cannot overlook. What is the value of science and
technology assessment? Can the process of scientific research or technological innovation be planned in the same way as that of developing
products? Can chance be calculated (in science and technology)?
Whatever the answer may turn out to be, the next question will be: Is
the realization that we cannot overlook the consequences of particular
research programs or particular technological research programs already enough of an argument for dispensing with research and the
development of technology, or at least with portions of these programs? The answer is probably not. And who could then distinguish
between the usual possibilities for development connected with all
human actions and consequences that have the tendency to become
independent, or between primary and secondary effects? Moreover,
the requirement that comprehensibility (of all possible effects) be a
condition for development would be ineffectual. Not only would it be
disobeyed in practice, but it would also hinder an essential part of
scientific and technological research: the step beyond the limits of
what we know or can comprehend, the play of the known with the
unknown, the pursuit of new paths, the vision of future scientific
worlds—but without our necessarily being reminded of Faust, for example, as the "Faust in us."[4]

In addition, the requirement that all the effects and risks involved
in man's scientific and technological research be determined and mas-

tered in advance would block progress, and along with it man's own future. This literally means that without research that explores the new and pursues new paths only stagnation or the way back would remain. And in view of scientifically and technologically induced problems, such as overpopulation, scarcity of resources, and ecological emergencies, this path would involve greater losses than even a path full of risks leading to an uncertain and unexplored future.

Second, scientists, not least because of the dominant role science plays in technological culture, have a special responsibility, but do they also have a special *ethics,* i.e., their own scientific ethics? Is there after all such an *ethics of science,* e.g., an ethics of the natural sciences? Not very likely. The sciences in society's view constitute a special form of *knowledge,* but not, at least not from an ethical point of view, a special *societal* form with a corresponding ethics. Whoever thinks this way not only confuses *methodologically* founded rationalities in the constitution of knowledge, with *ethically* founded societal rationalities, but is also being guided by a wrong notion of ethics—the notion that there is an ethical answer, *the* correct ethical answer, for all problems and in all situations. In other words, ethics is assumed to be a discipline (falling primarily within the competence of philosophers) that can say what is morally justified and what not in all conceivable cases. Such a notion, however, is completely misleading—some would say unfortunately so. It confuses ethics with a cookbook that can provide an answer for every question of taste. Thus the culinary 'take this' is turned into a seemingly unerring moral 'do this' (when one follows the misleading notion of ethics that I have described).

This notion, however, is not only aroused by common expectations towards ethics, but also by ethics itself, namely, in the form of the so-called *material ethics of values.* In such an ethics (as represented by such modern philosophers as Max Scheler and Nicolai Hartmann), an impressive order of values is constructed in a carefree manner, a 'realm of values' with generalized notions about the good, the just, and the reasonable—as their discoverers contend. In fact, particular options about the morality in the material sense are selected over others, without there being a principle that could justify such choices.

As opposed to such an ethics of material values, there is also a conception of ethics that restricts itself just to the formulation of such a principle. The paradigm for this conception is still Kant's categorical imperative according to the following formulation: "Act in such a way that the maxim of your will can also always be considered as the principle of a general law."[5] A philosophical encyclopedia from Con-

stance clarifies the situation in the following way: "This principle formulated by the categorical imperative defines precisely that possibility
of justification which results from renouncing the justification through
certain value judgements (i.e., particular ideas of what is good, just or
reasonable)."[6] In other words, ethics becomes a *formal principle* (in
contrast to the idea of a material order of values) or, putting it very
simply, a one-proposition ethics. The application of such a principle
to particular problems and situations, however, is the achievement of
the individual, i.e., the *achievement of subjectivity.* Ethics cannot take over
the burden of deciding what and what not to do in concrete cases.

This is another reason why there can be no such thing as an ethics
of science that can be separated from other ethical spheres and conceived of as a material order of values concerning scientific goods.
Moreover—and here I am returning to the difference between (ethically relevant) social forms and (methodologically relevant) forms of
knowledge—the addressee of moral claims is the scientist not as scientist, but always as citizen. Ethics is always *citizen's ethics;* it cannot be
divided socially (e.g., into a scientist's ethics and a nonscientist's ethics). We could also say that ethics is always the *product* and the *virtue*
of all (i.e., all citizens), guided not by textbooks on ethics or catalogues
of virtues, but by principles, such as the categorical imperative just
mentioned.

That there is from the point of view I have taken no special ethics
of science or ethics for the scientist, does not mean that the scientist
does not have or should not have a special *ethos.* On the contrary, this
is in fact absolutely necessary. What I mean by this is the *living form*
within which the individual, here the scientist, behaves subjectively
towards ethical orientations or an ethical principle. For the scientist,
such an ethos is necessary because of his special competencies, for
instance, his thinking, theoretical, or problem-solving skills, his in-
novatory and anticipatory skills. His responsibilities are also of a special nature because of the general inability of the nonscientific mind
to control scientific practice and because of the dependence of technological culture on the abilities of the scientific mind. These responsibilities make the acquisition of a special ethos a necessary virtue. If this
ethos degenerates, two complementary dangers threaten: 1. the danger that societal control over science weakens, and the citizen's ethics
loses its force, and 2. the danger that societal practice takes over
science and that 'social relevance' becomes the magic formula that
society uses to exercise its control over science. In both cases science
loses its status as a representative of rationality and (through its sub-

jects) as an institution with special responsibilities in technological cultures.

4.

But there is also another point: it is absolutely necessary to extend the concept of responsibility beyond the immediate results of our practice. The consequences of scientific (and technological) action in technological cultures concern not just us, who are living today, but also those who will follow us, and often *only those*. According to Hans Jonas, this extension lies in the transition from a type of responsibility based on "the ex-post-facto bill for what was done," to a type of responsibility based on the necessity of "determining what to do."[7] During this transition man takes the side of the future by conceiving of the 'future of mankind' as "the first duty of human collective behaviour in the age of a technological civilization that has become 'all-powerful' in a negative way."[8] Here, in the face of a technological culture that is rapidly becoming universal—particularly with the ecological consequences that follow in its wake—a difficult situation arises. We have to extend our previous ethical conceptions, which were based mostly on the concrete relations among persons, to all mankind, including future generations. By extending ethics in this way Jonas refers to this as 'long-term responsibility'—ethical orientations lose their 'emotional' basis. There are no feelings towards abstract quantities, such as 'mankind' or even 'future mankind.' They must also manage without a precise knowledge of the situation, which as a rule is indispensable for moral behavior.

But even these conditions do not justify our ignoring possible future developments. The customary and often irresponsible faith in the inventive ability of future generations to cope with the problems we have created could be a deception. There is no way of dealing with irreversibility, which as an aspect of change increasingly accompanies our scientific and technological practice. Such behavior, moreover, distinguishes all too hedonistically between that part of mankind that razes a house or scorches the earth, and the part that has to rebuild the house to be able to live in it, perhaps more cautiously. Everything seems so simple in principle. It would be enough to assume responsibility for future generations, so that these would be spared what we fear most for us and our children: a life on a biologically desolate, poisoned, impoverished earth.

Again, the burden of responsibility falls on the scientist, especially the natural scientist. Not, however, as a representative for what really happens—this he can do in a democratically constituted society only in his role as citizen—but with respect to the special role expertise plays in judging what is and what will be. Carl Friedrich von Weizsäcker speaks in this way about an 'unavoidable moral duty' for the natural scientist, particularly the physicist, in the face of the consequences of his doings.[9] According to Weizsäcker, it is not science that is impeded by the fulfillment of this duty, but, in the terminology I am using here, the dominant reduction of reason to technical reason in technological cultures: it would be

> "completely senseless to deduce from this that we will stop doing physics. One can only help change the political world—through one's own actions, one's own thoughts—as radically as the modern natural sciences have changed what we know. For with our knowledge and the political forms in which we traditionally live, the end—as we know today—can only be horrible."[10]

In other words it is not *science* that has to change, but the *political world*. Not, however, without the scientist fulfilling his responsibilities, though in this case, this is also related to his role as citizen. Let me repeat: ethics is always citizen's ethics; it cannot be divided socially. It is the product and the virtue of all citizens. The same is true of a rational politics.

Jürgen Habermas stated as much in 1966:

> "With the unplanned socio-cultural consequences of technological progress the human species has challenged itself not only to conjure up its own social fate but also to learn how to control it. This technological challenge cannot be met only through technology. More important is getting a politically effective discussion underway, which establishes a rationally binding relationship between society's potential in technical knowledge and ability and our practical knowledge and will."[11]

It is not technological knowledge and ability that require change (a demand, which in face of the rapid change in this area, would always come too late), but practical knowledge and will, that is, the political world, and this from the *perspective of reason*.

5.

If, in view of the nature of technological culture, an ethical problem exists concerning our responsibility for future generations, then we cannot separate this problem in a strict sense from a responsibility towards nature as a whole. Since the living conditions of future generations depend essentially, as did those of past generations, on nature being more or less 'intact,' nature is not only an object of economic or ecological judgment, but also of ethical judgment. A nature that is 'humane' is not just an economic problem involving the acquisition and maintenance of scarce resources. That was not always the case. Problems that rational cultures have with nature are due to the rupture between nature and (rational) life typical of these cultures. The rational individual no longer lives with or in nature; he faces it in his modes of work and production. The rational individual does not belong to nature; nature belongs to him. Technological culture has made this change the mode of living typical of rational individuals and of the reality of nature. Nature itself becomes part of a rationally organized reality; it acquires a new quality. The result of the development of natural science and technology in the modern age is not just a new society, the 'technological' society or the 'technological' culture, but also a new nature, the 'technologically appropriated' nature. Bacon's slogan that one can take possession of nature by following its laws,[12] and Hegel's proposition that man has "in his tools . . . the power over external nature"[13] are realized in technological culture.

This development also involves the replacement of the *nature paradigm* for all orders, including the order of human life, by a *technological paradigm*. This means that today discoveries in the natural sciences are due mostly to the conditions defining a technological practice, and no longer to the conditions defining a 'natural' order (consider modern chemistry or plasma physics). Thus the modern natural sciences as laboratory sciences mostly produce their own objects, in order to examine them either after or during their production. Decisive in our context is that modern physics, as opposed to classical (Aristotelian) physics, which sought to construct an *orientational knowledge in nature*, together with modern natural science wants to control or utilize nature or provide the scientific preconditions for such a *ruling knowledge of nature*. Let me put this in a different way. In the 'cosmological' or nature paradigm of Greek physics, a physics whose object of research was to all appearances an ordered nature, nature and life are inextricably intertwined. Nature remains as it is. In the technological paradigm of modern physics, life and nature are separated in the orientational sense I mentioned above; a new nature comes into existence—without an orientational meaning. A *history of progress (Fortschrittsgeschichte)*, namely, the gradual shift from a 'cosmological' to a 'technological' paradigm in natural research, also reveals in the process elements of a *history of losses (Verlustgeschichte)*: technological cultures that come into existence in the wake of this transition have enormous difficulties living 'rationally' with nature, in view of their overabundance of *Verfügungswissen* and their relative lack of *Orientierungswissen*.

Natural history thus reveals itself to be not only physical history but also *cultural history.* What nature is is a matter of nature *and* of culture, that is, the history of man in nature and the history of nature in the history of man. This is, moreover, also the origin of the peculiar problem of being able to say precisely what and where nature is. We celebrate it as a green world that should be before our windows, but has long been missing as 'untouched' nature. As a rule we look at nature merely as a source of raw materials managed by economic and technical expertise, or as the ground in which technological culture puts its waste products, or as a haven for free time that the tourist industry fills with its false dreams. Nature, again, has become a part of technological culture—a part of 'spaceship earth,' in the resolute language of technological culture. Wherever one goes 'in nature,' the knowing, constructing, economizing, and ravaging mind has already been there.

Surprisingly enough, it seems as if an idealistic conception, namely, that the mind recognizes itself in nature, finally managed to become accepted even in a materialistic world. In technological culture nature becomes *the other side of the subject,* entrusted to man for appropriation and cultivation. 'Evolutionary' reasons can also be given for this view of things. While the phylogenetic process of development among living creatures generally occurs as a process of adaptation to their respective environments, this is different for human beings. During his cultural development, man, remaining virtually unchanged as a biological species, adapted the environment (and hence nature) to his needs, which means simply, to himself. Man so controls, especially in technological cultures, the arrangement and organization of his environment that it is no wonder that the appearance of limitless independence and perfection, being dominant in these cultures, also influences how he deals with nature. As I already emphasized, natural conditions are no longer valuable as orientational elements that can be implemented in life, but as that realm in which man achieves mastery of his ability to utilize and control.

This superiority of man can, of course, also be conceived of as the ruthless completion of his 'nature,' of which his rationality—understood here (and also a little misunderstood) as a product of evolution—is a part. In human culture, that is, in man's way of appropriating and changing the world into his world, we find an unmistakable expression of man's nature and ecological success. Even his problems are testimony to this: "If this magnificent ecological success of our species . . . causes us increasingly more problems and at the same time to all of nature around us, then it is not because we would have strayed from the path of natural virtue, but because up to now we have been following it almost with blind determination."[14] Or put morally: "Where leaving nature behind in the sense of the progressive mastery over nature becomes an end in itself, the result is a relapse into pure earthiness."[15]

In man's 'nature' and his 'earthiness' too, however, something like *the natural* is no longer recognizable—and not only because nature and culture are no longer clearly divisible areas. That nature itself has a history, that is, a history that is not only part of the history of man, also means that it does not exist as something unalterably natural, as the great being behind all other beings that belong to our world. Nature also comes and goes: nature looks different over long periods of time. Neither the nature of the older paleolithic era, which provided pre-Neandertal man with scant nourishment, nor the younger paleolithic era, in which *homo sapiens* entered the scene, is *our* nature. Our nature is—and not just within the limits of technological culture—a 'cultural nature,'[16] a nature created by man, that is, by his continual interaction with 'natural' facts. All that is 'natural' is man himself and the world he has utilized, exploited, cared for, praises, and fears, a world that is never the 'pure' world of nature, but always man's world. In other words we are mistaken when we oppose the cultural to the *natural,* at least when we mean that something natural is the original, the timeless, the measure of all things, even the human.

6.

Nature is the quintessence of life. Where it is not conceived of in this way, not only 'external,' but also 'internal' nature, i.e., man's own nature, come under categories of appropriation. In fact, the utmost consequence of man, who realizes himself as *homo faber,* consists in his making his own nature. In this process, which in technological cultures almost has to happen, something that had originally been uncontrollable, something nature once stood for, dissolves into elements that technically are at least partially controllable. In the expanding possibilities for gene manipulation, what was once science fiction has gradually become an oppressive part of reality. We are partially capable of fundamentally changing ourselves—our nature, that is—to do to our 'inner' nature what we have long been doing to 'external' nature. Man has become not only ideologically, but also biologically, manipulatable. Thinking about nature becomes linked to *ethical* problems—among them the already mentioned problem of a responsibility towards future generations and, connected with it, the problem of a responsibility towards nature as a whole.

Up to now I have been talking about the question of our responsibility towards nature as a whole with reference to the dependence of future generations on an 'intact' nature. Another question, however, is whether there is or can be a responsibility towards nature *for its own sake.* With this question we enter the realm of a *teleological* conception or an anthropomorphic view of nature. Nature appears as a subject with its own aims and rights. Robert Spaemann speaks in this connection about the "moral right of nature" as the "right of a natural being to be treated in such a way that we can treat it as a good for its own sake."[17] Jonas states that we "do not have the right to choose or even to risk the nonexistence of future generations because of the existence of the present one."[18] For Meyer-Abich man is related not only to animals and plants, but also to the elements, earth, water, air, and fire: "In all of nature they are like us and we are like them."[19]

These conceptions go too far, at least with respect to the limits of ethical arguments. They do not even apply to man, if what we mean here is not only the right of future generations to humane living conditions, but over and above this, a right to exist. If mankind decided today not to have any more children—naturally, a completely fictive idea—much could be said against such a decision (from a violation of God's plans for mankind to the eventual loss of social security). We could not say, however, that the nonexistent have a right to exist. But what counts for man counts even more for nonhuman life and for nature as a whole.[20]

This is why philosophy has traditionally seen the question of our responsibility towards nature (for its own sake) as a question that concerns man's responsibility *towards himself.* Kant's view, for example, is that in

> "beholding what is *beautiful* but inanimate in nature . . . a tendency to mere destruction . . . is contradictory to man's obligation to himself because it weakens or eliminates that feeling in man which is not in itself already moral, but which nevertheless at least prepares that mood of sensuality which promotes morality: namely, to love something without the intention of use."[21]

In this context Kant particularly mentions the suffering of animals as a reason for moral responsibility and obligations towards nature. When man inflicts suffering on animals, his 'sympathy' for their suffering declines, so that "a natural disposition which facilitates morality in relation to other people weakens and is exterminated little by little."[22] This means that man's obligations towards nature are obligations towards ourselves. Endangering nature, in Kant's argumentation, endangers morality. Not because nature is itself a (moral) subject, but because in this sense, the interaction with nature also falls under moral categories.

However one judges this type of argument, this much is clear (as it is in Kant): an ethics of nature cannot be grounded 'in itself,' that is, it cannot be derived 'from the perspective of nature,' which would thus be understood as a moral subject. An ethics of nature can only be part of an ethics in which (rational) man is the subject. A *rational ethics* encompasses an *ethics of nature,* be it for reasons that Kant mentions or for reasons that I have mentioned here. To the extent that rational action begins to change nature in a way that endangers not only 'natural' but also 'reasoning' nature, we can say that nature in an *ethical,* and not just in a physical or economic, sense becomes the limit of our actions. No other rationalities can set this limit, but then neither can nature, that is, a nature that "opens its eyes."[23] As in any enlightened ethics, i.e., an ethics based on the view of reason, this limit is the limit of reason *(Vernunftgrenze).*

7.

Even if we incorporate an ethics of nature into an ethics of reason, we still cannot be sure what nature is and what it should be. For technological cultures, with their appropriating structures, the answer to such questions is basically a mystery. In a certain sense, this is even true of an *ecological* perspective, from which one would most likely expect the 'right' answer. Ecological judgments can also not say what a nonappropriated and noncultivated nature should be. Nor can they say how we should behave 'properly' towards nature. And just as medicine cannot say how 'healthily' we should live, but only how we should live once we know how healthy we want to be, so ecology can also not say how 'natural' nature should be, but only what nature is relative to our ends and how we achieve them. In other words, when ecology has to decide what the proper relationship between technolog-

ical culture and nature is it, too, presupposes a certain conception of what nature should be.

Ecology does not develop these conceptions by itself. This can be illustrated by using the central concept of ecological balance, which in ecology is mostly a descriptive concept. It defines the state of an ecosystem in terms of a fluid equilibrium. In general discussions, however, it is often used (and misused) as a normative concept to describe a state that should not be disturbed for its own sake. It can also be illustrated by indicating the grounding of ecology in man's (rational) self-interest. For example, protecting endangered species:

> "In answering the question which of the many species—apart from moral or aesthetic considerations—we will need most in the future, since they could be potentially useful to us later, the best answer is the least precise: as many as possible. The reason is simply that all species are gene banks which maintain themselves for us in the least expensive way. . . . This, of course, is especially true of the primary chemical producers, the hundreds of thousands of plant species. . . . This is why our first and greatest care, for mere utilitarian reasons, should be the preservation of as many plant species as possible."[24]

This is the way things are, even if it pleases neither the philosopher among the ecologists nor the teleologist among the philosophers.

Thus, ecological steps to a proper way of dealing with nature are also not simple or clear. They generally range from a rule of prudence (limiting exploitation), in which case they are themselves economically oriented, to moral commandments (responsibility for nature). In this respect they share problems with ethical orientations. There is also the attempt to develop a 'philosophical' way of looking at things in which teleological and evolutionary points of view constitute a mode of argumentation that is difficult to understand. The following conviction, for example, reveals this:

> "(a) The belief that humans are members of the Earth's Community of Life in the same sense and on the same terms in which other living things are members of that Community. (b) The belief that the human species, along with all other species, are integral elements in a system of interdependence such that the survival of each living thing, as well as its chances of faring well or poorly, is determined not only by the physical conditions of its environment but also by its relations to other living things. (c) The belief that all organisms are teleological centers of life in the sense that each is a unique individual pursuing its own good in its own way. (d) The belief that humans are not inherently superior to other living things."[25]

What is presented here as a 'biocentric' point of view follows the already mentioned 'teleological' idea of replacing an ethics of reason with an ethics of nature ('biocentric' ethics). Compared with the ideals of knowledge in science (nature as an object of knowledge) and the ideals of production in the economy (nature as a resource), both of which almost coincide in technological cultures, ethical and ecological orientations have difficulty finding their own way.

With the idea of an ethics of nature as 'biocentric' ethics, ethics does not just become dependent on a particular world view, in this case the conviction mentioned above. There is also the threat of a new 'biologism,' namely, the grounding of an ethical orientation in biological facts. Ethics becomes a part of a natural history of man. Mohr's questions, for example, point in this direction:

"Is our inability to react with reason to the challenges of our times a cultural misadaptation that can be (easily?) corrected, or is it the expression of an evolutionary inheritence that proves to be a misadaptation in the present cultural situation. Are they biological limits which block man's path to eternal peace and global ecological reason?"[26]

If the second of these options were true, man would be the victim of his own (biological) nature; enlightenment—and hence also an ethics of reason—would remain stuck in a biological dead end. Mohr's own suggestions contain little comfort:

"Man is a product of evolution, so his cognitive dispositions too (patterns of thought and patterns of knowledge) must originate in the course of Darwinian evolution. Our subjective patterns of knowledge correspond to the real world precisely because in the course of human evolution they evolved in adaptation to this world. The way in which we think and the range of our thoughts are anchored in our genes."[27]

Ethics arises out of a (problematical) evolutionary epistemology. Behind our moral deficits, stands a biological evolution that is not completed and cannot deal with us—with its inborn patterns of behavior and action (something that can be found already in Einstein): The

"human mind, adapted to the middle dimension of the Pleistocene Era [the age of gatherers and hunters] was not created for the purpose of understanding the modern world and its dangers. The pathological thoughtlessness with which we foolishly reproduce ourselves and completely exploit the planet, is our biological inheritance. We do not realize what we are doing."[28]

This is probably the case. It is precisely rational cultures that are often, with respect to their patterns of appropriation, struck by irrational blindness. But is biology here really an explanation or even an excuse? The way Mohr rounds off his ideas sounds more plausible: "Our future will depend on whether and to what extent man succeeds in his actions in breaking away from the obsolete fitness maxims of biological evolution and creating the decision-making freedom he needs for a good life."[29]

In fact, that is man's actual task as a rational being. Attempts to view the rationality of this being either as an evolutionary product or as running contrary to evolution both lead here in the wrong direction. What is at stake is not the playing of man's nature, including his rational nature, against biological evolution (or in favor of it), but making nature the expression of reason in man and his culture. An *ethics of reason*, however, does precisely this. An ethics of nature that teleologically or in whatever other way goes beyond the limits of an ethics of reason does not.

Notes

1. The following contribution relies on ideas used in two other publications and develops them further under the double aspect of an ethics of natural science and an ethics of nature: J. Mittelstrass, *Zur Ethik der Naturforschung* (Frankfurt, 1985) (Polytechnische Gesellschaft e.V.); "Leben mit der Natur. Über die Geschichte der Natur in der Geschichte der Philosophie und über die Verantwortung des Menschen gegenüber der Natur," in: O. Schwemmer (ed.), *Über Natur. Philosophische Beiträge zum Naturverständnis* (Frankfurt, 1987), 37–62. I want to thank Stephen Gillies (Constance) and John Fisher (Philadelphia) who assisted me in preparing the English text.

2. M. Weber, *Gesammelte Aufsätze zur Wissenschaftslehre,* ed. J. Winkelmann, 3rd ed. (Tübingen, 1968), 559f.

3. A. Einstein, *Über den Frieden. Weltordnung oder Weltuntergang?,* ed. O. Nathan/H. Norden (Bern, 1975), 494.

4. F. Hammer, *Selbstzensur für Forscher? Schwerpunkte einer Wissenschaftsethik* (Zurich, 1983), 57.

5. I. Kant, *Kritik der praktischen Vernunft,* A 54.

6. O. Schwemmer, "Ethik," in: J. Mittelstrass (ed.), *Enzyklopädie Philosophie und Wissenschaftstheorie,* vol. I (Mannheim/Wien/Zurich, 1980), 594.

7. H. Jonas, *Das Prinzip Verantwortung. Versuch einer Ethik für die technologische Zivilisation* (Frankfurt, 1979), 174.

8. *Op. cit.,* 245.

9. Introductory remarks in *Verantwortung und Ethik in der Wissenschaft.* Symposium of the Max Planck Society, Schloss Ringberg/Tegernsee, May 1984, (Munich: Max-Planck-Gesellschaft, 1984) (*Berichte und Mitteilungen,* vol. 3/84), 153.

10. *Ibid,* 153f.

11. "Technischer Fortschritt und soziale Lebenswelt" [1966], in: J. Habermas, *Technik und Wissenschaft als 'Ideologie'* (Frankfurt, 1968), 118.

12. *Novum organum* [1620] I 3, *The Works of Francis Bacon,* vols. I–XIV, ed. J. Spedding, R. R. Ellis, and D. D. Heath (London, 1857–1874), vol. I, 157.

13. G. W. F. Hegel, *Wissenschaft der Logik II, Sämtliche Werke. Jubiläumsausgabe,* vols. I–XX, ed. H. Glockner (Stuttgart, 1927–1930), vol. V, 226.

14. H. Markl, *Natur als Kulturaufgabe, Über die Beziehung des Menschen zur lebendigen Natur* (Stuttgart 1986), 358.

15. R. Spaemann, "Naturtheologie und Handlung," in: R. Spaemann, *Philosophische Essays* (Stuttgart 1983), 33.

16. See H. Markl, *Ökonomie und Ökologie. Wissenschaftliche Forschung und ökologische Herausforderungen* (Speech given in Mainz on May 13th, 1987 at the 75th Jubilee of the Industrial Association for the Protection of Plants (IPS) (separate publication, here 6).

17. Lecture quoted by H. Lenk, "Verantwortung für die Natur. Gibt es moralische Quasirechte von oder moralische Pflichten gegenüber nichtmenschlichen Naturwesen?," *Allgemeine Zeitschrift für Philosophie* 8 (1983), 3. See R. Spaemann, "Naturtheologie und Handlung," *op. cit.,* 57.

18. *Op. cit.,* 36.

19. K. M. Meyer-Abich, *Wege zum Frieden mit der Natur. Praktische Naturphilosophie für die Umweltpolitik* (Munich 1984), 24.

20. See also G. Patzig, *Ökologische Ethik—innerhalb der Grenzen blosser Vernunft* (Göttingen, 1983) (*Vortragsreihe der Niedersächsischen Landesregierung zur Förderung der wissenschaftlichen Forschung in Niedersachsen,* 64), 19.

21. I. Kant, *Die Metaphysik der Sitten. Tugendlehre* §17, *Werke in sechs Bänden,* ed. W. Weischedel (Frankfurt, Darmstadt, 1956–1964), vol. IV, 578.

22. *Ibid,* 579.

23. J. Habermas, "Technik und Wissenschaft als 'Ideologie'," *op. cit.,* 57.

24. H. Markl, *Natur als Kulturaufgabe,* 337f.

25. P. W. Taylor, *Respect for Nature. A Theory of Environmental Ethics* (Princeton, 1986), 99f.

26. H. Mohr, "Evolutionäre Ethik," in *Information Philosophie,* vol. 4, 1986, 4f.

27. *Ibid,* 5f.

28. *Ibid,* 9.

29. *Ibid,* 15.

Should Science Be Supervised, and If So, by Whom?

MARCELLO PERA

1. Science and Technology: The Differentiated Treatment View

The problem of the supervision of science can be split into three distinct, although connected, questions: 1. Should science be supervised, and if so why? 2. What technical and scientific activities or fields should be curtailed? 3. Who should have the right of curtailment? To anticipate my conclusions, I shall maintain that science *as such* should be supervised because it is not value free and has moral relevance; that *all* science should be supervised, not only those particular fields or applications of it that *prima facie* seem to be harmful or risky; that no supreme authority, however elected or appointed, should be granted the right to impose the rules governing the supervision of science. This last point does not deny the risks of science. On the contrary, these risks are recognized. What is questioned is the advisability of facing them by deputation. I start with a discussion of the first question, which is intended as a preliminary to discussions of the second and third.

The most typical answer to questions one and two stems from a widespread distinction among pure science, applied science, and technology. We may call such an answer the *differentiated treatment view*, according to which pure science and applied science should be left completely free, while technology and technological fallouts should be supervised and, if need be, restrained.

The justification for the differentiated treatment view is usually said to lie in the fact that science is good in itself, since it answers purely intellectual needs, while technology is merely an instrumental good that fulfills practical needs and aims. Only when such needs and aims are legitimate and morally right should technology be promoted. This is the case for robotics, medicine, and civil engineering, which tend to realize commendable and permissible aims, such as health, security, low-cost products, and precision instruments. They deserve to be encouraged, and the research programs from which they derive their basic know-how should be highly recommended. On the other hand, there are needs and aims that are neither necessary nor useful or that can easily be dispensed with without seriously damaging our lives or considerably lowering our standard of living. To give a few examples, the birth of a healthy child is desirable, but what about the selection of a child with predetermined sex or eye color? Happiness is so obviously desirable that some political constitutions include it among their aims, but what about total lack of strife or the painful tensions of our everyday life? Rapid means of communications are most welcome, but what about cars whose higher speeds entail higher pollution?

Technologies that aim at realizing these ends should not be promoted. For example, genetic engineering should be stopped before the border between improving physical conditions and manipulating human genoma is crossed. Likewise, pharmacology should be restrained when the bridge between health and deceitful states of happiness is crossed; biotechnology should be limited when it pursues whimsical ends (for example, the recently invented cross between a sheep and a goat) rather than genuine needs; civil engineering should also be regulated when it conflicts with fundamental goals of human life.

The distinction between pure science, applied science, and technology is sensible and conceptually useful, and I agree that some technologies could be dispensed with. However, I have two main complaints about the differentiated treatment view.

My first is that leaving pure and applied science free while imposing supervision on technology that does not pursue useful or necessary ends rests on a difficult distinction between *necessary ends* and *whimsical desires* or, in other words, between primary and secondary ends, between natural rights and cultural rights, between ends in themselves and instrumental aims. Such a distinction, however sensible, cannot easily be drawn.

Consider, for example, the prolongation of life, which seems a natural end. However, in some cases it clearly becomes a selfish act or does violence to the patient. Should we be allowed to pursue such an end even in these cases and allow medicine to develop the technical means it may need for them? Consider also mental health. It is a primary end, but can we always be confident that modern drugs are more effective, more charitable, or more humane than older therapies or no therapy at all? A distinguished Cambridge physician, Lord Rosenheim, has declared that "since benzodiazepines are available, we need much fewer beds at the mental hospitals, and the time of hospitalization becomes shorter."[1] Is this a sound argument? One might reply that a shorter period of hospitalization is an economic advantage, but not necessarily a human benefit. And pills and drugs are often psychological straitjackets, not dissimilar, in their consequences, to the old, material ones. Chemical therapy does not pursue the patient's health, since it does not restore mental capacities, but seems to pursue different ends, namely, the patient's (or his parents' and relatives') peace, harmlessness, and adaptation to current codes of behavior—that is, not primary ends or natural rights, but secondary ones. Or, to give another example, consider the case of sex predetermination. Should it be condemned or allowed in every case? Real-life situations are so rich and depend on so many variables that it seems to be impossible to make sharp distinctions: sex predetermination in one situation (for example, a family in Western Europe) may look whimsical; elsewhere (for example, in a developing country or even in a less developed Western country), it may be considered vital.

I do not want to argue that there is no sensible distinction between different ends or aims. Rather, I want to suggest that no such distinction can be drawn on *a priori* grounds and taken as definitive. No revealed codes prescribe which ends are intrinsically legitimate because natural, and which are not worth pursuing because cultural or simply fashionable. Moreover, even if one believes that there are such codes, there are no sharp, clear-cut, fixed criteria or for their interpretation and application.

The recent Instruction of the Congregation of the Faith of the Catholic Church concerning artificial fertilization and other bioethical questions may help clarify the problems we are discussing. The differentiated treatment view seems to be the official view of the Catholic Church. The Instruction starts by saying that

> "scientific basic and applied research is a remarkable expression of man's control over creation," but science and technology "cannot by themselves disclose the sense of existence and human progress. . . . Science and technology require, to have intrinsic sense, that the fundamental criteria of morality be respected; that is to say, they need to be subordinated to human personhood, to its indefeasible rights, to its true, integral good according to God's project and will."[2]

The fundamental maxim at work here is clear. If a technology T is intended to realize an end E, then T is admissible provided E is a member of the class N of natural rights or ends in themselves. Since the Catholic Church maintains that N is specifiable and actually specified (through revelation as interpreted by the Church itself), it can draw immediate consequences from its maxim. For example, no technological intervention is permitted, if it risks human life; no artificial fertilization is allowed, if it may be fatal to an embryo or harmful to its growth; no euthanasia is legitimate; no technological devices are justified, if they do not respect human personhood, and so on.

The problems sketched above can now be easily seen. First, there is the problem of the *content* of the moral code to which technology should be subordinated. The Instruction maintains that there exists "a natural moral law which expresses and prescribes the ends, rights and duties which are based on the corporeal and spiritual nature of the human person."[3] But this is far from being clear. We may grant that several rights and ends are so well entrenched in our culture that they may be taken as "natural," but what about others? Take, for example, the right to have children. The Instruction denies that couples have this right. But the argument that "a child is not something due and cannot be taken as a property"[4] is not very compelling, for sterile couples may want to have children for the children's sake, that is, as an act of love and not of mere egoism (just as there are fertile couples who adopt children, even handicapped children, because they love them and see it as their duty to help them).

Or consider another example, the case of unusual bone marrow transplantation (BMT) that has given rise to recent discussion. In 1984, a four-year-old girl was diagnosed as suffering from a chronic myeloid leukaemia. The parents were informed of the fatal prognosis and the possibilities of BMT (as well as the related risks), and were advised that if they had a second child he might be a compatible donor. Although the probability of compatibility was estimated as one in four, the parents decided to have a second child, who was born in 1985. He provided successful BMT, and now both the girl and his brother are leading normal lives and are in good health. Reporting the results of their intervention, the doctors write that "many unanswered questions, especially ethical ones, arise from this case of programmed generation of a potential bone marrow donor, but a life may have been saved."[5] However, many people, especially among Catholics, reacted negatively on the ground that a child has to be conceived for his own sake and not as an instrument, as a programed potential donor seems to be. But why? How can we be sure that the parents wanted the second child only as an instrument and that they were so egotistical as to be ready to sacrifice the life of the second for the survival of the first? Might they not have loved both children in the same way? Have we been ready to accept the second, even though he might be a noncom-

patible donor? Where is the assured code that states unequivocally
what is wrong and right in this case?

But suppose such a code does exist. We are now faced with our
second problem, the *justification* of the code. Catholics maintain that
such fundamental rights as the right to life and the right of the human
person to respect "can be recognized by all who wish to be guided by
proper reason and objective truth."[6] Accordingly, they maintain further that "the personalistic view is the only one that can be based and
justified theoretically."[7] But this is disputable because no ethical norm
can be rationally justified, and because we have no privileged, intuitive
access to a fundamental code of natural rights that is valid at all times
and places. That means that other ethical norms may be equally right.
If one replies that the Christian or any other religious code is the only
true one because it has been revealed directly by God, then Kant's
argument in his *Religion within the Limits of Pure Reason* may still be
invoked: even though God stated what is good and bad, it is always up
to us to accept his statements and to apply or violate them.

But suppose this problem could be solved, that is to say, suppose
a fundamental natural code N existed to which people could resort to
evaluate whether their behavior is legitimate or not. Then the third
problem crops up, the *interpretation* of the norms contained in N.

Let us take an example. Suppose N contains the maxim: "We must
respect human personhood." What does "human personhood" mean?
Who is a human person? When may a living organism confidently be
said to be a human person? Since the body is the physical expression
of personhood, it must be present; but obviously that is not enough—
there must be psychic life. But this too seems to be insufficient. One
author maintains that "a person is a unity of spirit and body";[8] another
writes that

> "man's life is intangible for man is a person. Being a person is not a
> psychological fact but an existential one; it does not depend on age,
> psychic conditions, or the talents of a subject. . . . Personhood may remain
> unconscious when we make a slip, but it continues and we must refer to
> it. It may be not developed as yet when we are children, but it claims
> moral respect since its beginning. . . . The existential difference between
> subject and object, personhood and things is rooted in an ontological
> difference according to which we are either persons or things, *tertium non
> datur.* "[9]

The least we can say about these definitions and philosophical distinctions is that they are vague if not tautological. How then can concrete,

practical consequences be drawn from them? Someone has written that "modern biological science and genetics sufficiently prove that an embryo is not a thing."[10] This may be granted, but if we allow science to define that an embryo is a person, we must expect the definition of a person to change along with changes in science.

Let us take another example. The Catholic doctrine lays down the norm: "In the conjugal act the procreative and the unitive dimensions must not be separated."[11] Can we say, as some Catholics maintain, that homologous artificial insemination (AIH) with drawing of sperm *after* the conjugal act is to be admitted, while AIH with drawing of sperm *distinct from* the conjugal act (for example, through masturbation) is to be condemned? All depends on the interpretation of the key word "separated": some authors maintain that in the latter case there is no morally relevant separation, for example, because husband and wife still act in a context of love; others, on the contrary, maintain that there is. Who is right? Who may be credited with the true interpretation of the norm? The fact is that even a fundamental code of natural rights, supposing it exists, suffers from a typical desease that affects all codes—vagueness. To face it, we can only resort to authorities or jurisprudence, but different authorities may give different interpretations of the same norm. Someone who believes in a supreme authority whose verdicts are final is not in a better position, for such an authority could render different verdicts in different situations. This happens even within the Catholic Church, and it is no scandal. Does it not indicate that the alleged fundamental code of natural rights is not a reliable guide for conduct?

Suppose, however, that a fundamental code N is fixed; its justification accepted; and its interpretation clearly specified. The last problem on our list now arises, that is, the *application* of the norms of N to given, concrete situations. Consider again the norm: "We must respect human persons." We may grant that a conscious patient suffering in his bed is a human person. But does the norm apply to a patient vegetating in a state of irreversible coma? Or consider the norm, "We must respect human life." It certainly obliges us to respect children. But what about embryos and other biological states? Different answers are possible.[12] For example, we might argue that human life begins when an ovule is fertilized, or when the fusion of the spermatozoon with the ovule starts, or when the cells are organized in the embrinal stripe, or when the last moment of possible twinning is reached, or when cerebral life starts, or when there is a capacity to react to stimuli or to feel pain. Many other criteria are also possible. How does the norm apply? Appealing to science is putting the cart before the horse, for science ascertains states of affairs (for example, that at a given moment in time there is such and such cell organization), but to establish that a certain state of affairs is an instance of "human life," we must already have a criterion (this is true for any universal term, but is especially relevant for a term such as "human life," which is not descriptive, but theoretical and axiological).

Faced with problems such as these, we have to admit that a fundamental code of natural rights is similar to other codes—to civil codes, for example. Jurists know that all codes, even the most detailed, are not only vague, but incomplete because new situations can arise for which there are no clear-cut rules. Moreover, codes are often antinomic and contain rules that prescribe contradictory behaviors. Our example of BMT is a case in point. Here we have a genuine conflict of rights: the right to health and normal life of one child, and the right to dignity of the other. Who will decide that one right is more fundamental or the only legitimate one? Do both rights not belong to the same class N of natural rights?

Or let us take another example. Consider again the norm: "In the conjugal act the procreative and unitive dimensions must not be separated." Even supposing that the norm is clear, when we apply it to concrete cases, we find borderline situations in which what the right behavior is is not clear. On the basis of this norm, the Catholic Church has condemned not only both homologous and heterologous *in vitro* fertilation with embryo transfer (FIVET), but also AIH "except when the technical instrument does not replace the conjugal act but facilitates and helps it to reach its natural aim."[13] The main reason is that, even if there were no loss of embryos, the instrument dissociates the two dimensions of the conjugal act. But is this application of the norm indisputable? What is the difference among AIH with drawing of sperm after the conjugal act, AIH with drawing of sperm distinct from the conjugal act, and FIVET? Could not all these techniques be considered as "technical aids" and evaluated according to the intentions of their users?

Summing up: first, it is doubtful whether there exists a code of natural rights that is fixed once and for all. What one culture declares to be natural is a value that that culture takes as fundamental. Second, even if such a code existed, it is doubtful—owing to the problems of content, justification, interpretation, and application—that it can serve as a reliable guide for promoting or restraining technology. Thus the differentiated treatment view, despite its merits, is an unsatisfactory answer to our question concerning which scientific activities should be restrained or promoted.

To avoid misunderstandings, I have to be clear in my criticism. I do not deny that technology should not be evaluated on ethical grounds; I believe that it should. However, I maintain that there can be no privileged ethical code, that codes are our own choices, and that any code gives rise to problems of interpretation and application that we have to solve personally. It is here that my second objection to the differentiated treatment view arises.

2. Science and Values: The Divorce View

The problem is the following: If we grant that technology must be subjected to moral standards, since it depends on pure and applied science, should not these also be subjected to the same standards? Many adherents of the differentiated treatment view say, no. Only technology, not basic science, should be supervised. They rest their case on the argument that science is a cognitive enterprise that states how the world is, whereas ethics prescribes how the world ought to be.

I call such a view the *divorce view,* and I do not intend to go into detail here.[14] I take the old, venerable distinction between *"is-statements"* and *"ought-statements"* to be sound and beneficial; it is sound because there is no logical way of passing from one kind of statements to the other, and beneficial because it has saved science from ideology and ethics and religion from scientism. I limit myself to two remarks.

First, I believe that the divorce view is based on too narrow a conception of how science ascertains truth, that is, it assumes that scientific truth depends only on objective comparisons between hypotheses and observational or experimental facts, without any pragmatic, personal, or cultural factors being involved in the process. This conception is intimately linked to the divorce view. It was not by chance that Galileo, who was firmly convinced that science reaches truth through "sensible experiences and necessary demonstrations," battled the Church to defend the divorce view.

But Galileo was wrong, as is shown by the way in which his heliocentric theory was finally accepted by the scientific community. Had this theory been based on, or tested by, empirical evidence alone, its adoption would have been delayed for centuries. It is well known that after our expulsion from the paradise of logical positivism (and from "World Three" as well) that a scientific theory, in particular a pervasive theory with many inter- and extrascientific connotations, has to pass different kinds of tests, including value tests, and therefore uses different kinds of arguments, including rhetorical ones. Galileo himself could have acknowledged this fact. He advocated "sensible experiences," but these are sometimes merely observational facts, sometimes experimental facts, and occasionally even idealizations. He commended "necessary demonstrations," but sometimes these are "flowers of rhetoric," as he calls them when criticizing their use by other authors. These include analogical arguments, pragmatic arguments, and arguments *ad hominem* or *ad personam*.

If science cannot be said to be value free, since value considerations enter into the method through which it ascertains its truth, how can the divorce view still be maintained? One might reply that value considerations pertain not to the *theoretical appraisal* of scientific theories, but to their *practical acceptance.* But this distinction is far from clear. Leaving aside the fact that theoretical appraisal also needs value considerations (for example, considerations about simplicity, elegance, and heuristic promise), theoretical appraisal can be distinguished, but not separated, from practical acceptance. Since we do not have independent access to truth, we can only admit as true those cognitive claims that have been ascertained through the best tests and arguments, that is, that are acceptable in the best test situations. Truth, as such, may still be considered independent of our acceptance procedures, but our *criteria* are not. And if our criteria of truth involve value considerations, our scientific truth is not value free.

One might object that this value dependence of scientific truth still does not prove the divorce view untenable, for the values entering into the scientific test procedures are epistemic, not ethical or religious. In this connection I introduce my second remark: even if the borders between epistemic and ethical values were clear (which they are not, since such values as simplicity or elegance are sometimes based on philosophical or religious views), we still cannot dispense with strictly moral considerations in pursuing and testing some scientific hypotheses. This is often the case with biological or genetic hypotheses involving experiments on animals and humans, or with psychological and sociological hypotheses, and even with certain physical hypotheses. Moreover, scientific fallouts can have unpredictable consequences, some of which are desirable and useful, others risky and even devastating.

The point I want to stress here is twofold. Not only are our statements of scientific truth not value free, the very decision to pursue a cognitive end, that is, an apparently pure end, requires at least a judgment of suitability, namely, that pursuing such an end is not harmful to men, animals, or the environment. Thus my answer to the question whether science should be supervised is that it should. Science is linked to ethics, religion, values—in short, to the rest of our culture—and is not an independent enterprise. However desirable, it must be brought into harmony with the whole of human life. Hence we should place all science under supervision, not only technology or some specific fields.

Even those who may agree with my answer to the first question may disagree with my answer to the second, and go back to the differentiated treatment view. What is the use, they may object, of supervising basic science? Does it not satisfy cognitive ends that are good in themselves, such as knowing the nature of the world and of man to prevent undesirable events or diseases or to find the proper remedies for them? My reply to this objection is, first, that pursuing basic science also involves moral considerations, as I have already remarked; second, that a good result may be used badly, as is well known; third, that even good ends pursued with goodwill may have bad consequences. Chemical pollution is a case in point, and the old saying that "the road to hell is paved with good intentions" still holds true. Finally, we can predict neither the use we can make of the products of science, nor their consequences. Thus I have to repeat myself: if we want science to be harmoniously integrated with all the other dimensions of our life, and be responsible men and not slaves of our own creations, then we have to supervise science.

This brings me to our final, third question: To whom should the supervision over science be granted? Before answering this question, let me explain why it is so topical. For centuries it was thought that science was good in itself and could be trusted unconditionally. When, in the face of undesirable results and grave risks, doubts were raised, we tended to suppose that science was the best remedy for its own shortcomings. Our confidence was so great that we transformed a healthy respect for science into a blind faith in it, and made scientists the supreme authorities in an ever-increasing number of fields. We even ask them questions about areas in which they are incompetent, for example, individual happiness and social constitutions, and they offer answers to questions that are completely outside their domain of expertise. The case of scientists who believe they have something valuable to say about God is the most glaring. The reaction was inevitable. Heideggerians, Nietzscheans, and neo-Parmenideans attacked the basis of the scientific enterprise and its "will to power." Romantic poets, humanists, and novelists began weaving panegyrics to the good old days; new mystics started to appeal to the true, real, meaningful world as opposed to the spurious one we live in. Socially, public opinion started to be frightened by the risks of unemployment, pollution, alienation, and lack of identity. Politically, radical Greens started to play on these fears and to raise antiscientific and antitechnological flags. Thus, in a relatively short period, we have passed from taking science as the savior to regarding it as the Devil himself.

I consider these reactions to be as irrational, uncritical, and emotional as the former faith in science. The *homo scientificus* or *technologicus* is neither a natural kind nor a fatal outcome of human history. It is one of our own cultural products that we have to evaluate. Both hosannas and exorcisms are to be avoided; they take us nowhere. If we do not want to jump from the frying pan of scientism into the fire of luddism— the former untenable because counter realistic, the latter unreasonable because counter historical—, we have to face the problem of the supervision of science in a realistic way. But how?

4. Four Guiding Principles on the Road to Responsibility

There are at least four guiding principles.

First: as Feyerabend has stressed,[15] we should take science neither as the only tradition nor as necessarily the best one. This principle seems obvious. Science, as we know it, was invented a few centuries ago and is likely to remain an integral part of our life in the future. Although it superseded other traditions, we cannot conclude that they were all childish and will no longer be useful. There is no historical law of the intellectual development of mankind. Contrary to what Comte maintained, any such law is an act of faith in disguise; it is not a scientific discovery, but a scientistic dogma.

Second: we should promote competition between science and other traditions, be they ascientific or antiscientific. On this, I also agree with Feyerabend. Many cases could be cited to show that competition is the best source of intellectual and moral progress. A recent case, still under discussion among experts, has especially confirmed for me the validity and suitability of this view. For years scientific medicine tried to convince us that alternative medical doctrines and therapies were unsound and useless. Homeopathy, for example, was condemned mainly by the argument that after repeated dilutions in water, the molecules of a drug completely disappear. The rare scientists who bothered to examine the problem repeated this argument *ad nauseam,* and always considered *ad hoc* the hypothesis that molecules of a drug may leave a "mark" in water. However, recent experiments cast doubt on this conclusion and suggest that the transmission of the biological information may be related to the molecular organization of water. Had not homeopaths maintained their view, and had not laboratories and journals given them the opportunity to prove their point, such a result (however disputable it may still be)[16] would never have been obtained.

Third: we should promote the sense of responsibility among scientists. All kinds of risk can be expected if scientists *qua* scientists do not consider themselves as having moral obligations. If they profess a form of scientism, according to which whatever scientists do is a contribution to progress, or if they stick to the divorce view and relegate the ethical questions stemming from their work to politicians, moralists, or priests, we are in trouble. The same holds if we keep them in ivory towers or under glass cups. Scientific fallout is ethically loaded, and, since scientists themselves are in the best position to assess at least the most immediate consequences, they should feel responsible for them.

Fourth: we should defend individual freedom and democracy. This means that, whatever role we may want science to play in our life, we should not forget man's right not to be indoctrinated, oppressed, or hurt; to live according to his own desires; to make his decisions personally; and to follow his conscience, even when he is in a minority.

If we stick to these principles, we will be in a better position to face the problem of who should be granted the right to supervise science. Different solutions are possible. I shall examine some of them in decreasing order of suitability in the light of these principles.

First solution: the state. Since the state is an organized community of citizens, this solution looks reasonable. But there is a problem with it. As Feyerabend has stressed, modern Western states are linked to science, and they impose science through education and in many other ways. How then could we trust a controller who is called on to control himself? We should separate the two roles and demand that the state defend and promote traditions other than science, precisely as it does with linguistic, ethnical, or religious minorities. The monogamous marriage of state and science conflicts with our first principle, since it favors one subculture alone, with the second principle, since it does not promote competition, and probably also with the fourth, since it represents a risk to individual freedom.

Second solution: committees of experts. Several good reasons militate against this old solution, which dates back at least to Plato. First, there are no authorities in ethical matters. Committees are not experts on moral questions, only people are. Second, there is the counterargument that even if we elect authorities, no one should be given the right to decide what is good for others. Moreover, we have to consider that if we delegate supervision of science to some authorities, they will automatically be transformed into uncontrolled controllers, like Egyptian or Mayan priests, or Plato's philosopher-kings. Finally, such a delegation would lower scientists' sense of responsibility. Hence, the idea of committees of experts has to be rejected because it conflicts with our third and fourth principles.

Third solution: scientists themselves should be granted the right to supervise their own work. This seems a step in the right direction because it considers the responsibility of scientists in accordance with our third principle. But for this principle be respected and the others satisfied, at least two conditions must be fulfilled, namely, that scientists must openly confront other subcultures and citizens, and, that scientists must be suitably educated. I doubt whether these conditions are fulfilled. On this point we have to be realistic even at the cost of being disagreeable. By transforming scientists into supreme authorities, we have put them in the worst condition to accept their own responsibilities. Few of them seem prepared to talk to ordinary people, to compare their approach to problems with those of others, to fully appreciate that other things are as important as science. In most cases they believe that they alone possess the truth, or know the only way to reach it. If you dare to question their work, they reply that you are incompetent or they simply ignore you. The level of specialization is so high that the same arrogant answer is usually given by scientists working in one field to scientists working in another. The current scientific training is unsatisfactory, if scientists are to be involved in the supervision of science, because such a training stresses mainly, if not solely, the technical aspects of science to the detriment of its historical, philosophical, and ethical dimensions.

This brings me to the fourth solution: the supervision of science should be granted to everyone. Conceptually this seems the most satisfactory solution. It is also the most obvious one because science concerns everyone, and thus everyone should be granted the right to thrust his own nose into it. In modern democracies citizens are invited to give their opinion on any kind of question that concerns their personal or social destiny. They are consulted about politics, economy, peace, war, social insurance, health care, and so on. Why should they refrain from expressing their views on science? Is not science an integral part of their own lives? Does it not affect their destiny?

I admit that when we pass from the conceptual to the institutional and educational levels, this solution is far from easy. We do not yet have supervisory institutions. Until a few decades ago, we had not even thought about it. Thus we are late and largely unprepared. But although the challenge is serious, we can meet it. We have invented parliaments to replace tyrants and to make ourselves heard, unions to control absolute economic power, courts to enforce our rights, schools to educate ourselves, referees and editorial boards to guarantee objective and pluralistic information, and advisory committees to take considered decisions. If we have been so good in these fields, we should not despair of science either.

Notes

1. Reported by W. A. Werner in his opening remarks at the symposium *Benzodiazepines: an Update. Where do we go from here?*, ed. by O.J. Rafaelson and J. Ward, (Basel: Editiones Roche, 1986).

2. See "Istruzione della Congregazione per la Dottrina della Fede su il rispetto della vita umana nascente e la dignità della procreazione umana," reprinted in *Il dono della vita*, ed. by E. Sgreccia (Milan: Vita e Pensiero, 1987), 10.

3. *Ibid.*, 11.

4. *Ibid.*, 37.

5. G. R. Burgio, *et al.*, "Programming of Bone Marrow Donor for a Leukaemic Sibling," in *Lancet*, June 27, 1987, 1484–1485 and "Bone Marrow Transplantation from Programmed Donor: One Year Later," in *Lancet*, April 23, 1988, 945.

6. E. Sgreccia, "Bioetica, eutanasia e dignità della morte," in *Corso di Bioetica*, ed. by E. Sgreccia (Milan: Franco Angeli, 1986), 182.

7. E. Sgreccia, "La bioetica: contenuti e fondamenti," in *Corso di bioetica, op. cit.*, 55. Father Sgreccia attacks liberal radicalism and utilitarianism (*ibid.*, 54–55). But not all Catholics seem to be of the same opinion. For example, Father Manuel Cuyas, Jesuit, professor of moral philosophy, maintains that genetic engineering is to be limited only by a "good anthropology" that "evaluates rationally and with good sense the cost/benefit ratio of the practical application of a scientific discovery." See his words as reported in *Tempo medico*, 266, 28 February 1987, 44–45.

8. E. Sgreccia, *La bioetica. Manuale per medici e biologi* (Milan: Vita e Pensiero, 1986), 65.

9. Romano Guardini, as quoted by Angel Rodriguez Luno, "Sessualità, matrimonio, procreazione responsabile, problemi etici della sterilizzazione e dell'aborto procurato," in *Corso di bioetica, op. cit.*, 110.

10. A. R. Luno, *op.cit.*, 110.

11. See the Encyclical *Humane Vitae* by Pope Paul VI (25 July 1968), 12.

12. For a review and critical examination of these possibilities, see A. Serra, "Quando comincia un essere umano. In margine ad un recente documento," in *Il dono della vita, op. cit.*, 91–105.

13. "Istruzione, etc.," *op. cit.*, 34.

14. See M. Pera, "Does Science Interfere with Ethics and Relgion?," paper read at the conference *The Ethics of Scientific Knowledge*, International Center of Theoretical Biology, Venice June 4–6, 1987, forthcoming in the Proceedings (Rome: Istituto dell'Enciclopedia Italiana).

15. P. Feyerabend, *Science in a Free Society* (London: New Left Books, 1978).

16. See the paper by J. Benveniste and his colleagues, "Human Basophil Degranulation Triggered by Very Dilute Antiserum Against IgE," in *Nature*, vol. 333, June 30, 1988, 816–818; see also the reply of the Editor and his collaborators, " 'High-dilution' Experiments a Delusion," in *Nature*, vol. 334, July 28, 1988, 287–290. The ways to science seem to be as many as the ways to the Lord; one of the editor's collaborators is a magician!

Ecological Theories and Ethical Imperatives:

Can Ecology Provide a Scientific Justification for the Ethics of Environmental Protection?

KRISTIN SHRADER-FRECHETTE

Introduction: Ecological Science as a Foundation for Environmental Ethics

Many of us probably believe that ecologists ought to play a central role in helping to formulate environmental policy and to justify many of our claims in environmental ethics.[1] Philosopher Paul Taylor, for example, explicitly affirms both our duty to preserve environmental integrity and the necessity for us to rely on biologists and ecologists to help us recognize the scope of our ethical obligations.[2]

Many other philosophers,[3] scientists,[4] and lawmakers[5] have made a similar point: good ecology is a necessary (but not a sufficient) condition for sound environmental ethics. Moreover, they claim, technological and industrial activities are harming the entire biosphere; ecologists, because of their expertise, have an obligation to help create wise public policy.[6] For example, we need trustworthy ecological data on species decline relative to reserve size,[7] if our ethical and policy conclusions about the optimal size of tropical forest reserves are to be justifiable. Similarly, we need to know whether ecologists are correct in believing that phosphorus is a limiting nutrient in causing lake eutrophication, if environmental policymakers are to have a clear scientific basis for not allowing pollution of fresh-water lakes with phosphorus effluents.[8]

According to Arthur Cooper, when he was president of the Ecological Society of America, the most direct example of ecological influence on environmental ethics and policy is the role that findings about coastal and estuarine ecosystems played in stimulating government programs for coastal zone management.[9] Cooper also claimed that findings of ecologists were directly responsible for environmental decisions limiting use of DDT; for national forest-management policies favoring the diversity of multispecies forests; and for drawing attention to the problem of acid rain.[10]

Given that environmental ethics relies at least in part on ecological data,[11] it is reasonable to ask how successful the science of ecology has been in informing environmental ethics. Although I wish it were otherwise, my main argument in this essay is that ecology, at least at present, cannot do the job many moral philosophers and environmental policymakers often assign to it,[12] perhaps because it is such a young science, and because its parameters are much more resistant to prediction than are those of physics.

To support this conclusion, I shall argue for three related claims. 1. Many philosophers who do environmental ethics presuppose that their normative conclusions gain support from certain ecological theories and hypotheses. 2. Ecologists cannot, at least at present, provide an uncontroversial account of two absolutely central ecological notions, biological holism and "equilibrium" or the "balance of nature"; these concepts are as problematic as is the notion of "species," for example (see the essay by Mauron in this volume). 3. Finally, although ecology may contribute at the general, first-order, or intuitive level to a correct world view in terms of which to conceive environmental ethics, it contributes little, at the second-order or critical level, to the resolution of particular controversies in environmental policy and ethics.

Philosophers and Policymakers Assume that Ecologists Can Help Justify Environmental Ethics

Insofar as moral philosophers look to ecology to support their views about environmental ethics, they often assume that ecologists can provide them with guidelines for a wholistic, ecosystemic ethics, and for maintaining some sort of balance in nature. In other words, they typically accept what I call, respectively, the "wholism presupposition" and the "balance presupposition."[13]

Discussing the role of the balance or homeostasis presupposition, Holmes Rolston in his classic essay distinguished two main species of environmental ethics. Environmental ethics in the secondary or anthropocentric sense focuses on "the paramount law in ecological theory . . . that of homeostasis,"[14] and connects morality with maintaining ecological balance or stability. According to Rolston, humans have an obligation to promote ecological homeostasis or balance, since it is a necessary condition for maximizing human well-being or survival. Paul Sears, Garrett Hardin, Thomas Colwell,[15] Paul Taylor,[16] and Bryan

Norton[17] are some of those who espouse an environmental ethics in this secondary sense and subscribe to variants of the balance presupposition.

Unlike environmental ethics in the secondary or anthropocentric sense, which hinges on the balance presupposition, Rolston claims that environmental ethics in the primary or ecocentric sense focuses on what I have called the "wholism presupposition." This ethics is based on the discovery of a moral ought inherent in recognition of the unified character of the ecosystem. It defines right actions as those that preserve the wholeness or integrity of the ecosystem, actions which "maximize ecosystemic excellences."[18]

In addition to Rolston,[19] Callicott, Dubos, Goodpaster, Leopold, Shepard, and perhaps Sagoff,[20] also subscribe to variants of the wholism presupposition and espouse an environmental ethics in the primary, non-anthropocentric sense.[21] Goodpaster, for example, invokes Lovelock's notion of Gaia,[22] suggests that "the biosystem as a whole" exhibits feedback behavior, such as being sustained by metabolic processes for accumulating energy and maintaining an equilibrium with its environment.[23] On the basis of the wholism presupposition, Goodpaster follows Leopold[24] and argues for extending moral considerability to ecosystemic wholes. Callicott says much the same thing, that ecology has made it possible to apprehend the biosphere as an "organic whole" of "integrally related parts,"[25] a whole that has rights on the basis of "ecological entitlement."[26]

Problems with Appeals to the Balance of Nature

Whether one appeals (like Bryan Norton) to the balance presupposition or (like Goodpaster and Callicott) to the wholism presupposition, one is unable to use either ecological notion as an uncontroversial foundation for resolving particular, second-order disputes in environmental ethics. In both cases, but for different reasons, ecology cannot do the precise job demanded of it by those who wish to use it as a basis for resolving environmental conflicts.

Perhaps the greatest problem with appealing to the balance presupposition is that there is no clear sense in which one can claim that natural ecosystems proceed toward homeostasis, stability, or some "balance."[27] In the ecosystemic view of the balance of nature, to which Norton and Taylor appeal, there is no consensus among ecologists.[28] Nor is there support for the diversity-stability view held by MacArthur, Hutchinson, and Commoner.[29]

The reasons for the disfavor attributed to the view of MacArthur, *et al.* are both empirical and mathematical. Salt marshes and the rocky intertidal provide only two of many classical counterexamples to the diversity-stability view. Salt marshes are simple in species composition, but they are stable, and they are not diverse ecosystems. On the other hand, the rocky intertidal is one of the most species-rich and diverse natural systems, yet it is highly unstable, since it may be perturbed by a single change in its species composition.[30] Empirically based counterexamples of this sort have multiplied over the last 15 years, and May, Levins, Connell, and others have seriously challenged the diversity-stability hypothesis on both mathematical and field-based grounds.[31] Yet, many policymakers continue to cite the hypothesis, the most famous version of the balance of nature, as grounds for supporting many tenets of environmental ethics and law, such as the Endangered Species Act.[32] Most ecologists, however, have either repudiated the thesis or cast serious doubt on it.[33]

Their doubts have arisen in part because we cannot say what it would be to hinder the balance of nature. Ecosystems regularly change and regularly eliminate species. How would one use an ethic based on some balance of nature to argue that humans should not modify ecosystems or even wipe out species, for example, when nature does this itself through natural disasters, such as volcanic eruptions and climate changes like those that destroyed the dinosaurs? Nature doesn't appear merely to extirpate species, or cause them to move elsewhere because their niches are gone. But if not, then one cannot obviously claim that it is wrong on *ecological grounds* for humans to do what nature does—wipe out species. Obviously, there are *anthropocentric grounds* for alleging wrongness (for example, because it is wrong for humans to cause unnecessary suffering or to destroy something wantonly or selfishly). But if one's only basis for condemning such actions is anthropocentric, because there are no adequate and universal theories of ecological "balance," then it is not clear how ecological theory can support an ecocentric environmental ethics.[34]

Moreover, the criterion for justifiable species extinction, for those who appeal to the balance presupposition, cannot be that what happens naturally is good, while what happens through human intervention is bad; this would be to solve the problem of scientific and empirical meaning with a purely stipulative and *ad hoc* definition. (See the essay by Colwell in this volume and his notes about Sober.) Nor can the difference be merely that humans do quickly (e.g., cause lake eutrophication) what nature does slowly. One must have some arguments to show that accelerating ecosystemic changes is bad, even if the changes themselves, e.g., wiping out species, are natural.

Medical science (if it is a science) also faces problems of defining what is "balanced" or "healthy," problems that are similar to those of ecological science. Both disciplines need to specify criteria for health or "balance," in order to evaluate the success of their scientific practice. It is relatively easy to do so in medical science because its goal is always the well-being of the *individual* patient. The analogue in ecology would be the well-being of an individual organism, e.g., the redfish, or species. Environmental problems, however, almost never focus on the health of one organism or species at the expense of others. Ecological prescriptions for what is healthy or natural must take into account thousands of communities, species, and individuals, all relative to the health of an entire ecosystem—or the entire biosphere, and then specify how to maintain the health or balance of the *entire system*. This is far more difficult than specifying the health of one individual within some system.[35] Because it is so difficult, it is not clear how one could specify an ecological "balance" without knowing precisely how to define the system that is allegedly being balanced. (This biological difficulty is analogous to the economic problems associated with defining a theory of social choice; here one of the difficulties is knowing how to specify the whole that aggregates, combines, or represents numerous individual choices.)

Problems with Appeals to Wholism or Organicism

As a foundation for environmental ethics, appeals to organicism or to the wholism presupposition likewise suffer from both ethical and epistemological problems. Let's sketch some of the ethical difficulties. First, to presuppose that ecosystems are wholistic units that maximize their well-being, as Rolston and Callicott claim, and that humans are bound to maximize ecosystemic well-being,[36] is to attribute interests to ecosystems. Yet, within the accepted philosophical tradition, "interests" logically presuppose desires, aims, or wants.[37] And ecosystems do not have desires, aims, or wants.[38]

Moreover the capacity for suffering or enjoyment is presumably a prerequisite for having interests.[39] If it were not, as Singer points out, then our obligations to beings with interests could multiply beyond reasonable limits. Hence we might be forced to say, for example, that automobiles had an interest in being lubricated and that water had an interest in not being drunk.[40] This means that attributing interests to ecosystems (via a first-order ethical principle) is incomplete and problematic (because of the multiplication problem) unless one likewise formulates second-order ethical principles for how to adjudicate conflicts among beings whose interests differ. In the absence of such second-order principles, it does not seem reasonable to attribute interests to ecosystems.

A second ethical problem with the wholism presupposition is that, if the biosphere or ecosystems were organic wholes having a good, then it would be difficult for us as moral agents to know what that good is, since they cannot tell us. Moreover, it is not clear (apart from human interests) why humans should care what the good for them is, since they cannot experience pleasure or pain. Obviously, there are purely anthropocentric grounds for condemning wanton destruction or misuse of the environment because such behavior manifests selfishness or greed. It would be difficult, however, to specify solely nonanthropocentric criteria for praising or blaming moral actions concerning ecosystems.[41]

Third, the wholism presupposition appears to lead to what Regan calls "environmental fascism."[42] If one follows an ethics of maximizing ecosystemic well-being, then one thereby presupposes that the good of the ecosystem or biosphere ought to come before individual human good. This means, for example, that massive human deaths or violations of basic civil liberties could be justified, even required, on the grounds that it would help check the population problem and contribute to the good of the biosphere. Garrett Hardin has already made such an argument in his famous discussion of "lifeboat ethics."[43]

Fourth, within a wholistic ethics, there is a dilemma: either we humans are on a par with other creatures on the planet, or we are not. Either we humans are equal members of the biotic community and therefore have no special responsibilities—contrary to what our ethical traditions have taught—or we are not. If we are not equal members because of our moral primacy, then we have no obligations to any nonhuman entity whenever its basic welfare conflicts with our own. Following the consequences of this dilemma, the presupposition of wholism appears to lead to actions that are either heinous (in the case of human equality with other beings), or inconsistent with the prescriptions of most environmentalists (in the case of human superiority over other beings).[44]

From the scientific point of view, the wholism presupposition is just as problematic. For one thing, most well-known ecologists have rejected the GAIA hypothesis, the basis of many accounts of wholism, as unproved speculation. Of course, they admit the ecological fact of interconnectedness and coevolution on a small scale. Second, an ecosystem, as the same collection of individuals, species, and relationships, does not *persist* through time. Hence any notion of the "dynamic stability" of an ecosystemic whole is unclear.[45]

Third, the selection of the "ecosystem" as the unit that is or ought to be maximized is peculiar.[46] Why not choose as the unit the community,[47] the association,[48] or the trophic level? Clements said that the community is an organism;[49] if so, then why is the ecosystem also an organism? Which is it, and what are the criteria for a wholistic organism? Or, if one is a wholist, why not choose the collection of ecosystems, the biosphere, as that which is maximized in nature and which we are morally enjoined to optimize? Once one abandons an individualistic ethic, then how, from a scientific point of view, does one choose among alternative nonindividual units to be maximized?[50] Such questions suggest that wholism or organicism is an arbitrary and imprecise notion, akin more to metaphysics than to empirical science.

Fourth, as an empirical notion, wholism is further undercut by the current reductionist dispute in ecology among Gleasonian individualists and Clementsian wholists. Their controversy indicates that the "levels problem" has not been solved in ecology.

Admittedly, various ecological conclusions are valid within particular spatial and temporal scales. Nevertheless, a given ecological conclusion (regarding balance) typically holds for some (but not other) "wholes" (e.g., populations, species, communities). For example, there may be some sort of stability or balance for a given species within a certain spatial scale, but not for other species, or not within another such scale. Ecologists cannot optimize the well-being of all these different wholes (having different spatial and temporal scales) at the same time. Because they cannot, there is no general level at which ecological problem solving takes place, and no general temporal or spatial scale within which a stable "whole" is exhibited.

Because of the absence of a universal ecological theory that can be appealed to in defining the "whole" that is balanced, ecologists are forced to work on a case-by-case basis. They recognize that there is no universal level (across species, populations, or communities) at which some balanced or stable whole exists. In part this is because numerous alleged "wholes," e.g., populations, exhibit density vagueness rather than density dependence, while other "wholes" do not.[51] This suggests, therefore, both that there is no universal level at which a balanced or stable whole is evident, and that there is a "levels problem" in ecology. But if so, then there is no clear, universal sense of wholism to which environmental ethicists can appeal.

A fifth scientific problem with the presupposition that ecosystems are wholistic units that maximize their well-being is that ecosystems are not agents in any meaningful sense. Moreover, it is scientifically wrong to suggest that ecosystems, rather than populations, adapt. Admittedly, species may evolve in a way that benefits a given ecosystem, but there is no selection at the level of the ecosystem.[52] Adaptation is restricted to heritable characteristics; no alleged knowledge of the past operates in natural selection, and the individual that is better adapted to the *present* environment is the one that leaves more off-spring and hence transmits its traits.[53] Given neo-Darwinian theory, Dobzhansky, Goodpaster, Lovelock, Mayr, Rolston, Wright, and other wholistic philosophers and ecologists are fundamentally wrong when they suggest either that natural selection operates to produce organs of a given kind *because* their presence gives rise to certain effects, or that ecosystemic processes operate in certain ways *because* they maximize ecosystemic excellence.[54]

Moreover, although it is possible to claim that adaptation maximizes individual survival in the sense already discussed, it is not clear what a community or an ecosystem maximizes. Traits advantageous to the individual are not always advantageous to the species or the ecosystem, as in the case of an individual's "taking all the food."[55] And traits advantageous to the species or to the ecosystem are not always advantageous to the individual, as in the case of dying young to hasten the cycling of nutrients.

Sixth, many ecosystemic or wholistic explanations are neither falsifiable nor even testable. This is probably why ecosystems ecology has been called by at least one scientist "theological ecology."[56] There is a clear definition neither of what it is to maximize some pattern of excellence, e.g., based on interspecific competition, nor of the ecosystem that is the subject of this alleged excellence. Theorists simply do not agree on the underlying processes that structure communities and ecosystems.[57]

Ecology and Its Contribution to Environmental Ethics

Although neither the balance nor the wholism presuppositions can assist us in developing environmental ethics and policy, there might be a sense in which ecology, considered more generally, could contribute to a correct paradigm for environmental ethics. However, the contributions do not seem to lie in the areas mentioned by Cooper in his 1982 Presidential Address to the Ecological Society of America. Recall that Cooper argued that ecological findings about the value of wetlands provided "the most direct example of ecological influence on public policy. . . ."[58]

Although Cooper cites the wetlands example as an ecological victory for environmental policy, it really appears to be a case in which environmental policymakers accepted the untested, highly doubtful beliefs of ecologists.[59] Indeed the acclaimed theoretical ecologist, John Maynard Smith, noted that "ecology is still a branch of science in which it is usually better to rely on the judgment of an experienced practitioner than on the predictions of a theorist."[60] As a consequence of this reliance, the battlefields of environmental policy are littered with the carcasses of untested, now rejected hypotheses (like the wetlands example and DDT biomagnification)[61] that were once used as ecological "facts" to support arguments for environmental protection.[62]

In the United States' longest legal conflict over environmental policy, for example, ecology was of little help. The controversy began in 1964 and was between the U.S. Environmental Protection Agency and five New York utility companies. The basic problem was that the disputants disagreed over the effect of water withdrawals by the utilities on the Hudson River striped bass population. After spending tens of millions of dollars, scientists could still not estimate the precise ecological effects of the water withdrawals. In other words, they knew at the level of a first-order ethical principle that they wished to avoid serious harm to the striped bass population. Because of the inadequacy of ecological theory, however, they were unable to specify some second-order principle for adjudicating the dispute between those attempting to protect the utility and those attempting to protect the bass.[63]

This suggests several reasons why it is difficult for ecologists to get a hold on fundamental processes allegedly underlying the balance and the wholism presuppositions.

1. Many important ecological problems, such as the causes and consequences of global CO_2 or acid rain, involve many parameters and a high degree of complexity and uncertainty. The presence of numerous parameters means both that too much is "going on" in natural communities to be captured by any model, e.g., Lotka-Volterra,[64] and that ecologists are not certain which factors are significant.[65]

2. Data bases in ecology are still so limited that they do not pro-

vide enough information for making environmental policy.[66] Because of inadequate data bases, different ecologists often claim evidential support for inconsistent hypotheses.[67]

3. Ecologists are encumbered with masses of untested hypotheses.[68] Just by mere dint of repetition, these hypotheses often achieve the status of facts.[69] Many of them are not testable in the first place;[70] some are mere tautologies;[71] and most are not evaluated against null models.[72]

4. Ecologists often advocate overly simple theories about ecosystem response because empirical data are hard to obtain. Such simple theories (e.g., regarding linear relationships between two parameters) are easily challenged, even though more complex ones are difficult to establish.[73]

5. Ecologists are forced to examine and understand ecosystems that are constantly changing in ways that are not always predictable or uniform. In other words, the natural-selection foundations of ecology undercut any uncontroversial notion of ecosystemic wholism, equilibrium, or balance of nature.[74] Moreover, even if ecologists could arrive at some noncontroversial notion of balance or equilibrium, it would not be very useful, for two reasons. First, unlike the mathematical models used to portray them, natural ecosystems are not typically at equilibrium; if they were, they would have far fewer species.[75] Second, it is not clear that adverse environmental effects come from loss of system stability rather than from direct impacts.[76]

6. Virtually every ecological situation can be said to be unique. Hence there may be no general theoretical laws in ecology, since the diversity of the biological community often fails to converge under similar physical conditions.[77]

7. Scientists often cannot make ecological measurements, e.g., for r (the intrinsic rate of natural increase of a population), as fine as legitimate use of proposed equations might require.[78]

8. Ecologists often must know how to optimize a situation involving many individual entities, species, communities, and populations. As was already mentioned, an analogous problem arises in economics: how to develop a theory of social choice that represents the interests of each person, but makes the good of the entire group paramount. We can't solve the problem either in economics or ecology.

Although the eight reasons just listed mean that ecology often cannot give us fundamental theoretical laws capable of informing particular environmental decisions, they suggest both useful methodological rules[79] and insights regarding what ecology can tell us.[80] It can tell us very general things, and can give us first-order ethical principles, such as: "behave as if everything is connected to everything else," or "do not exceed the carrying capacity of the area or the planet." But none of these generalizations is very helpful in practical, environmental decisionmaking, especially when we need a second-order ethical principle that tells us how to adjudicate disputes, for example, over precisely *how* everything is connected to everything else.[81]

Ecology can also tell us how to solve very specific problems whose solutions may be subjected to short-term empirical testing. Problems of this kind are exemplified by successful control of vampire bat populations, California red scale, and lake eutrophication.[82]

Likewise ecologists can often tell us, for example, which interventions in ecosystems are likely to reduce species diversity. *If* we define "balance" in terms of species diversity, *then*, indeed, ecologists can help us in environmental ethics and policymaking. That is, given the *end* of maximizing species diversity, ecology can tell us about the *means* of attaining it. Ecologists, however, cannot provide us with a general definition of an *end* or *goal* of ecosystemic activity, but they can often reveal the best *means* of attaining some goal, once it is specified. This is in part because, as a recent U.S. National Academy of Sciences report noted, there is typically no general, predictive ecological "theory" that can be applied to solve environmental problems, even though particular ecological facts, gained from specific cases, have often been useful in environmental policymaking.[83] In other words, ecologists can rarely tell us how to *protect* entire ecosystems or how to define such protection, although they can often help us *manage* particular species so as to benefit human interests.[84]

Summary

Where does all this leave us? Ecology can't tell us that more diverse ecosystems are more stable, that tropical rainforests contribute net oxygen to the atmosphere,[85] that there is a testable balance of nature, or that organochloride pesticides magnify along food chains. McIntosh puts the point well: all the schools of ecology have failed to provide it with a general ecological theory having predictive power.[86]

Until ecology is able to give us precise and predictive theoretical explanations as a basis for environmental ethics and policy, I have several interim suggestions: *first*, we ought to defend our views in classical anthropocentric terms, not by means of questionable ecological hypotheses like diversity-stability, or the wholism and balance presuppositions.[87] *Second*, following the example of the famous Hudson River controversy over the striped bass population, we ought to conceive of environmental policy, not as justified by appeals to questionable ecological hypotheses, but as established on the basis of a negotiated settlement for mitigating impacts.[88]

Third, just as we ought to avoid untestable grand theories in ecology as a basis for environmental policy, we also ought to avoid assuming, as Sagoff does,[89] that ecology can never become anything more than natural history. Environmental ethics and policy, like good science, must remain open to new discoveries.

Fourth, we can nevertheless argue, as does Robert Colwell,[90] that all aspects of nature have "instrinsic value," and we can thereby establish the presupposition that the burden of proof is on the person who aims to destroy, manipulate, or otherwise tamper with nature. In other words, we can claim that, all things being equal, we have a *prima facie* duty to recognize the intrinsic value of all beings and therefore also a duty not to interfere with anything in nature without good reason.

This duty might be said to exist, at least in part, because most nonhuman species existed on the planet before we did, and because all of us on the planet are interdependent. One could also argue that, because we did not create nature, we have a duty not to interfere with it without good reason. We might help others to recognize this duty by encouraging persons to have experiences in nature, e.g., backpacking, camping, birdwatching, and by trying to be aware of how we are dependent on nature.[91]

Once we make the first-order (or intuitive) ethical claim that all of nature possesses intrinsic value, we make it more difficult for humans to ignore their duties to the environment. Nevertheless, such claims do not provide *sufficient* conditions for practical decisionmaking; we still need second-order (or critical) ethical rules to specify criteria for how to adjudicate conflicting claims among natural entities, all of which have intrinsic value.[92]

For example, there might be a conflict between the first-order principles that all humans possess a right to life (and therefore can eat plants in order to live) and that all beings (including plants) have instrinsic value. If both principles hold, then we need to specify second-order principles to resolve the controversy. Presumably, these latter principles would enable us to justify the fact, for instance, that although plants have intrinsic value, nevertheless there are occasions when humans are justified in eating them.

As this example illustrates, merely agreeing with the first-order ethical claim that all of nature has intrinsic value does not resolve the most difficult environmental conflicts. This is because often those who destroy the environment do *not* deny (at the first or intuitive level) that nature possesses intrinsic value; instead they merely claim (at the second or critical level of analysis) that human concerns are superior to those of nature. In other words, they disagree (at the level of second-order principles) about how to resolve controversies when human concerns, e.g., jobs, are set against environmental well being, e.g., protecting wilderness. For this reason, an appeal to intrinsic value is a necessary first step in environmental ethics, but it is incomplete or insufficient as a basis for practical environmental decisionmaking. This is because most ethical controversy probably occurs at the second level.

One possible solution to some conflicts among first-order principles (as in the plant example) or among second-order principles (as in the jobs example) might be to specify additional second-order principles. These principles might be, for example, that only humans (or only sentient beings) have "interests" and therefore rights, and that only certain strong rights (as explained by Dworkin) "trump" other obligations arising out of considerations of intrinsic value.[93] In order to use these two second-order principles to resolve a conflict, however, we must be able to spell out and defend a notion of "strong rights," a task too extensive to be undertaken here. Nevertheless, this brief mention of rights, interests, and conflicts should suggest some of the possible ethical avenues still open to us, despite the limitations of ecology as a basis for environmental policymaking.

Objections to This Account

A number of persons, however, might object to these arguments that the theoretical ecological notions of "balance" and wholism or organicism provide little basis for environmental policymaking. They might claim, for example, that: 1. The earlier analysis amounts to "ecology bashing." 2. It ignores the human *need* for balanced, wholistic thinking, both for our own welfare and for that of the entire biosphere. 3. The earlier analysis also ignores nature's "right" to exist. 4. Moreover, objectors might claim that ecology does give us a number of answers to environmental questions.[94] Let's consider each of these disagreements in turn.

The first objection, regarding "ecology bashing," is warranted only if ecology is currently able to provide more of a foundation for environmental ethics and policymaking than has been alleged in the preceding analysis. If so, then this foundation needs to be demonstrated, even though there is no agreement on general ecological theory, and there are few, if any, successful predictions issuing from general ecological theory. In other words, a claim of ecology bashing is justified only if the bashing is unfair, if ecology is able to do more than has been alleged. In the absence of arguments to show this unfairness, this claim amounts to begging the question. Moreover, the preceding analysis has been bashing not ecology as such, but two interpretational concepts (balance and wholism) that threaten the clarity and testability for which most ecologists strive.

The second objection, that humans *need* balanced, wholistic thinking, also seems to miss the point. To posit the existence of something, e.g., ecological balance, just because we need it, would be wishful thinking at its worst, wishful thinking of the sort that Freud condemned in *The Future of an Illusion.* Moreover, just because we need something does not mean that it exists. We may need intelligence, for example, but that does not mean that we have it. The limits of reality are not determined by our desires, but by what exists and is defensible.

In particular, we may need wholistic thinking, but this does not mean that we can provide a rationally defensible account of wholism, an account robust enough to undergird environmental policymaking and likely objections to it. Earlier the analysis indicated some of the fundamental conceptual difficulties besetting wholistic/organismic ecology and ethics. If this account is correct, then although a given individual may be able to accept some sort of wholism at the *personal* or *moral* level, it is unlikely that wholism is defensible at the *societal* or *ethical* level because of the conceptual problems already noted. In other words, one *individual* may decide what "whole" to maximize, on the basis of his or her personal beliefs; to undergird a *societal* approach to policymaking, however, wholism must be free of the conceptual difficulties already noted, be precisely defined, be rationally defensible, and therefore be acceptable to many people. Moreover, the set of beliefs that are acceptable to all members of society is much smaller than the set that is acceptable only to one person. This is why society seldom legislates morals; it cannot typically do so successfully. For this reason, the content of environmental law and public policy must be narrower than the content of personal, environmental morality, since law must be acceptable to a variety of persons with different beliefs. This suggests that, although we may need a wholistic way of thinking, we may not be able to ground societal environmental policy on a wholistic framework, for the reasons already noted. Nevertheless, we may be able to adopt wholism at the level of personal morals.

Like the first objection, the objection that this analysis ignores nature's "right" to exist also begs the question. It can only be wrong to ignore something that is apparent. Yet, it is not apparent that nature has a right to exist, for reasons already explained earlier, viz., the fact that nonsentient beings do not have interests, in the philosophical sense, and therefore do not have rights.

If this objection is a proposal to accord rights to nature, then the proposal (if it is to be successful) must include at least two criteria: one by virtue of which nature is said to have rights, and another or second-order ethical rule that enables us to adjudicate rights conflicts. Without the first, it would be impossible to tell what/who has rights and why they do. Without the second, according rights to all beings would mean that none have them. If everything is said to have rights, and if there is no way to adjudicate among conflicting rights claims, then practically speaking nothing has rights. This is analogous to the observation that, if everything is said to be true, and there is no way to adjudicate among conflicting truth claims, then nothing is true.

According to most contemporary philosophers, natural rights are typically accorded only to humans, and on the basis of the criterion of rationality. Likewise rights claims, on the current view, are adjudicated on the basis of the *types* of rights in conflict, so that strong rights take precedence over weak ones (see note 93). It may be reasonable to change the criteria for according rights and adjudicating rights conflicts. Without specific, alternative criteria, however, such a proposal for change is at best incomplete or at worst unworkable as a basis for environmental ethics and policy.

Finally, the objection that ecology does give us a number of answers to environmental problems, in part because it has a notion of ecological "balance," is correct insofar as ecology can help us along the lines already suggested earlier. For example, ecology can give us environmental answers that are capable of being subjected to short-term empirical testing. It is incorrect, however, insofar as it postulates a universal notion of balance or equilibrium. There is no universal equilibrium both because not all populations, e.g., many insects, exhibit density dependence, because they are affected by unpredictable environmental factors, and because many populations never show a balance or equilibrium but instead exhibit cycles or chaotic changes.

Evidence of radical changes in community composition and structure throughout history also suggests that there are no stable or balanced community "types" existing through time; such types may appear stable only because our time frame of examination is relatively short. Moreover, communities cannot be classified (into balanced, stable types), on the basis of climate. Both spatial and temporal fluctuations/perturbations undercut any universal notion of balance.[95]

Conclusion

Although there appear to be no precise and predictive notions of "balance" and "wholism" that we can use as a foundation for environmental policymaking, the purpose of this essay has not been to leave environmental ethics without a foundation. Rather the purpose has been merely to point out that the foundation is not as simple as many persons currently suppose. As a recent U.S. National Academy of Sciences report on ecology noted:

> "the point of discussing the many obstacles to making accurate predictions is not to argue the futility of trying, but to show that the process of prediction must be viewed as complex and probabilistic. An appropriate approach to managing ecological systems recognizes the random component of population dynamics . . . Environmental manipulations will always be experimental to some extent, and our most promising course is to structure each one so that we can learn as much as possible from it."[96]

If the Academy report is correct, then ecological notions such as "balance" are not so much foundations on which to build an ethics. Rather they are idealizations that provide a useful context for learning more about the environmental perturbations and fluctuations that preclude precise prediction, balance, or stability in ecology. Once we have learned more about these perturbations and fluctuations, we may be able to provide a new paradigm for balance or stability, a paradigm that provides more guidance for environmental ethics.

Notes

An early version of this essay was presented in December 1985 at the annual meeting of the American Society for Value Inquiry, held in connection with the Eastern Division American Philosophical Association meetings. The author is grateful to Sara Ketchum and Bryan Norton for criticisms of this early draft. A much later version was presented in Switzerland in 1988 at a meeting sponsored by the Conference of the Swiss Scientific Academies, The author is especially grateful to biologists Robert Colwell and Earl McCoy for detailed, constructive criticisms of this later draft, as well as to Evandro Agazzi, Christof Burckhardt, Franz Furger, Alex Mauron, Bruno Messerli, Jurgen Mittelstrass, Hannes Pauli, Marcello Pera, Peter Saladin, William Shea, and Beat Sitter for helpful comments. Whatever errors remain are, of course, the author's responsibility.

1. See R. P. McIntosh, *The Background of Ecology: Concept and Theory* (Cambridge: Cambridge University Press, 1985), 289–323; hereafter cited as *Background.*

2. Paul Taylor, *Respect for Nature* (Princeton: Princeton University Press, 1986), 299; hereafter cited as Taylor, *Respect.*

3. Some philosophers have also claimed that understanding the biological or ecological universe provides us with particular directives about how we should live our lives. See, for example, Richard Watson, "A Critique of Anti-Anthropocentric Biocentrism," *Environmental Ethics* 5:3 (Fall 1983): 252–256.

4. Well-known sociobiologists have tried to derive ethical assertions directly from statements about conditions that make it possible for genes to be preserved. See Taylor, *Respect,* 49, and E.O. Wilson, *Sociobiology: The New Synthesis* (Cambridge: Harvard University Press, 1975). For a criticism of the attempt to use biological findings as a guide to life, see Michael Ruse, *Sociobiology: Sense or Nonsense* (Dordrecht: Reidel, 1979), esp. Chapter 9.

5. In part, U.S. scientists' views of their ethical responsibilities regarding environmental policy have been a result of the passage of the U.S. National Environmental Policy Act of 1969 (NEPA). This act gave ecologists a role somewhat like that of engineering scientists who provide information, so that policymakers can do what is right. See S.I. Auerbach, "Ecology, Ecologists, and the E.S.A.," *Ecology* 53:2 (Spring 1972): 205–206; W. Van Winkle, *et al.,* "Two Roles of Ecologists in Defining and Determining the Acceptability of Environmental Impacts," *International Journal of Environmental Studies* 9 (1976): 247–254; G. Suter, "Ecosystem Theory and NEPA Assessment," *Bulletin of the Ecological Society of America* 62:3 (1981): 186–192; hereafter cited as: *NEPA.* See also Mark Sagoff, "Fact and Value in Environmental Science," *Environmental Ethics* 7:2 (Summer 1985): 100; hereafter cited as Sagoff, *Fact;* see also D. Nelkin, "Ecologists and the Public Interest," *Hastings Center Report* 6 (February 1976): 39; hereafter cited as Nelkin, *Ecologists.*

    In addition to NEPA, a number of environmental laws also presuppose this ecologist-as-expert view. They speak of the "health" and "balance" of ecosystems and leave it to ecologists to define such concepts in scientific terms. For example, the Marine Protection, Research, and Sanctuaries Act of 1972 enjoins the nation to preserve the "health of the oceans." The Federal Water Pollution Control Act of 1972, similarly requires polluters to demonstrate that their effluents are such that they "assure the protection and propagation of a balanced, indigenous population of shellfish, fish, and wildlife." (Quoted by Sagoff, *Fact,* p. 101.)

6. See, for example, D.B. Botkin, "Can There Be a Theory of Global Ecology?" *Journal of Theoretical Biology* 96 (1982): 95 (hereafter cited as Botkin, *Theory*); L.B. Slobodkin, "Aspects of the Future of Ecology," *Bioscience* 18:1 (January 1968): 16; see also Nelkin, *Ecologists,* 38–44.

7. See, for example, R.F. Noss, "Dangerous Simplifications in Conservation Biology," *Bulletin of the Ecological Society of America* 67:4 (December 1986): 278–279. See also J. Diamond, "The Design of a Nature Reserve System for Indonesian New Guinea," and T.E. Lovejoy, *et al.,* "Edge and Other Effects of Isolation on Amazon Forest Fragments," in *Conservation Biology,* E. Soule (ed.) (Sunderland, Massachusetts: Sinauer, 1986), 485–503 and 257–285; hereafter cited as Soule, *CB.*

8. D. W. Schindler, *et al.,* "Eutrophication of Lake 227 by Addition of Phosphate and Nitrate: the Second, Third, and Fourth Years of Enrichment, 1970, 1971, and 1972," *Journal of the Fisheries Research Board of Canada* 30:10 (1973): 1415–1440.

9. Cooper claimed that ecologists were responsible for the discovery that coastal wetlands support high levels of both primary and secondary production of fish. This discovery, he said, formed the basis for the Coastal Zone Management Act of 1972 and for state environmental legislation to protect coastal wetlands. Arthur Cooper, "Why Doesn't Anyone Listen to Ecologists—and What Can ESA Do About It?" *Bulletin of the Ecological Society of America* 63:4 (December 1982): 348; hereafter cited as Cooper, *Why*.

10. Cooper, *Why*, 348–349.

11. Sagoff, *Fact*, 99.

12. According to Mark Sagoff, for example, ecologists not only can help policymakers achieve given objectives, e.g., increase the profitability of fisheries, but also can help them decide what their objectives should be, what to preserve and why (Sagoff, *Fact*, 100). Philosophers, naturalists, and policymakers such as Rolston, Leopold, Shepard, and McKinley maintain that the science of ecology provides us with a model to follow in the domain of environmental ethics. (See H. Rolston, "Is There an Ecological Ethic?" *Ethics* 85:2 (1975): 93–109 (reprinted in *Ethics and the Environment,* edited by T. Attig and D. Scherer (Englewood Cliffs: Prentice-Hall, 1983; Rolston hereafter cited as *EE,* with page citations to the 1983 reprint; Attig and Scherer hereafter cited as EAE.); Aldo Leopold, *A Sand County Almanac* (New York: Oxford University Press, 1966; hereafter cited as: *SCA*); and Paul Shepard and Daniel McKinley (eds.), *The Subversive Science: Essays Toward an Ecology of Man* (Boston: Houghton Mifflin, 1969). See also C. Little, "In a Landscape of Hope," *Wilderness* 48:168 (1985): 21–30; E. Partridge, "Are We Ready for an Ecological Morality?" *Environmental Ethics* 4:2 (1982): 175–190; and J.B. Callicott (ed.), *A Companion to the Sand County Almanac* (Madison: University of Wisconsin Press, 1987); hereafter cited as *Companion.*)

13. In subscribing either to the general belief that ecological science helps justify environmental ethics, or to the particular beliefs that I call the "wholism presupposition" and the "balance presupposition," their views are open to criticism on both ethical and epistemological grounds. Several general ethical objections have been formulated elsewhere by Paul Taylor, so I shall not discuss them in detail here. In general, Taylor claims that philosophers who maintain that ecology provides us with a model to follow in environmental ethics confuse fact and value; they confuse humans as biological organisms with humans as moral agents. In so doing, he argues, they ignore the human necessity to make choices, and they forget that biology cannot provide the standards for making normative or evaluative choices. They also err, says Taylor, in falling victim to anthropocentrism by assuming that human survival is a good. (See Taylor, *Respect,* 47–58.)

Instead of discussing the ethical objections, I want to focus on the two main epistemological criticisms of these presuppositions. These are, first, that there are no good reasons for believing that ecology can deliver the "truths" we need in environmental ethics, even if one assumes that ethics ought to rely on scientific findings and, second, that one cannot substantiate either the wholism presupposition or the balance presupposition.

14. Rolston, in *EE,* 42–46.

15. Thomas B. Colwell claims that "The balance of nature provides an objective normative model which can be utilized as the ground of human value. . . ." (Rolston, *EE,* 45.) See also Mark Sagoff, "On Preserving the Natural Environment," in Attig and Scherer, *EAE,* 28; Sagoff hereafter cited as *OP.*

16. Philosopher Paul Taylor presupposes one version of the "balance presupposition" when he argues that we ought to preserve ecological integrity. (Taylor, *Respect,* 299.)

17. Philosopher Brian Norton adopts another variant of "the balance presupposition" when he argues that we have an ethical obligation to pursue preservationism, which he characterizes in terms of maximizing "dynamic stability." For Norton, "dynamic stability" refers to the fact that a system is stable even through significant changes in structure and function, provided that those changes result from the "internal dynamic" of the system. In general, says Norton, barring highly unusual disturbances, homeostasis is higher, and predictability is greater in more mature ecosystems. For Norton, maturity is an indicator of stability, and more diverse *ecosystems* are more predictable/stable. (For ecologists MacArthur and Hutchison, complex *trophic systems* and diverse *communities* are more stable than less diverse, or simple, ones.) Given this ecological generalization, says Norton, the preservationists' ethical mandate is clear: we must exercise caution in altering ecosystems, lest the alteration not be in keeping with the balance established, or the "dynamic stability." We must protect biological diversity and we must maintain the dynamic stability or balance of naturally functioning ecosystems. (Bryan G. Norton, "Conservation and Preservation: A Conceptual Rehabilitation," unpublished essay, 29–31. See also Bryan Norton, *The Spice of Life: Why Save Natural Variety?* (Princeton: Princeton University Press, 1987), chapters 2, 4; hereafter cited as *Spice.* See R. Lewontin, "The Meaning of Stability," in *Diversity and Stability in Ecological Systems,* G. Woodwell and H. Smith (eds.) (Brookhaven: Brookhaven Laboratory Publication No. 22, 1969), for discussion of the claim that ecosystems are locally stable and globally unstable; see also D. Futuyma, "Community Structure and Stability in Constant Environments," *American Naturalist* 107 (1973): 443–446; G. Innis, "Stability, Sensitivity, Resilience, Persistence. What is of Interest?," in *Ecosystem Analysis and Prediction,* S. Levin (ed.) (Philadelphia: Society for Industrial and Applied Mathematics, 1974), 131–139 (hereafter cited as Levin, *SS,* L. Wu, "On the Stability of Ecosystems," in Levin, *SS,* 155–165; and D. L. De Angelis, "Stability and Connectance in Food Web Models," *Ecology* 56 (1975): 238–243, for notions of stability closely related to Norton's.)

There are three kinds of diversity in ecology (alpha, beta, gamma), and many types of stability have been postulated. For some of the most famous discussions of trophic and community stability, see R. MacArthur, "Fluctuations of Animal Populations, and a Measure of Community Stability," *Ecology* 36 (1955): 533–536 (hereafter cited as *Fluctuations*); G. E. Hutchison, "Homage to Santa Rosalia, or Why Are There So Many Kinds of Animals?" *American Naturalist* 93 (1954): 145–159; C. Elton, *The Ecology of Invasions by Animals and Plants* (London: Methuen, 1958), 143–153; Daniel Goodman, "The Theory of Diversity-Stability Relationships in Ecology," *The Quarterly Review of Biology* 50 (1975): 237–266; hereafter cited as *Theory.* The MacArthur-Hutchinson notion of diversity-stability, however, was challenged by authors such as May and Connell (see note 33). See also McIntosh, *Background,* 187, 252–256, and Donald Worster, *Nature's Economy: The Roots of Ecology* (San Francisco: Sierra Club Books, 1977), Chapter 15, for a discussion of wholism and stability in the development of ecology.

18. For an account of the wholism-versus-reductionism controversy in ecology, see See R. P. McIntosh, *Background,* 252–256.

19. Rolston claims that nature "has been enriching the ecosystem," and that we should get in gear with nature, which is maximizing ecosystemic excellences. (Rolston, *EE,* 53–54.)

20. Sagoff appeals to the wholism presupposition when he enjoins us to preserve nature for its own sake, (Sagoff, *OP*, 27) as if the whole of nature were a living organism that had interests of its own.

21. Rolston, *EE*, 46–54, esp. 52–54. Although Rolston identifies environmental ethics in the primary (nonanthropocentric) sense with the wholism presupposition, and environmental ethics in the secondary (anthropocentric) sense with the balance presupposition, it is not clear that the balance presupposition and the wholism presupposition are easily separable. This is because to recognize the wholistic character of the ecosystem is precisely to recognize the balance inherent in it or the homeostatic processes driving it to preserve itself as a whole. In other words, it appears that principles of homeostasis or balance are the engine that helps to drive the machine of the ecosystem. Without such principles, it would be difficult to define what the whole was. See also note 12.

22. J. E. Lovelock, *Gaia* (New York: Oxford University Press, 1979); hereafter cited as: Lovelock, *Gaia.* See also J. Hughes, "Gaia," *The Ecologist* 13 (2/3) 54–60; hereafter cited as Hughes, *Gaia.*

23. K. Goodpaster, "On Being Morally Considerable," in Attig and Scherer, EAE, 39; hereafter cited as *OB.*

24. Goodpaster's move here is a more sophisticated version of what Leopold did years earlier. Leopold claimed, in "Conservation as a Moral Issue," that the parts of the earth—soil, mountains, rivers, etc.—could be regarded as organs with coordinated functions, and that the whole earth underwent growth processes like a living being. Leopold argued that because the earth is indivisible and its parts are interdependent, it is a living organism. (A. Leopold, "Conservation as a Moral Issue," in Attig and Scherer, *EAE*, 139–149. See also Lovelock, *Gaia.*) University of California ecologist Daniel Botkin claims that ecosystems as a whole maintain life-sustaining functions; see Botkin, *Theory*, 97. Some of these same Leopoldian sentiments are found in other writings, such as those of Chief Seattle of the Duwanich tribe, in his famous statement to President Pierce in 1867. Seattle wrote: "How can you buy or sell the sky—the warmth of the land? The idea is strange to us. Yet we do not own the freshness of the air or the sparkle of the water. How can you buy them from us?" (Quoted in C. Haar and L. Liebman, *Property and Law* (Boston: Little, Brown, and Company: 1977), 15.)

25. B. Callicott, "Animal Liberation: A Triangular Affair," in Attig and Scherer, *EAE*, 61–62; hereafter cited as *AL.*

26. "Ecological entitlement" refers to the fact that natural beings are part of living biotic processes in ecosystems. Because nature has ordained that organizations of living and nonliving natural beings combine in an ecosystem that maximizes its excellences, Callicott claims that we too are bound by our moral theories to do whatever maximizes ecosystemic excellence. (Callicott, *AL*, 68.)

27. P. Taylor, for example, urges us to "preserve ecological integrity" (Taylor, *Respect*, 299), but he never tells us what it is.

28. Taylor, for example, denies that ecology can inform environmental ethics (Taylor, *Respect*, 8).

29. See Sagoff, *Fact*, 107–110, and Taylor, *Respect*, 8.

30. Sagoff, *Fact*, 109, and M. Sagoff, "Environmental Science and Environmental Law" (College Park, Maryland: Center for Philosophy and Public Policy, March, 1985), unpublished essay, 8; hereafter cited as: *ES.*

31.   See works by May, Levins, and Connell cited in note 33; see also Sagoff, *Fact,* 109, and McIntosh, *Background,* 187–188.

32.   See, for example, U.S. Congress, Senate, *Congressional Record,* 93rd Congress, First Session, 119 (24 July 1973): 25668; B. Commoner, *The Closing Circle* (New York: Knopf, 1971), 38; and N. Myers, *A Wealth of Wild Species* (Boulder: Westview Press, 1983).

33.   See Sagoff, *Fact,* 107. See also R.T. Paine, "A Note on Trophic Complexity and Community Stability," *American Naturalist* 103 (1969): 91–93; R. Lewin, "Fragile Forests Implied by Pleistocene Data," *Science* 226 (1984): 36–37; R.M. May, *Stability and Complexity in Model Ecosystems* (Princeton: Princeton University Press, 1973); R. Levins, "The Qualitative Analysis of Partially Specified Systems," *Annals of the New York Academy of Sciences* 231 (1974): 123–138; J. H. Connell, "Diversity in Tropical Rain Forests and Coral Reefs," *Science* 199 (1978): 1302–1310; Daniel Goodman, "The Theory of Diversity-Stability Relationships in Ecology," *The Quarterly Review of Biology* 50:3 (September 1975): 237–266. See also M. E. Soulé, "Conservation Biology and the 'Real World'," in Soulé, *CB,* 6–7, who argues that diversity-stability can be said to be a working hypothesis, even though it fails to have the empirical backing to satisfy experts and even though there are several categorial exceptions to it. Finally see R. P. McIntosh, *Background,* 142.

35.   B. Norton expressed his views about his variant of the diversity-stability hypothesis in a phone conversation with the author on December 13, 1985. Norton's variant of the *ecosystemic* diversity-stability hypothesis, however, fares no better than earlier versions because concepts like succession cannot be operationalized. For him to maintain that diverse and mature ecosystems are hence stable is to assume both that there is a pattern by means of which ecosystems proceed toward maturity—even though he cannot state what it is—and that there is some neutral way to define a *mature* ecosystem.

Moreover, even if various balance or stability hypotheses could be shown to yield correct predictions and satisfying explanations, for a moral philosopher to use these ecological "facts" to support his ethics could still be questionable. To postulate a balance of nature is to postulate a property of nature as an object of consideration of conscious, sentient human beings. Only realists, not instrumentalists, believe that nature itself could be said to have these alleged properties apart from some viewer or valuer. Hence there may be no ecological basis for using the balance presupposition to affirm an ecocentric environmental ethics. Indeed, if current scientific instrumentalists are right, a nonanthropocentric ecology is not possible.

While instrumentalist claims are nothing new, they could bode ill for ecology in a way that does not trouble the other sciences, such as physics. This is because ecology is used to undergird theses about what is natural and therefore about what ought, on moral grounds, to be preserved. None of the other sciences, except perhaps economics, is used to support claims about what it is natural, and therefore moral, to do. For this reason, the possible instrumentalist nature of science presents a special burden to those who hope to use ecology to support public policy.

If stability or balance is a property of human descriptions of nature, not necessarily a property of nature, then one ought not affirm that stability is good on grounds that it is "in nature," and that what is "in nature" is good. Hence the balance presupposition does not necessarily support either claims about values *in nature* or a nonanthropocentric environmental ethics.

34.   Paul Taylor clearly recognizes this point, since he argues that natural ecosystems provide the criteria for human actions regarding the environment. (Paul Taylor, *Respect,*

4–6, 81, 85, 174–176.) Note, however, that Taylor also claims that ecology provides no help to environmental ethics (Taylor, *Respect*, 8).

Following the principle that nature knows best, even when it eliminates species, Taylor also consistently argues that humans have no obligations to rescue or restore species diminished by nature. (Taylor, *Respect*, 50, 52, esp 177.) What follows, if Taylor and I are reasoning correctly, is that it may well be impossible to argue consistently that "nature knows best" and yet to argue (as many environmentalists do) for giving species more protection than nature itself gives them.

35.   Imagine how difficult the practice of medicine would be if every medical doctor, instead of taking as the goal the survival of the individual patient, had to take the health or well-being of the entire system of which the individual was a member. Following such a goal, a doctor might worry whether to save the life of a 20-year-old severely retarded person, since that person would never be a contributing member of society. Or, the doctor might worry whether to prescribe moving to the sunbelt for an arthritis sufferer, since the patient might have to relocate in an area whose environment had already exceeded its human carrying capacity.

In other words, if individual doctors had to worry about patients' allocation of financial resources, about ultimate societal well-being, and about conflicting means for maximizing the health of different family members (just as ecologists following the balance presupposition would have to worry about the well-being of large natural systems, rather than only about the well-being of individual members of the systems), then they could rarely make a clear-cut decision about a particular patient. Once their criteria for medical action became societal or global, rather than based on the Hippocratic Oath and on an individual patient's well-being and rights, then medical doctors would face some of the same problems ecologists face in attempting to use the balance presupposition to dictate particular environmental policies.

36.   See notes 24–26.

37.   For discussion of the philosophical notion of 'interest,' J. Feinberg, "The Rights of Animals and Unborn Generations," in *Philosophy and Environmental Crisis*, W. T. Blackstone (ed.) (Athens: University of Georgia Press, 1977), 49–51 and W. Frankena, "Ethics and the Environment," in *Ethics and the Problems of the 21st Century*, K. Goodpaster and K. Sayre (eds) (Southbend, Indiana: University of Notre Dame Press, 1979), 11; hereafter cited as Goodpaster, *Ethics*, and Frankena, *Ethics*.

38.   An ecosystem, as a whole, is not a living thing; hence it is unclear how it could either have interests or be a beneficiary. It has no analogue to human sentience on which to base interests, so assigning interests to it or claiming that it is a moral subject is highly arbitrary, at least from a philosophical point of view. See John Rodman, "The Liberation of Nature," *Inquiry* 20 (1977): 91, for an analysis of the view known as sentientism, that it is only possible to benefit or harm a conscious, sentient human being. See also Taylor, *Respect*, 18.

39.   Australian philosopher Peter Singer makes a similar point when he notes that the capacity for suffering or enjoyment is a prerequisite for having interests. P. Singer, *Animal Liberation* (New York: Avon, 1977), 8; hereafter cited as Singer, *AL*. See J. Heffernan, "The Land Ethic: A Critical Appraisal," *Environmental Ethics* 4:3 (1982): 235–247, and B. Callicott, "Animal Liberation," *Environmental Ethics* 2:4 (1980): 311–336, who argues against Singer's view. For responses to Callicott and Heffernan, see text of essay following this endnote.

40. Even if assigning interests to ecosystems or organic wholes somehow made sense, Singer points out that we would begin using the term 'interest' in a very nonphilosophical, loose sense. (P. Singer, "Not for Humans Only," in Goodpaster, *Ethics,* 194–195 ff.) Moreover, our obligations to meet such interests would multiply to preposterous and counterintuitive levels. And if our obligations to meet interests multiplied to unworkable levels, then claiming that nonsentient beings had interests would result in a philosophical dilution of the notion of an "interest." We might have to say that air had an interest in not receiving any human industrial effluents. Hence, by *reductio,* it follows that one ought not to define 'interests' so loosely as to allow nonliving wholes, such as ecosystems, to be said to have interests.

To this *reductio,* however, proponents of according interests to ecosystems might point out that if sentiency were the criterion for according interests to beings, then one would have no obligations to (permanently) nonsentient humans, such as completely anaesthetized, hypnotized, or deeply comatose persons, or individuals afflicted with a well-documented condition known as "congenital universal indifference to pain." (See D. Baxter and J. Olszewski, "Congenital Universal Insensitivity to Pain," *Brain* 83 (1960): 381–393.) Yet we do believe that we have moral obligations to such persons; hence it is not clear that sentiency is always a criterion for having interests that one is morally bound to recognize.

The response to this counter-argument is that we do not typically accord rights or interests to beings, even human beings, who have no possibility of being sentient. Even according to the American Medical Association criteria, there is no obligation to keep brain-dead persons (those with flat EEG's and who are incapable of ever being sentient again) alive. "Pulling the plug" is allowable because such patients are not sentient beings whose interests can be harmed, even though they are still breathing and their hearts are still beating. This suggests that it might be difficult for Leopold and others to argue that ecosystems have interests and are members of our moral community, even though we do not consider living, breathing, brain-dead humans as having interests and as being members of our moral community. See H. K. Beecher, "Report of the 'Ad Hoc' Committee of the Harvard Medical School to Examine the Definition of Brain Death, A Definition of Irreversible Coma," *Journal of the American Medical Association* 205 (5 August 1968): 85–88.

Even if those who subscribe to the wholism presupposition could make a case for nonsentient beings like ecosystems having interests, the basic conceptual problem they face is that they have no criterion to replace sentiency. Presumably there must be a criterion, like rationality or linguistic ability, to replace sentiency, and according to which to determine the limits of moral obligation. Without such a criterion, proponents of the wholism presupposition have left themselves open to the charge that they have imposed an ethic that is impossible to fulfill; with no criterion to delimit moral obligation, virtually everything could be said to have interests that we are obligated to respect. If proponents of wholism wish to move their ethics from the realm of poetry and place it in the realm of practical, realistic action, then they need a criterion. The alternative is to give virtually everything interests, thereby devaluing interests and giving nothing to those said to have interests.

41. Frankena, *Ethics,* makes a similar point.

In response to this second difficulty, environmental philosophers would likely respond that finding criteria for moral action appears problematic only if one presupposes the truth of speciesism, i.e., the view that only humans have rights and interests, and that humans are the only species whose needs and interests need to be considered by moral persons. (Singer, *AL.*)

While this response is undoubtedly correct, the point of the objection is that ethicists employing some new, nonanthropocentric, nonspeciesistic paradigm must bear the burden of proof and must give reasons for their positions. Taylor's book, *Respect for Nature,* is a first step in that direction. Taylor warns us about how difficult it is to avoid thinking according to old, outmoded paradigms of speciesism and anthropocentrism; see Taylor, *Respect,* 23.

42.   T. Regan, *The Case for Animal Rights* (Berkeley: University of California Press, 1983), 262, uses the term "environmental fascism." See Taylor, *Respect,* 118, who makes a similar criticism of Leopold and Rolston, both of whom hold organicist views; he says that they give no place to the good of the individual.

43.   Several thinkers, among them Holmes Rolston, have attempted to respond to the charge of "environmental fascism." Rolston's basic position is that, of course, we must interpret wholism so that we recognize inalienable, individual human rights. (See H. Rolston, "Duties to Ecosystems," in Callicott, *Companion.*) While this response is reasonable, it does not resolve difficulties with a new environmental ethics based on wholism or organicism. The difficulties remain because we still have no clear criteria for when to give primacy to an ecosystem or to the biosphere and when to give primacy to human rights. This is not an easy question since presumably according primacy to human rights (e.g., to private property) is precisely why the biosphere and ecosystems have been harmed in the past. Thinkers like Rolston simply can't respond that human rights take priority over the well-being of the biosphere or an ecosystem, since presumably the whole point of attempting to maximize ecosystemic well-being, through the wholism presupposition, is to insure that nature receives consideration in the face of emphasis on solely human interests.

For a discussion of "lifeboat ethics," see Garrett Hardin, "Living on a Lifeboat," *Bioscience* 24 (October 1974): 561–568.

44.   On the one hand, if we are on a par, as equal members of the biotic community, then it is no more wrong for humans to kill and eat other humans than it is for wolves and alligators to do so. This is because, as equal members of the biotic community, we have no special rights and, consequently, no special responsibilities. On the other hand, if we are not on a par with other members of the biotic community, owing to our special moral responsibility and our alleged free will, then we share moral community only with other beings who also have moral responsibility and free will. But in this case, then neither the biosphere, nor any ecosystems, nor land, nor any nonhuman entity is a member of our moral community, since none of these has responsibility or free will. And if they are not members of our moral community, then we have no obligations to them, no obligations to land or to the biosphere, or to any other nonhuman entity. See P. Fritzell, "The Conflicts of Ecological Conscience," in Callicott, *Companion.*

On a more general level, environmental philosophers face a similar problem when they argue for "species impartiality" and for a nonhierarchical view of nature, yet maintain that humans have special rights and duties to the environment and to nonhumans. See Taylor, *Respect,* 45–46, 225–226, 246, 259, 281–282. They can't have it both ways and remain consistent.

45.   See Norton, *Spice,* Chapter 4, section 2; see also MacArthur, *Fluctuations,* and Goodman, *Theory,* 239.

46. The main reason for this peculiarity is that different camps of ecologists would probably claim that different units ought to be maximized.

47. This is the response that many community ecologists would probably make.

48. Ecologists who follow Clements are likely to make this claim. See McIntosh, *Background,* 44, 79, 107.

49. McIntosh, *Background,* 228, 252–256.

50. B. Norton, "Environmental Ethics and the Rights of Nonhumans," *Environmental Ethics* 4 (1982): 17–36, raises a similar point. See McIntosh, *Background,* for a discussion of community ecology (69–146, 263–267), population ecology (146–193), and ecosystems ecology (193–242).

51. Many ecologists follow the Platonic, wholistic paradigm of reifying and studying organic entities such as ecosystems, while others follow the nominalistic and reductionistic paradigm of examining the individual or the species, and refrain from creating higher-level wholistic entities such as ecosystems. Neither side has won acceptance, but most of the predictive power is on the side of the reductionists, although advances are possible through wholistic approaches. McIntosh, *Background,* 126 ff., 157 ff., 181–182 ff. and 252; see K. Shrader-Frechette, "Organismic Biology and Ecosystems Ecology," in *Current Issues in Teleology,* N. Rescher (ed) (Pittsburgh: University of Pittsburgh Center for the Philosophy of Science, 1986), 77–92; hereafter cited as *Biology.* For information on density dependence, see D. Strong, "Density Vagueness: Abiding the Variance in the Demography of Real Populations," in *Community Ecology,* J. Diamond and T. Case (eds) (New York: Harper and Row, 1986).

52. I am grateful to R. Colwell of the Biology Department of the University of California, Berkeley, and to D. Botkin of the Biology Department at the University of California, Santa Barbara, for discussions of natural selection and adaptation.

53. Rather than that each species adapts to its present environment, Lovelock (*Gaia,* 109, 127–128) claimed that whole ecosystems, as well as individual species, adapt.

Despite such assertions, he assumed that the "world evolves through Darwinian natural selection" (Lovelock, Gaia, 127.). To the extent that moral philosophers presume this erroneous interpretation of natural selection, their environmental ethics rest on an erroneous interpretation of Darwinian natural selection.

54. According to neo-Darwinian theory, an organism possesses heritable traits because of genes it carries; which genes it transmits to its progeny are determined by random processes taking place during division and fertilization of the sex cells, not by the effects that the genes produce in the organism carrying them or in its offspring and not by the effects that the genes are alleged to produce in the ecosystem. Since mutation of genes, as well as which genes are transmitted to offspring, is determined by random processes, natural selection does not operate to give rise to certain effects, whether in individuals or in ecosystems. Although genes mutate as a consequence of environmental changes to which the organism responds, both the specific mutation involved, as well as which genes mutate, is *independent* of the effects that the mutation may have, either on successive generations or on the future of the ecosystem. To presuppose otherwise is to confuse environmental poetry with biological science. In sum: flamingos didn't get their long legs by trying; Darwin didn't welcome the maker of Paley's famous watch; and ecosystems didn't go through successions of species by "desiring" excellence. (See Shrader-Frechette, *Biology.*)

55. Thanks to Sara Ketchum for this example. Even were this erroneous interpretation of natural selection technically correct, it would still not be clear what it is that an ecosystem maximizes. Rolston says it is "excellence," but excellence is neither a clear nor precise notion.

56. McIntosh, *Background*, 193. Ecosystems ecology is allegedly empirical, but the ecosystemic entity about which it centers is not clearly defined. Ecosystems can be of many kinds and many sizes. This being so, it is not precisely clear that particular claims about ecosystems are falsifiable. In fact, the claim that ecosystems maximize excellences is not falsifiable.

57. What pattern of excellence does an ecosystem maximize? Ecologists cannot answer the question. Theorists such as Diamond and Gilpin, following MacArthur, claim that interspecific competition is a major factor in patterning natural processes of ecosystems. Other ecologists, such as Simberloff and Strong, argue that the Diamond and Gilpin theories are untestable. Strong and Simberloff have created numerous null models, which (they claim) indicate that observed patterns of species occurrence do not depart from what one might expect if associations were purely random. (See M. Cody and J. Diamond (eds.), *Ecology and the Evolution of Communities* (Cambridge: Harvard University Press, 1975); D. Strong and D. Simberloff (eds.), *Ecological Communities* (Princeton: Princeton University Press, 1984), especially M. Gilpin and J. Diamond, "Are Species Co-occurrences . . . ?," 298–315. See also note 72.) Moreover, the evolutionary foundations of ecology seem to suggest that many different happenings in ecosystems might be stable, integral, and balanced. It is not clear that there is a moral reason, short of human welfare, to prefer one temporal arrangement or stability over another. In other words, the evolutionary foundations of ecology seem to undercut a precise definition of stability, at least a definition formulated in purely nonanthropocentric terms. This, in turn, seems to undercut both the balance and wholism presuppositions.

Admittedly, it is easy to formulate some definition of stability in terms of human needs and interests, but this is precisely what proponents of the balance and wholism presupposition typically want to avoid doing; they want a nonanthropocentric environmental ethics.

But if ecosystems that are "maximizing excellence" follow no accepted natural process, then how did competition become so entrenched in "explaining" ecosystemic processes? One scientist claims that competition has survived as an hypothesis merely because it fits in with our notions of homeostasis and the balance of nature. (R. Lewin, "Santa Rosalia Was a Goat," *Science* 221 (12 August, 1983): 636–639.) If this is so, and I think it is, then ecology is in the midst of a revolution, Kuhnian or not, to overthrow entrenched and untestable competitionism. This is a significant revolution because competitionism allegedly provides the major explanation of the processes underlying natural systems; it allegedly explains the "machine" that drives the ecosystem to maximize something or other called "excellence."

58. Cooper and other ecologists claimed that coastal wetlands both support great numbers of species and are necessary to the existence of fisheries. Marshes, they claimed, are like food pumps that feed adjacent areas. See Sagoff, *Fact*, 104.

59. If one examines the scientific (as opposed to political or public-policy) status of Cooper's ecological claim that wetlands support many species and are necessary to the fishing industry, then the claim is highly doubtful. All the classic studies allegedly supporting the claim, like those of Teal and Odum, are unsupported by empirical data.

Six years after Odum's paper, when the marsh theory of the "outwelling" of nutrients from marshes to adjacent waters began to be tested empirically, the data tended to disconfirm the correctness of the theory about the value of wetlands. The upshot is that this paradigm, accepted for so long without evidence, is now being questioned. It is not clear that or how salt marshes play a nutritive function in estuarine systems. (Sagoff, *Fact,* 107. See, for example, S. W. Nixon, "Between Coastal Marshes and Coastal Waters," in *Ecological Processes in Coastal and Marine Systems,* R. J. Livingston (ed.) (New York, Plenum Press, 1979), 437–525; see also Mark Sagoff, "Environmental Science and Environmental Law" (College Park, Maryland: Center for Philosophy and Public Policy, March 1985), esp. 5 ff.

60.　Quoted in McIntosh, *Background,* 321.

61.　Not only do ecologists now believe that wetlands do not supply nutrients for estuarine production, as Odum and others presupposed, and that more diverse ecosystems often are unstable, but they have rejected other hypotheses as well. One example is the frequent environmentalist claim that persistent pollutants such as DDT and PCBs concentrate and accumulate along the food chain, leading to biomagnification. (See K. S. Shrader-Frechette, *Environmental Ethics* (Pacific Grove, California: Boxwood Press, 1981), 294–301.)

62.　Although the biomagnification hypothesis has now been largely dismissed, it was used for several decades as an argument against the use of persistent organochloride pesticides. (See Sagoff, *Fact,* 110; see E. Hunt and A. Bischoff, "Inimical Effects on Wildlife of Periodic DDD Application to Clear Lake," *California Fish and Game* 46 (1960): 91–106, for a tentative statement of the hypothesis. See F. Moriarty, *Ecotoxicology* (New York: Academic Press, 1983), 135–154, for a review of the literature leading to the demise of this hypothesis.) While there are excellent grounds for arguing that organochloride pesticides should never be used, the biomagnification argument is not one of them. Such cases point up the difficulty of using specific ecological claims to support specific environmental policies.

　　This is why a number of policymakers and scientists have pointed to the failure of ecology to provide clear directives for decisionmaking. They have claimed that ecology "has not been able to deliver the facts, understanding, and predictions" needed for environmental reform. (R. Carpenter, "Ecology in Court . . . ," *Natural Resources Lawyer* 15:3 (1983): 573–595; see also 44 *Federal Register* 71456 (December 11, 1979); S. Levin and M. Harwell, "Environmental Risks Associated with the Release of Genetically Engineered Organisms," *Genewatch* 2(1): 15; Suter, *NEPA;* W. Murdoch and J. Connell, "The Ecologist's Role and the Nonsolution of Technology," in *Ecocide—and Thoughts Towards Survival,* Clifton Fadiman and Jean White (eds.) (Santa Barbara, California: Center for the Study of Democratic Institutions, 1971), 57; Cooper, *Why;* and M. Sagoff, "What Ecology Can Do," unpublished essay, 1986.)

63.　The controversy focused on the potential environmental impacts of Con Ed's proposed Cornwell Project, a pumped-storage facility to be built on a mountain overlooking the Hudson valley. At the focus of the debate was the potential impact of the facility's water withdrawals on the Hudson River striped bass population. As several authors in *BioScience* put it, "the Hudson River controversy was a unique test of the ability of biologists to use their science to aid public decisionmakers in achieving an equitable solution to an important environmental problem. . . . After more than a decade of study and the expenditure of tens of millions of dollars, it was still not possible to draw definitive conclusions about the long-term effects of entrainment and impingement on fish populations in the Hudson River. We do not believe that this failure can be blamed on lack of effort, on the incompetence of the biologists involved, or on the use of the wrong model. We believe that it occurred because of insufficient understanding of underlying biological processes [even though,] . . . in the Hudson River controversy, the scientific issues were more clearly defined, and the research effort greater, than for any other major environmental dispute known to us." (L. W. Barnthouse, *et al.*, "Population Biology in the Courtroom: the Hudson River Controversy," *BioScience* 34:1 (January 1984): 17–18.

The final settlement of the Hudson River case was negotiated between EPA and the utilities; it called for the utilities to deviate from the outage schedule, provided that the overall degree of mitigation of impacts was not reduced. The credit allowed for shutting down a given generating unit during a given week is determined by the contribution of that unit to the conditional entrainment mortality rate for striped bass.

The classic Hudson River case suggests that ecologists may influence public policy, but that their influence derives largely from appeals to their authority, rather than from empirical evidence for their specific claims. Ecology simply cannot come up with specific, practical claims, in many cases because the science does not yet have a hold on the underlying natural processes that allegedly support some balance of nature or some wholistic, ecosystemic maximization of excellence.

64. See Mark Sagoff, "On Explanation in Ecology," unpublished manuscript, 1986, 17; hereafter cited as: Explanation.

65. Scientists often are not even sure which factors are relevant to understanding the problem. Hence they have found a dearth of regularities and few fundamental ecological theories. When they are able to find regularities, they often attribute causality to mere correlations whose significance is uncertain. (Cooper, *Why*, 350. See also McIntosh, 247, 249, 268, 273–74, 278, 284.)

66. Most environmental-impact statements are forced to employ data bases that are inadequate because of the lack of complete resource inventories (e.g., soils, vegetations, fauna), even for federal lands, the lack of knowledge about the state of environmental variables such as air and water, and the lack of knowledge of process phenomena such as physiology, population, and functioning of ecosystems. (See Cooper, *Why*, 350–351.)

67. Some ecologists, for example, claim that stressed ecosystems are less resistant to additional stress than unstressed ones, and they substantiate this claim with the observation that bark beetles invade oxidant-weakened pines; meanwhile, however, they often ignore masses of counterexamples. This allows other ecologists to promote the inverse claim that stressed systems are more resistant to added stress than unstressed ones. (This example is from Suter, *NEPA*, 186.)

68. See D. Simberloff, "The Sick Science of Ecology," *Eidema* 1:1 (1981), and T. W. Poole, "Periodic, Pseudoperiodic, and Chaotic Population Fluctuations," *Ecology* 58 (1977): 210–213. See also McIntosh, *Background*, 249, 269–270, 273, 284.

69. This is what happened with acceptance of the diversity-stability view, the estuarine production view, and the food-chain biomagnification view, all of which were accepted for decades without any real testing. (See Sagoff, *Fact*, 110–111.)

70. See D. S. Simberloff, "Competition Theory, Hypothesis Tesing, and Other Community Ecological Buzzwords," *American Naturalist* 122 (1983): 626–635.

71. See, for example, R. H. Peters, "Tautology in Evolution and Ecology," *The American Naturalist* 110: 971 (January-February 1976): 1–12. See also the previous note. Although there are some deficiencies in Peters' account, his basic point, that ecologists need to use null models, remains sound.

72. See note 70.

73. See Suter, *NEPA*, 186, who makes this point; see also McIntosh, *Background*, 244, 268. For an analysis of when use of criteria of simplicity might be desirable in ecology and population biology, see Richard Levins, "The Structure of Model Building in Population Biology," *American Scientist* 54:4 (December 1966): 421–431.

74. See E. Johnson, "Animal Liberation Versus the Land Ethic," *Environmental Ethics* 3:3 (1981), and A. Desmond, *The Ape's Reflexion* (New York: James Wade, 1979).

75. One ecologist affirms, "ecosystems are rarely if ever at equilibrium. They are continually being perturbed . . . and are therefore in a permanently unstable state. . . . If they ever did come to equilibrium I don't think we would like them very much. The reason is that, in coming to equilibrium, the rich ecosystems we see today would inevitable lose many of their species." (Roger Lewin, "In Ecology, Change Brings Stability," *Science* 234 (28 November 1986): 1072.) In other words, even if there were an equilibrium, it would not describe or explain the real world, and it would not obviously fulfill environmentalists' goals of species preservation.

76. In a similar vein, another scientist claimed recently that preservation of some sort of ecosystem stability would not necessarily help conservation and the environment. He noted that the threat of habitat destruction and pollution derives primarily from direct impacts rather than from loss of system stability. (R.E. Ricklefs, "Community Diversity: Relative Roles of Local and Regional Processes," *Science* 235 (9 January 1987): 171; hereafter cited as *CD*.)

77. R.E. Ricklefs, *CD*, 167. Or as another researcher put it: one can present numerous criticisms of any "test" using natural systems because each is literally unique. Hence a single field study is not enough to falsify or support an ecological hypothesis. (See Amyan Macfadyen, "Some Thoughts on the Behaviour of Ecologists," *Journal of Animal Ecology* 44: 2 (June 1975): 351.)

Because of the variety of ecological situations and the necessity of using limited observations, ecologists often extrapolate these limited observations into regularities; because this extrapolation involves neither an understanding of what the relevant regularity means nor a knowledge of the domain in which it operates, (McIntosh, *Background*, 273.) the regularity often turns out not to be a suitable candidate for the status of fundamental theoretical law.

78. Ecological equations and models tend to be extremely sensitive to small increments, for example, in the value of r; this means that a slight error, even to the second decimal point, may yield an outcome vastly different from the correct one. Thus, it is difficult to establish the correctness of the equations in the first place. (See Sagoff, *Explanation*, 18.)

79. The existence of these difficulties suggests that ecologists need to pay careful attention to their techniques and to the methodological presuppositions underlying them. It also suggests that a healthy antidote for what has been called "theological ecology" is an increased emphasis on field experimentation and testability. (See E. C.

Pielou, "The Usefulness of Ecological Models: A Stock-Taking," *The Quarterly Review of Biology* 56: 1 (March 1981): 17–31; Suter, *NEPA*, 189.

80.   Apart from the scientific reasons for emphasizing the testability of ecological hypotheses, it is also politically important for them to be scientifically sound, especially if decisionmakers and ethicists attempt to use ecological findings as the basis for public and environmental policy. Often ecological prescriptions go against change, growth, progress, development, and other activities our society views positively. This means that the ecologist is often cast as a "gloom and doom" person in opposition to most prevailing societal mores. For example, ecological injunctions designed to protect food webs and ecosystem processes on land in one area often oppose the alleged right of the individual to do with his private property, in another area, as he wishes. They often oppose the common belief that technology, rather than sound ecological actions, can protect environmental resources. Perhaps most importantly, they often oppose traditional neoclassical economic prescriptions. For all these reasons, there are strong practical grounds for careful attention to ecological method and justification. (Cooper, *Why*, 351.)

81.   At the level of case-by-case decisionmaking, general ecological statements, such as "don't exceed the carrying capacity," are only a little more useful to the person doing environmental ethics than is the dictum "do good and avoid evil" to the person doing normative ethics. In both cases, real problems arise at the level of interpreting exactly what ought to count as good, and exactly what level is the carrying capacity.

Thorny problems of normative ethics cannot be solved by vague appeals either to "do good and avoid evil" or to remember that "everything is connected to everything else" and that "there is no free lunch." For example, if a utility wants to build a nuclear power plant and to discharge its cooling water with a thermal gradient of three degrees into a local lake, this action may be difficult to attack on grounds of environmental ethics supported by ecology. Suppose the ecologists claim to show that the lake ecosystem will be altered and that the existing balance will be upset. Such an argument is a paper tiger if, indeed, the ecologists have no clear definition of what constitutes a balance and if such ecosystems are naturally modified anyway. Precise specification and predictive control of the relevant ecological parameters are absolutely necessary, especially in the borderline cases involving things such as small amounts of thermal pollution. The cases that are not borderline, such as destroying a watershed, or polluting groundwater, or destroying a rainforest, are not difficult because there are usually anthropocentric grounds for opting in favor of the welfare of nature. This means that the very cases, the borderline ones, in which environmental policymakers and moral philosophers look most to ecologists for help, are precisely those in which the ecologists cannot offer much help. And they cannot offer much help because it is not clear that we are yet able to define, precisely, a balance of nature, stability, or species succession in any clear nonprobabilistic, testable sense.

82.   The vampire bat and red scale examples are taken from Daniel Simberloff, "Can Basic Ecology Guide Environmental Policy?" an address given at the University of Florida, December 11, 1986. This information is also in G. H. Orians, Chair, Committee on the Applications of Ecological Theory to Environmental Problems, Commission on Life Sciences, National Research Council, *Ecological Knowledge and Environmental Problem-Solving* (Washington, D.C.: National Academy Press, 1986), 151–190; hereafter cited as: Orians, *EKEP*.

See R. H. Peters, "From Natural History to Ecology," *Perspectives in Biology and*

Medicine 23:2 (Winter 1980): 197 ff. and his account of the transformations of phosphorus in lakes; this is a good example of the precise, empirical sort of work at which ecologists can be quite successful.

83. Ecologists cannot tell us what contributes to the integrity, stability, and beauty of the biosphere, for the sake of the biosphere but, if we humans can agree upon some of those goals, e.g., promoting species diversity, then ecologists can often provide details about the *means* for attaining those ends. For example, if we humans want to maximize production of rockfish in a particular area (this example is from Sagoff, *Facts*, 101) then ecologists can often tell us how to do this, just as they can tell us how to maximize long-run production of certain natural goods and services. But this is a largely anthropocentric and economic goal. The problem arises when our goal is something like preserving the health of the biosphere or maintaining the alleged natural equilibrium of some ecosystem. Ecologists cannot typically tell us these things.

For the National Academy of Sciences report, see Orians, *EKEP*, esp. 1.

84. See Sagoff, *Fact*, 103, for the management/protection distinction.

85. See Sagoff, *Fact*, 111.

86. McIntosh writes: "It is unfortunate that the demand for theoretical ecological insights with which to support rhetorical ecology [ecology at the service of environmental ethics and policy] comes at a time when ecology is in a condition sometimes described as . . . confusion. The press in recent decades to produce a theoretical ecology has coincided with a multiplicity of theoretical ecologies philosophically and methodologically at odds with each other." All schools have failed to provide the hoped-for predictive capacity for ecology. (McIntosh, *Background*, 321.)

Given the highly problematic character of the balance and wholism presuppositions, ecology appears to be in a stage of "paradigms lost." But if so, then prescribing ethical directives, such as "it is good to maintain the greatest numbers of species possible," on the alleged ecological grounds of the stability-diversity hypothesis is both a false and a misleading way to ground environmental ethics. The moral is that scientifically naive ethics do not bear up under epistemological scrutiny. Environmental ethics so grounded is no better than Kantian philosophy built on false physics.

87. This is what Brian Norton argues in his forthcoming book, *The Spice of Life*. He also argues for the ethical obligation to promote diversity on grounds that ecosystemic diversity promotes stability/predictability, and stability is a good. This is a problematic approach, for many of the reasons already given. His other argument for maintaining diversity is that future generations would derive value from species diversity, and therefore that we should promote it. Admittedly, Norton's argument focuses only on human welfare, but it has the merit of not risking the demise of our environmental ethics because of its dependence on a questionable nonanthropocentric argument built on vague or erroneous ecological presuppositions.

88. Such a mitigation would not require that we be able to predict the effects of certain environmental actions, but merely that we work out details, perhaps on a benefit-cost scheme, of how to mitigate adverse impacts. (See Barnthouse *et al.*, in note 63. See also Sagoff, *ES*, 14–55.)

89. Just as we ought to avoid begging the question that ecology can provide fundamental laws, we also ought to avoid begging the question that ecology cannot provide fundamental laws. (See Sagoff, *Explanation.*)

90.   See the essay by Colwell in this same volume.

91.   All these points need more justification than can be given here. See Taylor, *Respect*, who makes them a central theme of his book.

92.   R. M. Hare, in *Moral Thinking* (New York: Oxford, 1981), makes the distinction between first-order, or intuitive, ethical principles and second-order, or critical ethical principles.

93.   For a discussion of strong versus weak rights, see R. Dworkin, *Taking Rights Seriously* (Cambridge: Harvard University Press, 1977).

94.   The first objection was formulated by Berkeley ecologist Rob Colwell, the second by Colwell and by University of Bern (Switzerland) geographer Bruno Messerli. Philosopher Beat Sitter and attorney Peter Saladin made the third objection, and Saladin made the fourth objection.

95.   See the Strong reference in note 51. See also M. B. Davis, "Climatic Instability, Time Lags, and Community Disequilibrium," and R.W. Graham, "Response of Mammalian Communities to Environmental Changes During the Late Quaternary," in *Community Ecology*, J. Diamond and T. Case (eds.) (New York: Harper and Row, 1986), 269–284 and 300–313.

96.   Orians, *EKEP*, 91–92.

In Defence of Nonanthropocentrism in Environmental Ethics

BEAT SITTER

Neither the notion of a balance of nature nor the concept of ecosystems as wholes[1] similar to organisms provides a solid foundation for environmental ethics and politics, since both are vague and unclear. We face serious methodological and empirical difficulties when we try to operationalize them. Therefore, we ought to defend our respective views in classical anthropocentric terms.

This appears to me to be Kristin Shrader-Frechette's central thesis.[2] Although I share some of her ethical and scientific scruples, I cannot fully agree with the first part of her thesis, and I do not think that the second part logically follows from the first. From a moral point of view, I consider it wrong, if taken as the only guide for an environmental ethics. I maintain that such an ethics needs a firm nonanthropocentric pillar, i.e., a foundation whose material and structure correspond to a timely outlook on the world. Although talking of one pillar only, I do not mean to exclude others, and I favor an ethics that combines both nonanthropocentric and anthropocentric aspects. Since I propose here to plead the cause of nonanthropocentrism, I shall concentrate on this aspect of the issue.

1. An Interpretation of the Expression 'Balance of Nature' and 'Ecosystemic Wholes'

The ecosystemic outlook and analysis of nature (where nature is understood to be not just man's environment, but the world encompassing human beings) follow the axiom that all objects of knowledge are in some way interconnected and interfere with others. Ecosystemic analysis is guided by the idea that the elements of the world, viewed as an overall system, may be arranged into smaller or larger units whose holistic interpretation explains important aspects—especially processes—of the world we live in.

For ecosystemic science, it is imperative to engage in holistic analysis if we wish to understand the behavior of individuals and groups, the history and the development of situations and processes, and to influence them.

Ecosystemic explanation borrows its instruments from systems theory; we find among them the axioms concerning the tendency to self-preservation, the faculty of learning and adaptation, and the balance of systems. This balance is conceived of in three different ways: we speak of stable or elastic balance, of unstable balance, and finally of indifferent balance of systems. The three notions refer to the different ways in which systems react to internally or environmentally caused impacts. None of them would be appropriate if applied exclusively to ecosystemic reality. In nature we observe the adaptive preservation, modification, and, eventually, vanishing of systems. The preservation of propitious states of order by negative feedback will be found together with the integration of favorable innovations through amplification of a particular direction of fluctuation, which results in an irreversible modification of the original state of the system. "The faculty of instability is a constitutive trait of any ecosystem; it is of deep significance for the genesis and the evolution of an ecosystem."[3] Looked at in this light, the claim to conserve existing elastic balances of definable ecosystems at any rate would be wrong. The notion of an enduring ecological balance makes sense only if applied as a Kantian ideal to nature, i.e., as an axiom whose empirical rightness will never be definitely established, but remains indispensable for the interpretation of natural processes.[4]

These considerations lead to three assertions: 1. the expression 'balance of nature' refers to a conception proper to systems theory and applied to the world as a whole; it is not of any relevance to our actions. The balance of nature, if it truly exists, produces itself as a metastable balance, and thus transcends the domain of possible human responsibility. 2. The concept of balance does not become irrelevant or superfluous because we cannot recognize a state of balance in a concrete ecosystemic situation. As a heuristic principle, the concept remains indispensable for all ecosystemic analysis of reality, notwithstanding the difficulties that may show up when we try to apply it to empirical facts. 3. Whereas it is indeed useless to make the balance of nature an object of human action, the preservation and enhancement of the balance of definable ecosystems may still be an aim and a task for us. If we understand 'balance' in this restricted sense, then it is not yet disqualified as a normative principle.

This enables us to sharpen the objection that Shrader-Frechette raises against the normative usefulness of the idea of balance (p. 76): Indeed, "we cannot say what it would be to hinder the balance of nature." However, given a defined ecosystem actually displaying a favorable, relatively enduring state of order, we may—applying human time scales—show what it would be like to disturb the balance of this concrete ecosystemic unit. From which it follows that not the balance of nature as a whole, but the natural balances of ecosystemic situations may become objectives for human action and, therefore, objects of our responsibility.

In this context it is sufficient that ecologists admit the fact of the coevolution and the interconnectedness of the elements of our world, at least on a small scale. It is not important whether they accept the Gaia-hypothesis (Lovelock, 1979) or think that the overall balance of nature is a meaningful concept.

Thus far, I have only shown that the expression 'balance of nature' can indicate a significant goal for human action. But to avoid misunderstandings, we should speak of natural balances of ecosystemic situations. This leaves unanswered the question whether we are always morally obliged to respect and preserve such balances. Only if we succeed, could the idea of balance become the cornerstone of the foundation of an ecological ethics.[5]

But before providing the required evidence, I have to define ecosystems in a way that is sufficiently clear for my practical purposes. I started from the presupposition that it is possible to identify ecosystemic units, and that we can show what we mean when we talk about affecting existing balances.

2. A Way to Define Ecosystems

Obvious difficulties appear when we try to apply the term 'system' to concrete cases: in the first instance, the term refers to an idea, not to an empirical unit. Systems theory does not tell us which empirical unit should become an object of systematic analysis;[6] our choice will depend on our standpoint. If we apply this to ecosystemic research, we may say that defining ecosystems depends on the questions we actually raise, "on the momentary aim of investigation," generally speaking on the observer's attention which is biased by his interests.[6a] The definition looks arbitrary, and this appearance is used as an argument against holistic and organismic views to discredit the acceptability of the claim to enhance wholes and to preserve their balances (cf. Shrader-Frechette, pp. 79, 82).

However, the definition of systems as such is not arbitrary. First, we may—without necessarily counting ourselves among the realists "of the most naive sort"—maintain that, though 'system' is an intellectual notion, we can also speak of systems as real entities.[7] A real system is not a set of random things, but a unit "of elements connected by reciprocal action" that "form a whole with its proper qualities" (Bertalanffy); the system, therefore, is more significant than the mere sum of the qualities of its parts.[8] The notion of system does not allow us to link events without any empirical connection, e.g., my writing with the rain falling on the Maldive Islands, unless we engage in metaphysical speculation or are writing a fairy tale. Hence, the structural aspect of the notion of system does not allow for arbitrariness, and, consequently, the hierarchical aspect does not admit it either. When proceding from a once accepted system to a wider or more particular order, we have to respect the following limitations: in the first case, the original system must become an element of the higher order, integrated in it by reciprocal action on at least one of its elements; whereas in the second case, it must remain the reference unit for systems placed on a more particular level.

The restriction that we must not use the term 'system' unless the elements defining it have mutual effects, may be expressed in a different way, namely, by saying that only a set of elements sufficient to satisfy the balance requirements (Küppers, 1068) may be labelled a system. This is not begging the question; rather it is a support provided by systems theory for the definition of factual systems, and a way of excluding arbitrary combinations. Entities of no significance to the conceived state of balance of a set do not belong to the system. They may be part of its environment (if we allow the concept of environment to include entities that do not affect the system). The balance requirement entails that ecosystems, conceived as a "texture of mutual effects for living beings and their anorganic environments",[9] maintain their basic order through self-regulation, compensating fluctuation in number and strength of species as well as in flux of energy and matter (Küppers, *ibid.*). The requirement implies another essential trait of ecosystems: passages from one state to another are clearly discernible, as well as the moment when ecosystems disintegrate. Hence, injuries to ecosystems by human inference are in principle knowable.

Systems theory provides the necessary means to define and isolate systems; but they are not sufficient. We can still restrict or enlarge the circle encompassing the elements.[10]

But this is a matter of choice, and is thus an act that must be answered for. The definition of the system will not be based on lack of knowledge. We must be conscious of the relations we want to neglect, and be in a position to argue for such neglect by referring to the aim of the investigation.[11] Only then shall we dispose of the sufficient conditions for defining a system. In the case of ecosystems, it will be particularly advisable to regard definitions as dynamic; for in scientific work, it may prove indispensable to consider interrelations that were screened off in the first instance. But this does not show that ecosystems cannot be defined in principle, and successful work has been done on the basis of such definitions.

However, in the context of ethical issues, the fundamental definability of systems might sound odd. Confronted with a moral claim, one may well object that it is not clear which ecosystems should be taken care of. It is not *the possibility* of defining ecosystems that is called in question; rather, the objection suggests that *the way* to the definition is, though perhaps within certain limits, optional and in this sense arbitrary, i.e., related to subjective goals.

To settle this query, I suggest an intersubjectively acceptable argument, bearing in mind that in ethical issues it is easier to come across negative rules than to discover positive norms, and that the first are more readily universalizable. An example is the golden rule: while I may never be sure that what looks desirable to me will be good for others, I ought to refrain from doing to others what would be bad or wrong in my eyes.[12] The positive claim to preserve and enhance ecosystems, to maximize their excellences, does entail difficulties. However, it is easy to agree that elements of our environment have been damaged or have vanished. If one is willing to remedy this state of affairs, then one is compelled to pay attention to all the elements, connections, and processes that affect the condition of what one considers to be damaged. Knowledge of the effective elements and interrelations must be deepened as far as possible. Conscious neglect of only a few of these elements or relations would be wrong because inconsistent with the autonomously fixed goal. The definition of the ecosystem in question becomes independent of subjective option and in this sense complete. This does not mean that it is also objectively complete, but from the moral point of view, we may declare respect for the prohibition of arbitrariness. In the light of practical requirements, the definition is sufficiently clear and precise.

Hence, we have to define ecosystems with regard to practical requirements. We should not begin by trying to maximize something; rather our starting point should be the assessment of a negative fact, and our willingness to correct it.

The same can be said when we consider activities that interfere with existing structures in the world. An ecosystem is sufficiently defined with regard to practical needs, when it encompasses all the elements, the relations, and the processes that will be acted on. In this case the descriptive content of the claim to respect and preserve the *balance* of an ecosystem is sufficiently clear for practical purposes.[13]

3. Wholism as a Defendable Presupposition

We may now say that ecosystems can be clearly determined as far as practical concerns are involved. Furthermore, as systems they may be investigated under the threefold aspect of balance. They are identifiable as wholes that preserve themselves by processes of self-regulation, which in turn lend themselves to description in terms of systems theory. Indeed, the idea of balance and the wholism conception are not separable; they illustrate two aspects of the same phenomenon, i.e., the systemic whole. The balanced aspect of the ecosystem relates to a whole that, for a shorter or longer time, is preserved by homeostatic processes.[14]

We can now determine holistic entities when we describe and analyze nature. If we consider the tendency towards self-preservation and the necessary self-regulation of the processes that characterize each whole and differentiate it from the environment, then we may speak of organisms. However, this notion is ambiguous;[15] therefore, I shall not use it. The following consideration is of much higher significance for the interpretation of ecosystems as wholes. Even with humans as parts of ecosystems, the processes that govern the systems remain ultimately out of human control.[16] We may be able to describe and explain the processes, calculate and control them; but we cannot create or abolish them in an original and definitive sense. Like natural laws they are not an object of human whim.[17] This is irrespective of whether we shall ever be able to grasp general laws underlying all ecosystems, or whether we are limited to specific rules that govern a certain ecosystem.[18]

Hence, the two following assertions: 1. it is possible to assess holistic environmental entities with regard to practical requirements. 2. Since the regulation of these environmental entities ultimately remains independent of human will, it makes sense for our practice to realize such assessments.

4. Is There a Moral Obligation to Respect Ecosystemic Wholes and Their Balance?

Although we may succeed in determining ecosystems as environmental wholes with their balances, ought we to—and are we obliged to—respect the wholes with their balances? The dispute between economic interests and the maintenance of the natural environment reveals that this question is open. Few argue for and act with respect to the thesis that ecology is identical with long-term economics (B. Messerli, et al., 5), and thus endeavor to conciliate economics with ecology. The fundamental difficulty resides in the fact that, not unlike the representatives of the narrow and short-sighted economic view, appeal is made to human interests, truly engaging in anthropocentric arguments. We can, of course, argue against the blind predominance of economic selfishness from an anthropocentric standpoint. We can recall that human existence and economic prosperity depend on natural conditions; that, if we wish mankind to continue, everything must be done to keep natural systems intact or to restore them when they have been seriously damaged; that, to be fair, self-restraint and even substantial renunciation must be admitted, since it would be immoral to make future generations pay for our depletion of natural resources. However, these arguments are not convincing unless linked to three decisions that rational arguments alone cannot account for: 1. that I and others ought to exist; 2. that mankind ought to exist, not just now, but also in the future; 3. that we ought to assure for future generations, as far as we can, conditions as good as those we enjoy.

I do not deny the desirability of these decisions or the importance of the arguments that ensue, but I believe that they need to be supplemented. They do not fully correspond to the possibilities of contemporary moral consciousness. Their flaw consists in relating all nonhuman beings to human interests, thereby considering them instruments of human well-being. They do not allow for a *direct* obligation to look at nature in a holistic way and preserve its balance.[19]

I shall therefore omit anthropocentric arguments but illustrate the obligation to respect holistic environmental entities and their balances. But before doing this, I wish to discuss the term 'anthropocentrism' to clarify what is meant by a nonanthropocentric position.[20]

4.1 Anthropocentrism Is Not Inevitable in Ethics

The suggestion to rely on classical anthropocentric terms when justifying environmental ethics and politics sounds all the more plausible when we are told that, in so doing, we stand on firm ground and use precise concepts. Yet looking more closely at this claim, we soon observe that it is not at all clear what is meant by classical anthropocentric terms.

4.1.1 The Claim of Anthropocentrism Is Not Clear

Pleading for anthropocentrism in ethics means connecting moral norms and duties with human wants, desires, and goals—in short, with human interests. And those interests are considered the decisive point of reference in value conflicts.[21] But whose interests are at stake—those of the individual or the group? But in groups different individuals have different needs and contradictory desires. Or should we refer to the interest of the human species? And if the interests of our species (or of a group) are decisive, will this allow us to sacrifice the individuals to the species (or to the group)? Is it clear whether a species can be the subject of interests, if we prescind from specific self-preservation?

Even if we succeeded in giving satisfactory answers to these questions, other queries would still lurk in the background: Which interests should be considered ethically relevant—the physiological, instinctive ones that are hardly accessible to arguments, or the rational interests open to discursive justification? If both, are they equal or is one subordinate to the other? Would such a relation be unambiguous, so that we could always know which to prefer? I do not think that we can expect to see this question answered in a generally accepted way. The claim that life, or survival, is the fundamental, hence most important value[22] is contested by the Christian or Islamic teaching. But even among the clearly individual interests that are related to earthly life, there does not seem to be any generally admitted order; rather, such orders depend on culture, education, biography, and innate personal inclinations.

What, then, are the generally admitted classical anthropocentric terms we are supposed to refer to in ecological ethics and politics? We simply are not in a position to state them in an unambiguous way. The question raises difficulties "which traditional anthropocentric ethics is relatively helpless to deal with."[23]

The attempt to rely on anthropocentric arguments is neither clear nor precise. Would the same apply to a nonanthropocentric starting point in ecological ethics? To answer this query, I first wish to list various meanings of 'anthropocentrism' and examine in what way they are ethically relevant. This will allow me to illustrate the sense in which we may speak of a nonanthropocentric foundation of ecological ethics.

4.1.2 Seven Ways of Using the Word 'Anthropocentrism'

Protagoras' "man is the measure of all things" illustrates *cosmological anthropocentrism.* Here, the human being is the center and the goal of the world whose elements are the material he may dispose of, as suits him best. *Theological anthropocentrism* corresponds essentially to this view, although in this conception the human being is subordinated to a transcendent God. But this renders humans prominent among all beings; they are the cherished object of His concern, the object of redemption, His only image in the world. Devotion to God is man's essential duty; it may, but need not, free him from all responsibility for the rest of the world. The world, however, is still the material to be dominated for the sake of human life. When secularized, theological anthropocentrism turns into *humanistic anthropocentrism.* [24] This relieves man from transcendent dominance, and sharpens the necessity to ensure his existence by lording it over his fellow lodgers in the world. Man's claim to domination knows no limits, as there is no deity to make everything good and just in the end.[25] I call a species of this outlook *anthropological anthropocentrism.* It focuses on the particular position man holds among all other beings of this world because he can himself fix the aims of his existence, use language and assume responsibility for a moral life. This particular condition grounds the human being's predominance over other beings and his ability to possess rights, i.e., with respect to his superiority, absolute privileges. All other beings remain rightless, mere instruments, handed over to human favor or disgrace, even if that outlook did not exclude humanitarian behaviour towards nonhuman beings (Teutsch 1987, 16).

Anthropological anthropocentrism has a *legal* aspect. Actions are judged solely in the light of their compatibility with normative systems that protect human rights and dignity (cf. Taylor 1981, 197). This form of anthropocentrism has been dominant for centuries; it is mitigated only hesitantly and rarely, e.g., by animal protection acts.[26] It is defended by protests against laws that would be nonanthropocentric. This is done with reference to *interest-oriented anthropocentrism.* Although highly questionable, this form of anthropocentrism firmly sticks to the principle "humans come first!" and declares human interests to be the ultimate reason and the best means for settling normative queries.

I would call the last form of anthropocentrism I wish to consider *epistemological anthropocentrism.* It reflects the fact that all knowledge and value are mediated through human perception, thought, and emotion. In consequence all objects of our knowing and valuing are not, to use Kant's words, things in themselves; they can only be perceived within the framework of human faculties as phenomena.

It seems obvious that all these varieties of anthropocentrism, except the last, are relevant to ethics. They result in man's preeminence and establish his prerogatives. Man is the absolute value, an end in himself; other beings are his instruments. Legal anthropocentrism illustrates the fundamental ethical consequence of this way of thinking: nonhumans have no claim to legal or moral status.[27] In consequence, a nonanthropocentric approach to ecological ethics must first renounce the claim of human *predominance.* Yet this does not hinder it from choosing man's *particular condition,* e.g., his rationality, as a subject for investigation, and to examine this condition by focussing on the particular responsibility it may entail for man.

4.1.3 Epistemological Anthropocentrism and Ethics

Epistemological anthropocentrism differs from the remaining varieties that I shall now subsume under the title 'plain anthropocentrism.' Epistemological anthropocentrism gives expression to the prerequisite of ethics: that man is a rational being. Looked at in this way, one may say that there can only be an anthropocentric ethics. However, this manner of speaking is misleading, when we take into account the remaining ways of using the word anthropocentrism. The statement that, as far as we know, only man exists as the center of ethical reflection, does not entail that man must always and exclusively make his proper interests the ultimate reference point for ethical considerations. An example of a wrong inference from anthropotrope[28] to plainly anthropocentric ethics appears when we are reminded that nature does not have any "alleged properties apart from some viewer or valuer"; or that, "if current scientific instrumentalists are right, a nonanthropocentric ecology is not possible" (Shrader-Frechette, note 35); and when all this happens in a context ending in a demand to use classical anthropocentric terms in environmental ethics. The fallacy again supports the thesis that it is only with reference to plain anthropocentric views that we can decide whether our actions are wrong or right: the fact that only humans can make the distinction between right and wrong is turned into the claim that right and wrong depend on human interests.[29]

In conclusion, we may say that epistemological anthropocentrism neither justifies a plainly anthropocentric foundation of ethics, nor renders it unavoidable. On the other hand, ethical reflection searching for a not plainly anthropocentric base for morals is not turned into a plainly anthropocentric endeavor by the anthropotrope nature of all reflection. The anthropocentrism such ethical reflection wishes to avoid is that which styles man to be the absolute value and the necessary reference point for all valuing of other beings, with the consequence that the prevailing criterion for valuing nonhuman entities is human interests, wants, desires, and aims.[30]

4.1.4 Human Evaluations, Judgments, and Actions Are Not Necessarily Anthropocentric

Showing that the anthropotrope nature of all reflection does not justify a plainly anthropocentric[31] ethics does not yet disprove the assertion that all our valuations refer ultimately to interests. This means that all our actions, including those that appear altruistic, are motivated and justified by reference to interests (of all kinds, be they cultural, intellectual, genetically determined, physiological, or sociological). The mere fact that the claim is shaped into a universal statement that is not directly verifiable does not invalidate it. If we wish to refute it, we must produce at least one counterempirical example, or else we have to make plain that it is of no practical use in certain contexts of justification. This is what I wish to do.

Let me mention here that Rawls provides the following example of nonanthropocentric valuing. There is a meaningful way, he says, of employing the word 'good' when we refer to the coat of an animal or the root of a plant. If we adopt the point of view of the animal or the plant, then 'good,' referring to the coat or the root, means that these display properties that the animal and the plant need to remain alive (1972, 403). In this case, our judgment refers to objects outside our sphere of interests. Neither the judgment nor its justification necessarily depends on our valuing coat and root because we take an interest in the existence of the animal or the plant. Content and justification are separated from our interests (which may have caused the judgment) and may even run against them.[32]

On the other hand, our behavior *after* judging is no longer independent of content and justification. Our behavior towards the object of our judgment cannot but refer to the valuation, either by paying attention to or neglecting it. The acquired knowledge makes us responsible for the object of our valuing. Only if we could get rid of our essential relation to rightness and truth would we be able to free ourselves from that responsibility. This is plainly impossible.[33] Hence, judgment leads to consequences that are independent of our interests.

The example of the good Samaritan (Luke 10, 30–37) is interesting in this context. Both the priest and the Levite notice the robbed and wounded man; they value his condition and his wants without referring to their own interests. Even if they used their imagination to feel what it would be like for them to be in an analogous position, their evaluation refers to the condition of another person. Their further behavior is related to the result of their cognitive valuing; manifestly remorse could torment them if they neglected someone else's urgent needs. The Samaritan's behavior illustrates an evaluation of the needs of the person concerned, and not his own. He takes the new knowledge gained by cognitive valuing into account and subordinates his own interests to the other's needs.

In the first instance, I only wish to show that it is possible to make value judgments without directly referring to the valuer's own interests. But then I also think that, being such a valuer, we can respect others' values and interests for their own sake, in the course of our behavior, i.e., without further recourse to our own interests. To note that "a large element of selfishness . . . is a quite ineradicable part of human nature" (Mackie 1981, 132) does not invalidate my opinion; it just stresses that it is difficult for us to take up the correct attitude and act accordingly. It is, of course, possible to ask what interest might have motivated the Samaritan to adopt an altruistic position; and every answer hinting at an unselfish reference point may again be scrutinized with a view to find the concealed self-love. However, if we thus proceed, we have to pay attention to the fact that it is not the actor himself, but *the observer* analyzing the acting person, under the heuristic presupposition of complete determination by interests, who *constructs* proper interests as motivations. The motivations *the actor himself* vindicates, may contradict the constructions; it is not clear from the beginning that the analytic construction hits reality, and hence is right despite the actor's statements. The contrary opinion that would turn the heuristic viewpoint into a theory and ward off any possible critique would be disastrous.

Daily experience reveals that an analysis of proper interests that determine human behavior may bar the understanding of existential decisions in practical situations. Take the example of the woman who, left alone after the death of her husband, has to earn her family's livelihood and take care of her three sons' education. They prove a source of sorrow for her, not only because of the trouble they have at school and in society, but because they treat her badly. She experiences situations where only her sense of responsibility sustains her will to keep on living. It would obviously be wrong to explain her choice by self-love and proper interests. Practical decisions often demand reasons that go beyond selfishness.

Examples such as the one just given do not make it impossible to have recourse to self-love and proper interests to justify ethical norms. But they emphasize that proceeding this way may be irrelevant from a practical viewpoint, since it entails blindness with respect to the essence of the situation.

Therefore, this way should not be made into a principle and declared relevant to all kinds of practice. Moreover, the claim that we *always* rely on our own interests when engaged in valuing and choosing our actions is invalidated.[34] We are not compelled to deny the experience according to which many of our judgments are directed by our own interests, when, from a practical point of view, we maintain the following *thesis:* we are rational beings, in principle capable of recognizing the wants of our fellow beings for their own sake, i.e., without any regard to our own interests; and we are, in principle, able to admit these values and wants as goals of our action. This is possible even in contradiction to our own interests; from a practical view, the faculty remains significant even when, in the end, we prefer our interests to measures that are imperative from the stand point of those affected by our actions. The perception of another's inherent worth and proper needs affects the domain of our responsibility; it is not without consequences for the justification of our practice, and it may modify that practice if we take the new insights into account.[35]

4.2. Towards the Obligation to Respect All Natural Beings

There seems to be no dispute concerning ecology as a science opening a way to holistic and systemic thought. But ecology has its own historical side. It makes us understand to how much man depends on autonomous developments and modification of natural ecosystems. Climatic changes, for example, may be prerequisites of flourishing human cultures, but also the cause of their vanishing.[36] Today we are worried by climatic changes that are partly the results of human activity. In analysing and interpreting these changes, e.g., the so-called greenhouse-effect, we perceive that we are, to a great extent, delivered to far-reaching processes. We may be searching for a means to control them, not by attempting to change the undisposable processes themselves, but by trying to change our behavior.

Historical and current ecology only confirms the anthropocentric attitude. It does not help us resolve the question whether a duty could be conceived that obliges us to respect, protect, and enhance ecosystemic wholes and their balances. Yet this query may now be settled. I do this in two phases. First, I shall argue for our duty to respect all natural entities; and second, I shall apply the result to ecosystemic wholes and balances.

4.2.1 Clearing the Concept of 'Nature'

The word 'nature' is employed in various ways; the meaning of the expression 'natural being' (or 'natural entity') varies accordingly. Thus, in the first instance, I indicate how I use these expressions. I wish to distinguish five aspects of nature that are intimately linked to each other:[37]

1. 'Nature' is what man has not made himself, what he is not able to create, what happens without his being able to interfere even in principle. It is what is given to man without his cooperation.[38]

2. Nature is for man (a natural being himself) an historical prerequisite as well as a necessary condition of his being—i.e., what he needs to exist, what he cannot produce, and what does not yield to his will.[39]

3. Moreover, nature is what man has to recognize as a prerequisite of his cultural activity, what may become an object of this activity, yet remains its necessary condition. This view is correct even if we rarely come across "purely natural" objects, and when we recall that all human perception passes through filters shaped by culture and personal biography. The specific manner in which we deal with nature does not invalidate nature as its prerequisite, although it may sever our consciousness from nature so interpreted.[40] This happens, for example, when nature is defined as that which we objectify by our knowledge and abilities in an historical way.[41] Such an interpretation presents nature as a mere "unit of regulations constituted by artificial arrangements" (Böhme, 1988, 42). Of course, the distortion caused by this interpretation might be corrected by considerations on personal death. If this does not take place or if the distortion stays in place, it turns into ideologically conditioned blindness.[42, 43]

4. We have learned that linear, monocausal analysis is not appropriate for understanding reality, since the latter is governed by structures of order and relations that are far too complex to be grasped by reductionist thought (P. Messerli 1986, 15). Conceiving of systemic interconnections proves particularly indispensable when we analyze damages in our environment and try to mend them. In consequence, 'nature' has become the overall notion for all ecosystemic contexts. We perceive every organic and inorganic being as woven into diverse reciprocal actions. A web of further relations connects those ecosys-

temic contexts that form, as elements, a superior whole, the biosphere or encompassing ecosystem on whose condition all living beings depend. Hence, we may say that natural being is essentially ecosystemic. Ecosystemic coinage turns out to be a new ontological category; it discloses beings to be functional in contexts which are ruled by the principles of self-preservation, compensation, and stability, yet which are not less dynamically open[44] for modification. Nature as the whole embracing all natural beings—among them humans—is ecosystemically constituted.[45]

5. The last aspect of the notion of 'nature' sheds light on nature's vulnerability. Though an undisposable prerequisite of human existence, nature is no longer an infinite instance and a material to be exploited without limits. To both our experience and our imagination, it has become a sensitive context; human interference and consumption, particularly when harnessed by science and technology, disturb it and can, in the extreme case, abolish the natural prerequisites for life. Nature as the spring of and the provision for life has become fundamentally endangered by man, not just for human beings, but for all living beings. Hence, vulnerability is a crucial aspect.

Combining these five aspects we reach a definition of 'nature' as the overall notion encompassing everything that is given to man beyond his disposal; all that he needs to exist, create, and develop; all that is ecosystemically constituted; everything that man may injure so as to render life impossible. 'Nature' includes human beings.[46]

4.2.2 The Obligation to Respect Natural Beings

Various reasons may lead us to respect natural beings. The first reason emerges when we consider the first three aspects of the meaning of 'nature' that reflect man's dependence on nature as a presupposition of his existence and a never-to-be-disposed-of limitation of his will. Not only to live well, but to live at all, we must use natural beings that are given to us. We may transform what we find, but whenever interfering to shape nature we remain dependent on the given 'material.' Ultimately, we cannot create anything, but are limited to transformation. This holds true even if we synthesize substances, or interfere with the hereditary control of the genesis of living beings. A chimera or a transgeneous animal remains a product of transformation, and is not a creature in the radical sense. What remains untouched by our shaping but provides a necessary presupposition for it reveals some independence. This independence of natural beings on which we depend as long as we want to exist appears to me to be a good reason for respect.

A second reason lies in the consideration that natural entities not only transcend our creative power, but oppose our free will with unsurmountable restraints. It is precisely for ecological science to teach us that man should not undertake what does not agree with nature. If he is able to do it, he ought not to do it. If he trespasses on the limit indicated in the form of ought, then nature is likely to open the way to his destruction. As Frankel puts it: "Nature never bends to a human purpose without charging a price" (Frankel 1976, 103). In so far as man depends on the existence of some being that for its part does not in any way owe its existence to him, we may credit that being with *dignity* and derive from it the claim that man should *respect* it. For "respect is properly the conception of a worth which thwarts my self-love."[47] This is exactly what natural beings as necessary and therefore not disposable prerequisites of human existence and actions do. They cannot be arbitrarily bargained away, and in this sense they do not have "any price," "no equivalent against which they could be exchanged"; it is for this very reason that showing them due respect implies recognizing their dignity.[48]

If one accepts theses two reasons, one may still maintain that they are clearly anthropocentric. However, a nonanthropocentric argument can be arrived at by paying attention to a certain equality among all beings. In ontological terms, we can interpret it as equality with reference to a fundamental mode of being. Martin Heidegger has underlined it with regard to human existence (Dasein) as "thrown-ness" ("Geworfenheit").[49] I propose to apply this ontological character also to nonhuman beings. Like man, all other beings can be said to be thrown into their existence and delivered onto themselves.[50] Looking at the history of nature, we perceive the equality of man and other natural objects as rooted in their common *ground* of existence. If we set apart man-made evaluations, there is no reason to prefer the existence of one being over that of another.[51] We may, therefore, maintain that *in principle* all beings possess an equal natural right to existence, whether man acknowledges it or not.

In recognizing this right, I do not deny either that the various natural beings are differently constituted and equipped, nor that man occupies a special place in the world due to his rational competence, his reasoning capacity, and his moral being. And I do not argue against his being bound to making use of other beings to provide for his own existence. But I stress the responsibility that emerges from his special position. For as soon as man understands that all beings are, in some way, ends in themselves because centers of relations independent of his will, he realizes that they are, in this respect, equal to him. As a being capable of rational insight and moral responsibility, he should behave towards nonhuman beings in the light of that fundamental equality. If we agree to that, then we ought to transfer the *principle of equality* from the social sphere to the overall community of beings. This principle requires that equal things should be valued and treated equally as far as their equality is concerned, and that, on the ohter hand, what is different should be valued and dealt with differently and in accordance with the differences in question.[52] By thus transferring the principle of equality to the overall community of beings, we might give life to a moral and, eventually, to a *legal community of nature.*[53] In this community, man as a moral agent is obliged to ask what is due to every individual being in a given situation. He ought to do it, since he is capable of doing it.[54] This may direct his actions away from or against the particular interests of other members of the community or even his own. What is due to each of the concerned beings in the light of their equal right to exist must be sought for in the interest of limiting human arbitrariness. This also applies to the case in which resolving the conflict of concurrent rights inevitably leads to the abolition of the existence of some being—e.g., if I have to kill an animal to nourish myself.

Negatively speaking, we can hold that in the legal community of nature man may not indisputedly destroy what he has not wholly made himself.[55] This rule entails that there should be compensation for harm inflicted and damage done. *Positively* speaking, the legal community of nature requires respect for the quality of—though it may be limited—self-reliance in all beings, and therewith a limitation on the arbitrariness of others at any time and in every respect, i.e., it requires man not to deal with other beings as if they were mere instruments. Kant's categorical imperative, addressed to rational beings, should not only apply to that kind of being, but should also govern the relations of these beings to nonrational members of the overall legal community.[56]

4.2.3 The Correct Application of the Equality Principle

In referring to the equality principle and, at the same time, maintaining that human beings have a special responsibility towards natural beings, I find myself at variance with an opinion of Shrader-Frechette's that is a main argument for her anthropocentric position (Shrader-Frechette, p. 78 and note 44). She contends that, if human beings are equal members of the biotic community, they do not have any special responsibility. It is no more wrong for us "to kill and eat other humans than it is for wolves or alligators to do so." Being on a par with other members of the biotic community, we do not have any special rights and therefore no special responsibilities. This use of the equality principle is clearly inconsistent with its widely accepted meaning, which requires that we carefully distinguish equalities and inequalities when comparing two or more entities. Equality does not imply identity; it is always tied to a certain aspect and is therefore compatible with differences under other aspects. That humans are biotic entities does not mean that they are not rational beings, capable of distinguishing right from wrong and thus of leading a moral life, i.e., of assuming responsibility for their actions. They are, under that aspect, simply not comparable with beasts of prey. Likewise, while it is true that, under the mere aspect of our biotic membership, we do not have any prerogative to exist, it is wrong to maintain that, as rational beings and thus potential moral agents, we are not bound by our responsibilities. Our being is not exhausted by its biotic character. Not to have prerogative right does not imply being divested of all rights. If humans possess the same right of existence as other beings, this does not exclude the requirement that they must pay attention to the same right of existence in other beings.

4.2.4 Obligation Can Be Independent of Reciprocity

The second part of Shrader-Frechette's argument, alluded to in the preceding section, is not conclusive either. It claims that humans have no obligation to any nonhuman entity, since they are endowed with moral primacy and therefore are not equal members of the biotic community. The moral community is formed of beings who have moral responsibility and free will. Thus, no nonhuman entity is a member of that community, and moral agents do not have any obligation towards nonhuman beings.

That, morally speaking, man is not the equal of nonhuman beings is not sufficient to exclude *a priori* any moral obligation towards those beings. This would not even be the case were it unambiguously correct to state that nonhuman beings are not members of the moral community. If we define the moral community as the unit formed by rational beings, by persons able to commit themselves and to assume responsibility, then, of course, nonhuman natural beings would be excluded from such a community. But again this would neither logically nor empirically make it impossible for members of the community to have obligations to nonmembers. If it can be shown that such obligations can be conceived and exist, then it becomes a mere matter of expediency and definition whether we include all objects of moral action in the moral community, or only the moral agents.

The idea that moral obligation can only take place between rational beings and on the basis of reciprocity is Kantian.[57] But it is wrong, since we generally admit moral obligation towards the feeble-minded or the heavily handicapped, even towards comatose humans who have never been and never will be capable of responsibility and reciprocity.[58] We give them moral consideration, recognize their moral status, and thereby admit the obligations that bind us, but this does not mean that these obligations are merely rooted in our reason. We recognize the beings themselves as the ultimate source of obligation. Their inherent worth gives rise to our acknowledgment of being obligated.

4.2.5 Nonhuman Natural Beings as Sources of Obligation

The case is similar with nonhuman natural beings. They exist without our creative activity, as centers of relations that we can know, but not bring forth. They are, as it were, self-reliant and ends in themselves, originally independent of our will. This existential and teleological independence gives them a right of existence over and against our whims. This proper right—of which we become conscious—corresponds to our duty not to affect natural beings in any arbitrary way. Since we have no right to freely dispose of what we have not entirely made,[59] we ought not to look on natural beings as mere means to serve our interests, wants, and desires. We ought to keep in mind that the scientific and technological tools we have developed have become powerful enough to damage and even destroy everything in our reach. The mightier our power, the more pressing our responsibility towards everything exposed to it. Not simply natural, but historical, intentionally realized conditions made everything fall under our disposal. As moral agents, we have to answer for it, and we must moreover admit that the capacity of interference and control implies the obligation to take care of what is capable of manipulation.[60] This obligation in no way depends on reciprocity. It lies in the inherent worth of beings and in our capacity for affecting them. But it is a testimony of man's particular position in the world. This makes him feel "responsible also for other natural entities and systems that depend on him" and in which he recognizes "quasirights" that he defends and enforces as their trustee, thus giving evidence of his specific dignity.[61]

4.3. The Obligation to Respect Ecosystemic Wholes and Their Balance

What has been said about human beings' interrelations with nonhuman natural beings and the obligations those interrelations imply may now be applied to ecosystemic wholes. We only have to keep in mind that ecosystemic wholes are defined in the way shown above, i.e., by starting from concerned individual beings and constructing the ecosystemic web that supports them. Ecosystemic entities or wholes may then be interpreted as necessary conditions of the existence of those individual beings that demand our consideration, and in that quality become objects of reflection, preservation, care, and furtherance.

Ecosystemic units are not just the sum of the properties of the elements that form them. The linkage of the elements is a property of its own, giving the embracing whole its unique character and thus bestowing on it the quality of independent, clearly recognizable individuality without, of course, turning it into a living organism. The individuality of the unit depends on time and change, but this does not exclude its being considered as an historical individual, although lacking self-consciousness, just as our own changing and dying does not deprive us of our historical personality. Ecosystemic entities may therefore be thought of as complex natural beings, and become objects of our concern and a source of obligation in the same way as simple nonhuman natural beings. In so far as dynamic balance is a necessary condition of their preservation, it becomes a proper object of concern for human actors.

Let us recall that such entities exist primarily without our doing. They form units whose functions have goals independent of human purpose. We have good reasons to believe that many of these units of interconnected elements lack self-consciousness and free will; nevertheless, it would be false to deny them a meaning and a purpose related to themselves and not to human beings, notwithstanding the fact that humans are needed to verbalize such meaning and purpose.[62] "The element of value, of being valuable, of having value, of being an end in itself, of being something which is for its own sake, must not be omitted in any account of an event as the most concrete actual something."[63] This is precisely what is meant when we speak of worth inherent in a being, be it an individual or a functionally definable complex of beings. This way of speaking emphasizes the difference between what belongs to the being, and the act by which the inherent worth is recognized. Since this worth is not a human product, but given to man in a way he is not able to dispose of, it may become the object of due respect and thus, mediated by reflection, a source of obligation for humans.[64]

It is again man's ambiguous scientific and technological power to interfere with ecosystemic units that yields, when we hold it against the inherent worth of such systems, definite obligations. I wish to glance at it once more, this time highlighting the ethical relevance of ecology as a science.

4.4. The Weakness of Scientific Ecology as a Source of Its Ethical Relevance

Ecologists cannot provide any solid foundation for environmental ethics and politics because they use questionable hypotheses and unclear notions that frequently give way to assertions and previsions that are later proved wrong or unreliable.[65] Ecological knowledge is not of much use when decisions must be taken that need ethical and political orientation (Shrader-Frechette 1989, pp. 82f.).

This thesis sounds plausible, for how should it be possible to ground responsible behavior on ambiguous data and uncertain theories. But the plausibility resists only a first and quick glance. If scrutinized, the uncertainty of ecological knowledge discloses a particular ethical relevance.

4.4.1 Weakness of Ecology Reconsidered

If we examine the reasons for the tentative character of ecological assertions and previsions, we note that the previsions are not in the first place questionable because of unsatisfactory methodological principles (e.g., the notion of dynamic balance or the path of wholistic explanation). Much rather our intellectual capacity, our elaborated methodologies, and the acquired knowledge of laws and empirical data remain insufficient for detecting, let alone understanding the highly diverse facts and complex interrelations we are confronted with. It is precisely ecological science, with its stress on a wholistic outlook on the world that has confronted us with the finiteness of our understanding.[66] These limitations are not easily seen as long as we stick to the recipe that has proved so successful throughout the history of science: reductionism, i.e., cutting down the complexity of nature to a few processes that can be measured and hopefully repeated, questioning nature by focussing on a single parameter.[67] In an exemplary manner, ecology has taught us to exchange this paradigm for a systemic and wholistic appraisal of nature—without, it must be stressed again, compelling us to conceive of such wholes as living organisms.[68] They remain heuristic constructions, but with heuristics founded in a daily experience of the world we live in.[69]

As soon as we have accepted the ecological approach to nature, realized the interconnectedness of our own behavior and the poor range of our knowledge, the weakness of ecological science becomes ethically relevant. Notwithstanding this weakness, we are in a position to isolate things and processes from their support and are manipulating or destroying them. The difficulties essential to ecology teach us that our activities interfere with things we do not even know of, that they cumulate in synergetic effects that we are simply unable to conceive of, that we cannot forsee how these effects will determine the existence of human and nonhuman living beings in the near and in the far-distant future that we shall never personally experience.

4.4.2 Applying the Fairness Principle

The combination of far-reaching and blind power that can affect individual beings, ecosystemic entities, and indeed the whole biosphere, with our poor knowledge about such effects does not in itself yield any moral obligation. Neither does the mere establishment of some equality between ourselves and those affected by our actions. To morally direct these actions, we need ethical principles.

Two have already been introduced, namely, the principle of equality and the negative norm that we do not have any right to injure what we ourselves have not entirely created. Both these principles may be summed up by the fairness principle that reminds us that we should not enjoy profits that others have to pay for without adequate return from our side. This implies that we have to be prepared to renounce personal interests when the situation of those we interfere with to satisfy these interests demands it. The fairness principle is a moral guideline for human interrelations and is rooted in the recognition of every human being as an end in himself. This may be extended to all natural beings, since they are under certain aspects ends in themselves, particularly living beings and ecosystemic units.

If we consider our ignorance of the results of our power in the light of the fairness principle, we come across an ethical imperative that obliges us not to interfere with natural beings or ecosystems unless there is an existantial and urgent need.[70] Since we cannot live without making use of natural entities, the imperative further obliges us to act with the utmost circumspection, i.e., to enhance our knowledge as much as possible, and to spare and take care of what we cannot avoid affecting. In any case, the recommendation that we build our environmental ethics and politics on anthropocentric grounds alone, i.e., only with a view to human welfare, is not compatible with an ecologically enlightened position that does not arbitrarily confine the fairness principle to the domain of human interaction.

I conclude that ecosystemic analysis of nature urges us—particularly when we consider its difficulties—to give up the idea of an anthropocentric standpoint in environmental ethics, and that ecology is of high ethical relevance.[71]

5. The Absolute Necessity of General Principles

Whenever we are placed in particular situations that require an ethically guided decision, we may indeed be confronted with thorny problems: it may be impossible to clearly foresee the various effects of our decision or assess all their advantages and disadvantages. The question then arises whether the general principles provided by ethics are of any help when we try to justify ourselves before the court of our conscience and of the moral community.[72]

No true decision can be taken without a guiding principle. This does not mean that we always have such a principle in mind when factually deciding a case. But the principle could be reconstructed: the reasons for a decision must be scrutinized, and going back to the very root of our decision, we reach more and more general stages until our search for good reasons ends—though perhaps only in a provisory manner—with what we call a highest principle. This is our real point of reference when we justify decisions.

Unless we want to give up the notion of decisionmaking—which would mean leading our lives in an incoherent and chaotic way—we must have recourse to general principles for our actions. The degree of generality we need in the particular case may be left open; it will not always be necessary to go back to the most fundamental convictions that guide our existence.[73]

Looking at principles from another perspective, we may say that they furnish us with a basic value structure without which we would not be able to make any decisions. Principles are signposts indicating *directions* of actions; they do not determine the *detailed course* of these actions. Without principles we could not act at all; but to act, we obviously need not only principles, but empirical information. Actions are the application of principles to concrete situations. But normative principles do not enable us to grasp clearly the empirical conditions under which we are to act. This function is left entirely to experience without the achievements of which we would remain as incapable of assuming responsibility as when divested of principles. Responsibility rests on two pillars: on normative direction and empirical knowledge. If the latter is uncertain, the first cannot be blamed. Moreover, difficulties in applying normative principles do not deprive these principles of their validity. And difficulties of application are certainly not a good reason for exchanging one set of general rules for another, e.g., ecocentric against anthropocentric principles. A simple exchange does not abolish the character of generality, and the anthropocentric terms we use in justifying our decisions and actions are still general points of reference.[74][75]

There remains a third aspect of principles, perhaps the most relevant to practical affairs. Once a principle is stated and accepted, it uncovers parts of reality by its descriptive element: it urges us to consider the new aspects when deciding about our way of acting. Thus, it places potential actors under an obligation they may not have been aware of before, and it definitely removes the possibility of their acting as if they did not know what was at stake. It changes the actor's situation in an essential way and compels him to enter into considerations and valuations even against his own immediate interests. Such is the case with the general rule to do good and avoid evil. It does not allow us to act without further reflection, but forces us to ask what the good really is, since the good is not merely what suits us best. It is the gateway to morality, independent of the concrete manner in which we eventually determine the 'good.'

Accepted principles of ecological ethics entail analogous consequences. To demand that we should not violate the carrying capacity of a given area tells us first that this capacity is an important point of reference, and then compels us to assess it. The immediate pursuit of our interest is no longer possible. Again, if we are told that everything is connected and that we should take account of this interconnectedness while determining our goals and our means, we are morally bound to scrutinize not only the effects and side effects of realized goals, but also those entailed by the means. We thus discover beings that are affected by our actions and about which we might not have thought. These become new objects of moral consideration.

General principles open up and stake out the field of our moral responsibility. They are as indispensable in ethical decisions as in political negotiations, as long as we admit a moral point of view.

6. Four Principles for Environmental Ethics

Considering the necessity of general principles and looking back to our defence of a nonanthropocentric foundation of environmental ethics, I think I can now propose four principles to serve as that foundation. The first is a reformulation of the second formula of Kant's categorical imperative;[76] the other three explain the first and form the core of a theory of ecological justice (cf. Sitter 1987).

Since universalizability is generally accepted as an essential property of ethical norms, and taking into account that every natural being, either individual or complex, possesses an inherent worth, as something that cannot be appropriately understood as a means for human aims only, the first principle reads as follows:

1. Act only on those attitudes and rules that you can at the same time will as a universal law; always respect the inherent worth of everything affected by your actions (nonhuman no less than human beings) and consider it in a fair way; never regard and use anything in the world as a means only.[77]

This general imperative can be rendered more concrete when we recall what has been said above about man's condition. Our ecological knowledge is still poor, whereas our scientifically and technologically harnessed actions entail uncontrollable consequences. Like all living beings, we depend on the use of other natural beings to keep us alive. That we are bound to cultivate and consume other beings does not bestow on us a moral or legal privilege in relation to those beings. Apart from human valuation, there is no foothold for granting existential preeminence to one natural being over others. Human pleonexia is a dangerous trait, and it is prudent to allow priority to ecosystemically coined natural beings over human interests, as far as these are random, unweighed, and unjustified.

Three principles for environmental ethics can be drawn from these sketchy considerations:

2. *The principle of preservation:* the existence of natural beings, be they individuals or systems, must not be interfered with or destroyed without justification.

In justifying interferences we have to apply the equality principle when considering and weighing the inherent worth and the corresponding rights proper to any natural being.

3. *The principle of use:* interferences with the existence or the state of natural beings should be based on the ecological knowledge available.

They should be shaped so as not to disturb ecosystemic entities and complexes beyond what is necessary, and to preserve the systems in our reach undiminished, as far as this depends on our faculty.

4. *The principle of knowledge:* our understanding of existence, functioning, and meshing of ecosystems must be continuously extended and deepened.

Human behavior and its effects on ecosystemic entities must be scrutinized.

These principles sound abstract. They are not prescriptions for particular actions, but guidelines for case-by-case decisions. But they can be concretized in different directions even before we come to particular actions (Sitter 1987, 283–288). I wish to illustrate this with a consideration of the duties that they entail for scientists and their institutions.

7. Obligations the Scientific Community Ought to Meet

Modern science rests on a few elements that do not automatically tally with the outlook advocated above. The reductionist attitude to consider the investigated entities as mere objects of control and manipulation tacitly underlies all research. Reductionism owns a morally important aspect: as a rule, the object of scientific research is divested of any moral significance or status possibly connected with it.[78] This nonmoral approach may abolish our faculty of grasping the moral significance of beings with which we coexist in our world, including man himself. The idea of human dignity may, and has, in fact,[79] fallen to pieces; the rarely accepted concept of the dignity of all natural beings may never become generally admitted.

Scientists are first and foremost obliged to neutralize the reifying and alienating effect of their doing. They ought to present their outlook on the world as one tradition among others (cf. Feyerabend 1980, esp. part I, cap. 2, part II, cap. 9; Weisskopf 1984, 11), justified by what it has achieved for human welfare, but nonetheless just one and, moreover, an ambiguous factor in the search for truth. Since science is widely considered the source of welfare and happiness, scientists ought to use their authority to show that this is correct only in a limited sense.

Like all language, scientific language is a means of understanding and representing our world in a certain manner. To choose that language is not an absolute necessity. Therefore, scientists must clearly state where their concepts, terms, and theories come from, what they serve, and that these concepts, etc. are only appropriate for a specific context. They have to justify their choice and may not withdraw from public discussion by appealing to the scientific character of their terms and methods. They have to assume responsibility for the view of the world they develop and propagate.

Moreover, it might be fruitful for scientists to consider changes in their language, to learn other descriptions of the world, since this could lead to a modification of their scientific goals. If we look at the world with wonder and love, regaining thereby a sense for the inherent worth of all natural beings and their various relations, our scientific aims might become different. Responsibility for the existence and the enhancement of nonhuman beings might become a major drive of our scientific undertaking.[80]

This being the case, and because scientific research easily leads to forgetting about the inherent worth of the objects studied, scientists ought not simply to tolerate a wholistic, emotionally enriched outlook on the world, but to propagate it. They ought to plead for respect for nature. The four principles suggest that scientists should engage in ecologically relevant issues more than is actually the case.

It goes without saying that this duty also concerns research councils and similar bodies. By increasing the means they already allocate to ecologically relevant projects, they might attract more scientific potential to this domain of scientific endeavor. We have, I think, good ethical reasons to demand at least a reconsideration of the traditional distribution of funds available for scientific research. That urgent scientific reasons plead for such a change has been shown by Shrader-Frechette's penetrating remarks on the weakness of ecology as a science.

With regard to this weakness, Shrader-Frechette considers a number of obligations residing in what may be called the ethos of science itself. She emphasizes that ecologists should carefully consider their hypotheses, methodological presuppositions, and techniques; that they must render them testable and indeed examine them in field research. This is not just a matter of scientific interest, since the findings of ecologists influence social values and attitudes and thus acquire political relevance (cf. Shrader-Frechette 1989, cf. notes 79f.). I wish to highlight yet another ethical and political consequence for scientists that arises from the same weakness of ecology. Ecologists ought to lay bare their epistemological difficulties as well as the uncertainty of their findings to demonstrate how difficult it is to take and justify environmental decisions. They ought to elaborate the provisional character of their knowledge and by that the difficulty of assessing the effects of interferences with natural conditions. It might be scientists' duty to fight a political battle precisely because they are not in a position "to get their science right." If we allow for the principles discussed above, scientists are obliged to suggest caution and reserve, and to plead for the reversal of the traditional distribution of the burden of proof: if we plan to interfere with natural beings and systems, we first have to make sure that this interference will not be to the detriment of those entities.

If it is detrimental, then we not only have to provide ethically satisfactory arguments to go ahead, but indeed to mitigate impacts and to provide for maximal therapeutic measures. The goal for therapeutics is quite clear, for it is a function not of natural processes, but of our own doing. It is the restoration, as fully as possible, of the situation preceding our intervention, and this with special regard to the living beings that may have been affected. To do this properly, we need scientific advice; scientists are morally bound to provide it, and therefore to concentrate on the necessary research.

There follows a further obligation for scientists and those supporting their work: much more attention—and funds—must be destined for the investigation of the effects, especially the long-term ones, that follow our scientific, technological, and economically motivated interferences with nature. This claim may go against the very interests driving scientific and economic activity. But it has, if we accept the four principles, obvious priority over short-term wants and interests. It actually justifies the warning against an all-too-quick and optimistic development of biotechnology based on genetic engineering.

This confronts scientists with an even more difficult duty: they should give an account of their dependence, in a more or less direct way, on society and, more specifically, on their employers, when fixing or accepting the objectives of their research. These objectives are not necessarily compatible with the principles stated above. If they are not, scientists accepting the principles ought to show how incompatible they are, and how the objectives could be modified or abandoned.

To oppose public goals is, as a rule, less risky, since one can mount platforms specially designed for public argument and political controversy. It is, however, far more delicate to do in private industry and with one's economic well-being menaced. The obligation to follow truth and to stand up for what one considers to be right persists nonetheless. This difficulty might lead to the creation of some sort of trade union of scientists that would protect individuals prepared to engage themselves not only for moral, but also for factual and legal assessment of the claims implied by the four principles. But I must content myself with indicating these problems without venturing to propose a general solution. I should only argue that since the obligations I roughly sketched concern scientists as persons and the supporting bodies as institutional individuals, it is primarily their affair to assume the corresponding duties and make them effective in the scientific and engineering communities, and through both in the economic world. But if scientists do not realize their responsibility or do not comply with it in a satisfactory way, or if their influence on economic decision makers fails, then society must have recourse to political instruments.

Notes

1. Shrader-Frechette terms them the balance and the wholism presuppositions (p. 74).

2. Cf. pp. 74, 83f. The explicitly identified "main argument" on p. 74 is specified by the three related claims (*ibid.*) and should be combined with the author's suggestions on p. 83f., especially the first one. The second suggestion, i.e., "to conceive of environmental policy . . . as established on the basis of a negotiated settlement for mitigating impacts" (p. 84), is a corollary of its forerunner. If impacts on environmental conditions entail a risk to human welfare, it is, from an anthropocentric viewpoint, in the immediate interest of those involved to mitigate them once they have been admitted. I shall not discuss the third conclusion further. Of course, I agree that environmental ethics and politics should be open to new discoveries, but the suggestion is not relevant for the ethical controversy in question.

3. Küppers, 1069, to whom I refer in sketching some ecosystemic rules.

4. Küppers, taking up an evolutionary viewpoint, calls the ecological balance "metastable" (1069).

5. I prefer the term 'ecological ethics' to 'environmental ethics,' stressing that man is a member of nature.

6.   Considered in this way, the notion of system, applied to empirical entities, remains of necessity vague; cf. Seiffert, 182. Yet although every systemic unit is a relative entity in so far as it is defined by a particular level of integration, and although it needs complementation since "all systems known to us are integrated into systems at more complex levels," it does make sense to define and analyse particular systems; cf. Pauli/ von Uexküll, 172.

6a.   Remmert, 193. Cf. P. Messerli, 26; Pauli/von Uexküll, 172; Ulrich/Probst, 28.

7.   The difference between the objective notion of system and the intellectual notion of system is illustrated by Seiffert, 95–97.

8.   Bertalanffy, cited by Seiffert, 125; cf. *ibid.*, 97, 114, as well as von der Stein, 5, again cited by Seiffert, 98. Cf. Pauli/von Uexküll, 160f.; Ulrich/Probst, 30–35.

9.   G. Osche, cited by Küppers, 1068.

10.   Shrader-Frechette, p. 79, and note 51; for the hierarchical conception of systems, see Ropohl, 18, cited by Seiffert, 131f.

11.   Of course, the objective of this investigation is again liable to justification.

12.   To recall it briefly: the positive and the negative version of the golden rule read, for instance, as follows: 1. do to others what you wish to be done to you, and 2. do not do to others what you do not wish to be done to you.

13.   I agree to Shrader-Frechette's objection that demanding to maximize some pattern of excellence neither tells us anything about the pattern in question nor what the concerned ecosystem is like (p. 79, notes 55–57). However, these uncertainties vanish if one takes up the negative starting point I suggested. This is, I suppose, the main reason why Sagoff does not adopt Rolston's suggestion "to maximize the ecosystemic excellences" (108), but contents himself with the recommendation that "ecologists should not seek to define the "health" and the "integrity" of biological systems as if these were positive, measurable qualities. Rather, what is to be measured, quantified, or defined is various kinds of environmental injury, insult, and distress" (113).

14.   In this respect, I am in complete agreement with Shrader-Frechette; cf. her note 22.

15.   Thus, we should have to decide whether and by what criteria we wish to distinguish living organisms from nonliving ones, whether ecosystems could be conceived of as living organisms under certain aspects, and so on.

16.   When glancing at the past 18,000 years of the history of the earth, we note how important climate changes have influenced the rise and fall of cultures and civilizations. A short but impressive illustration is given by B. Messerli, et al., 8f., referring to events in North Africa.

17.   Ecosystems comprising human beings function without the assent of the latter, and independent of human valuation. This is precisely the case when humans interfere with these systems, when they damage or destroy them; cf. Rehbinder, 87; also Lenk 1983, 3f., who stresses, though in a different context, that man as a partial system cannot be considered the goal of the overall system. Interpreting this passage, I would say that man as a partial system may own and be aware of his proper rules, but this does not render him capable of disposing of the rules proper to the encompassing system.

18. It has been stressed that each ecosystem is, as it were, unique and that there may be no general laws to understand it adequately, i.e., to make predictions about its behavior; cf. Remmert, 193, 195; Seiffert, 133; Shrader-Frechette, notes 64 and 88. But this is not relevant to my argument.

It is worth noting that the essential point, veiled by the historical process of secularization and subjectivism, had been lucidly stated centuries ago, e.g., by Nicholas of Cusa. What must be regained today, though in different terms, and revalued was then still evident. Consider the following statements from *De mente:* "Scis, quomodo simplicitas divina omnium rerum est complicativa. Mens est huius complicantis simplicitatis imago. Unde, si hanc divinam simplicitatem infinitam mentem vocitaveris, erit ipsa nostrae mentis exemplar. Si mentem divinam universitatem veritatis rerum dixeris, nostram dices universitatem assimilationis rerum, ut sit notionum universitas. *Conceptio divinae mentis est rerum productio; conceptio nostrae mentis est rerum notio.* Si mens divina est absoluta entitas, tunc eius conceptio est *entium creatio:* et nostrae mentis conceptio est *entium assimilatio* (c. 3, 57, 8; my italics).—Inter enim divinam mentem et nostram interest, quod inter facere et videre. Divina mens concipiendo creat, nostra concipiendo assimilat notiones seu intellectuales faciendo visones; *divina mens est vis entificativa, nostra mens est vis assimilativa* (c. 7, p. 75, 1; my italics). I am grateful to R. Zihlmann for drawing my attention to Cusanus (Zihlmann, pp. 125f.).

19. The decisions correspond to the Kantian stage in the development of moral consciousness. Kant denies that man can have obligations *towards* nonhuman beings, see *The Metaphysics of Morals, Part II: Doctrine of Virtue,* §16. For a critical discussion of Kant's position cf., e.g., Birnbacher, 115–118; Burckhardt, 404–408; Maurer 1982, 20, 23–26; Meyer-Abich, 599–601; Sitter 1984b, 165 f., and 1988.

20. The meaning of the central terms is not always clear when the practicability or the indispensability of anthropocentric reflection in ethics is discussed. See the debate between Taylor and Spitler in *Environmental Ethics* 3, 1981, 197–218; 4, 1982, 255–260; 5, 1983, 237–243. Shrader-Frechette also uses the term 'anthropocentrism' in more than one sense: epistemological (note 35), utilitarian (e.g., p. 78, ref.), or undetermined (note 41, p. 96). Murdy goes so far as to maintain, in his defence of "a modern view of anthropocentrism," that an "anthropocentric attitude towards nature does not require that man be the source of all value, nor does it exclude a belief that things of nature have intrinsic value" (15). This divests the term 'anthropocentrism' of its most characteristic trait, that of referring to one source for all valuation—human self-interest.

21. Shrader-Frechette, p. 77; Taylor 1981, 198; Teutsch 1987, 17. The general statement that "to be anthropocentric is to affirm that mankind is to be valued more highly than other things in nature—by man" (Murdy, 13) is correct, but not precise enough. It does not account for the anthropocentric trend to make human well-being the reference of all decisions leading to action. Taylor's circumscription focussing on human welfare is more to the point (1981, 198).

To say that anthropocentrism makes humans the *central* value, while leaving room for *other* values, is a useful, though not sufficient, clarification. It does not exclude the possibility for human interests to remain without exception the ultimate and decisive reference point, when value conflicts must be solved. Thus, the statement that other than human values might be taken into account is not much help. The discussion revealed, on the other hand, that maintaining the idea of ecocentrism is not in contradiction with the view that human beings as parts of ecosystems have a particular position and value in the systems. While ecocentrism is not compatible with the principle of preferring, without exception, human interests, it allows for the possibility of prevailing human interests, provided that such a preference is justified by a careful and respectful weighing of the values in question.

22. Jonas 1979, 86–92; Tammelo, 212, 250, 254.

23. Lenk 1983, 6; as to the predominance of anthropocentric humanism in traditional ethics, cf. Teutsch 1987, 10ff., and the literature indicated there.

24. Teutsch 1987, 16ff. uses this expression in essentially the same way.

25. Cf. for an instructive sketch and critique of secularized theological anthropocentrism, Maurer 1988, 21; also Murdy for an enlightening outline of the three forms of anthropocentrism just dealt with, 12f.

26. Among the few jurists who still plead for positively recognizing inherent rights of nature we find, after Stone, Stutzin, Tribe, Rehbinder, and now, well advanced, because tackling detailed aspects of codification, Saladin and Leimbacher, and finally Bosselmann.

27. Cf. Larenz, 29–31, 75, 168, for a clear statement of ethical personalism as a prerequisite of owning legal rights. A critical comment to this in Sitter 1984a, 38f.

28. Teutsch uses the expression 'anthroponomous' in an analogous context (1987, 18).

29. See Shrader-Frechette, p. 76.

30. For a useful illustration of the fact that we are apt to conceive of values that are not in any relation to our proper interests, though every valuation be anthropotrope, see Scherer, 74–74. In a thought experiment, he takes us to a planet out of human reach and that never influenced our world. Nonetheless, we (as uninterested observers) can recognize valuable entities, conditions, and processes proper to that planet.

31. From here on I shall speak of anthropocentrism when referring to plain anthropocentrism. Epistemological anthropocentrism will be labelled as such.

32. The definition of 'good' elaborated by Mackie corresponds to what is explained here. 'Good' means *"such as to satisfy requirements (etc.) of the kind in question."* The requirements, i.e., wants, wishes, and interests, do not necessarily and exclusively refer to the valuing human being. Mackie's definition relies on man's faculty to place himself in the position of the object of his valuation, on his capability of assuming the viewpoint of that object and thus extinguishing himself as a reference point; cf. 55f., 58f. Mackie maintains that 'good' always hints at something such as interests or wants, even if they are only "theoretical." However, he places much emphasis on a case that is decisive in our context: In "calling something good, we are saying something about how it is in itself; we are referring immediately to its qualities, its intrinsic features, rather than directly to any relation that it has to anything else, as we would be if we said that it satisfied, say, some interest" (56).

33. For man's existential and inseparable relation to truth and rightness, cf. Sitter 1984a, 18–23.

34. It is therefore not sufficient for ethics "to take men as they are and moral laws as they might be," as Mackie correctly states (133). We must also propose arguments for ethical norms that correspond to existential practice and do not simply satisfy—if at all—the claim of theoretical consistency.

35.   We cannot avoid destroying other living beings if we wish to survive. This is agreed on by ecocentric ethicists (cf., e.g., Lenk, Maurer, Rolston, Sagoff), as well as by those justifying ethical norms by anthropocentric views. Those beings are, together with us, members of the biotic community (Taylor 1981, 198) and in so far own an equal right of existence. Yet the "hideous necessity" (Schweitzer, 387) to destroy some living beings does not annul the precept to respect other living beings. It entails some important consequences: If, to build my house, I fell a tree, knowing that I thereby infringe on its right to exist, if I am conscious of this act as an offence, then this will not be of much help to that tree and the trees I may still have to fell. But it will be of help to other trees. For the acknowledgment of guilt will make me ask, whenever I shall be in front of a tree, if it is really indispensable for me to fell or injure it. This question affects the building of a house: the intention itself must be revised. The immediacy of the intention and of the action is broken, and the sense of responsibility roused. (I am borrowing the tree example from Meyer-Abich (1982, 597), elaborating it slightly.)

Taylor has been successful in defending his biocentric standpoint against Spitler's thesis that we cannot but think in anthropocentric terms (see note 20). He does not deny that the *motivation* to engage in nonanthropocentric views may be guided by interest and become an object of psychological investigation. However, this is not true for the *contents* of the biocentric outlook on the world: the inherent worth of a living being and its requirements, once recognized, no longer depend on the motivation of the person recognizing them. Neither are the consequences of this insight dependent on its motivation; they might even run against the desires and interests of the person who has them; cf. 1983, 239 f.

36.   Cf. note 16.

37.   Cf. Sitter 1984a, 46; 1987, 179ff.

38.   The material conception of nature, cf. Vossenkuhl, 169. If we control processes we count on them, and we know how to calculate them. This is different from shaping new processes as in technology. But in the end, technology is based on processes created by nature.

39.   Metaphysically speaking, we might say that nature is that force that appears through man, not in its entire essence, but always in a form that hints at its essence.

40.   See Vester's discussion of the alienation of nature as a result of the conditions set by our scientific-technological civilization (158). Similarly, Murdy, 16; Sitter 1985, 59f., 63–65. P. Messerli (1986) considers technology as a means of satisfying inflationary human wants, and entailing alienation between man and nature (14). Cf. also Biser, as cited by Zihlmann (1984, 27), and Zihlmann himself (1984, 22–27).

41.   Moscovici, cited by Böhme, 44.

42.   A nice illustration of how nature (as understood in the indicated third sense) is authoritative even for scientific research, was given already more than 20 years ago by Polanyi. A scientist's questions and choices are highly personal acts, but they happen in a framework of dependency: what he does is not simply a result of his free will; rather he engages in his research work because what he wishes to disclose compels him to do so. The freedom of putting questions is a conditional freedom. The scientist does not "hit on discoveries merely by trying everything as it happens to cross" his mind. His guesses anticipate something that attracts him. His groping for it is his choice and a matter of his responsibility; "but what he pursues is not of his making; his acts stand

under the judgement of the hidden reality he seeks to uncover. His visions of the problem, his obsession with it, and his final leap to discovery are filled from beginning to end with an obligation to an external objective. In these intensely personal acts, therefore, there is no self-will. Originality is commanded at every stage by a sense of responsibility for advancing the growth of truth in men's mind. Its freedom is perfect service" (76f.).

43.   M. Sagoff highlights how inappropriate it would be to say that nature must be understood as a mere construct of human culture, since what we know and conceive of nature is but the result of cultural mediation. How far something can be said to be fundamentally natural may be grasped when looking at the process of its generation. This proves no less correct for ecosystems than for individuals: "The factory method by which rainbow trouts are produced in vats in Idaho are quite different from the 'natural' processes by which these fish grow in wilderness streams. One may not be able to distinguish the products by look or taste; the processes, however, are hardly the same" (101).

44.   Cf. Dubos, Leopold, and Shepard, cited by Rolston, 106, and Rolston himself, *ibid.*

45.   Cf. Rolston, who uses the expression 'ecological nature' as if it went without saying, 99.

46.   Another characterization, might read as follows: nature is that instance that forms beings, brings forth life, that shapes itself into man, acquires language and reaches self-consciousness, and returns through man to itself.

47.   I. Kant. *Foundations of the Metaphysics of Morals,* trans. by L. W. Beck, ed. by R. P. Wolff (Indianapolis, [6]1978), 21, note.

48.   I. Kant. *The Metaphysics of Morals, Part II: Doctrine of Virtue,* §37.

49.   *Sein und Zeit,* §29, esp. 135 (Max Niemeyer Verlag, Tübingen, [13]1976).

50.   I follow here a proposal made by Burckhardt, 417. We are, of course, leaving the Heideggerian context when using this mode of expression.

51.   Taylor uses this argument for all living beings and convincingly defends it in the context of his biocentric outlook on the world (1981, 211–216; 1983, 241f.). But the argument does not only apply to living beings; we may generalize and apply it to every being as such. See also Schweitzer who refuses to acknowledge different values for different levels of life. They are but the expression of man's whim—of man taking himself for the ultimate measure of all things (vol. II, 389). In a more general way and not only with reference to living beings, Böckle recalls that all values remain contingent, and that this is true, too, for the superiority man vindicates for himself (308). Finally, an impressive statement of the case is made by Murdy: "To be anthropocentric is to affirm that mankind is to be valued more highly than other things in nature— by man. By the same logic, spiders are to be valued more highly than other things in nature—by spiders. It is proper for men to be anthropocentric and for spiders to be arachnocentric. This goes for all other living species" (13). Murdy is pleading for anthropocentrism, precisely on the ground that there is no natural prerogative for man to exist.

52.   Cf. Teutsch 1987, 76–81, and the numerous references indicated there.

53. "Rechtsgemeinschaft der Natur"—a notion elaborated by the German physicist and philosopher K. M. Meyer-Abich (1982, 602), but prepared by Rolston's idea of nature as a commonwealth (1974–1975, 101) and reflected by Taylor's notion of "Earth's biotic community" (1981, 198). Consider also White's conception of a "democracy of all God's creatures," cited by Murdy, 14 (referring to White's contribution to *Science* 155, 1967, esp. 1205).

54. As an evolutionary product, man has become a moral agent. It is his faculty and becomes his duty "to enhance values beyond himself" (Murdy, 12). To be able to take on responsibility for others is an essential trait of his dignity (Maurer 1982, 33f.; Lenk 1983, 9, 11f. 14–16; Meyer-Abich 1984, 65 f.). To extend moral and legal rights to other than human beings is but a matter of further evolution (Tribe, 58). "In ethical terms, the golden rule applies to man's relations with nature as well as to relations between human beings" (Huxley, 24, cited by Murdy, 14). See also Teutsch's comprehensive article on "Humanity" and the many literary sources he refers to or cites (1987, 91–97).

55. This rule represents only one of the possible concrete forms of the well-known prohibition of traditional natural law "alterum non laedere"—not to harm others. Cf. also Burckhardt, 418.

56. Cf. Sitter 1988 with the citation of various versions of a new categorical imperative.

57. I. Kant. *The Metaphysics of Morals, Part II: Doctrine of Virtue* §§16f.. Cf. Sitter 1984c, 95; Meyer-Abich 1984, 70–74; Birnbacher, 117f..

58. A well-known argument, cf. for many, Birnbacher, 122; Feinberg, 145; Singer, e.g., 17, 52f., 59; Sitter 1984a, 38; 1984b, 169; Wolf, 11f.; Saladin, implicitly passim, esp. 198ff., 211f..

59. As Burckhardt, 418, 429; Meyer-Abich 1984, 48f.

60. For example, Jonas, esp. 175f.; cf. Sitter 1984b, 160f., with various authors referred to in note 30, 161.

61. Cf. note 48, Lenk, 14, 17, and Sitter 1984c, 96.

62. As Taylor rightly points out, consciousness is not a necessary precondition of teleological constitution (1981, 210). A teleological being need not itself know about its particular structure.

63. Whitehead, 93, cited by Murdy, 15.

64. This is all the more true when we recall further how human existence depends on the intactness of an indefinite number of such ecological units. Because the interconnectedness of ecosystems is far from being transparent to human intelligence (Passmore, 213; P. Messerli, 27), even those complexes that do not seem to be of vital significance to man should be given careful consideration and cautiously dealt with. Yet since this is a clearly anthropocentric argument, it would not be consistent for me to dwell on it.

65. Remmert, 263 ff.; Sagoff, 104–110; Shrader-Frechette, 81.

66. See for an excellent example P. Messerli's final report concerning the Swiss contribution to UNESCO's program "Man and Biosphere," parts 1 and 2. Cf. also K. Shrader-Frechette's list of weaknesses of ecology as a science, especially items: 1. (too many

parameters), 2. (limited data bases), 5. (ever-changing objects of investigation), 6. (uniqueness of ecological situations), 7. (difficulties in realizing fine enough measurements), 8. (lack of a sufficient theory of social choice; 11).

67. Cf. Staudinger, 8; M. Born, cited by Hammer, 46; Ulrich/Probst, 14–18.

68. Cf. Taylor, 1981; Scherer 1983 (1982).

69. Hence, it is not the heuristic principle of ecological enmeshment or wholistic appraisal that fails if the story about the nutritive function of salt marshes is wrong (cf. Shrader-Frechette, 76, 81, notes 59–61; Sagoff, 104ff.) or if an inadequate account of the relationship between diversity and stability in ecosystem is given (cf. Sagoff, 107ff; Shrader-Frechette, 00, notes 31–35). For a more conclusive account see Remmert, 260–266. He shows that stability had been confused with constancy of an ecosystem. Diversity and constancy may well go together, since highly diverse ecosystems develop only under constantly optimal conditions. But this means that they are very sensitive to changes in these conditions and therefore possibly unstable. An example for factual instability is the tropical rain forest in the Amazon and the Congo regions. Yet the rain forests in many parts of southern Asia do not seem to be liable to the same instability, although they are no less diverse. Apparently, the soils in this region dispose of the resources needed to make up for the stress human inference puts on the forest. Stability is compatible with inconstancy. It implies the elasticity of an ecosystem that is exposed to various affections, reacts to these by respective modifications, but returns regularly to a more or less original state.

70. Küppers words the first part of his new categorical imperative as follows: "Never change your environment without any compelling reason!", 1071.

71. Compared to the lines of arguments followed by Rolston (1974–1975), Sagoff (1985), and many others, my argument may seem scanty. Whereas I hope to show that man has obligations towards nonhuman natural beings, they stress emotionally motivated respect for the beauty, the harmony, the autarky, etc. of natural beings and systems. Ecology provides a wider basis for an environmental ethics than I have considered. Our convictions are not formed by rational arguments alone. Rolston, Taylor (1981), and Sagoff make it clear that they do not produce arguments deduced from universally accepted principles, but urge a new outlook on the world, which bears on our moral behavior towards natural beings, and should become a cornerstone in the foundation of environmental ethics and politics. They are defending general guidelines, not seeking clear and precise theories and concepts that allow for prediction. Ethics does not deal with "precise and predictive explanations" (Shrader-Frechette, 83); these are only—but then indeed—needed when we apply ethics to concrete problems.

72. According to Shrader-Frechette, general rules, such as "there is no free lunch," "do not exceed the carrying capacity of the area," or "do good and avoid evil," are not very helpful in practical, case-by-case decision making; cf. 83 and note 81.

73. Of course, our reason for stopping at a given degree of generality may be investigated, and this might again lead us back to fundamental convictions.

74. Cf. Mackie who, while maintaining that to "identify morality with something that certainly will not be followed is a sure way of bringing it into contempt" (132), would "advocate moral principles that are in conflict with established habits of thought and behaviour, that prescribe a degree of respect for the claim of others—and of distant others—which can flourish only by overcoming ingrained selfishness and limitations of

generosity that are authorized by the existing law and the real conventional morality" (133f.). Note, however, that he does not accept "the fantasy moralities of utilitarianism and neighbourly love" (134).

75. Normative principles can only be criticized with reference to the weakness of an empirical discipline if they are derived from it. But then, of course, they would be wrong in an even more radical way as the outcome of the naturalistic fallacy. The weakness of ecology will never be a reason for refuting normative principles that guide our behaviour towards nonhuman beings, as long as we do not venture to deduce such principles directly from empirical results of ecological investigation. This does not exclude taking account of the ecosystemic outlook on the world when we endeavor to establish normative principles for environmental ethics.

76. Kant's categorical imperative in its second form reads as follows: "Act in such a way that you treat humanity, whether in your own person or in the person of another, always as an end and never as a means only" (*Foundations of the Metaphysic of Morals*, BA, 66f.).

77. Cf. Sitter 1988, where formulations offered by other authors, such as Maurer, Spaemann, and Löw, are stated.

78. "Dismoralization has become a prerequisite of scientific research" (Lepenies, 548).

79. Recall B. Skinner's suggestion to go "beyond freedom and dignity" or R. Dawkin's interpretation of man as a "survival machine" controlled by the egoism of his genes. For ethical and moral effects of scientific reductionism, cf. Feyerabend 1980, 143, 149, 256; Jonas, 29f., 57f., 236; Sitter 1988, 125 (F); Weisskopf, 10f.

80. "Ecologists would then help society to assess, mitigate, or prevent risks to the health and welfare of ecosystems and not simply to the health and welfare of human beings." (Sagoff, 102, cf. also 116).

81. This as a comment on Scott Nixon as cited by Sagoff, 109f.

Bibliography

Bertalanffy, L. von (1972): "Vorläufer und Bergründer der Systemtheorie," in *Systemtheorie* (Berlin: Colloquium Verlag), 17–28.

Birnbacher, D. (1980): "Sind wir für die Natur verantwortlich?" in *Oekologie und Ethik*, ed. by D. Birnbacher (Stuttgart: Reclam Verlag), 103–139.

Böckle, F. (1973): "Wiederkehr oder Ende des Naturrechts?" in *Naturrecht in der Kritik*, ed. by F. Böckle and E.-W. (Böckenförde, Mainz: Matthias-Grünewald-Verlag), 304–311.

Böhme, H. (1988): "Verdrängung und Erinnerung vormoderner Naturkonzepte. Zum Problem historischer Anschlüsse der Naturästhetik in der Moderne," in *Kunstnachrichten. Zeitschrift für internationale Kunst*, 24, Vol. 2, 35–47.

Bosselmann, K. (1985): "Wendezeit im Umweltrecht. Von der Verrechtlichung der Oekologie zur Oekologisierung des Rechts," in *Kritische Justiz*, 18, 345–361.

Bosselmann, K. (1986): "Eigene Rechte für die Natur? Ansätze einer ökologischen Rechtsauffassung," in *Kritische Justiz*, 19, 1–22.

Bosselmann, K. (1987): "Die Natur im Umweltrecht. Plädoyer für ein ökologisches Umweltrecht," in *Natur + Recht, Zeitschrift für das gesamte Recht zum Schutze der natürlichen Lebensgrundlagen und der Umwelt*, 9, no. 1, 1–6.

Burckhardt, A. (1983): "Kant, Wittgenstein und das Verhältnis der relativen Ethik zur absoluten: Zur Begründung einer ökologischen Ethik," in *Zeitschrift für Evangelische Ethik*, 27, 391–431.

Dubos, R. (1972): *A God within* (New York: Charles Scribner's Sons).

Feinberg, J. (1980): "Die Rechte der Tiere und zukünftiger Generationen," in *Oekologie und Ethik*, ed. by D. Birnbacher (Stuttgart: Philipp Reclam jun.), 140–179.

Feyerabend, P. (1980): *Erkenntnis für freie Menschen. Veränderte Ausgabe* (Frankfurt a.M.: Suhrkamp Verlag).

Frank, F. (1988): "Trotz UVP sind die Spiesse alles andere als gleich lang," in *Der Bund*, 139, no. 19 (22.08.1988), 6.

Frankel, C. (1976): "The Rights of Nature," in *When Values Conflict. Essays in Environmental Analysis, Discourse, and Decision*, ed. by L. H. Tribe, et al. (Cambridge Mass.), 92–113.

Hammer, F. (1983): *Selbstzensur für Forscher? Schwerpunkte einer Wissenschaftsethik* (Zürich: Edition Interfrom).

Heidegger, M. ([13]1976): *Sein und Zeit* (Tübingen: Max Niemeyer Verlag).

Huxley, J. (1963): *The Human Crisis* (Seattle: The University of Washington Press).

Jonas, H. ([5]1984): *Das Prinzip Verantwortung. Versuch einer Ethik für die technologische Zivilisation* (Frankfurt a.M.: Insel Verlag).

Kant, I. (1965): "Die Metaphysik der Sitten," in *Immanuel Kant. Werke in sechs Bänden*, Vol. IV, ed. by W. Weischedel (Darmstadt: Wissenschaftliche Buchgesellschaft), 301–614.

Kant, I. (1966): "Grundlegung zur Metaphysik der Sitten," in *Immanuel Kant. Werke in sechs Bänden*, Vol. IV, ed. by W. Weischedel (Darmstadt: Wissenschaftliche Buchgesellschaft), 7–102.

Kant, I. ([6]1978): *Foundations of the Metaphysics of Morals*, transl. by L. W. Beck, ed. by R. P. Wolff (Indianapolis).

Küppers, B.-O. (1984): "Oekologie," in *Enzyklopädie Philosophie und Wissenschaftstheorie*, Band 2, ed. by J. Mittelstrass (Mannheim/Wien/Zürich), 1068–1073.

Larenz, K. ([5]1980): *Allgemeiner Teil des deutschen Bürgerlichen Rechts* (München).

Leimbacher, J. und Saladin, P. (1988): *Die Natur—und damit der Boden—als Rechtssubjekt*. Bericht 18 des Nationalen Forschungsprogrammes 'Boden' (Bern) (ISBN 3-907086-10-4).

Lenk, H. (1983): "Verantwortung für die Natur. Gibt es moralische Quasirechte von oder moralische Pflichten gegenüber nichtmenschlichen Naturwesen?" in *Allgemeine Zeitschrift für Philosophie*, 8, no. 3, 1–17.

Leopold, A. (1949): "The Land Ethic," in *A Sand County Almanac* (New York: Oxford University Press), 201–226.

Lepenies, W. (1983): "Historisierung der Natur und Entmoralisierung der Wissenschaften," in *Merkur. Deutsche Zeitschrift für europäisches Denken*, 37, no. 5, 545–554.

Lovelock, J. E. (1979): *Gaia. A New Look at Life on Earth* (Oxford: Oxford University Press).

Mackie, J. L. (1981): *Ethics. Inventing Right and Wrong*, Harmondsworth (Middlesex, England): Penguin Books Ltd.

Maurer, R. (1982): "Oekologische Ethik?" in *Allgemeine Zeitschrift für Philosophie,* 7, no. 1, 17–39.

Maurer, R. (1988): "Oekologische Ethik als Problem," in *Oekologische Ethik,* ed. by K. Bayertz (München/Zürich: Verlag Schnell & Steiner), 11–30.

Messerli, B., et al. (1987): *Umweltprobleme und Entwicklungszusammenarbeit* (Bern: Geographisches Institut der Universität Bern).

Messerli, P. (1986): *Modelle und Methoden zur Analyse der Mensch-Umwelt-Beziehungen im alpinen Lebens- und Erholungsraum.* Schlussbericht zum Schweizerischen MAB-Programm Nr. 25 (Bern: Bundesamt für Umweltschutz).

Meyer-Abich, K.M. (1982): "Vom bürgerlichen Rechtsstaat zur Rechtsgemeinschaft der Natur," in *Scheidewege,* 12, 581–605.

Meyer-Abich, K.M. (1984): *Wege zum Frieden mit der Natur. Praktische Naturphilosophie für die Umweltpolitik* (München/Wien: Carl Hanser Verlag).

Murdy, W.H. (1983): "Anthropocentrism: A Modern Version," in *Ethics and the Environment,* ed. by D. Scherer and Th. Attig (Englewood Cliffs, New Jersey: Prentice-Hall), 12–21.

Nicholas of Cusa, (1960): "De mente," in *Nicholai de Cusa opera omnia,* iussu et auctoritate academiae litterarum Heidelbergensis ad codicum fidem edita, Leipzip 1932ff., Vol. V. Citations according to Zellinger, E. (1960): *Cusanus Konkordanz* (München: Max Hueber Verlag), 124f.

Osche, G. (³1975): *Oekologie. Grundlagen, Erkenntnisse, Entwicklungen der Umweltforschung* (Freiburg/Basel/Wien).

Passemore, J. (1980): "Den Unrat beseitigen. Ueberlegungen zur ökologischen Mode," in *Oekologie und Ethik,* ed. by D. Birnbacher (Stuttgart: Philipp Reclam jun.), 207–246.

Pauli, H. G., and von Uexküll, Th. (1986): "The Mind-Body Problem in Medicine," in *Advances. Journal of the Institute for the Advancement of Health,* Vol. 3, no. 4, 158–174.

Polanyi, M. (1967): *The Tacit Dimension* (Garden City, New York: Doubleday and Co.)

Rawls, J. (1972): *A Theory of Justice* (Oxford: Clarendon Press).

Rehbinder, E. (1979): "Oekologisches und juristisches Denken im Umweltschutz," in *Hestia 1978–1979* (Bonn), 83–107.

Remmert, H. (³1984): *Oekologie. Ein Lehrbuch* (Berlin/Heidelberg/New York/Tokyo: Springer-Verlag) (English edition (1980): *Ecology*).

Rolston III, H. (1974–1975): "Is There an Ecological Ethic?" in *Ethics,* 85, 93–109.

Sagoff, M. (1985): "Fact and Value in Ecological Science," in *Environmental Ethics,* 7, no. 2., 99–116.

Saladin, P., and Leimbacher, J. (1986): "Mensch und Natur: Herausforderung für die Rechtspolitik," in *Menschengerecht,* ed. by H. Däubler-Gmelin and W. Alderstein (Karlsruhe: C. F. Müller Verlag), 195–219.

Scherer, D. (1983): "Anthropocentrism, Atomism and Environmental Ethics," in *Ethics and the Environment,* ed. by D. Scherer and Th. Attig (Englewood Cliffs, New Jersey: Prentice-Hall), 73–81.

Schweitzer, A. (n. d.): "Kultur und Ethik," in *Albert Schweitzer. Gesammelte Werke in fünf Bänden*, Vol. 2, ed. by R. Grabs (Zürich: Buchclub Ex Libris), 95–420.

Seiffert, H. (1985): *Einführung in die Wissenschaftstheorie*, Band 3 (München: Verlag C. H. Beck).

Shepard, P., and Mc Kinley, D., eds. (1969): *The Subversive Science* (Boston: Houghton Mifflin Co).

Shrader-Frechette, K. (1989): "Ecological Theories and Ethical Imperatives," in *Scientists and Their Responsibilities*, ed. by W. R. Shea and B. Sitter (Nantucket, Mass.: Watson Publishing International), 73–104.

Singer, P. (^{8}1983): *Practial Ethics* (Cambridge: Cambridge University Press).

Sitter, B. (1984a): *Plädoyer für das Naturrechtsdenken. Zur Anerkennung von Eigenrechten der Natur* (Basel: Helbing & Lichtenhahn).

Sitter, B. (1984b): "Ueber das Recht der Natur im Naturrecht der Gegenwart," in *Vom normativen Wandel des Politischen*, ed. by E. U. Heyen (Berlin: Duncker & Humblot), 145–172.

Sitter, B. (1984c): "Aspekte der Menschenwürde. Zur Würde der Natur als Prüfstein der Würde des Menschen," in *Manuskripte. Zeitschrift für Literatur*, 23, 93–96.

Sitter, B. (1985): "Hat Ethik in der Wissenschaft nichts zu suchen?" in *Wissenschaft in der Verantwortung*, ed. by B. Sitter (Berne/Stuttgart: Verlag Paul Haupt), 37–78.

Sitter, B. (1987): "Wie lässt sich ökologische Gerechtigkeit denken?" in *Zeitschrift für Evangelische Ethik*, 31, no. 3, 271–295.

Sitter, B. (1988): "The New Categorical Imperative. The Ethical Principle for a Technological Age," in *Revolutions in Science: Their Meaning and Relevance*, ed. by W. R. Shea (Nantucket, Mass.: Science History Publications), 205–220.

Sitter, B. (1988): "Konstruktive und destruktive Wechselwirkungen zwischen Wissenschaft und Ethik," in *Freiburger Zeitschrift für Philosophie und Theologie*, 35.

Spitler, G. (1982): "Justifying a Respect for Nature," in *Environmental Ethics*, 4, no. 3, 255–260.

Staudinger, Hj. (1980): "Verantwortung und Fortschritt in der Wissenschaft," in *Merkur. Deutsche Zeitschrift für europäisches Denken*, 34, no. 1, 1–16.

Stone, Chr. D. (1974): *Should Trees Have Standing? Toward Legal Rights for Natural Objects* (Los Altos, California: William Kaufmann, Inc.).

Stutzin, G. (1980): "Die Natur der Rechte und die Rechte der Natur," in *Rechtstheorie*, 11, 344–355.

Tammelo, I. (1975): *Zur Philosophie des Ueberlebens. Gerechtigkeit, Kommunikation und Eunomik* (Freiburg/München: Verlag Karl Alber).

Taylor, P. W. (1981): "The Ethics of Respect for Nature," in *Environmental Ethics*, 3, 197–218.

Taylor, P. W. (1983): "In Defense of Biocentrism," in *Environmental Ethics*, 5, 237–243.

Teutsch, G. M. (1985): *Lexikon der Umweltethik* (Göttingen: Vandenhoeck & Ruprecht, and Düsseldorf: Patmos-Verlag).

Teutsch, G. M. (1987): *Mensch und Tier. Lexikon der Tierschutzethik* (Göttingen: Vandenhoeck & Ruprecht).

Tribe, L. H. (1976): "Ways Not to Think about Plastic Trees," in *When Values Conflict. Essays on Environmental Analysis, Discourse, and Decision,* ed. by L. H. Tribe, et al. (Cambridge, Mass.: Ballinger), 61–91.

Ulrich, H., und Probst, G. J. B. (1988): *Anleitung zum Ganzheitlichen Denken* (Bern/Stuttgart: Verlag Paul Haupt).

Vester, F. (²1985): *Unsere Welt—ein vernetztes System* (München: Deutscher Taschenbuch Verlag).

Vossenkuhl, W. (1977): "Natur," in *Lexikon der Ethik,* ed. by O. Höffe, et al. (München: C. H. Beck Verlag), 169f.

Weisskopf, V. F. (1984): "Frontiers and Limits of Science," in *Mitteilungen der Alexander von Humboldt Stiftung,* vol. 43, 1–11.

Whitehead, A. N. (1925): *Science and the Modern World* (New York: Macmillan).

Wolf, J.-C. (1985): "Ethische Aspekte des Tierversuchs," in *Arbeitsblätter für ethische Forschung,* no. 14, October, 11–19.

Zihlmann, R. (1984): "Umweltkrise. Streifzüge durch das geistesgeschichtliche Vorgelände," in *Zeitschrift für Ganzheitsforschung,* Neue Folge 28, 16–30.

Zihlmann, R. (1986): "Betrachtungen zum Ethos der Neuzeit," in *Zeitschrift für Ganzheitsforschung,* Neue Folge 30, 124–134.

What Does It Mean to Be Responsible and Free? A Philosopher's Viewpoint

GERHARD SEEL

I am afraid that I am going to do what philosophers usually do and what philosophers are usually blamed for, namely, to discuss freedom and responsibility on a universal and abstract level without entering into the concrete debate indicated by the title of this book. Though I am convinced that philosophy should not limit itself to abstract and fundamental questions, but should contribute to solving the concrete problems of our time, I think it would still be of some use in assessing the responsibility of the scientist to know even on an abstract level what exactly 'responsibility' means and where we have to seek its foundations.

To answer this question I will proceed as follows: First I will attempt to give a precise definition of the term 'responsibility.' Since, as we shall see, responsibility presupposes both freedom and valid norms, I also intend to clarify these notions. In my second step, I will distinguish three concepts of freedom, establish their mutual relations, and discuss the theoretical difficulties that we encounter in attempting to assess them. Finally, I will raise the question of where the norms that responsibility presupposes are to be found and inquire into the grounds for the social responsibility of the scientist.

I.

Philosophers usually define the term 'responsibility' as follows:

x is responsible to y for z if and only if there is a valid norm n that entitles y to call x to account for z.

In other words, 'to be responsible' is a three-place predicate. For the sake of further clarification, let us look at the domains of the variables of this function. The domain of the variable x is in most cases restricted to free human individuals or institutions; the same holds for the variable y. The variable z, on the other hand, is limited to contingent events or states of affairs.

146

To clarify the notion of responsibility, it is extremely interesting to see how the substitution of one of the variables by a constant restricts the domains of the two others. It is obvious that a certain human individual is responsible only to those entitled by a norm to call him to account. Such persons will not normally be all human beings, but only one particular group or individual that is given that function. But, as we shall see, there is an important exception to this general principle. Furthermore, a definite human individual is not responsible for all contingent events or states of affairs, but only for those that fulfill the following two conditions: their realization must depend, wholly or in part on the agent's free will and free action; they must fall under the norm which by binding or obliging the agent's will makes him responsible.

This means that there is no responsibility without freedom, and no responsibility without valid practical norms. These two points are of particular importance. They lead me to the second and third steps of my argument.

II.

Freedom being, as we have seen, one of the presuppositions of responsibility, I should first of all like to clarify the exact meaning of the term and then show the obstacles to a clear-cut demonstration of the existence of freedom. The difficulties start with the notion of freedom itself. For we use the term on three different theoretical levels, and on each of these it has a different connotation:
a. *the metaphysical or ontological level* (here 'freedom' means "absence of causal necessity in a process.");
b. *the anthropological level* (here 'freedom' means "capacity of decision and action.");
c. *the socio-political level* (here 'freedom' means "independence from the constraint of another's will.").

These notions are by no means identical; nor do they include one another. The logical relations between them are, all things considered, highly controversial, though some of them are obvious. This becomes evident when the three notions are given precise definitions, which is what I shall now attempt to do.

Let me start with the ontological concept of freedom. Normally it is introduced as the modality of an event. Under which condition do we call an event 'free' or 'causally undetermined'? Consider Figure 1.

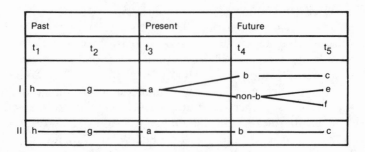

Figure 1.

I and II present series of events. In series II every time-point is occupied by a single event. That means that at every moment one and only one event can happen, and thus this event must happen. We speak in this case of a causally necessary event. Series I shows a completely different structure. Here only the time-points in past and present are occupied by a single event, whereas for every future time-point, there are at least two events. This means that each of these future events is possible, and none is necessary. They are what philosophers call 'future contingent events.' This leads me to the definition of the term 'contingent event.'

> An event x is contingent if and only if there is at least one time-point t' such that a) t' precedes the time-point occupied by x and b) x is a contingent future event at t'.

Note: not all contingent events are future contingent events. This is not only because they can change their time mode, but also because they can change their time-bound modal status. For instance, event c in series I is a future contingent event at t_3, but at t_4 it necessarily changes its modal status: if b is realized at t_4, c becomes a necessary future event; if non-b is realized, it becomes an impossible future event.

A causal chain, which, like series I, contains contingent events, is a causally undetermined process. If all processes in the world were causally determined, there would be no ontological freedom. That is what universal determinism states. This thesis is the following[1]:

T_1: (x) (t') (t'') ($R_{t'}x \cdot t'' < t' \rightarrow N_{t''}R_{t'}x$)

For all states of affairs x and for all points of time t′, the following holds: if x is the case at t′, it is true for all time-points t earlier than t′ that at t it is necessary that x will be the case at t′.

The negation of T_1 would be the following thesis:

$$T_2: \; \exists \, x \; \exists \, t' \; \exists \, t'' \; (R_{t'}x \cdot t'' < t' \cdot C_{t''}R_{t'}x)$$

There is at least one state of affairs x and one time-point t′ such that if x is the case at t′, there is at least one time-point t which precedes t′ and at which the future reality of x is a contingent event.

I would like to stress that T_2 is not identical with the stronger thesis T_3 which states universal chaotism.

$$T_3: \; (x) \; (t') \; (t'') \; (R_{t'}x \cdot t'' < t' \rightarrow C_{t''}R_{t'}x)$$

T_3 denies the existence of any causally necessary chain of events in the world. Logically speaking, all three positions are noncontradictory and therefore possibly true. To prove or refute one of them, we must therefore look for a demonstration from premises that are not purely logical.

Now, what do we mean when we speak of 'freedom of decision' and 'freedom of action'? First, it is important to emphasize that these two notions are neither identical nor equivalent. The first concerns the mental process of self-determination of the mind; the latter refers to the determination of an exterior process by the mind.

What self-determination of the mind really is and how it is possible remain unsettled philosophical questions. I do not pretend to have a sufficient answer to these questions, but I would like to attempt a sketchy description of the problem that confronts us. Self-determination of the mind is a causally undetermined process. But unlike similar processes that we encounter in the external world, it is a process in the human mind. The events which compose this process are therefore mental acts. By itself, this is not sufficient to characterize 'self-determination,' since the mind must also be aware of the events happening in it. Moreover, to have real self-determination, the mind must have perfect control over these events. How is this possible?

For the sake of explanation, let us start with an example. A young woman and a young man are sitting in a coffee shop. As he behaves rather timidly and hesitantly, to push things forward she suddenly says: "Well, at the end of this cigarette I must go." This provokes in the young man's mind what we call a 'decision process.' What could be the structure of this process?

We have to distinguish at least three periods in such a process. *First period:* (a) when the young man thinks, "When she has finished her cigarette, I will want either to ask her to stay or let her go. In the meantime I have to make up my mind and decide between the two possibilities." *Second period:* (b) when he thinks, "Until now, my wanting to ask her to stay and my wanting to let her go were equally possible, but now I necessarily will want to ask her to stay." *Third period:* (c) when he thinks, "I want to ask her to stay."

We can represent this structure by the following pattern[2]:

t_1	a	t_2	b	t_3	c	t_4
acts	S: At t_4 S:a or S:b; at t_3 Sd:a or Sd:b		S: Until now at t_4 S:a or S:b but now at t_4 necessarily S:a	S:a		
modalities	C_{t_1} S:a$_{t_4}$ C_{t_1} S:b$_{t_4}$ C_{t_1} Sd:a$_{t_3}$ C_{t_1} Sd:b$_{t_3}$		R_{t_3} Sd:a$_{t_3}$ N_{t_3} S:a$_{t_4}$	R_{t_4} S:a$_{t_4}$		

Figure 2.

It is worth mentioning that in the three mental acts, other (past or future) mental acts of the same person are reflected on. In doing so, the person confers on his past and future acts a certain modal status. But this modal status is not only represented in thought, it is also partially created by thought, as can be clearly seen in the pattern of modalities in Figure 2. In this context the mental act (b) is of particular interest. It is the very act of decision-making because it effects a real change of modalities concerning the future act in question. S:a which had been simply a contingent future act becomes, in virtue of Sd:a, a necessary future act. It remains completely enigmatic how a mental act of this kind can have such an effect. The solution of this enigma is a permanent challenge to philosophical insight.

As a result of our analysis, we may give the following definition:

A conscious being x has freedom of decision if and only if x is capable of producing decision-act sequences in his mind.

Normally the decision-making act (b) does not immediately follow the decision-begging act (a); between (a) and (b), other acts are interpolated by which the person seeks a rational foundation for his decision in suitable criteria. In the ideal case, at the end of his reasoning, he comes to the conclusion—for instance—that he should make up his mind in favor of S:a. The question arises whether the thinking of unequivocal clear-cut decision criteria entails the decision as its necessary consequence. If that were the case, the possession of sufficiently strong criteria would preclude liberty. But the thinking of such criteria is never a sufficient cause for the corresponding decision. We are free to apply or not to apply criteria we are familiar with, just as we are free to follow or not to follow norms we are aware of. This point has important implications for the attribution of responsibility to a person.

Let me now come to freedom of action. It is defined as the capacity of a human being to realize the objects of his free will in the external world. In this respect we speak of the power that a person has over a state of affairs:

A person S has power over a state of affairs x, if and only if the probability of x being realized rises in virtue of S's decision to want x.

A person can have more or less power over future states of affairs. Here we must distinguish three aspects of power: extent of power; degree of freedom; and powerfulness of action possibilities.

'*Extent of power*' means the overall totality of states of affairs depending, in whole or in part, on a person's will. The '*degree of freedom,*' on the other hand, is measured by the number of alternative possibilities that a person has for action. Finally, only a limited number of states of affairs can be realized within one and the same possibility of action. Regrettably, often only a subclass of the class of states of affairs, each of which we can realize separately, are realizable together. That is why we have to distinguish the 'extent of our power' and the '*powerfulness of our action possibilities.*' Furthermore, one person may have only a few but very powerful action possibilities, while another has a great degree of freedom with comparatively powerless action possibilities.

I come now to the third notion of freedom, namely, socio-political freedom. Kant defined it as "independence from another's constraining will" (*Metaphysik der Sitten* in the standard German critical edition, Akademie Ausgabe (AA) VI, 237).

The first question we must answer is how, by what means, one man can constrain another man's will? We must distinguish two main possibilities: direct physical obstruction of his actions, and influence on his decision-making process through persuasion or threats. Blackmail is doubtless the strongest means of doing so.

Whereas ontological and anthropological freedom cannot be lost or gained, since we simply have it or we do not, socio-political freedom is an object of human aspiration. We can care about it in almost as many ways as it can be endangered. But there are two main ways of defending one's own freedom: direct physical action against the adversary who threatens our freedom—here the extreme case would be to kill him—and mental influence by means of persuasion, threats, etc.

What are the relations among the three types of freedom we have distinguished? Most philosophers believe that freedom of decision presupposes ontological freedom; that freedom of action presupposes both freedom of decision and ontological freedom; and that socio-political freedom depends on all three types of freedom. On the other hand, philosophers normally hold that there may be causally undetermined processes in the world without any freedom of decision, and that both freedom of decision and freedom of action can exist without political freedom.

Common sense convinces us that all three kinds of freedom exist. But when it comes to certainty and demonstration, things look different. The ancients tried to prove determinism by means of modal logic. Kant did the same by transcendental argumentation. Classical mechanics was supposed to offer an empirical demonstration of universal determinism. Modern physics, especially quantum mechanics or modern theories of evolution, on the other hand, are supposed to provide us with empirical proof of ontological freedom. But logical and philosophical analysis in recent years has clearly shown that these endeavors failed. We must now acknowledge that there is in fact no proof, be it logical, transcendental or empirical, that establishes the existence of freedom. This skeptical view holds also for our freedom of decision and our freedom of action. In fact, freedom of decision could be just an illusion. That would mean that in Figure 2 only the act scheme would be correct, and the corresponding modalities would be wrong. This would mean that we only think we make decisions, but in reality the decisions are already made by factors unknown to us. There is also the possibility that we have real freedom of decision as we defined it without the corresponding freedom of action. For instance, the moving of my hand in this case would not be caused by my willing it to move, but by a material cause independent of my will. Though these suggestions are implausible, they are by no means impossible.

These skeptical considerations lead to the question of what happens to our responsibility if freedom, which is its necessary basis, cannot be established. Could not every criminal decline responsibility for his actions if there is no possible certainty that he was free to do them?

First, we must take into account that not all types of freedom are equally presupposed in the assessment of responsibility. The foundation of responsibility is our freedom of decision and our freedom of action. The case of socio-political freedom, on the other hand, is more complicated. If someone physically prevents another person from doing something, this other person's responsibility is completely nullified. But if the influence is on the mind, say by blackmail, responsibility for one's actions is certainly modified, but not completely eliminated, because his will is still free to yield to or to oppose the blackmail.

Now, to the sceptical question of whether responsibility will be completely undermined if there is no demonstration of liberty, Kant has found a convincing answer. In the *Groundwork* he writes:

> . . . every being, which cannot act otherwise than under the idea of freedom is thereby really free in a practical respect. That is to say, all laws which are inseparably bound up with freedom hold for it just as if its will were proved free in itself by theoretical philosophy (*Grundlegung Zur Metaphysik der Sitten*, AA IV, 448).

Now it is doubtless the case that no human action worthy of the name can be accomplished without the agent's firm conviction that he is free to decide and act on his own. Therefore, if any laws oblige him to act in a certain way, he is by that very fact responsible for those actions. The question of whether those laws really exist and what their foundation is will be the issue of our third and last section.

III.

In our first section, we showed that responsibility depends on two facts: the freedom of the responsible agent, and the validity of the norms under which he acts. We dealt with the first condition in our second section. Now the last point remains to be settled.

We have to distinguish two types of norms as the basis of responsibility: positive and transpositive norms. They are to be defined as follows:[3]

> A norm x is *positive* if and only if x's validity is due to a positive act of legislation, which put x into force.
>
> A norm x is *transpositive* if and only if x must be observed regardless of whether it was enacted by positive legislation.

Positive norms create legal responsibilities, and with the responsibility, they institute the authority that receives the account. The question of the responsibility of the scientist would therefore be easily settled if there were pertinent positive laws. But as Peter Saladin shows in his article in this book, this is not the case, and it is not yet clear if it really should be the case. In the absence of positive norms, we must therefore look for a transpositive basis for the responsibility of the scientist.

In so doing we are immediately confronted with the old debate between natural-right philosophers and the positivists. The latter categorically deny the existence of any nonpositive norm. The strength of their position is due to the weak arguments that natural-right philosophers have long been using for a correct thesis. Indeed, they tried to found natural rights in the will of God, in the laws of nature, or in the intrinsic value of the essence of a being or a state of affairs. The theological foundation depends on religious convictions that are not shared by everyone; the argument from the laws of nature was critized as a naturalistic fallacy, i.e., illegitimate inference from 'be' to 'ought'; and the value theory failed because of the unquestionable social and historic relativity of values. In this situation, if we do not wish to yield immediately to positivistic criticism, we must look for a stronger basis for transpositive norms.

In my opinion the only way out of the dilemma is to analyze the concept of positive legislation itself. In this way we carry the war into the enemy's camp. A precise analysis of what positive legislation is and how it works will show that the participants in any legislation whatsoever must accept and recognize a certain number of rules before even starting their work if they wish to bring about what they aim at.[4] These rules are therefore to be considered as transpositive norms. For instance, no positive legislation is possible without recognition of the metanorm "pacta sunt servanda." The validity of this norm therefore cannot depend on convention.

Furthermore, the question of whether we should bind one another by positive legislation is not subject to arbitrary decision. Reason demands that every reasonable being avoid practical contradiction in his private and social life. But the only efficient way to stay in agreement with everyone is to follow rules everyone has accepted. This is what positive legislation brings about.

What, now, are the transpositive norms every positive legislation presupposes and no positive legislation is entitled to abrogate? These usually come under the title of 'human rights.' The highest and most important of these rights concerns the respect we owe to every human being as a potential legislator. Kant discovered the classical formula for the universal duty corresponding to that fundamental human right: "Act in a way such that you use the mankind in yourself as in the person of anybody else always also as an end and never only as a means (AA IV, 429)."

To get a strong philosophical basis for protecting the environment, many philosophers actually argue in favor of analogous rights of animals and plants. These arguments fail because animals and plants, whatever their excellence, can never be considered potential legislators. They therefore lack the only property that would oblige us to consider them not only as a means, but also as an end in themselves.

Does that mean that there is no philosophical justification for environmental protection? I think there are cogent arguments in favor of such a policy, that are based not on animal or plant rights, but on human rights.

According to the ethics of reason, the foundations of which we exposed in the last section, the highest aim of positive legislation must be the protection of liberty. This results clearly from Kant's famous definition of right: "Right therefore is the totality of the conditions under which the will of one person can be put into harmony with the will of another person according to a universal law of liberty."
But there are two ways of hindering another's action—by direct impediment, and by withdrawal of the necessary means.
According to this distinction there are two classes of human rights: liberty rights, and social rights.

The first binds us to respect, within the limits of law, the free decisions and actions of others; the second obliges us not to deprive others of the means for their realization. Among the second group of human rights figure not only the right to property and the right to labor, but also the right to an intact environment, which is doubtless one of the most important conditions for a decent human life.

This obviously holds also for future generations. I certainly agree with Günter Patzig[5] that it is nonsense to postulate that those who do not yet exist have a right to exist. But if we don't renounce having

children, we are obliged to respect the human rights of future generations. Therefore, we are bound to preserve the conditions of life for
generations to come.

To conclude, let me add some considerations on the responsibility of the scientist. As we have seen, there are transpositive norms that
create responsibility even where positive norms are lacking. This is a
responsibility that not only the scientist, but everyone has to assume.
Therefore, I agree with Jürgen Mittelstrass that scientists have no
special ethics. But Mittelstrass rightly stresses that scientists have a
special responsibility. Let me explain this last point.

We have seen in our first section that responsibility goes as far as
the real power of the agent. Now, the power of man has dramatically
increased in the last century. We live today in a completely new historic
situation, which admits of no comparison with other periods in the
history of man. In fact, as a consequence of scientific and technological
progress, man has for the first time in his history the power to exercise
complete control over the thoughts, feelings and actions of anyone
else; change his essence by manipulation of genetic information; and
put an end to the existence of humanity itself by nuclear weapons or
the destruction of the natural basis of life. This dramatic change in the
power of man also gives us dramatic new responsibilities.

The increase of power is to a great extent due to science and
technology. This gives the scientist his special responsibility. To this
thesis it is often objected that science and technology are purely instrumental and that the responsibility lies in the hand of the users not of
the producers of such instruments. The responsibility of those who use
modern technology is not questionable. But does that mean that the
producers have no responsibility at all? If arms are used by criminals
for morally bad aims, do those who gave them those arms have no
responsibility? To convince ourselves of the contrary, it is sufficient to
realize that the bad ends would not have been attained had the means
not been placed in the hands of the users. Certainly, most of the means
can be used for both good and bad purposes. But in certain cases, it
is not sufficient to guarantee the possibility of good use; we must also
exclude bad use. Here lies the difference between a knife and nuclear
technology. With a knife one can kill only a limited number of persons.
With nuclear technology one can kill all of humanity. That is the
reason for the special responsibility of scientists in certain 'hot' research fields. Even if they don't do the killing themselves, they make
killing possible and in certain cases even highly plausible.

We normally base our ideas of responsibility on a one-cause

model of causation. The agent's will is considered a necessary and sufficient cause of the event. But this is seldom the case. Usually an agent's will is not sufficient to bring about the effect, and in some cases it is not even necessary. Should we in the latter cases absolve responsibility and reserve it for the first? In my opinion, to attribute responsibility to an agent, it is sufficient that his willing the effect increases the probability of its realization and that his not willing the effect diminishes this probability. But we can by no means waive responsibility if the agent's will is a necessary cause of the effect. For in this case, even if it is not in his power to bring about the effect, it is up to him to stop it. That is what counts when the effect is undesirable. Whether the terrific instruments of self-destruction are produced is in the hands of the scientists in the 'hot' research fields. If they are not able to stop their production, they should at least care about which hands they fall into.

This does not mean that research must stop. Again I agree with Jürgen Mittelstrass that there is no way back. Romantic adoration of the 'good old days'—which after all were not that good—does not solve our problem. The difficulties that are due to scientific and technological progress can only be mastered by using science and technology. All we need is the right use of science and technology. That means that the scope of research and the direction of scientific and technological development must be redefined. In this work scientists have to play an important role. But as science today depends largely on important financial means, and private interests decide to a great extent what means are placed at which person's disposal, we are confronted with a *political* problem. So, without diminishing the special responsibility of the scientists, I would like to stress the political responsibility of all citizens for the survival of humanity. This responsibility must also find its application in international politics.

Notes

1. In our formalization we use the following symbols: t′ and t″ are time-point variables; N stands for: "it is necessary that"; R means: "it is the case that"; C stands for: "it is contingent that."

2. In our pattern we use the following symbols: S:a means: "the concrete subject S thinks the thought a." Sd:a means "the concrete subject S makes a decision in favor of the thought a." As a general rule, the expression on the left side of the double point means the content of a mental act of S. For instance $Ct_1 Sd:bt_3$ reads: "It is contingent at t_1 that S will at t_3 make his mind up in favor of b."

3.   See my paper: "Légalité et légitimité: leurs rôles respectifs dans la garantie de la liberté," in *Studia Philosophica*, 44, (1985).

4.   That is the proposal of K. O. Apel, *Transformation der Philosophie*, Vol. 2 (Frankfurt: Suhrkamp, 1973), 359ff.

5.   See G. Patzig. *Ökologische Ethik-innerhalb der Grenzen blosser Vernunft.* Göttingen 1983.

Should Science Provide an Image of the World?

CATHERINE CHEVALLEY

Science is like a fish out of water whenever it does *not* undergo a crisis. However, 'ordinary' foundational crises deal with internal contradictions or with the interpretation of new phenomena. They may involve conceptual revolutions with far-reaching consequences, as was the case with the heliocentric hypothesis or the birth of quantum physics, but crucial choices remain inside the realm of a reassessment of methodological or philosophical orientations. A different situation develops when the general appreciation of what the task of science ought to be comes into discussion. The crisis then leaps from outside, clearly merging today from antiscience movements on the one hand, and from the confusion and ambiguity of the scientific community about what should be done in such and such cases, on the other. As far as ethical and political issues are concerned, scientists are now confronted with unexpected requirements, and the question arises of who should be in charge of ethics, if not scientists themselves. Before this question can be answered, it may be useful to explore the reasons for putting this ethical demand on science, and to venture to express general doubts about the clarity of our philosophical concept of contemporary science. My contribution here will be to suggest a possible orientation along these two lines of argument, by tracing our *image of science* to some of its origins and stressing the inadequacy of this image to the present state of scientific knowledge.

The image of science is not immediately well defined, even among practitioners. There is no reason, except in particular circumstances, why one should try to give a clear-cut answer to the question 'what is science,' since it is doubtful whether such knowledge could be of any use. However, a plausible cause for the intricate situation met by physics, biology, or ecology seems to be the tension or contradiction between different features of this image of science, blurred as it is. Nuclear fission, genetic manipulation, or the destruction of ecosystems have given clear evidence of the unlimited and uncontrolled power of scientific achievements. On the basis of this evidence, it has been expected that scientists would solve the difficult problem of a limitation of scientific research. On the other hand, scientific activity has up to now been ruled essentially by some internal, though often unexpected, logic of its own development. The traditional concept of science had no room for any self-limitation on the ground of anticipated evil consequences. An essential feature of this concept was to view science as a set of universal principles reflecting the unity of the human mind. When the idea of such a science developed in connection with ethical and political valuation of its consequences, only good effects were taken into consideration. The tension experienced today may come therefore from a contradiction in the premises. If science is universal, how are we to introduce in its concept limitations due to ethical considerations? *Mutatis mutandis,* the problem is similar to the one stated by Leibniz, among others: Why is there evil in the world? The question 'why is there evil in science' may ultimately appear as a merely inconsistent formulation. Nevertheless, to understand its meaning requires a clearer view of the various elements that compose our image of science, of when it was formed and how it could be criticized.

Science as *Mater Universalis*

The suggestion has often been made that science inherited during the eighteenth century the burden of providing *values* as well as methodological principles and ontological description because of the decreasing influence of religion and Christian morals. Though such a straight-forward interpretation lacks subtlety in many respects, the reordering of the relationships among metaphysics, logic, physics, and ethics did end with science replacing metaphysics at the bottom, after metaphysics had replaced religion. This at least is the story told by Auguste Comte; such a move is also clearly seen in the work of Condorcet. Both were so influential in the popularization of the image of science that it may be useful to recall briefly some characteristic statements of their view. I shall restrict myself here to Condorcet, who will possibly sound anachronistic—though a comparison with the 'manifesto' published by the Vienna Circle in 1929 would be interesting in this respect.

Condorcet's optimistic view of modern times, as expressed in the *Esquisse des Progrès de l'Esprit Humain,* [1] was based on absolute confidence in the liberating power of science, about which he did not foresee any possibility for bitterness or disappointment. The "mathématique sociale" was to secure "happiness and perfection for humanity." Rationality would prove strong enough to destroy evil feelings and passions:

"one day will come when our interests and passions will have no more influence on the judgments which guide our will than they have today on our scientific views."[2] Objectivity of mathematics and physical science being rooted in the stability of the axes of the universe—as Laplace had shown—ensured continuous progress of the understanding of nature.[3] Therefore, one could reasonably hope to extend the certainty proper to exact sciences into the realm of moral and human sciences: "Thinking over the nature of the moral sciences, one cannot but see that they must work with the very method of the physical sciences, obtain similar accuracy and preciseness in their language and reach the same level of certainty, since they are supported by the observation of facts exactly like the physical sciences."[4] Such progress will be ensured, Condorcet thought, through the application of probability calculus, and his mathematical works were partly devoted to showing that the applicability of the probability concept could provide a secure basis for freedom[5] and moral behavior.[6] Progress of mankind would thus be made possible by the development of scientific method: "Any scientific discovery is a blessing for Humanity."[7]

Above all, said Condorcet, Descartes was to be praised for such a development. Comparing the achievements of Bacon, Galileo, and Descartes, Condorcet enthusiastically underlined the influence of the last. While Bacon possessed "to the highest degree the genius of philosophy," he was not a scientist, and therefore "his methods for discovering truth, of which he gave no example, were admired by philosophers but had no effect on the development of sciences."[8] Similarly Galileo, who was able to give the sciences their sole foundation on experiment and computation, was not a philosopher, and "since he restricted himself to mathematical and physical sciences, he failed to provide the impulse that was needed."[9] Only Descartes knew how to be simultaneously a scientist and a philosopher: "he conjugated examples and precepts." He extended his method to everything: God, man, the world. "His boldness was fascinating, his enthusiasm was stimulating." Reason and metaphysics were at last united and given a firm foundation on a set of "first principles and certain truths."[10] Finally this metaphysics "applied to the whole realm of human knowledge" succeeded in raising *"an everlasting barrier between mankind and the former mistakes of its youth."* Descartes's children were Locke, the progress of the sciences during the eighteenth century, the American Revolution, and finally the French Revolution. All this together amounted to a second birth of mankind, "a birth to happiness."

How are we to appreciate this unabashed optimism, so contrary to Condorcet's own tragic end? It would, of course, be outrageous—and a reductionnist interpretation—to restrict the spirit of the Enlightenment to an activist conception of scientific rationality. However, it should be pointed out that any assessment of science as 'providential' risks generating countereffects that may give rise to strong irrationalism. What happened during the nineteenth century was that the crystal-clear image of a rational scientist devoted to democracy and the happiness of mankind was gradually transformed into that of a tormented and solitary genius led by his very despair to transcendant understanding of the mysteries of nature and destiny. Romantic literature profusely illustrated this dark image. An image that nevertheless seems to be the exact counterpart of the first one, since both concepts shared a common feature in the belief that science provided a deep and universal kind of knowledge of nature and man. Though the romantic scientist does not wish to contribute to technological or moral progress, he 'sees' the truth, and he builds a world all the same; science and 'Weltanschauung' remained closely connected. Even though, when it came to political involvement, there were usually wide and significant differences between rationalist and irrationalist trends of thought, one is left with striking similarities in the premises of their arguments. In one case, rational knowledge—the science praised by Condorcet—provides rules for rational action (the building of a happy and democratic society); in the other case, irrational knowledge—the science of Faust—provides rules for irrational action (suicide, despair, rebellion against rationality, etc.). But in both cases, rules of action—ethical and political issues—are immediately derived from the kind of knowledge given through science.

The implications of such a continuity between ethics and the theory of science should be more thoroughly discussed than have been hinted here. I shall, however, restrict myself to underlining a coincidence. Obviously science is confronted today with ethical and political dilemmas, and obviously scientists are often at a loss when it comes to making decisions. Powerful antiscience reactions spring from this confusion, together with irrational pangs of love for anything that looks 'natural.' The ultimate inability of science to provide technological happiness, its remarkable ability to create ecological disasters, give arguments in favor of rejecting science itself. If then we assume that to a large extent this rejection is based not on any conceptual weakness of science, or any lack of beauty [or success] in it, but solely on its being ethically impotent, it seems reasonable to question the belief that science ought to be different. Apparently the situation results from the *petitio principii* that science was originally supposed to generate freedom and happiness, the good and the goods. If one assumes at a given time that there must be a natural connection between the progress of science and the progress of mankind, failure in this respect leads naturally to disappointment. In other words, there seems to be a fairly obvious coincidence between too much faith in the expanding power of scientific rationality and too much rejection of the ability of scientists to master complex situations.

Should science be freed from such expectations? Is it possible to disjoin our image of science from this obligation to exhibit ethical and political competence? Is it possible, conversely, to conceive rational ethics and politics independently from scientific knowledge? It would be preposterous to suggest any general answer to these questions, since progress in this matter will most probably be made only as the result of well-defined and localized particular cases. However, following the former line of argument, it might be interesting to recall that, apart from any restriction of their theoretical value, Condorcet's views on science had been criticized on the ground that it was perfectly illusory to set so many hopes on scientific progress.

Politics and Education

Opposing the claim that the rationality of exact sciences would in time secure the development of moral progress, Rousseau had previously aimed at a more realistic assessment of the importance of politics and education for a free society. Rousseau became involved in a painful fight with his former friends, Diderot and d'Alembert, because he strongly opposed the view that science could give rise to political freedom. Such a belief, in Rousseau's opinion, was inadequate to meet the actual requirements of the situation. "Man is born free. He is a prisoner everywhere"—with this first sentence, the *Contrat Social* meant to stress a major *contradiction*. In the face of such a blunt reality, faith in the power of arts and sciences suddenly looked futile. The only appropriate tools had to be politics and the education of individuals. That Rousseau published the *Contrat Social* and *Emile* in the same year was no coincidence.

Rousseau's criticism of the idealistic attitude shared by the Encyclopaedists is already clearly stated in the early, almost juvenile *Discours sur les sciences et les arts*. What are the real social consequences of the spreading of arts and sciences? They amount, Rousseau argued, to a general corruption of the soul. Fallacious needs are created: luxury,

ostentation, idleness, the desire to show off, the striving to be published, the tendency to argue one thing and then the contrary to
display rhetorical virtuosity. In many cases, the origins of the sciences
are sheer perversions or moral and intellectual blemishes: "Astronomy
was born out of superstition; eloquence out of ambition, hatred, flat-
tery, lies; geometry out of stinginess; physics out of idle curiosity.
. . ."[11] A maxim of Rousseau is that sophisticated intellectual knowledge and craft have grown out of passions and the 'will to dominate,'
in contrast with actual needs. Nature did not anticipate that man would
be willing to damage or even destroy her to unveil her secrets. Actually
nature had kept her secrets so well hidden precisely to protect man
from doing harm to himself out of idle curiosity: "Nature's intention
was to keep you away from science, as a mother who snatches some
dangerous weapon from the hands of her child."[12] Arts and sciences
thus do not provide or guarantee freedom: "We have physicists, we
have mathematicians, we have chemists, and poets, musicians, paint-
ers; *we do not have citizens any more.*" To believe in the sheer power of
reason to break the chains of slavery would be naive.

However, Rousseau by no means recommends giving up speculation and going 'back to Nature' or to breeding sheep. The goal of the
Discours sur les sciences et les arts is to make a careful distinction between
science itself and the show of 'rationality.' In its essence, science is a
private matter, like philosophy, art, etc., ruled by individual destiny.
Great scientists and philosophers did not profit much from socialized
and institutional support, they went their own way by themselves:
"Those whose fate was to be the disciples of Nature had no need for
any master." They acted out of a kind of internal necessity; they fed
on obstacles: "*Verulam, Descartes, Newton, these men who taught mankind,
. . . what guide would have led them to where they arrived by their genius? They
first learnt to make efforts through the obstacles they met. . . .*"[13] Should
therefore society leave them on their own, in isolation? Not at all,
Rousseau answers again. Society must give them expectations suited
to their ambition and genius. In other words, society must provide for
them the *highest responsibilities:* "The prince of eloquence was a consul
in Rome, while the greatest philosopher was Chancellor of England!"[14] Had Cicero or Bacon been offered an academic position in
a university or a research center, they would have done little.[15] Scientists being "the tutors of mankind" should not be transformed into a
crowd of assistant teachers: "Let the first-rate scientists be given some
respectable refuge in the Courts; let them obtain the only reward
which is worthy of them, namely, let them contribute through their

influence to the happiness of the nations to which they taught wisdom. Only then shall one realize how much virtue, science and authority can achieve together for the good of the human species when inspired by a noble competition."[16] Given political power, true scientists and philosophers would be able to allow intellectual knowledge to serve freedom and increase happiness, along with political institutions. Since Rousseau claims elective aristocracy to be the best possible government for middle-sized countries,[17] scientists and philosophers will quite naturally find a part to play that will be neither Plato's philosopher-king nor the modern all-rational intellectual.

Thus, Rousseau's first philosophical work gives—*cum grano salis*—an example of the possibility of conceiving criticism of the connection between science and power independantly of any irrational dismissal of science itself. Rousseau merely insists that science cannot be a substitute for laws and education. One needs to address citizens and to consider society as a system more complex than a mechanical set of physical points. Freedom for men will depend essentially on good 'social contracts' and cannot be secured by the sheer liberating influence of scientific rationality. The essence of man is to be free, which does not entail that mankind behaves rationally; freedom therefore calls for stronger protection and more stability than those that science can provide.

Is it unreasonable to suggest that the situation that scientists face today exhibits similar complexity? Instead of going back and forth between optimism and bitterness about science, it might be necessary to renounce the belief that science can serve as a universal model and provide rules of action, including rules for its own development and consequences. Many misunderstandings probably arose because too much was expected from science, while the premises that linked science to the task of giving some kind of 'Weltanschauung' remained unquestioned. Therefore, arguments for and against are bound to move inside a circle. Science requires freedom, but freedom first seems to require appropriate laws and education.

What Is Science?

To a large extent, the recognition of a restricted validity of the image of science that was inherited from the eighteenth century is also forced on us by fundamental new features of contemporary science, and here we hit on the theoretical weakness of this image. The basis for Condorcet's conception was the statement that science is 'objective', meaning that science is the true transcription of the essence or structure of an independent reality. From this statement, one could derive the belief that scientific knowledge could be expanded outside the realm of the exact sciences to a different area, such as morals. This was a paradoxical move; science was viewed as objective—free from valuation—and *thus* it could become the origin of values. In any case, the main question that arises here is whether contemporary science has retained the same concept of objectivity. Clearly, if it has not, its ontological privileges must be given some new interpretation.

First, the debates about the objectivity of science in the twentieth century are frequently restricted to debates between the classical views on rationality and irrationality. It has been argued that quantum mechanics is basically irrational physics, and it has been argued that, since physics must be the expression of the structure of independent reality, quantum physics has to be incomplete. But what is rational physics? Interpretation bounces back and forth between concepts that arose initially in connection with classical mechanics. Definitions of 'physical reality,' for instance, remain so closely connected with localization in space and time, continuity, visualization or independence with respect to the means of observation, that one will easily deny it to quantum objects, or support the idea that quantum physicists despise 'physical reality'—while they only change the definition of the concept. Similar remarks could be made about biology, and the eternal debates for and against vitalism or mechanism. On the whole, one might suggest that the image of science that was inherited from classical mechanics (and reinforced during the nineteenth century) is too restricted to account for the paradoxical features of contemporary science. There is no need to look for 'irrationality' whenever the classical conception of reason is defeated, if 'objectivity' has to be defined otherwise.

Strikingly, the inadequacy of the classical image of science was pointed out for purely philosophical reasons by phenomenology in the 1930s. The reassessment of the meaning of Descartes's philosophy together with a new interpretation of Galilean science was a central theme for both Husserl and Heidegger. Despite diverging conclusions, both shared a view of the rise of modern metaphysics as the development of 'objectivism,'[18] namely, as the determination of first principles ruling the being in its totality. From these principles, the 'things' of the world had derived definition of their existence from their mathematical essence,[19] the privilege of geometry being further supported by a distinction between secondary and primary qualities; our own relationship with the world was described as a confrontation of subject and object,[20] truth depending on the certainty of representation; physical theory was given the privilege of being *the* theory of reality. From then on, the major goal of philosophy itself had to concentrate on theory of knowledge, and Descartes becomes in Husserl's description a starting point for the two traditions of rationalism and empiricism. Classical 'objectivism' was thus the generalization of the mathematical reinterpretation of nature that found its way through the work of Galileo, Kepler, and Newton. However, should the mathematics change, the ontology of objectivism might appear inadequate. Despite their opposition about which goals to achieve, phenomenology and logical empiricism both stressed such a possibility, and the suggestion was almost common sense in the 1930s. Even Cassirer departs strongly from any strict obedience to neo-Kantianism when he comes to the interpretation of quantum physics.[21] The general feeling was that new questions about science had to be elaborated to take into account the fundamental changes that took place in mathematics, physics, and biology. Little progress has been made since, but this is not sufficient reason for concealing the necessity of such a renewal of the image of science.

Finally, the physicists who invented quantum mechanics themselves insisted that no extension of physical theory into a general concept of the world could any longer be hoped for. Such an extension was possible for classical mechanics because of the coincidence between things that we experience in the world and the objects of mathematical physics. However, since in quantum theory the objects were no longer 'things encountered in a direct and immediate experience,' that could be thought of as permanent substances with changing attributes, this state of affairs made it impossible for anyone to make scientific knowledge serve as a foundation for any Weltanschauung.[22] Not that anyone ever encountered in immediate experience the classical principle of inertia; but things nevertheless were expected to conform in principle to rational mechanics, even extended into electromagnetism and statistical mechanics. However, the tracks of an electron inside a cloud chamber seem to be outside the realm of any link with the world of our perception. Therefore, science may appear more like a beautiful work of art, with differences due to differences in styles, than like the foundation for a universal understanding of the essence of things. The unique contemporary homologues of Descartes and Leibniz stubbornly refused to provide a general ontology that might serve as some new foundation for a new monument: logic, physics, ethics.

Only strong commitment to the former vision of science could conceal the advantages of making a distinction between two very different aspects of scientific activity. One would be the setting up of new schemes, the building of new theories, in absolute freedom, and the other an expansion of these new schemes into a general theory of being, entailing ethical and social consequences. This second move seems to have been a specific feature of what is sometimes called 'modernity,' from the seventeenth century on. If there is a crisis, it is probably confined to the second aspect. As Husserl wrote as early as 1935: "This is the right place to denounce the naiveté of this kind of rationalism, which was interpreted as unconditional rationality, and which marks the whole of modern philosophy since the Renaissance."[23] Should science keep on replacing ethics and metaphysics? It seems difficult to find firm ground for this assumption, since we do not have a clear and unified notion of what science itself is, in what is sometimes called 'postmodernity.' On the whole, the old image of science that gave rise to Condorcet's enthusiasm does not allow us to escape polarisation between scientism and antiscientism. Such a debate, however, looks already anachronistic in view of the new ethical and political problems faced by scientists. Freedom has to be secured by law and politics, while philosophical understanding of science is confronted with the difficult task of finding a way through objectivism, reductionnism, and mysticism towards a new conception of reason.

Notes

1.   J. A. Nicolas Caritat de Condorcet, *Esquisse d'un tableau historique des progrès de l'esprit humain* [1793–1794], in A. Condorcet et F. Arago, *Oeuvres complètes* (Paris, 1847–1849).

2.   *Ibid.*, introduction: "un jour viendra où nos intérêts et nos passions n'auront pas plus d'influence sur les jugements qui dirigent la volonté que nous ne les voyons en avoir aujourd'hui sur nos opinions scientifiques."

3.   *Ibid.*, "sans doute ces progrès pourront suivre une marche plus ou moins rapide, mais elle doit être continue et jamais rétrograde tant que la terre occupera la même place dans le système de l'univers."

4.   "Discours de réception à l'Académie française," in Condorcet, *Oeuvres complètes*, l. c., I, 392.

5.   See the case of elections, in *Essai sur l'application de l'analyse à la probabilité des décisions rendues à la pluralité des voix* (Paris, 1785). A facsimile edition was published by Chelsea Publishing Company (New York, 1972).

6.   See the demonstration that it is useless to gamble, in *Elemens du Calcul des Probabilités et son application aux jeux de hasard, à la loterie et aux jugements des hommes* (Paris, an XIII [1805]).

7.   "Discours de réception . . .", l. c., 390: "Toute découverte dans les sciences est un bienfait pour l'humanité."

8. *Esquisse* . . ., 8ème période: "Mais Bacon, qui possédait le génie de la philosophie au point le plus élevé, n'y joignit point celui des sciences; et ces méthodes de découvrir la vérité, dont il ne donne point l'exemple, furent admirées des philosophes, mais ne changèrent point la marche des sciences."

9. *Ibid.*, "Mais, se bornant exclusivement aux sciences mathématiques et physiques, [Galilée] ne sut imprimer aux esprits ce mouvement qu'ils semblaient attendre."

10. *Ibid.*, "il subjuguait par sa hardiesse, il entrainait par son enthousiasme. . . . c'est ce dernier pas de la philosophie qui a mis, en quelque sorte, une barrière éternelle entre le genre humain et les vieilles erreurs de son enfance."

11. Rousseau, *Discours sur les sciences et les arts,* in Rousseau, *Du Contrat Social* (Paris: Garnier, 1962), 4: "l'astronomie est née de la superstition; l'éloquence de l'ambition, de la haine, de la flatterie, du mensonge; la géométrie de l'avarice; la physique d'une vaine curiosité. . . ."

12. *Ibid.*, 11: "Peuples, sachez donc une fois que la nature a voulu vous préserver de la science, comme une mére arrache une arme dangereuse des mains de son enfant, que tous les secrets qu'elle vous cache sont autant de maux qu'elle vous garantit. . . ."

13. *Ibid.*, 22: "Les Verulam, les Descartes et les Newton, ces précepteurs du genre humain, . . . quels guides les eussent conduits jusqu'où leur génie les a portés? . . . C'est par les premiers obstacles qu'ils ont appris à faire des efforts, et qu'ils se sont exercés à franchir l'espace immense qu'ils ont parcouru."

14. *Ibid.*, 23: "Le prince de l'éloquence fut consul de Rome; et le plus grand peut-être des philosophes, Chancelier d'Angleterre."

15. *Ibid.*, 23: "Croit-on que si l'un n'eût occupé qu'une chaire dans quelque université, et que l'autre n'eût obtenu qu'une modique pension d'académie, croit-on, dis-je, que leurs ouvrages ne se sentiraient pas de leur état?"

16. *Ibid.*, "que les savants du premier ordre trouvent dans leurs cours d'honorables asiles; qu'ils y obtiennent la seule récompense digne d'eux, celle de contribuer par leur crédit au bonheur des peuples à qui ils auront enseigné la sagesse; *c'est alors* seulement qu'on verra ce que peuvent la vertu, la science et l'autorité animées d'une noble émulation et travaillant de concert à la félicité du genre humain."

17. Rousseau, *Contrat Social,* III, 5: "il y a . . . trois sortes d'aristocratie: naturelle, élective, héréditaire. La première ne convient qu'à des peuples simples; la troisième est le pire de tous les gouvernements; la deuxième est le meilleur: c'est l'aristocratie proprement dite. . . . En un mot, c'est l'ordre le meilleur et le plus naturel que les plus sages gouvernent la multitude quand on est sûr qu'ils la gouverneront pour son profit, et non pour le leur."

18. See, for instance, Husserl, *Die Krisis der europaischen Wissenschaften und die Transzendantale Phänomenologie* (1954).

19. See Heidegger's comments in *Die Frage nach dem Ding* [1935] (Tubingen, 1962), 82: "Die Frage nach dem Ding ist jetzt in der reinen Vernunft verankert, d.h. in der mathematischen Entfaltung ihrer Grundsatze."

20. Optical metaphors are crucial in Descartes' description of this relationship. For statements about the connexion between this and the history of the concept of truth, see Heidegger, *Sein und Zeit* [1927].

21. E. Cassirer, *Determinismus und Indeterminismus in der modernen Physik* (Göteborg, 1936).

22. W. Heisenberg, *Das Naturbild der heutigen Physik* [1953]. Similar statements are found in his paper "Wandlungen in den Grundlagen der Naturwissenschaft," *Die Naturwissenschaften* 40 [1934].

23. E. Husserl, *Die Krisis der europäischen Menschentums und die Philosophie* [1935]: "Hier is nun die Stelle [. . .] die Naivität desjenigen Rationalismus zu enthüllen, der für die philosophische Rationalität schlechthin genommen wird, aber freilich für die Philosophie der gesamten Neuzeit seit der Renaissance charakteristisch ist und sich für den wirklichen, also universalen Rationalismus hält." Husserl, of course, takes great care to make himself clear: one can criticize 'naïve rationalism' only to fight the claims of irrationalism. The crucial issue is to elaborate some rationalism of the second generation.

The Epistemology of the Opposition to Science

YEHUDA ELKANA

1. An Historical Overview

In every culture there are intellectuals who are carriers of the cultural heritage and actively participate in the creation of knowledge. Knowledge of all kinds: religious, political, economic, agricultural, technological, or scientific. Indeed, if we understand science broadly as knowledge dealing with the metaphysical and physical aspects of the world surrounding us, including our own body and soul, then no culture is without some kind of scientific enterprise. In Western society the quest for scientific knowledge was never negligible, but certainly in the last four or five hundred years, it is justifiable to call Western culture primarily a culture of science in the same broad sense as it can be said that previously it was a religious culture, and in the same sense as other cultures are primarily technological or musical or political, and in the same sense that nineteenth-century Bali is for Clifford Geertz a 'theatre state.'[1]

Ever since we have written down our history, we know that intellectuals—and in the last few hundred years specifically the magi, the natural philosophers, the scientists—have periodically come under attack. This attack was often mild, and even exerted a positive influence in its very challenge, causing a critical dialogue with the intellectuals; yet from time to time, the attack became so uncontrolled and dangerous that the very legitimacy of the whole intellectual enterprise was put in question. We seem to be going through such a period now, and all who believe in the legitimacy and even necessity of our joint enterprise need an historical diagnosis of the causes of such periodic attacks and then some guidance about how to react.

Historical, sociological, and psychological studies of antiscience movements abound. Since I cannot do better than most of them, nor do I see any major synthesis of them on the horizon, I shall confine my diagnosis to one descriptive thesis: antiintellectual movements become ferocious and uncontrolled in those periods when intellectuals themselves cannot agree that one intellectual domain has higher status

171

than all others, and in the framework of which by consensus all intellectual differences are fought out. Without such agreement the culture is in a disarray. We live in such a period. But before we touch on that, allow me to give a birds' eye view of the cultural history of the West seen from this vantage point.

The second and third centuries of our era were periods of disarray; so was the period between the late Renaissance and the Reformation, and the period of the religious wars in the seventeenth century. On the other hand, in the fifth and fourth centuries B.C., the *idea of the polis* with its politics, art and philosophy constituted the agreed upon domain. After its collapse, followed by the Alexandrian period and the emergence of Christianity, the culture was again in a total disarray by the second, third, and fourth centuries. It is against this background that the Gnosis, the Eastern mystical sects, and other pagan and Christian heterodoxies have to be viewed. Never before did intellectuals feel under such a populist attack and were so physically endangered or put under such psychological strain.

Just as the critical dialogue between orthodoxy and opposition, inside the community of intellectuals, fosters creativity and innovation, so do the frontal attacks of antirational waves on the activity, life style, and very existence of intellectuals, move them to defend themselves and reach legitimacy in new and original ways; if they survive, they thereby contribute to the reemergence and strengthening of the very phenomenon that the attackers came to abolish. The disarray of the second and third centuries brought about, or at least contributed to, what is known as the secondary breakthrough of late antiquity—the need of intellectuals to reformulate the aims of knowledge and the images of its validity by concentrating on the second-order concepts of 'proof' and 'experiment'; these were reactions to the popular— religious, mystical, and gnostic—attacks on all kinds of knowledge.

The resolution came with St. Augustine. In his works, and even more in his impact, the message was that henceforth there was a new 'superdiscipline,' namely, Augustinian theology, in which all differences could be hammered out. There is intellectual space there for reforming the dogma of the Church, for inclusion of pagan Neoplatonism, Eastern mystical trends, and even some elements of Gnostic and Manichean dualism, and for the exclusion (but in the same cognitive terms) of the Donatist and Pelagian heresies. The domain is available to all, and intellectually can deal with all these problems. Though not in these terms, that is what E. Troeltsch saw in the works of Augustine, and this emerges from the many magnificent studies of Late Antiquity by scholars like Peter Brown, Glen Bowersock, and Arnaldo Momigliano. The Thomistic synthesis almost a millenium later was of a similar kind.

The early Renaissance was united in the image of the *'virtú,'* replacing earlier dependence on *Fortuna* and having political, economic, and also purely intellectual implications. When the humanistic reaction abandoned the virtú and again pointed to a contemplative life style, it bitterly attacked the muscle-flexing, self-certain stand of the Renaissance activist; the consensus was torn apart, and the disarray reached a new peak before the Reformation. When it finally came, the Reformation and the Counter-Reformation together constituted a newly formulated theological-political framework in which all differences could be fought out: the differences between the two dogmas; their different economic implications; the contrary soteriological meanings of science, mathematics, and astronomy; the debate on the meaning and legitimacy of polyphonic music in the Council of Trent. The late sixteenth-century skepsis tore this fabric apart, and there was no longer a shared framework within which post-Erasmian humanism, the different varieties of religious dissent, the alchemists and Rosicrucians, the mathematical practitioners, the popular medics, the artisan-intellectuals and artist-craftsmen, the Aristotelians and the Neoplatonists could agree or disagree. The disarray reached its cruel climax in the wars of religion. When in their aftermath a new intellectual enterprise was created under the generic name of *natural philosophy,* it also created, consciously and systematically, an ideational framework, a language, and a style for rational argument in which all critical dialogue would be conducted. This reached its peak and excess in eighteenth-century rationalism, the last overarching cultural domain that was not only above disciplines, but above national differences too. The next major attack on rationality and science was orchestrated by early nineteenth-century Romanticism, and in reaction to it, for the first time in history, the responses were formulated on a national basis. In Germany philosophy became the superdiscipline; in England it was a utilitarian pragmatic world-view; in France it was a mathematical or rather geometrical conception of all intellectual discourse. Rorty in a brilliant paper drew attention to this phenomenon:

> Philosophy thus gets to be both a science (for has it not solved a problem science was unable to solve?) and a way to regain what science had seemed to take away—morality and religion. Morality and religion could now be encompassed within the bounds of reason alone. For reason had

been discovered by philosophy to be wider than science, and philosophy had thus shown itself to be a superscience.[2]

Around the end of the nineteenth century, the Newtonian synthesis was canonized; science, especially natural science, and above all physics, was seen as international, objective, empirical, and above human frailty and differences. Science now put forward its claim to be the superdiscipline, the modern equivalent of Augustinian theology, of the Thomistic synthesis, the Reformation and Counter-Reformation, the Scientific Revolution of the seventeenth century, the eighteenth-century Enlightenment, and Kantian philosophy. This claim was not only not weakened during the early twentieth-century upheavals in the body of knowledge (i.e., Einstein, quantum theory, and molecular biology), but became stronger and stronger. The social sciences accepted the ideal and the framework, as did the humanities, and public opinion looked at and up to science as the agreed upon framework in which humankind could conduct its critical dialogues and hope to better its fate.

By the end of the Second World War and after the bomb, all this was shattered, and today we are again in complete and dangerous disarray. The very advances in the sciences and in science-based technology create an ever-widening chasm between the successes in the body of knowledge and our Victorian images of knowledge. While the natural sciences produce more and more sophisticated knowledge and beneficial as well as harmful technologies at an ever-growing cost to society, other intellectual domains, such as the social sciences, or rather the sciences of man, increasingly throw off the yoke and straitjacket of the natural sciences. The legitimacy of the whole enterprise is being questioned more often and in stronger terms than ever before by a shrill and critical public opinion. In most Western democracies, the mood is populist and antiacademic, and greater public accountability of the sciences is being demanded by a chorus of scientifically illiterate groups and often also by their elected governments. The intellectuals are incapable of presenting a united front or of convincingly determining the framework and the language in which the debate is to be couched, and in terms of which the demand for public accountability is legitimate. If this trend continues and gains more support, the very intellectual enterprise itself will be in danger. What is to be done?

I shall first make a few distinctions and refinements, then take up a short excursus on technology. I will then concentrate on one major issue in which, in my opinion, we have to put our own house in order:

problem choice in scholarship and science. Finally, I shall ask the question: Can science be redirected to avert the frontal attack on its legitimacy?

2. Some Distinctions

In a recent lecture held at the American Academy of Arts and Sciences in Boston, Carl Schorske compared the music and world-views of Gustav Mahler and Charles Ives—both were populist subverters of the established musical order. They fought the "Cartesian view of the world [which] saw the surface heterogeneities of the physical universe to be unified by rational principles immanent in Nature."[3] They both introduced 'vulgar' folk-music and shattered "the pure but confining ideas of consistency and coherence that had governed the classical tradition."[4] And, once more: "In the same era when Nietzsche and Freud opened the intellectual order of reason to the psychological claims of repressed instinct, Mahler and Ives opened the musical order of reason to the repressed musics of the common man, past and present."[5]

This was an antirational revolt with vulgar, popular elements, yet it was also a battle waged by intellectuals for the sake of other intellectuals. Similar antirational trends in science repeatedly occurred in the past, and their representatives were scientists debating with other scientists. The tension and critical dialogue between rational and antirational approaches to nature, between the quest for unity and the quest for diversity, is the most important source of creativity and innovation. It is not to be mistaken for the other recurring pattern in history: the attack by the ignorant on the very legitimacy of intellectuals' mode of thought and not less on the intellectuals' style of life. Thus, it is important to distinguish attacks from within from those outside the intellectual community. Yet the two different phenomena[6] are not disconnected, and intellectuals' populism often supplies some of the tools for the vulgar attack on science, just as the ideology of the vulgar antiscience movement often supports the spirit and zeal of the intellectual antirationalist. This interaction has to be carefully studied.

One further distinction seems appropriate. Lay attacks on science and scientific rationality do not occur only from what is calle 'the left,' involving romantic, holistic nostalgia for feeling and nature as against cold rationality and technological exploitation of nature and man, which thus dehumanizes man and denaturalizes nature. Dangerous and counterproductive as this attack may be, it is at least not couched in nationalistic language—rather it belongs to youthful, somewhat immature international antiscience groups, environmentalist 'greens,' etc. Much more dangerous is the 'right-wing' fundamentalist, populist attack on the very core of the scientific ethos, namely, its internationality. The ideology of those who attack the scientific community from the right is: let science serve the direct interests of our group, social layer, or nation, if it is to justify our investment in it.

As an example of this nationalistic mood, we read in a recent editorial of *Science* the warning: "It is of real concern that, within this decade, admission of foreign graduate students to U.S. research universities, presentation at international forums of frontier work by American researchers, and collaboration with colleagues abroad in areas perceived as key to the country's international standing may be considered as contrary to U.S. interests as would be internationalization of the corn belt."[7] The danger applies to other countries as well—remember the effort of the British U.G.C. to introduce different fees for foreign students who wish to study in Britain. The rationale for this attack from the right is often formulated and used by intellectuals who belong to the scientific community.

A further distinction has to be made between the demand for understanding what sciences and scientists are about and the demand for a detailed control of the whole scientific enterprise. This distinction is important because of the seemingly new and unprecedented fact that with modern technologies we can do things without understanding them—the exact opposite of what we have been accustomed to for hundreds of years. This point is forcefully made by Joseph Weizenbaum: he talks of "the near impossibility of relating modern scientific understanding to the real world and to human wisdom."[8] His examples:

> ... the order of magnitude of the half-life of certain elementary particles is a pico-second ($10-12$ sec) on one extreme, and of others at the opposite extreme a mega-year (3×10^{13} sec). Neither time nor space is comprehensible to the human mind ... Philip Morrison, the MIT physicist has computed how long an American freight train, each of whose cars is filled to capacity with TNT would have to be in order, that its load of TNT would be one megaton: 30,000 cars long. ... We have now many computer programs which require that on the order of 1×10^{13} computorial events occur faultlessly in order for the program to be executed without error. ... I believe that the essential comprehensibility of computer systems provides a kind of core metaphor for much else going on in modern science and technology.[9]

Historians never took seriously the often repeated claim that 'this time it is really different.' Yet, funny as it may sound, this time it may be really different! Or so Weizenbaum claims. Is it indeed so? Or is it a temporary situation? In any case we must take this into account. More importantly, antiscience attacks often concentrate on attacking the very nature of science and of rational argument. There is an ongoing scientific-philosophical debate as to what constitutes valid scientific knowledge—as to what science is. Despite the divergence of opinions, there is almost a consensus about some characteristics of science: science is characterized by a drive for order; it presupposes the intelligibility of nature; it seeks experimental confirmation of its claims; it insists on internal coherence of its theoretical structures; it aims at as complete a view of the world as possible; it seeks the quantifiable aspects; it aims at predictivity; its ideals are images of knowledge, such as: objectivity, repeatability, quantifiability, etc. Each and every one of these is often under attack both from inside and without. The distinction to which I wish to draw attention is that it is not the contents of the attack in themselves that characterize it as antiscience or antirational, but rather the identity of those who are doing the attacking. Bacon attacked scholastic ratiocination in the name of empirical science; as early as the fourth century B.C. Aristotle attacked in rational political terms mathematics as a nonpractical luxury; nineteenth and twentieth-century evolutionary biologists often attacked reductionism and scientism. These were not really antiscience attacks. On the other hand, the names and theories of intellectuals, such as Nietzsche or in our own days Herbert Marcuse, were used to attack the very use of rational argument.

It is also important to distinguish the rational elements in the fear of science from the irrational opposition to it. Harvey Brooks makes this point:

> In all probability nothing has engendered fear of science as much as some of its major by-products: weapons of mass destruction, toxic and polluting synthetic chemicals, manmade radioactivity, depersonalizing applications of computers, and large-scale impersonal organizations made possible by modern information technology and communications.[10]

For a better understanding of these currents, it is important to study in detail the interaction between the antiscience trends inside science and the 'external,' antirational attacks. Such a study is initiated in an extremely interesting recent book by Richard Olson.[11]

3. The Aims of Knowledge—a Special Distinction

An additional distinction that can only be hinted at here is between the different aims of knowledge as held by different cultures and at different times. The first issue is the biological role that intellectual pursuit has for the human species. If we hold with Aristotle[12] and the vulgar Marxists (not Marx himself) that the species seeks to satisfy its physical needs before it can afford cultural pursuits, then science and technology are, so to speak, the result of a cultural choice; if, on the other hand, we believe that man is a cultural species in the sense that his intellectual—artistic preoccupations are as primordial, biologically speaking, as his concentration on his physical well-being, then there is no question whether we should have science or rather stick to our pristine innocence by not pursuing it.[13] This results in a debate on the aims of knowledge, and—whether an intellectual field emerges as a response to a utilitarian quest or the exact opposite—is again a dialogue among intellectuals. Olson reminds us that Herodotus saw the origins of geometry in the need for parcelling out land in Egypt while later Aristotle saw in geometry a result of leisure. In the mid-fifth century, Proclus agreed that pure knowledge was more dignified than utilitarian knowledge, but united the views of Herodotus and Aristotle. The serious external attack comes from popular Gnostic movements, which attack all science, nay all rational intellectual activity. This is a genuine clash between the intellectual community and strong 'external' antirational forces.

It is paradoxical and interesting that the seventeenth century, which, starting with Bacon, emphasized more than ever before the utilitarian aspect of science and technology, actually never delivered the goods. That very period when the utilitarian image of knowledge became the strongest advocate and legitimator of science and technology, when the argument was first clearly formulated that all 'pure sciences' would sooner or later lead to practical results for the benefit of man, actually saw "no dramatic major alteration in the way in which men earned their living, grew their food, transported themselves and their goods, communicated with one another, attacked their enemies and defended their countries, cured diseases and protected their health."[14] The claim turned out to be justified only from the nineteenth century onward—it is still with us and used in all arguments for requesting research funds. Again a fascinating tension: while the community of scholars leads a life of scientific research and considers it as the only possible way of life, indeed, as a road to salvation, it argues for its support by society in the name of utilitarianism. While its quest for truth is passionate and 'religious' (in a broad sense of the term), its propaganda uses objectivity and the dispassionate search for truth for the benefit of man as its legitimization. An activity, a way of life (a monastery, a via moderna . . .) that in the Middle Ages, Renaissance, and early Reformation allowed the individual to seek salvation needed no further justification. Now, beginning in the seventeenth century and continuing to our own times, an individual soteriology is considered self-indulgence and has to be justified in terms of its contribution to the well-being of mankind or at least of society. The mirror image of this state of affairs is that an activity is attacked and attempts are made to prohibit it if it involves potential danger to society. Society pays for the welfare of society; it is not responsible for the happiness or salvation of the individual. The aims of knowledge are formulated only in terms of collective representations.

4. Technology as a Bone of Contention: from the Middle Ages to Our Times

Clearly the cultural role of technology is a bone of contention in the antiscience debate. The often heard simplistic argument of the antiscience movement is that science and technology are Siamese twins, that technology is the golem of capitalist society, that it is impersonal and thus potentially cruel, and in deep contrast to our most cherished human values. Thus, if we wish to save humanity or at least to ensure the humane nature of man, we should either tame and humanize the sciences and technology, or, if we cannot—and there is enough to prove that so far we have not succeeded—then let us abolish science and technology, pay the price in comfort and riches, and settle in Arcadia or Walden.

The presuppositions in the above formulation are: that science and technology are inseparably linked; that science is basic research, while technology is applications; that science or technology as such are not value free; that a primitive, nontechnology based life is more humane; that science or rather the quest for knowledge can be abolished for ideological reasons; and finally, that Walden exists outside ourselves.

The conservative establishment of the scientific community has its own fairly simplistic response to the above argument. According to the establishment, basic scientific research is a response to a fundamental human quest for knowledge and involves the pursuit of truth; science and technology are indeed value free, in so far as they produce the objective results of their research; society is free to decide how to use these results—for the benefit of mankind or for its detriment. Moreover, the balance between the beneficial uses of science and technology and their harmful application is still heavily tilted in favor of the former. Finally, a fully computerized, labor-saving, food producing, and leisure-supporting world *is* Walden, not a "Brave New World."

Both of these attitudes were given here in their most simplistic formulation, but it will serve no purpose to refine them. Rather, let me concentrate on some basic disagreements that I have with both approaches, and, especially, let me point out when the two, in an unholy alliance, merely reinforce each other.

First, technology is not at the mere applicative end of a continuum, at the other end of which is basic science. Science differs from technology mainly in the *aims of knowledge*—not in its problem choice or method. Knowledge can be seen to serve for the glory of God, for the pursuit of truth, for subjugating nature or other people, for climbing the social ladder, for impressing others or oneself. Technology is generally perceived as the pursuit of ways of subjugating nature, and its problem choice is suitable to that purpose. In the framework of this quest, some basic scientific problems have to be solved—sometimes by 'goal-oriented' engineers and sometimes by 'basic' scientists. The present-day sharp distinction is a result of professionalization and the modern equivalent of guild formation, rather than a genuine description of the intellectual content, i.e., the body of knowledge. Indeed, for many an illustrious student of nature in the seventeenth, eighteenth, or even nineteenth century, it is difficult to say whether he was a scientist or an engineer! Were Robert Hooke, Antoine Lavoisier, Oliver Heaviside, William Thompson scientists, or grand masters of technology? For that matter is the laser a technical invention or a scientific discovery?

Once a problem is chosen, whether in science or in technology, work progresses towards its solution, and if we disregard fraud or self-delusion, the activity is value free. However, the most important aspect of both their activities, namely, problem choice, is not value free (on this more below).

It is often claimed that technology was always an antihumane activity, and the only difference today is that it has grown to dangerous dimensions. Lynn White[15] in one of his beautiful studies on technology shows that the spiritual value of hard work is not of Calvinist origin, but has Judaeo-Christian roots. He reminds us of the Benedictine Regula Magistri: "laborare est orare," in the wake of which medieval "moral enthusiasm for engines" followed. As a result of the identification of advanced technology with high morality, the Renaissance raised the classical virtue of *temperantia* to become one of the more prominent cardinal virtues; its "essential character had become Measure," and it became identified with technology.

> About 1450 the novel productive system of Europe, based on natural power, mechanization and labor-saving invention, which has been the backbone of capitalism, received the sanction of religious emotion and moral sensibility. The iconography of Temperance furnishes pointer-readings of pressure not easily identified by other means. . . . The late medieval affirmation that technological advance is morally benign was effectively unanimous.[16]

Another, powerful formulation of Lynn White's point is "The Virgin and the Dynamo are not opposing principles permeating the universe; they are allies."[17]

The Benedictine rule was in opposition to the classical scorn of manual work. Lopez reminds us that "Seneca confessed to admiring sculpture but despising sculptors because they dirtied their hands," and that in the sixth century Cassiodorus "eliminated from the gentlemanly course of studies the only practical crafts that Varro had included it it, medicine and architecture"; even in the twelfth century, "when Hugh St. Victor tried to put in a good word for what he called the adultarine science of mechanics, he recommended it only as a plebeian study intended to cater for material needs."[18] Thus, again a change of images: medieval acceptance of technology even though its manual work aspect has to be forgiven. By the seventeenth century, great scientists will try to mute the criticism that their speculation is arrogant by showing the experimental-crafts-connected nature of their science, and these characteristics symbolize modesty, humility, and harmlessness from the point of view of religious sentiments. Hooke, Huygens, and even Newton were seen and often wished to be seen as mechanical inventors.

In the Middle Ages, and during the Renaissance, actually up to the eighteenth century, antiscience and antirational trends were not directed against technology. It was only the Industrial Revolution and the ensuing social changes that resulted in the Luddite and other similar antitechnology movements.[19] Thus, what actually happened was a complete turn:

We are not afraid of pure science, which we identify with the dispassionate quest for truth, but uneasy about applied science, or technology,
which is powerful but may be used for evil as well as for good. In the
Middle Ages, the opposite view prevailed: there was fear of scientific
speculation for its own sake, a legitimate but dangerous path which could
lead closer to God, the supreme truth, or mislead to the Devil.[20]

As we have seen above, technology was considered beneficial or
at least harmless because it *did not constitute a threat to salvation.* Today
technology does constitute such a threat in the eyes of many. Does, on
the other hand, science, pure and speculative, answer the perennial
soteriological quest, albeit in a new form?

5. Science as a Doctrine of Salvation

The thumbnail sketch of history given in the first section of this
paper can be looked at in another way: from the point of view of the
quest for salvation. Whatever the core of a culture is—religion, arts,
politics, or science—that core must have in its framework a soteriological guidance that must be open and available to all. While the framework may be created and worked out by the intellectuals, it must be
so formulated that the road is open to all who seek salvation; otherwise
a major attack on all privileged access to salvation will be pitilessly
launched by the vulgar.

The attitudes of Christian Europe and later of the whole Western
world towards science and technology—or rather towards knowledge
in general—were heavily influenced first by Augustine's own personal
synthesis between Christian dogma and pagan Neoplatonic philosophy; this synthesis constituted Augustinian soteriology; then came the
Thomistic synthesis between revived Aristotelianism and the dogmas
of the Catholic Church, the first fully established and powerful conceptual framework since the fifth-century synthesis of Augustine; finally
from the thirteenth century onward, the tension and ongoing dialogue
between the Augustinian and Thomistic attitudes to knowledge helped
shape the intellectual mood of the Renaissance, the Reformation, the
Counter-Reformation, and finally the modern, Western, capitalistic
world-view, according to which *knowledge* and *especially science lead to
salvation.*

Augustine is ambivalent about the role of secular knowledge. Secular knowledge *(scientia),* although it may lead to divine knowledge,
may also lead mankind astray—man being evil and sinful. In any case

divine knowledge *(sapienta)* is enough; this can be easily gained from reading the Scriptures, which are easily understandable. In Augustine we find the root of the later Lutheran "the meaning is in the text."[21] As Lopez[22] shows, the Jesuit *Enciclopedia Cattolica* follows Aquinas in describing three attitudes towards the pursuit for knowledge: "Too little interest in knowledge is 'culpable ignorance,' a vice; a natural amount of interest is 'studiousness," a virtue; an excessive craving for knowledge is 'curiosity,' a sin."[23] This approach allowed one to investigate nature without, however, transgressing the limit of the search. God provided the complete theory of the world, and there was no need for any human replacement. This meant that more and better people (intellectually speaking) permitted themselves to apply rational thought to natural phenomena and expected from themselves greater precision and concreteness. These same people also dabbled in magic, as part of secular knowledge; as long as it did not interfere with religious wisdom and was not too blatantly practiced, it, too, was acceptable. All this new knowledge stemming from technology, mechanical studies, magic, alchemy, astrology, and engineering was either taught at the universities or practiced and taught privately by the same scholars who taught at the universities.

In Augustine's world *scientia* cannot lead to salvation. In the work of Thomas Aquinas and in his synthesis, the seeds are sown for a full legitimation of "studiousness" as a virtue and thus a prerequisite of the road to salvation. Occam's attack on the Thomistic synthesis further emphasized secular, even empirical, knowledge, as a fully legitimate enterprise separate from and independent of faith. After the Reformation, the reaffirmation of the Augustinian "the meaning is in the text," which presupposed one, natural interpretation and violently opposed a rationalistic, multiinterpretative, Thomistic Catholicism, the debate opened on all levels: literalism versus hermeneutics, realism versus instrumentalism, empiricism versus rationalism, critical constructive scepticism versus lethal, gnawing doubt. This complex, multifaceted debate temporarily coincided with the breakdown of medieval hierarchies in the Renaissance, with astronomical and scientific discoveries shattering the old view of the world of nature and the world of man. The fundamental issue was: Can knowledge lead to salvation, and if yes, which kind of knowledge? By the end of the seventeenth century, after heavy destruction in Europe following the religious wars, a growing number of intellectuals sought a contemplative style of life, followed their quest for knowledge of a kind to which maximum possible consensus applied, and increasingly considered this quest and this way of life as the surest way to salvation. Science as soteriology (i.e., a doctrine of salvation) was on the way.

Though not formulated in these terms, the idea of a soteriological role of modern science permeates the thinking of John Passmore.[24] The social role of knowledge occupied him in his magisterial *The Perfectibility of Man* (1970), in his *Man's Responsibility for Nature,* and then in his excellent *Science and Its Critics* (1972) dedicated to this very issue. His perspective is long term and genuinely historical, his cultural-religious interest is comparative and his view of knowledge is broad, comprehensive, and detailed in a sophisticated way. Passmore gives a thoughtful and sympathetic analysis of the humanistic antiscience mode of thought and gently chastises positivistic science for sometimes overshooting the mark in its over optimism, but in the last resort, he is a staunch defender of modern science, its aims and methods. He remarks on the last page of *Science and Its Critics:*

> Whatever our decision on particular questions, we most certainly never forget in the flurry of reappraisal that aristoscience has brought us great gifts, both intellectual and practical. It has made plain how much can be achieved by intellectual cooperation, by imagination and hard work in close alliance by high standards of honesty, directness, and concern for truth. "Scientists," C.S. Pierce once wrote "are the best of men." No scientist myself, I am still inclined to think that this is true. . . .

In other words, despite all, science is a road to salvation!

In his book, Passmore distinguishes the different types of anti-science moods among humanist intellectuals: extreme sceptics like Blake[25] as against the limited dogma of scepticism of Kierkegaard or F. H. Bradley. Following Hume, many scientists and agnostics denied that science could ever discover nature's hidden causes or essences, and the various branches of positivism and paradoxically also of religious metaphysics attacked the over optimistic claims of Bacon, Descartes, and their followers, according to which science discovers the "causes and secret motions of things."[26] All this is intrascience. There are debates or fights, if you wish, between antiscience intellectuals and those who represent what Passmore ingeniously called *aristoscience* ("the most prestige-earning kind of science"[27]). Aristoscientists are the intellectual elite, the modern equivalent to the medieval theologians. "Aristoscience does generate an attitude to the world which is peculiarly favorable to its technological transformation, peculiarly unfavorable to the contemplation of nature or its sensuous enjoyment.

This arises from the fact that science in its aristoscientific form has a special concern: to look at the world sub specie aeternitatis."[28]

6. Problem Choice in Science and the *Redirection of Science*

"Science in its aristoscientific form" is indeed what has failed to become that superdiscipline to which a consensus of all intellectuals and laymen alike could appeal as showing the road to salvation and in the framework of which all could agree that all metaphysical differences can be hammered out in a critical dialogue. Indeed, its concern is "to look at the world sub specie aeternitatis," thus objectivizing and the dehumanizing the intellectual enterprise. It is this form of science that introduced the demon of freedom from values. Around the ideal of value free science, the unholy alliance was created between positivistic-scientific practitioners of science, and positivistic-nonscientific politicians. These practitioners seek freedom from responsibility by claiming that in their pure pursuit of truth they only deal with fact finding; their results are then deposited in the hands of the policy maker and politician to apply them as they see fit. The politicians, on the other hand, justify their support of science by claiming that they represent the general population and act for its benefit and will see to it that the value-free results of scientific research be used to the best social purposes. Both groups accept that science and its results are predetermined, that the road to truth is one, and that the discipline dictates its own problem choice.

But this is not true. Physics does not tell us what to research, nor does biology. Problem choice is a social decision, not only in terms of trivially true social considerations, such as feasibility, career-promoting value, grantability, competition considerations, etc., but also in the cognitive considerations in terms of which problem choice is usually put: interesting, important, frontiers of knowledge, beautiful, of high symmetry, simple, mathematically formulable, etc. These are often considered as determined by the discipline, but when looked at carefully, they are the real socially determined images of knowledge. Thus, if the intellectuals and the community at large are to accept science and scholarship as the legitimate domain of a superframework, then there must be agreement on the images of knowledge that influence problem choice.

This brings me to my last normative point about science. To eliminate or at least weaken the attack on science, we must interfere with science. To announce repeatedly that science is objective, value free, autonomous, and thus answering a basic human need for a quest for truth will not do. On the other hand, science is autonomous, value free, and as objective as one can ever get, once its problems have been formulated, and its practitioners are working towards solutions. The only point where redirection is possible and thus genuine dialogue between scientists and laymen is open is in spelling out the images of knowledge held by society at large and by the scientific communities in its midst. In terms of their images of knowledge, problem choice can be discussed in a way understood by all; after that, even if on the final choice there is no agreement, a framework will have been established in which the critical dialogue or problems to be chosen can be conducted. Thus, a new superframework can be created. It is the fundamental, self-imposed task of intellectuals to help define and delimit that conceptual framework, which will then be considered the shared superframework for all critical dialogues. Individuals or small groups have in the past and will probably again in the future create the language and images of knowledge that constitute such a framework, but only with the help of the intellectual community at large will it be accepted and established as a shared framework. Only the existence of and consensus about such a framework can save a culture from total intellectual disarray, and thus make possible a fruitful, cooperative dialogue on the source and aims of knowledge between intellectuals and society.

Notes

1. Clifford Geertz, *Negara: The Theatre State in Nineteenth-Century Bali* (Princeton University Press, 1980).

2. Richard Rorty, "Nineteenth-Century Idealism and Twentieth Century Textualism," in *Consequences of Pragmatism* (Harvester Press, 1982), 149.

3. *Bulletin of the American Association for the Advancement of Science* XXXVII (1983), no. 1, 20

4. *Ibid.,* 21

5. *Ibid.*

6. This distinction is rarely made. A recent volume to which we shall refer often is A. S. Markovits and K. W. Deutsch (eds.), *Fear of Science—Trust in Science* (Cambridge, Mass., 1980). From among the many distinguished historians and students of science, only Harvey Brooks makes this point: "It must be admitted that much public fear and distrust of science has been fostered from within the scientific community itself, not by the lay "enemies" of science. If one looks at the source of opposition to large technological

projects, one always finds that the original impetus came from scientists, usually a minority who chose to appeal to the majority of their colleagues," in Markovits and Deutsch, 100.

7.   Anne Keatley, Senior Executive Staff Officer, National Research Council, Washington, D.C. 20418, in *Science,* 18 November 1983, Vol. 222, no. 4625.

8.   Joseph Weizenbaum, "Fear of Science—Trust in Science: A Meditation," in Markovits and Deutsch (eds.), *op.cit.,* 130.

9.   *Ibid.,* 131–132.

10.   H. Brooks, *op. cit.,* 105

11.   Richard Olson, *Science Deified and Science Defied* (University of California Press, 1982). For me, his book illustrates what I, following a series of studies by Clifford Geertz, called elsewhere: "Science as a Cultural System." See Yehuda Elkana, "A Programmatic Attempt at an Anthropology of Knowledge," in E. Mendelsohn and Y. Elkana (eds.), *Sciences and Cultures,* (D. Reidel, 1981). This way of looking at Olson's book is mine, and I am not sure whether he would agree with it.

12.   Exs: Aristotle in *Metaphysics* 981 b 20–25: "Hence all such inventions [i.e., those produced for necessities and conveniences of society] were already established, the sciences which deal neither with the necessities nor the enjoyment of life were discovered. And this took place earliest in the place where man first began to have leisure. That is why the mathematical arts were founded in Egypt, for there the priestly caste was allowed to be at leisure," as quoted by Richard Olson, *op. cit.,* 31.

13.   A. Marshack, *The Roots of Civilization.*

14.   This important insight is formulated by I. Bernard Cohen "The Fear and Distrust of Science in Historical Perspectives: Some First Thoughts," in Markovits and Deutsch (eds.), *op. cit.,* 35.

15.   Lynn White, "Temperantia and the Virtuousness of Technology," in T. K. Rabb and J. E. Seigl (eds.), *Action and Conviction in Early Modern Europe* (Princeton, N.J., 1969), 197–219. Reprinted in Lynn White, *Medieval Religion & Technology* (University of Calif. Press, 1978), 181–205.

16.   White, *Medieval Religion and Technology,* 217–219.

17.   Lynn White, "Dynamo and Virgin Reconsidered," in Lynn White, *Machina ex Deo* (The MIT Press, 1968), 72.

18.   Robert S. Lopez, "Wisdom Science and Mechanics: The Three Tiers of Medieval Knowledge and the Forbidden Fourth," in Markovits and Deutsch, *op. cit.,* 18.

19.   For a contemporary discussion of the phenomenon, see Dan Lyons, "Are Luddites Confused?" Inquiry 22 (1979), 381–403.

20.   Lopez, *op. cit.,* 15–16.

21.   For Augustine, see Peter Brown's magisterial, *Augustine of Hippo* (University of Calif. Press, 1967). For Augustinian influence on the Reformation, see *Heiko Oberman, Masters of the Reformation.*

22.   Robert Lopez, *op. cit.,* 16.

23. *Ibid.*

24. John Passmore, *The Perfectibility of Man* (N.Y. 1970); *Man's Responsibility for Nature: Ecological Problems and Western Traditions* (N.Y. 1974); *Science and Its Critics* (N.J. 1978).

25. Passmore, *Science and Its Critics*, 3.

26. *Ibid.*

27. *Ibid.*, 52.

28. *Ibid.*, 64. While I agree with the breadth and sophisticatedness of this point of view, I miss in it a clear distinction between opposition from within the intellectual community and the attack from without; the emphasis on the role of the critical dialogue between opposing views among the intellectuals as well as the role of the external attack in calling forth new legitimizing points of view leading to new types of creativity; the conclusion, which should follow from the historical point of view, that not only is there no science 'sub specie aeternitatis,' but there is no direct correlation between given bodies of knowledge or social groups and an antiscience or the opposite point of view. The core group of an intellectual elite is sometimes for science and sometimes antiscience; sometimes imagination is on the side of humanity opposing technology, while at other times and in another body of knowledge, humanistic technology opposes inhuman, antirational obscurantism.

The Epistemology of
The Disillusionment with Science

WILLIAM R. SHEA

Introduction

Civilization is a very thin veneer. Scratch the surface and you find not the noble savage, but man in the raw. In his essay, "The Epistemology of the Opposition to Science," Yehuda Elkana has wrestled mightily with the threat posed to reason and knowledge by the contemporary anti-intellectual backlash.[1] He stresses that scientists themselves are largely to blame for failing to provide a coherent platform to consider, evaluate, improve, or reject the outcome of current scientific practice. But whatever the nature of our current predicament, since the Scientific Revolution of the seventeenth century the so-called developed nations have been propelled to eminence by science and technology, and other countries have followed suit or long to do so. Jawaharlal Nehru, the great Indian leader and prime minister, was not unique in his frequently repeated belief that *the* answer to all the problems of his subcontinent was science.[2]

We have become less sanguine in our expectations, and science has lost much of its pristine glamor. Contemporary sensibilities, among the educated and the uneducated alike, are easily alarmed by a science that is suspected of creating long-term woes in its eagerness to secure short-term benefits. It has become difficult to talk about the advancement of science without having its burdens, real or imagined, thrust to the fore. A few decades ago, science was described as Promethean; it now seems more Mephistophelean, and what is being questioned is not some peripheral application of science and technology, but the very nature of the scientific enterprise itself. Our civilization, characterized by science and until recently revelling in such a description, is undergoing a soul-searching experience that is dangerous, not because it is visceral (this only shows that it is deeply felt), but because it is generally couched in a language that is frought with irrational imagery. Whereas it sufficed, not so long ago, to dismiss an objection on the grounds that it was not scientific, it is now up to the person who presents an argument as scientific to prove its validity in broader (e.g.,

189

social, political, ecological) terms. If we are brought back to the beginning, it is not to give names to "all the birds of the air and all the beasts of the field" (**Genesis** 2, 20), but to be mocked by the serpent and told, "Your eyes will be opened" (**Genesis** 3, 5).

The sudden inability to discuss calmly and serenely (I was almost tempted to write "scientifically") the uses and abuses of science has become a feature of the cultural climate of this departing twentieth century. Elkana rightly points out that problems of such an overarching nature can only be suitably addressed if there is a common language in which they can be posed and answered. But I would urge that, above and beyond a common idiom, we need a shared ideal, perhaps a collective myth, if we are to journey together towards truth. Elkana reminds us of the role played by the ideal of the *polis* for the Greeks and the *respublica christiana* for the Middle Ages. These key words served to focus the discussion because they were acknowledged as goals towards which the whole community (indeed, the entire civilization) was willing to strive. The means to this end were the object of intense and frequently acrimonious debate, but the ends themselves were perceived as beacons for all wayfarers whatever their individual road, pace, or companions.

Can we learn something from this? Thumbnail sketches of history are bound to differ according to the vantage point from which they are drawn, and my own would probably emphasize aspects of the landscape that Elkana has left out, but I would agree entirely with him when he states that modern science acquired soteriological connotations. When the medieval synthesis was shattered into the several confessions of the Reformation, the wars of religion that followed provided evidence that man has to live not by revelation alone, but by reason. The disagreement of philosophers and the much vaunted unanimity of scientists ensured that only the latter were recognized as the genuine spokesmen of reason. By the nineteenth century, science had become a new church in which scientists presided over the twin rituals of computing and experimenting. But the church did not go unchallenged, and I wish in the following pages to examine the two major assaults to which science has been subjected. The first was at the hands of the Romantics in the nineteenth century. The second is the one we are now experiencing and which, I believe, is much more serious because it is mounted by enemies from inside as well as from outside the camp. It is an intellectual crisis with moral overtones, and it accounts for the disillusionment with science and the scientific worldview that many profess.

The Scientific Revolution and the Romantic Imagination

Science as we know it and the scientific method as we practice it were fashioned in the seventeenth century by two or three generations of brilliant minds whose eponyms are Bacon, Galileo, Descartes, and Newton. The mechanical philosophy they devised may be described in a general way as mathematical physics or the successful combination of the techniques of computation with the art of experimentation. A blend of idealization and contrivance unlocked the secrets of nature, and scientists were buoyed by a feeling that they had finally mastered the language of nature itself. Bacon, who saw himself as performing for the senses "the office of a true priest"[3] prophesied, with all the eloquence of a Lord Chancellor, that science would "establish and extend the power and dominion of the human race over the universe."[4] Descartes expressed the conviction that his new philosophy would enable us "to know the power and action of fire, water, air, the stars, the heavens and all the other bodies in our environment . . . and thus make ourselves the lords and masters of nature."[5] Better still, it would revolutionize medicine and prolong life. He confided to Constantin Huygens that he hoped to live more than 100 years,[6] and his close friend and translator, the abbé Picot (unperturbed by the fact that Descartes died in Sweden of pneumonia at the age of 53), claimed that he had discovered how to "make men live four or five hundred years."[7] As for Newton, improving our physical surroundings or our physical health was not enough, and he saw science as a means to a higher morality:

> And if natural Philosophy in all its Parts, by pursuing this Method, shall at length be perfected, the Bounds of Moral Philosophy will also be enlarged. For so far as we can know by natural Philosophy what is the first Cause, what Power he has over us, and what Benefits we receive from him, so far our Duty toward him, as well as that toward one another, will appear to us by the light of Nature.[8]

Despite his unbounded faith in science, Bacon was too much of a politician not to recognize the dangers inherent in the extension of man's dominion over nature. What was to guarantee, for instance, that the new learning would not be put to base use or perverted to evil ends? Bacon did not face this issue squarely in the *Novum Organum,* but there is a brief and remarkable passage in the Utopian *New Atlantis* in which he acknowledges the need for protecting science from foolish or vicious exploitation at the hands of politicians:

we have consultations, which of the inventions and experiences which we have discovered shall be published, and which not: and take all an oath of secrecy, for the concealing of those which we think fit to keep secret: though some of those we do reveal to the state, and some not.[9]

Galileo, Descartes, and Newton were not even visited by such limited doubts, and in the following generation, science became another name for reason and objectivity. Newton's *Opticks* was celebrated in verse, and Pope may be said to have captured the spirit of the age when he wrote his famous epitaph:

> Nature and Nature's laws lay hid in night,
> God said, 'Let Newton be!' and all was light.

Less than a century later, a group of poets met in London in the studio of the painter Benjamin Haydon on 28 December 1817. In his diary, Haydon tells us how Wordsworth,

in a strain of humour beyond description, abused me for putting Newton's head into my picture; 'a fellow,' said he, 'who believed nothing unless it was as clear as the three sides of a triangle.' And then Keats agreed that he had destroyed all the poetry of the rainbow by reducing it to its prismatic colours. It was impossible to resist him, and we all drank 'Newton's health, and confusion to mathematics.'[10]

Not long after this toast, Keats wrote the familiar lines in *Lamia:*

> Do not all charms fly
> At the mere touch of cold philosophy?
> There was an awful rainbow once in heaven:
> We know her woof, her texture; she is given
> In the dull catalogue of common things.
> Philosophy will clip an Angel's wings,
> Conquer all mysteries by rule and line,
> Empty the haunted air, and gnomed mine—
> Unweave a rainbow. . . .

The wheel of fortune had come full circle. Worshipped, almost deified by the Augustan poets for his successful explanation of the nature of light, Newton was now damned for destroying its numinous character. But science withstood this onslaught, partly because the image of the scientist as a solitary thinker appealed to the Romantics, but more importantly because science remained intelligible and useful. A striking instance of this commonality of science can be seen in

Jefferson's democratic concern with the improvement and dissemination of new technology.

An engineer at heart, but a farmer to the bones, Jefferson never failed to examine the agricultural implements that were used in the countries he visited. As Minister to France in 1788, he was struck by the unwieldy plough that the peasants used, and he proceeded to design a better mouldboard that would raise the soil at a proper angle, so that it would topple by its own weight. Three years later, back in America, he described his progress as follows:

> I have imagined and executed a Mould board which may be mathematically demonstrated to be perfect, as far as perfection depends on mathematical principles, and one great circumstance in its favour is that it may be made by the most bungling carpenter and cannot possibly vary by a hair's breadth in its form but by gross negligence.[11]

In 1805, he took off half a day from his onerous duties as President of the United States to recalculate the shape that the mouldboard and the ploughshare should have to offer the least resistance. He published his design, and presented a model to the American Philosophical Society. He also planned to have the plough cast in iron for widespread distribution. In 1808, he came across an article about an improved plough in a French journal, and he arranged to have one shipped to America despite the embargo that his government had placed on French goods. He tested it with a dynamometer and had the great pleasure of finding it inferior to his own version. Jefferson also promoted the contour method of ploughing instead of straight furrows to avoid the erosion that ruined agriculture on hilly ground.

Jefferson's procedure is an excellent illustration of what the "scientific method" is supposed to be all about: the research is motivated by the quest for a practical solution to a socially significant problem; the design is an application of mathematics to physics (i.e., calculating the best angle for moving weights); the model is subjected to experimental testing; the results are published; the model is improved for mass production; and the invention is seen to benefit both people and land.

Achievements of this nature, and the triumphs of medicine, notably pasteurization and vaccination, ensured that science retained public support. Even the railway (against which Wordsworth railed) contributed to the alleviation of man's woes, not only by making travel faster and more comfortable, but by making people aware that human beings need not starve, and hence that they were morally responsible because they could do something about it. The outcome was public recognition of science as the embodiment of rationality, and this great consensus is illustrated in the writings of historians, philosophers, and sociologists of science alike.

Science as Rationality

The popular conception of science as inevitably progressing received its canonical formulation (and an apparently immaculate geometrical presentation) in George Sarton's *The Study of the History of Science* first published in 1936 and reissued in 1957:

> *Definition:* Science is systematized positive knowledge or what has been taken as such at different ages and in different places.
> *Theorem:* The acquisition and sytematization of positive knowledge are the only human activities which are truly cumulative and progressive.
> *Corollary:* The history of science is the only history which can illustrate the progress of mankind. In fact, progress has no definite and unquestionable meaning in fields other than the field of science.[12]

Among philosophers of science, logical positivists took it for granted that science is culturally unique and sharply distinguished from other fields such as philosophy, theology, or literary criticism. It was clear that consensus was possible in science, whereas it was a forlorn hope elsewhere. This was assumed to be the case because science dealt with matters of fact (as opposed to armchair theories) and resolved its disputes by invoking appropriate rules of inference (instead of mere rhetoric). Given this climate of opinion, it comes as no surprise that Popper saw the most important task of epistemology as the demarcation between science and nonscience. Where philosophers of science differed was in the interpretation of the evidentiary rules. Some, following John Stuart Mill, believed that these rules were already at hand and merely had to be "unpacked" or codified; others, less sanguine, felt that the kit was sitll incomplete. Some emphasized the logical side of theories; others stressed the empirical. But all, whether more mathematically or more empirically minded, concurred that such rules existed and accounted for both scientific agreement and scientific progress. Should the rules fail to yield an immediate solution, all that was required was the gathering of more facts. Disagreement among scientists was only possible when the evidence was too thin or too vague. The scientific method itself was unassailable since it implicitly relied on an inductive logic whose canons philosophers like Carnap and Reichenbach looked forward to explicating in short order.[13]

The view that science possesses a unique set of progressive norms was also embraced by sociologists of science. In a characteristic utterance, Robert Merton listed these norms as "universalism, communism, disinterestedness, and organized scepticism,"[14] as if there was nothing incongruous in lumping together intellectual, moral, and political qualities.

This unquestioning consensus combined the hallmarks of a dogma with the messianic promise of the good life for all. The challenge to this creed was slow to come because the devotees were able to shift their ground from the empirical lowlands to the logical heights or *vice versa* when they were attacked. In the end, they were routed on both fronts.[15]

The intellectual crisis that spelled the demise of this consensus may be considered as a fourfold argument, two of a more historical and two of a more philosophical nature.

Neither Intelligible nor Good

Dissent is endemic in science

The "scientific methodology" that all scientists allegedly share is at best an idealization. Controversies are rife in science, and they cannot be ascribed to ignorance or dismissed as the manifestation of personal idiosyncracies. The unfolding of science could be written as the history of a debating society discussing such topics as, Is the Earth or the Sun at rest? Do bodies fall because they are heavy or because they are attracted? Is the present shape of the Earth the result of gradual or sudden change? Was the agency water or fire? Do we need one or two fluids to explain electricity? Is combustion due to the release of phlogiston or the absorption of oxygen? Are acquired characteristics transmitted to offsprings or are all mutations random? Is light a corpuscular or an undulatory phenomenon? Is quantum physics really indeterministic? and so on. All these debates involved prominent scientists who offered genuinely different theories while ostensibly accounting for the same empirical data. Equally important is the fact that discussion often went on for decades. For instance, distinguished scientists such as Johann Bernoulli and Maupertuis were still weighing the pros and cons of Newtonian gravitation 50 years after Newton's *Principia Mathematica* had appeared.[16]

Dissent Is the Life of Science

Not only is controversy ubiquitous, it is necessary to scientific change. Great scientists usually modified or abandoned the canons that were accepted by their peers and can be seen, in retrospect, to have exerted a stultifying effect on research. More often than not, scientists who had the courage to innovate were also willing to ride roughshod over objections or even apparent refutations of their position. As Galileo put it, "One doesn't tear the house down because the chimney smokes!"

The Data are Under-determined

Controversy is not only rampant; it is inevitable because the rules of evidence do not and cannot pick out one theory unambiguously to the exclusion of all others. This argument takes two forms: one is associated with the names of Pierre Duhem and Willard van Orman Quine and aims to show that no theory can be logically proved or refuted by any body of evidence; the other is displayed in the writings of Nelson Goodman who criticized the rules of scientific evidence as radically open to different and even inconsistent interpretations. Science can only be said to be a rule-governed activity in a profoundly ambiguous sense. A more radical version of this problem was made fashionable by Paul Feyerabend for whom rival theories, if they are more than trivially different accounts of the same hypothesis, each belong to radically different conceptual universes.[17] This is the fourth challenge to which we now turn.

Theories Are Incommensurable

In its starkest form, this argument would have us believe that advocates of one scientific paradigm literally do not understand what their rivals are saying. On this view, contending theories are not really opposed since they are about different things that merely happen to wear the same linguistic label. How can the fire of Aristotle, for instance, be the same as Lavoisier's since the first is a state of matter, and the second is not matter at all! But whatever the change in the interpretation of fire, it is always related to the common experience of burning, heating, and cooking that we associate with the phenomenon produced by applying a lighted match to kindling wood! Some continuity seems inescapable, and more recently Thomas Kuhn has suggested that the problem should be discussed on the analogy of translations for which there exists a long tradition of scholarly discussions. Whereas no great poem has ever been rendered to one's utter satisfaction in a foreign language, some modern novels seem to have gained by being translated. But in both cases, a full translation is impossible because words in one language do not mirror the world in precisely the same way as the corresponding words in another language. For scientific paradigms, the pitfalls of translation are greater because the advocates of different paradigms subscribe to different methodological standards and do not share the same cognitive values. A failure of communication is inevitable somewhere along the way, and the common standards of scientific practice become impossible to determine. Only a short-term, short-lived view creates the impression of consensus, for scientists like all men,

> . . . are here as on a darkling plain
> Swept with confused alarm of struggle and flight,
> Where ignorant armies clash by night.[18]

This intellectual crisis could not come at a worse time. The perplexity of the philosophers and historians is nothing compared to the malaise in the community at large where the intelligibility and the usefulness of science are considered more and more problematic.

Knowledge Veiled

The organization of science has become increasingly complex, and the image of the scientist as a lonely thinker and the engineer as an inspired tinker has been replaced by the corporate image of a specialized "team" of experts who work in mysterious laboratories, often behind high fences under the surveillance of grim security guards. A dark curtain has descended on many scientific projects that are sponsored by either the government or the private sector. The use of increasingly sophisticated technology means that the public progressively loses access to the scientific phenomena of nature. Indeed, the *nature of the scientist* becomes less and less like the *nature of the common man*. This development already worried Einstein who warned, "I can think of nothing more objectionable than the idea of science [only] for scientists. It is almost as bad as art for the artists, and religion for the priests."[19]

The once useful distinction between an onlooker's and a participant's language becomes hopelessly blurred when only participants can see what they are talking about. It is a characteristic of modern science that the vast majority of our citizens are excluded from it. The problem is compounded because the industrialization of technology has led to the transformation of our daily lives, from fast food to instantaneous telecommunications. Our houses and our offices are full of more and more gadgets that we understand less and less, and our ignorance inhibits our ability to evaluate their real impact and to assess their ethical implications. Blind faith in the benign influence of science and technology has been waning at the very moment when they are encroaching more and more into our daily lives!

Some modern projects are so vast and call for such a variety of expertises that even the members of the scientific community can no longer embrace all their aspects. The heads of such mammoth projects have to rely on the scientific competence and moral responsibility of the people involved, whether they know them personally or not. Since no one sees the whole, everyone has to believe that the parts will fit, and in the struggle to get things to work, it is only too easy to forget the implications of the grandiose scheme for the world at large.

"If we only had time!" is not a complaint that originated yesterday, but there is no doubt that earlier generations had more time to come to terms with new technologies. Take, for instance, electrification. The idea of harnessing energy at a distance and conveying it almost instantaneously as far as cables can go was immediately attractive, especially when the source was a cheap and self-replenishing waterfall. We can hardly imagine the modern city without electricity to provide it with the power for its lighting, transportation, communications, and entertainment. Yet the introduction of electrification was a success not only because the side-effects on the environment were negligible (at least before the construction of mega-dams such as the one that has transformed the area above the Iguacu Falls), but because there was time for intellectual and political adaptation to it. The design of commercially viable generators took nearly 50 years after Faraday built his first model. Various problems of electrification engaged citizens at every level, and alternative schemes were publicly debated and examined in detail. The system that was eventually adopted was the result of a compromise between divergent interests and was experienced as the outcome of a genuinely democratic process. Such public involvement is becoming more difficult at the rate of increase of our science and technology. Thus, the rapid deployment of nuclear stations in the United States turned out to be a disaster for the industry itself.

Most of the funding for these mega-projects has to come from the state. How are the large sums involved to be accounted for in terms that are intelligible to the citizens or their representatives? This at a time when everyone has suddenly become morally accountable: the *engineer,* who is told that it is not enough to design an efficient plant, as he has been trained to do, but that he must gauge its impact on the environment, for which he has no training whatsoever; the *administrator,* who is asked to consider the long-range consequences of computerization on his personnel; the *manager,* who has to assess the social implications of automation in his factory; the *doctor,* who is faced with new ethical problems posed by a technology that enables him to initiate or prolong life almost at will; the *parents,* who have to decide what additives are acceptable in the food they give their children; and the *banker,* who is expected to respect privacy and to safeguard the computerized network from becoming a vehicle for fraud.

To whom or what are people to turn, since science is no longer a charismatic profession capable of training men and women to look at nature in an objective and self-detached way? While we wring our hands (at conferences or in the seclusion of our studies), the list of problems grows: more pharmaceuticals are discovered to have dangerous side-effects; the ozone layer is being depleted; our lakes and rivers become more polluted. Add to this the knowledge that over one-quarter of the world's scientists and engineers are actively engaged in research that is related to the development and manufacture of weapons. . . . Why should we be surprised if the unavoidable question is raised, Is all knowledge worth pursuing? As we have seen, science was supported not only because man is a naturally curious animal, but because it made implicit promises, which can be summarized as better jobs and better health, with, as a possible added benefit (for an additional small premium), the joy of understanding what scientists were up to.

What is the current image of the scientist? Is it akin to that of the apprentice sorcerer who unleashed untold misery upon himself and others by memorizing and using formulas that he did not understand? Or is the latent fear captured in *Frankenstein,* Mary Shelley's early classic of science fiction? Her monster still lives on our TV screens as the archfiend, and he is usually called Frankenstein. In the novel, however, Dr. Frankenstein is the scientist who pieces him together from living matter, and the creature has no name. It is not his innate malevolence, but his horrible appearance that causes people, including the person who made him, to flee in terror. It is the scientist's gross ineptitude and lack of responsibility for the work of his own hands that is the real cause of the creature's subsequent antisocial behaviour. Confronted with his misdeeds, the creature pleads with Dr. Frankenstein:

> Remember, that I am thy creature; I ought to be thy Adam; but I am rather the fallen angel, whom thou drives from joy for no misdeed. Everywhere I see bliss, from which I alone am irrevocably excluded. I was benevolent and good; misery has made me a fiend. Make me happy, and I shall again be virtuous.[20]

With this plea, the monster persuades Dr. Frankenstein to return to the laboratory and make him a helpmate with whom he will retire to the wilderness of South America away from all humans. As Dr. Frankenstein is about to breathe life into the female of the new species, he is arrested by the vision of "a race of devils" that would overrun the earth and subjugate mankind. "Had I a right," he asks, "for my own benefit, to inflict this curse upon everlasting generations?"[21] Under the eyes of the monster who watches him through the window, he destroys her. Now all fury is unleashed, but the threat to mankind is averted.

In 1817, the first readers of this gothic tale considered it merely an ingenious method of producing a pleasurable *frisson;* in 1989, when scientists and their corporate sponsors argue before the courts their rights to patent new life forms (genetically engineered bacteria today, higher forms tomorrow), it has become a cautionary tale. Unless, of course, we are to swallow our pride, and admit machines into the human family, as Bruce Mazlish urges us. Only then, will we have shed "the substratum upon which the distrust of technology and an industrialized society has been reared."[22] Welcome Frankenstein!

Locating his own contribution along the continuous spectrum of scientific "progress," Sigmund Freud saw his *psychological* revolution as the third major change in human consciousness, following upon the *cosmological* revolution of the sixteenth and seventeenth centuries, and the *biological* revolution of the nineteenth. The new astronomy destroyed the notion that the Earth is at the centre of the universe and reduced man's abode "to a tiny speck in a world-system of a magnitude hardly conceivable"; the Darwinian theory robbed man of the privilege of special creation and relegated him to a descendant of the animal kingdom; and Freud's psychoanalysis then informed him that he was not master in his own house, but only dimly aware of what was going on unconsciously in his own mind.[23] The fourth revolution might be the "scientific" news that man is just a machine. . . .

Can we be surprised if some are disillusioned with science? Science and machines have made us what we are, and we could not forsake science and technology without having to pay an enormous cost. But then it might be a question of saving our souls, for reasons analogous to those invoked in Samuel Butler's novel *Erewhon* (nowhere spelt in reverse) first published in 1872:

> Man's very soul is due to the machines; it is a machine-made thing; he thinks as he thinks, and he feels as he feels, through the work that machines have wrought upon him, and their existence is quite as much a *sine qua no.* for his, as his for theirs. This fact precludes us from proposing the complete annihilation of machinery, but surely it indicates that we should destroy as many of them as we can possibly dispense with, lest they should tyrannize over us even more completely.[24]

Herein lies our dilemma. The air we breathe is hardly more necessary than the machines on whose strength we have built our civilization. Yet the day may be near when we have to decide whether we have not asked too much of our creatures. Only a sadly disillusioned mankind would predicate its future happiness on the ability to be in some way profitable to machines. . . .

Notes

*The author wishes to thank the Institute for Advanced Study in Berlin, the Social Sciences and Research Council of Canada, and McGill University for their generous support of his research.

1. See, for instance, Yehuda Elkana, "Science as a Cultural System: an Anthropological Approach," in V. Mathieu and P. Rossi (eds.), *Scientific Culture in the Contemporary World* (Milan, 1979), 269–289; "A Pragmatic Attempt at an Anthropology of Knowledge," in E. Mendelsohn and Y. Elkana (eds.), *Sciences and Cultures* (Dordrecht: D. Reidel, 1981), 1–76.

2. See B.V. Subbarayappa, "The Impact of European Science on Colonial India," in W. R. Shea (ed.), *Scientific Revolutions: their Meaning and Relevance* (Canton, Mass.: Science History Publications, 1988), p. 280.

3. Francis Bacon, *The Great Instauration*, in *Works of Francis Bacon*, 14 vols., J. Spedding, R. L. Ellis, and D. D. Heath (eds.), (London, 1857–1874, reprinted Stuttgart: Friedrich Frommann, 1962), vol. IV, 26.

4. *Ibid.*, *Novum Organum* CXXIX, vol. iv, p. 114.

5. Descartes, *Discours de la méthode*, in *Oeuvres de Descartes*, C. Adam and P. Tannery (eds), (Paris, 1897–1913, reprinted Paris: Vrin, 1964–1976), vol. VI, 62.

6. Letter of 4 December 1638, *ibid.*, vol. 1, 647.

7. Adrien Baillet, *La Vie de Monsieur Des-Cartes*, 2 vols. (Paris, 1691, reprinted Geneva: Slatkine, 1970), vol. 11, 452–453.

8. Newton, *Opticks* (London, 1704, reprinted New York: Dover, 1962), 405.

9. Bacon, *New Atlantis,* in *Works* (n. 3), vol. 111, 165.

10. Benjamin Haydon, *Autobiography and Memoirs,* T. Taylor (ed.), (London, 1926), vol. 1, 269, quoted in Marjorie Hope Nicolson, *Newton Demands the Muse* (Princeton: Princeton University Press, 1966), 1.

11. Quoted in Gerald Holton, *The Advancement of Science, and Its Burdens* (Cambridge: Cambridge University Press, 1986). I am much indebted to this stimulating book.

12. George Sarton, *The Study of the History of Science* (Cambridge, Mass.: Harvard University Press, 1936), 5.

13. See Larry Laudan, *Science and Values* (Berkeley: University of California Press, 1984), 2–6.

14. Robert Merton, *Sociology of Science* (Chicago: University of Chicago Press, 1973), 268–269.

15. William R. Shea, "Beyond Logical Positivism," *Dialogue* 10 (1971), 223–242.

16. William R. Shea, "The Quest for Scientific Rationality: Some Historical Considerations," in J.C. Pitt and M. Pera (eds.), *Rational Changes in Sciences* (Boston: Reidel, 1987), 155–176.

17. Quine's version of Duhem's thesis is that "our statements about the external world face the tribunal of sense experience not individually but as a corporate body" (Willard Van Orman Quine, "Two Dogmas of Empiricism," in *From a Logical Point of View* (Cambridge, Mass.: Harvard University Press, 1959), 41. The consequences he draws from this thesis are the following: (a) it is misleading to speak of the "empirical content" of an individual statement; (b) any statement can be retained as true provided that sufficiently drastic adjustments are made elsewhere in the system; and (3) there is no sharp boundary between synthetic statements whose truth is contingent upon empirical evidence, and analytic statements whose truth is independent of empirical evidence (*ibid.,* 43). For Nelson Goodman's views, see mainly *Fact, Fiction and Forecast* (Cambridge, Mass.: Harvard University Press, fourth edition, 1983).

18. From the last three verses of Matthew Arnold's poem "Dover Beach."

19. Cited in Holton, *op. cit..*

20. Mary Shelley, *Frankenstein* (London: Dent, Everyman Library, 1979), 101.

21. *Ibid.,* 177.

22. Bruce Mazlish, "The Fourth Discontinuity," *Technology and Culture* 8 (1967), 4.

23. Sigmund Freud, *General Introduction to Psychoanalysis,* trans. by Joan Riviere (New York: Pocket Book, 1970), concluding paragraph of lesson XVIII, 296.

24. Samuel Butler, *Erewhon* (London: Page, 1923), 247.

Responsibility: the Genuine Ground for the Regulation of a Free Science

EVANDRO AGAZZI

Introduction

An unlimited confidence, unshaken optimism, and unconditioned approval for the growth and conquests of science and technology have been replaced in the last decades by widespread mistrust, fear, denigration, and rejection. Our society seems to have passed from scientism to antiscience, i.e., from the evaluation of science (and technology) as absolutely and unconditionally good, to seeing them as intrinsically evil. Both attitudes—despite having been backed by philosophically sophisticated arguments—are essentially irrational. Scientism has charged 'external' agencies with the responsibility for the negative consequences of scientific and technological development, thereby reducing the responsibility of the scientists to the correct performance of their specialized professional work. Antiscience, on the other hand, has made science and technology as such responsible for all the negative impacts mentioned, and has, therefore, denied that science deserves any freedom. Both positions have a kind of deterministic or fatalistic view of the course of science.

However, both positions are wrong: science and technology are certainly good, but not unconditionally good, and several negative aspects of their development have undeniably emerged (especially in recent times). This does not justify the proposal to stop them. But even if we reject (and we have the right to do so) the claim that science and technology are intrinsically perverse, we still have the problem of eliminating their negative impacts. The remarks that follow are meant to help clarify this issue.

Of course, that actions can or even must be subject to regulation does not imply that they cannot be free. On the contrary, the progress of mankind has consisted largely in increasing its freedom of action in various fields; indeed, only free actions are specifically 'human.' On the other hand, we must also recognize that mankind's progress was realized by introducing useful, wise, and opportune regulations in many

203

fields in which their absence had led to abuses, injustice, and dangers to individuals and the community.

The conclusion is therefore clear: it is our right (and duty) to defend freedom for science and technology. But, exactly as with other rights, the exercise of this freedom must be limited whenever it infringes other rights.

The Autonomy of Science

The modern age—which at least for so-called Western civilization may be identified with the historical period that began with the Renaissance—may be seen as a progressive disruption of the intellectual unity that had characterized the ancient world and, especially, the Middle Ages. Among the most significant manifestations of this decomposition, was the emergence of 'autonomies' in different sectors of the spiritual and practical life of man: the autonomies of politics (Machiavelli), of natural science (Galileo), of economics (British liberalism), and of art (Kant and the Romantics). At first these vindications of autonomy mainly expressed a particular stress on the *specificity* of the corresponding domains, which entailed the determination of *purely internal* criteria for the fulfillment of their restricted and specific goals. However, this autonomy quickly turned into a search for a kind of 'freedom' or 'liberation.'

The transition from autonomy to *freedom* may be understood in the sense that the admission of autonomy led to the rejection of any form of tutelage or interference from 'outside' the various domains. This vindication of freedom was understood in different ways and had different degrees. In one sense it was conceived as an *independence in the criteria of judgment,* e.g., a decision might be considered politically sound despite being economically disadvantageous, a behavior economically profitable despite being morally objectionable, a picture artistically beautiful despite being indecent. A common way of expressing this position is to say that politics, economics, and art are "value free," and this is especially said to be true of *science.* Indeed, the claim that science is and must be value free quickly became a widespread tenet of Western culture.

But it can also be said that this autonomy entails *independence in action.* In the above examples, this would mean that one is entitled to *perform* a political action despite its being economically disadvantageous, an economic action despite its being morally objectionable, a work of art despite its being indecent. This means that the politician "as a politician," the business man "as *homo oeconomicus,*" the artist "as an artist"—and we can also add the scientist 'as a scientist'—are allowed to act according to the *pure* criteria of their profession, at least to the extent that they are working *within* the profession. Autonomy can also mean refusing *controls or limitations* by external agents.

Such a process of 'liberation' has had several unacceptable results. In particular, this is being recognized in science: the need to protect the environment, to avoid technological catastrophes, and to regulate genetic manipulations (to cite the most common examples) is producing a demand for the regulation of science and technology. Therefore, we now confront the delicate problem of effecting a critical revision without becoming obscurantists.

We shall first try to understand in what sense those domains for which autonomy is claimed are to be considered 'value free.' This cannot mean that they are 'devoid of any value,' or that those who operate within these domains have nothing in view. Indeed, no human action (if it is really human) is performed without a purpose, i.e., without a goal that the agent considers worth pursuing. In this sense this goal or aim represents a 'value' that inspires action. It is sensible to establish criteria for evaluating how to pursue this aim.

This stage does not involve moral problems, since it is only related to action in an indirect and *hypothetical* way, i.e., by suggesting which course of action should be taken *if* the specific goal envisaged were the *only* goal. It does not *imply* that this is the unique or supreme goal of human action, or that one should disregard the impact that the fulfillment of this goal might have on the fulfillment of other human aims or values. Those who accept this 'implication' make a transition from the first to the second of the above mentioned meanings of 'autonomy,' i.e., to the meaning of 'independence in action,' and become immediately involved in a specific and highly debatable *ethical claim.*

Considering the Ends

Let us now consider science. It is useful to distinguish pure from applied science, not because a clear-cut separation is always possible or recommended in concrete cases, but because these notions constitute two 'ideal types' that should not be confused. Both can be considered as endeavors to provide *knowledge,* but for pure science the goal is the discovery of *truth*—in the sense of establishing 'how things are'—while in applied science, this goal is a practical *result.*

Admitting the specific aim of pure science to be the search for truth, it is clearly immune from moral objections in itself (i.e., it constitutes a perfectly legitimate value). The effort to reach sound and reliable knowledge in different specialized fields has given rise to certain prescriptions that constitute what is usually called "the scientific methodology." These have no ethical meaning, being simply *instrumental* to the achievement of the cognitive aim of science.

Yet pure science seems to imply some kind of truly moral requirement, such as the obligation not to manipulate data; the readiness to accept criticism, to recognize one's errors, and to credit other people's priorities; and a devotion to hard work. However, these virtues are not *specific* to science; rather, they are human virtues in a general sense (such as intellectual integrity and self-discipline) that find in scientific practice a privileged opportunity to be exercised. This is why scientific 'deontology' in matters of *this* kind is not really relevant to the relations between science and ethics, since its rules simply reinforce the fulfillment of the *specific and internal* aim of science.

Quite different is the situation of applied science. Here the search for truth is only a secondary end, the primary aim being some practical utility, which immediately implies the possibility of ethically relevant issues, depending on the particular *ends* an enterprise of applied science envisages. The point is clear enough in itself not to deserve extended discussion. To put it briefly: while it is in principle morally acceptable to *know* everything, and there are *no morally prohibited truths*, not everything that can be *done* is acceptable, and there are *morally prohibited actions*.

Considering the Means

It would be too hasty to conclude, as a consequence of the above considerations, that pure science can never be morally objectionable. This was said regarding its ends, but its *means* must also be considered, and the general principle that the end does not justify the means holds for science as well. Might the acquisition of pure knowledge require the use of morally questionable means? The answer is yes. In fact, at least in *experimental* science, truth cannot be discovered simply by thinking or observing; it requires the performance of operations, which implies the *manipulation* of the object that is submitted for investigation. Since manipulation is *action* and not knowledge, even when the acquisition of knowledge is its explicit aim, a particular act of manipulation may not be morally admissible in itself. When experimental research on man implies manipulating man, moral criteria become imperative. Experiments on human embryos and genetic manipulations for research purposes are widely discussed issues. They show that moral problems may arise in *pure science* and may imply restrictions on its freedom.

It is easy to see that these considerations about the ethical relevance of the means may also be transferred to applied science. The moral acceptability of the goal of a particular applied research does not free us from considering the moral acceptability of the means used in performing this research.

Considering the Conditions

Among factors involved in moral considerations, the *conditions* of the action also have special importance. They are similar to the means, but while means are tools for reaching ends, conditions make the action possible, and thereby serve ends only indirectly. This distinction is useful for understanding that an action seeking the realization of a morally legitimate goal through the adoption of morally acceptable means still remains open to moral questioning until its conditions have been analyzed. The most recent example of this kind of problem that has been discussed with reference to science is that of allocating funds for research. The money allocated to science has to be subtracted from other possible uses, such as hospitals, schools, social security, and environmental protection. Since the satisfaction of these needs corresponds to aims or values that are not only legitimate, but necessary to pursue, a problem of moral choice inevitably sufaces. The moral problem may be easier in applied science because it is usually easier to show how an applied research could 'compensate' through its expected results for the sacrifices the community makes. It is more difficult to demonstrate this for the simple acquisition of knowledge. This example shows how spurious the idea is that ethical problems are typical of applied science and hardly concern pure science.

Considering the Consequences

The last point of this analysis concerns the possible *consequences* of scientific research. This is often the *only* point that is considered in discussions about the ethics of science. Such an attitude is certainly too restrictive, but we should not underestimate the relevance of the consequences in the moral evaluation of actions, since it is an obvious moral principle that one is responsible for the consequences of one's actions, and therefore must try to foresee them. This problem has become the focus of ethical discussions regarding science because of the dramatic impact of certain unexpected tragic consequences of technological development. The problem is not new in ethics, however, where the the so-called 'double effect principle' is applied to those cases in which the intended end of an action (though legitimate in itself) entails morally unacceptable consequences. It also applies to cases in which consequences are only highly probable. In such cases one must first determine whether the pursuit of the goal can be renounced—to avoid the unacceptable consequences. If this is possible, it is a moral duty to renounce it. Here we have a counterpart of the principle that 'the end does not justify the means,' since 'the end does not justify the consequences.' Both principles are opposed to the contention that all that matters in ethics is one's *intention* in performing an act.

But there are other situations in which pursuing a goal is a moral obligation. In these cases one has to compare the importance of the two values (the value that the action serves, and the value that the consequences of the action violates), and sacrifice the less important one, or, to put it differently, 'choose the lesser of two evils.' A classical case in which this principle is advocated is that of 'therapeutic abortion,' when omitting a certain therapy would mean risking the life of the mother, while implementing it would *imply* the death of the fetus. Losing the fetus is considered the 'lesser evil' (a situation not to be confused with killing the fetus as a *means* of saving the mother). Situations of this kind are not rare in applied science.

Even though a consideration of the consequences is chiefly a problem for applied science, it is not totally alien to pure science where the *communication* of a discovery may raise moral questions. Scientific discoveries or theories are often communicated to the public in a sensational way with negative impacts on society's ways of thinking and on its appreciation of life and values. This is a fault of the media, but also of more or less distinguished scientists, who indulge in superficial popularization or even in partisan interpretations or extrapolations. At a time when science has such a tremendous influence on the thoughts and feelings of men, the honest and morally scrupulous dissemination of scientific truth has become a major ethical imperative.

The Particular Position of Technology

For the sake of our discussion, it is advisable to distinguish between science and technology. This distinction is based on the different *specific aims* of each: the specific and primary aim of science is the acquisition of *knowledge;* the aim of technology is the realization of certain *processes* and/or *products.* The goal of science is that of *knowing* something; the goal of technology is that of *making* something. Science is essentially a search for *truth;* technology essentially involves making something that is *useful.* This does not minimize the relations that exist between science and technology: on the one hand, science in general (and contemporary science in particular) cannot pursue its goals without relying on a massive use of highly sophisticated technology; and on the other hand, modern technology may be seen as a skillful application of scientific discoveries.

Indeed, technology is not mere technique, since it relies on the application of scientific knowledge. Mere technique is the accumulation of practically useful operating procedures that have been tested and improved over many generations and represent a *"know how"* without necessarily implying a *"know why."* This explains why some civilizations have existed with highly developed "technique" but poor science, while others have had a rich science but rudimentary "technique." Western civilization established a correlation between science and technical skills: first, by investigating *why* certain technical procedures are successful (*i.e.,* by looking for an *explanation* of this success that would give the *reasons* for it), and second, by *deliberately designing* instruments appropriate for reaching certain results. This second step has led to the establishment of *technology* as something distinct from mere "technique," and accounts for the strict interdependence between science and technology that could lead one to believe (mistakenly) that they are the same thing.

What we have being saying about *applied science* clearly applies to technology also. But the specific and direct aim of technology is to *make* something, while that of applied science is still to *know* something, though its goals are different from those of pure knowledge.

This distinction is relevant to the problem of freedom and regulation, since we may readily admit that everyone is free to *think* whatever he wants, but we are not usually ready to admit that everyone is also free to *do* whatever he wants. In other words, action is typically submitted to rules and regulations, both moral and legal. While there is no *ought to be* in the field of knowledge (the only imperative is to avoid error, which is a 'defining condition' of knowledge), there is an *ought to be* and an *ought to do* in the domain of actions. These give rise to moral norms from a subjective point of view, and to legal norms or regulations from a social point of view. Such norms indicate which actions are permitted, obligatory, or prohibited.

Here we can see major differences with regard to the limitations of pure science. In that case—as we have seen—limitations to the freedom of research, or regulations about how to perform it, are essentially imposed by considering the *means* or the *conditions* involved, while the *goal* (the discovery of new truths) is always considered legitimate. In technology, on the contrary (much more than in applied science itself), the choice of the goals may also be regulated, not only because some goals might be considered morally or socially unacceptable in themselves, but also because the goals of a particular technological enterprise may conflict with other legitimate goals. To put it concisely: technology may be seen as the search for ways of realizing any project. But while one has the right to know any truth, one does not have the right to implement all possible projects.

This amounts to saying that the regulation of technology must also be concerned with its goals; but this idea is not generally accepted nowadays, since technology has been gradually reduced to a series of procedures that are not expected to interfere with the goals. This is strange, since technology is by its very nature an activity in which knowledge is put at the service of a goal. It is important 'to do something *good,*' and 'to do it in a *good* way': the mention of the 'good' (in the first occurrence) indicates a relation to the moral sphere and to the problem of norms and regulations. However, owing to an historical evolution that we shall briefly outline, the consciousness of this double dimension has been lost.

The Evolution of Technology

In earlier societies technical skills were developed on a practical basis through successive refinements of empirically discovered procedures. In the Renaissance, when modern science was about to appear, several thinkers—among them Bacon and Descartes—advocated the domination of man over nature. This was to be achieved by uncovering nature's secrets and putting them to the service of man. This proposal foreshadows the spirit of technology proper, which assigns to *science* the task of providing the most efficient tools for human action, but also recognizes that these tools have a fundamental propose—the service of man. However, when the new science actually began to be applied, it did not result in the *domination* of nature, but rather in the *replacement* of nature by a world of *artifacts* that were supposed to perform 'better than nature itself.' These artifacts, designed by applying the knowledge the new science provided were *machines*.

Machines were not designed and produced to satisfy human needs proper, but rather to perform certain special *operations,* which were previously performed by men or animals, more efficiently. Moreover, since machines are expensive to construct, they were not built for sheer enjoyment, but for *profit.* The Industrial Revolution based on the diffusion of machines quickly became the most powerful propeller of technology, but it also made technology seek *profit.* This did not prevent technology from occasionally being used 'for the benefit of mankind,' but this was not its most significant employment. Even when the individual inventor was moved by such a noble purpose, his invention was normally financed only if it could produce a significant profit.

Recently an additional factor may be found in the acceleration of technical developments: the aspiration to realize all possible projects and objectives, to overstep all practical limitations. From this point of view, the fascination of the new, the pride of making what used to be considered impossible, the ambition of indefinitely expanding the power of man have clearly become intrinsic motives for the advancement of technology. The motive is no longer to serve other goals. The production of a *new* artifact is seen as positive in itself, the way the discovery of a new truth is.

The Divorce of Technology and Wisdom

Technology has become less and less a *goal-oriented* activity. But an activity that ceases to be aware of its goals simply becomes meaningless, devoid of sense. When men used their skills to satisfy their fundamental needs, these skills were embedded in a context of values, of goals that made it reasonable and meaningful to perform them. This had nearly ceased to be the case when technology started to be driven by the profit motive.

This corrosive attitude was reinforced by the narrow focus of technology. Technological rationality is purely *instrumental* and works in *isolated* compartments. It is sensitive to the problem of *how* to reach a goal but insensitive to the problem of *which* goal should be aimed at and *why.*

The consequences of this divorce are evident: environmental pollution, the waste of natural resources, threats to the survival of mankind, deep and sudden subversions of social and economic structures, devastation of traditional cultures, and the loss of respect for human life and dignity. They all share common features: they are *global* in scope and constitute clear evidence of how limited technological rationality is. Indeed, as we have seen, technological rationality points to the pursuit of a *single* and *isolated* goal, but the *consequences* of reaching this goal are *numerous* and *widespread*. Moreover, in ancient times these consequences remained within a restricted sphere. They were produced using more primitive skills and could be evaluated and mastered by an individual or a small community. By contrast, modern technology has *far-reaching* consequences and tends to affect *all* mankind.

It is thus *absurd* to stick to purely technological rationality—absurd because rationality is conceived as the solution to *local* problems, while its effects have a *global* impact. We master *isolated* difficulties, but create other, *large-scale* difficulties that we are unable to master. To put it briefly, technological rationality tends towards *simplification,* while reality is *complex.* Therefore, we need a kind of *complementary rationality* that would provide a more comprehensive framework in which it could operate in a meaningful way. This rationality would reconcile technology and wisdom. But would that necessarily imply *regulating* technology?

The Question of Regulation

Modern man does not easily accept regulations that limit his freedom of action. This is a consequence of the individualism that has characterized Western culture during the last four centuries. According to this view, only regulations that prevent people from directly injuring other people are acceptable. A kind of automatic protection against abuses and injustice is believed to arise from the spontaneous mechanisms of human commerce in which everyone 'offers' something that can be freely accepted, demanded, or refused. The idea that from the action of this 'local' mechanisms a 'global' harmony would arise was at the basis of the 'free-market' model of pure liberalism, which supposed that the law of supply and demand would correct the price of commodities and produce general wealth. But it is worth noting that some 'regulations' had to be introduced (such as antitrust or antidumping laws) to assure that the 'free market' functioned as it *ought to function.* Furthermore, not *everything* was freely sold. In fact the sale of heroin and of other dangerous products has been forbidden in almost every country even though customers were 'free' not to buy them if they so wished. In some cases regulation must be introduced to protect people from the risks of using freedom improperly, e.g., cigarette advertisements, which show smoking under an attractive light, but are counterbalanced by public regulations that require a warning about the dangers of smoking to be displayed on the ads. These elementary examples show that even in the idealized model of the free market, regulations are introduced to protect the exercise of freedom.

In scientific research and technology, some regulation already exists: standards are regulated: many countries have laws regulating the sale of new drugs, laws against the adulteration of food-stuffs, regulations imposing the use of noninflammable materials in certain buildings, regulations for avoiding accidents in industrial plants. Other examples could easily be given. These regulations are specialized and 'local,' in the sense that they concern specific risks, dangers, and possible abuses. Of course, they are far from useless, but it is highly debatable whether they would be sufficient for the global problems mentioned above.

The existing regulations are to a large extent 'protective' and aim at 'avoiding' dangerous or undesirable situations, but they do not have something 'positive' in view. On the contrary, regulation with a global range must be inspired by the intention of reaching certain important goals, by certain priority choices, by some strategy concerning the development of science and technology as an element of the general progress of mankind. We need a model of rationality that is open to *value judgments.*

The Plurality of Values

Ethics must start with an awareness that men are motivated by a wide variety of motivations that they consider to be legitimate in themselves, but that making a single value absolute (be it pleasure, wealth, power, family, fatherland, friendship, beauty, truth, love, or religion) would amount to admitting that anything is permissible in pursuit of this value. This statement remains true even if one admits a hierarchy of values. Indeed, we usually concede that we act on a subhuman level when we are motivated exclusively by pleasure or wealth. This judgment does not depend on the lower rank of these values, but on their having been made (consciously or unconsciously) into absolute values. To be persuaded of the truth of this, remember how many morally reprehensible acts have been or could be the consequence of making even the higher-ranking values absolute. Science does not constitute an exception to this rule. If we consider science only as a system of knowledge (i.e., if we consider *only* its contents), it has no ethical relevance. But as soon as we consider it as a human activity—i.e., the activity that aims at producing this knowledge—we must conclude that it cannot help being subject to the general conditions of any human activity, namely, that of being guided by choices inspired by value judgments. The plurality of values then comes into consideration.

The Spirit of the Regulation

Some corollaries follow from the considerations developed thus far. Specifically ethical limitations and regulations may affect the practice of scientific research. In fact, as soon as we admit that moral principles must govern human actions, we are obliged to accept that *not everything* is permissible. What *is permissible, obligatory,* or *prohibited* must be specified through concrete *norms.* But these norms must apply to situations and actions that are 'complex' because they involve the interaction of a number of principles and values.

This consideration has two consequences. First, criteria, standards, or norms elaborated for evaluating one domain cannot be automatically applied to another. Hence, moral evaluations have to be based on ethical criteria and are, as such, independent of scientific considerations. Second, ethics should take into account what is the most satisfactory fulfillment of all human values in a specific situation. This means that it is a real ethical commitment to grant science the freedom compatible with the respect due to whatever other values are involved. Hence, the *freedom of science* is part of the ethical consideration of science.

As we have seen, the regulation of science and technology is necessary because there are global goals and values that cannot be taken into consideration from within the restricted domain of any one scientific or technological enterprise. An effort should be made to think according to some criteria of *generality,* i.e., from the point of view of all mankind, of future generations, and of general happiness. This is not impossible, since it simply corresponds to the adoption of an attitude of *responsibility,* which is not alien as such to modern men, but simply not much practiced because of our standardized way of living, in which we 'execute' certain tasks without feeling really responsible for them.

The Ways of the Regulation

The legitimacy of explicitly establishing norms to regulate scientific activity cannot be denied. We are already accustomed to norms that regulate the security or secrecy of pure and applied research. Why should norms of a more general *moral* character be excluded? But which agency should be entitled to formulate these norms, and supervise their application? I believe that these norms should express a systems-theoretic harmonization of different values and be the result of a multilateral assumption of *responsibility.* The scientific community must accept other values in society and the right of other social agencies (economic, political, religious, etc.) to affect the rights of science. To reach this stage of responsibility, a process of education and *participation* is needed, whereby scientists become more sensitive to the existence and significance of more universal human values. But this also requires that moralists, theologians, and politicians become more sensitive and better acquainted with the issues involved in the practice of scientific research.

The Agencies of Control

An easy solution to the conflicts of values, rights, and interests seems at hand. Let us constitute full *social control* of science to steer it towards the solution of socially relevant problems. This is advocated by many people today, but it is plagued with problems. To begin with, the envisaged planning could only be effective if entrusted to public authorities. But this would transform the "social control" of science into "political control." Indeed, the successful control of science is the privilege of totalitarian regimes, which already indicates that a substantial reduction of freedom might be the hidden prerequisite for such 'discipline.' But even in democratic regimes, political control would inevitably mean submission to partisan evaluation, ideological intrusion, and pressure from political groups. In other words, this alleged solution would simply make science into a "servant of power."

More important than these practical considerations, however, is the question of principle: if we were to accept social control of science, meaning total planning of scientific research to make it completely goal-oriented, we would also have to accept two highly undesirable consequences. First, we would have to limit the freedom of science at the very moment that we seek to harmonize all rights. With the excuse that some research is 'socially useless' or even 'socially dangerous,' we would revert to external control of intellectual activity, against which modern science has won an historic battle.

Second, if we were to admit that scientific research has to be exclusively 'goal-oriented,' we could not avoid the question: "Who will determine the goals?" It would be naive to answer: "The goals will be determined by society," because society is an abstract entity that cannot formulate explicit goals for specific scientific projects. We would therefore have to have 'someone' to interpret the needs of society and determine which scientific goals are instrumental to the satisfaction of these needs. We would thus be confronted with the problem of political power.

The Right of Free Research

Whatever the limitations we might be inclined to impose on science, they should never eliminate freedom. No fundamental right or value should be totally supressed. But beside this principle (which is an immediate consequence of the respect that must be granted to freedom of thought in general) there is another equally important reason, namely, that scientific growth needs personal creativity, which cannot be produced by order of any person or institution. Science could not continue to flourish without an atmosphere of freedom and without feeling entitled to pursue knowledge for its own sake.

It is not difficult to see, on the other hand, how the need to grant science freedom for research is by no means inconsistent with the recognized duty to remunerate society for the price it pays for fostering scientific activity. It is 'in the interest of society' to preserve creativity, personal initiative, critical attitude, and freedom of spirit, as qualities of its members. If science fostered these qualities, it would be contributing to a better society.

The Responsibility of Science

Nonetheless, goal-oriented research is fully justified, and it would be highly desirable that such 'orientation' be more and more directed towards promoting basic values and satisfying fundamental human rights. But the *whole* of scientific research cannot be *forced* to become applied or goal oriented. Scientists themselves must have the right to participate in determining the goals of their research. Of course, this cannot be understood in a naive sense but rather in the sense that the scientific community should become more and more involved in discussing and determining the structure of society. It should exert considerable influence in specifying goals that, besides being of general social interest, involve the application of advanced scientific knowledge or sophisticated technology. Appealing to science for the needs of society has a moral character; it does not express an imposition or an obligation proper, but rather an appeal to the *responsibility* of single scientists and, in a way, the scientific community as a whole. Only free, rational beings can be credited with a sense of responsibility.

When we see the problem in this light, most of the difficulties involved in an abstract opposition between the rights of science and the rights of society vanish, since the scientist is part of society and *must* therefore be sensitive to the problems that concern it. By saying "must" we have evoked the category of *duty,* which is the only category capable of combining obligation with freedom and which fully corresponds to human dignity. A responsible person may be defined as one who is aware of his duties and ready to fulfill them. Scientists are already accustomed to respect some duties in their profession. These are mostly connected with what we call "intellectual integrity," but scientists have been less accustomed to considering other duties related to the 'context' of their research activity. The time has come for them to do so because this is the only way mankind can continue to trust science rather than fear it. Indeed, many people seem to be afraid of science and technology because they see them as a kind of blind force, growing without control.

But if people could become confident that this process is not blind because fellow men are behind it and steer it, they could again look at science and technology with a positive attitude. After all, one major root of the insecurity that characterizes our present societies is the declining concern about duty that has been obscured by an over emphasis on rights. Indeed, we can feel secure in a community only if we can be confident that everyone fulfills his duties, since this is the basic guarantee that our rights will be respected. What is true for individuals is also true for institutions and big enterprises: we can trust them only if we think that they include among their duties that of respecting our rights.

The Impact of Science on Ethics

What we have said concerning the cooperative spirit that should inspire the establishment of ethical and legal regulations of science does not simply express the obvious need of some 'democratic' way of solving this urgent problem, but corresponds to a much deeper understanding of the relations between science and ethics, an understanding that involves the systems-theoretic view mentioned above. In fact, in speaking of the relationships between science and ethics, it is insufficient to consider the influence that ethics has to exert on science, as we have mainly done thus far. An equally interesting investigation concerns the influence of science on the elaboration of ethical and moral norms. We shall confine ourselves to only a couple of examples. Ethics uses certain fundamental concepts such as freedom, normality, and human nature, and a concrete specification of these concepts, and of their *applicability* to actual human actions, requires taking into account the results of several sciences, especially of those concerning man (from biology, to genetics, neurobiology, psychology, and sociology). Without correct information from these sciences, the ethical discourse will be unable to speak to the man of today, who has a new 'image' of himself, and may feel that ethics is obsolete and backward looking.

The progress of science has already created and will continue to create new and unexpected situations, to which the existent moral norms can hardly apply. It could also open unforeseen possibilities of action, and therefore of choice in situations that in the past were totally beyond human decision. All this indicates that the growth of science influences ethics. If ethics in general expresses the need of 'doing what is right,' without the contribution of other fields, it cannot answer the question: *"What* is right to do?"* in concrete situations. Without pretending to answer this question (which is not a scientific question), science can nevertheless help formulate the answer.

Conclusions

It follows from the above considerations that self-regulation of scientific research and technology is to be recommended. However, a pure and simple self-regulation of the scientific community would not be sufficient in practice, and would be objectionable in principle. The scientific community has no right to consider itself a closed system that rejects external control. Some legal regulation is appropriate. The historical challenge of our age is to produce, through fruitful, *responsible participation,* such legal regulations.

On the other hand, a reasonable flexibility should characterize these regulations, except in very grave cases, which should be controlled through the usual means that any public authority uses to control the implementation of laws. The more flexible norms should be subject to the mechanisms usually prescribed by the deontological codes of the different professions. However, the most important problem is not that of *norms.* Of course, norms are needed, but what is more basic is the habit of making correct *moral judgments* that concern actual situations, in which conflicts of values may render the application of the pertinent norm (or norms) problematic. Here, again, the ability to assume one's *responsibility* is the best guide for keeping science under reasonable control without giving up its intellectual and practical conquests.

Further References:

"Oggettività e neutralità della scienza," *Civiltà delle macchine*, 24/1–2 (1976), 17–30.

"Freedom and Responsibility of Science," *Epistemologia*, VI (1983), special issue, 5–16.

"L'ideologia tecnologica," *Nuova civiltà delle macchine*, II/2 (1984), 5–14.

"Les enjeux éthiques de la science," in *La responsabilité éthique dans le développement biomédical, CIACO*, Louvain-la-Neuve, 1987, 23–42.

Weisheit im Technischen (Verlag Hans Erni-Stiftung, Luzern), 40.

"A Systems-theoretic Approach to the Problem of the Responsibility of Science," *Zeitschrift für allgemeine Wissenschaftstheorie*, XVIII–/1–2 (1987), 3–49.

Should Society Make Laws Governing Scientific Research? Is It Reasonable, Necessary, and Possible to Ensure Responsibility of Researchers by Law?

PETER SALADIN

The Notion of Research

Scientific research is a qualified process of widening man's knowledge of the world; oral or written presentation of scientific research results is a qualified way of human expression. For the moment, these two definitions may be a sufficient basis for developing our subject; however, in discussing the legal aspects indicated in the title of this paper, we shall have to reconsider that basis and ask ourselves whether our subject requires a deeper penetration into what we should call research. (It seems to be clear enough—but by no means sufficiently recognized by constitutionalists!—that for determining the legal sense of "science" or "research," we ought to take notice of what the "science of science" thinks should be thought of it. This has been admirably done by the Swiss scholar Hans Gruber. I largely base myself on his findings.)

> The German Bundesverfassungsgericht defined, in a famous decision of 1973,[1] scientific activity as "everything which has to be considered, according to its content and its form, to be a serious planful attempt to seeking the truth" ("alles, was nach Inhalt und Form als ernsthafter planmässiger Versuch zur Ermittlung der Wahrheit anzusehen ist"). This definition has been criticized by German constitutionalists as being merely cognitive and not taking into account the "social dimension" of science.[2]

Research, whether "scientific" or other, means a basic human activity growing out of man's "natural" curiosity.[3] Again, this statement may suffice, although I am well aware of its critical aspects (What does "natural" mean? Is there sufficient anthropological evidence for presenting it in such a general way? Is curiosity man's privilege—how does animals' curiosity, which we all know from experience with our pets, come into the picture? These questions, important as they may be, need, for the moment at least, no particular discussion for the aims of this paper).

Freedom of Research as a Legal Concept

If our definition of research is adequate, is it legitimate and necessary to make research the object of a *fundamental right?* In fact, the modern concept of fundamental rights and their legal recognition (in national constitutions as well as in international declarations, covenants, and charters) are based on the convictions that all basic human needs should be covered and that all fundamental developments of human personality should be, in principle, free and therefore protected against encroachments planned and executed by state or private power. Thus, it seems reasonable to look for respective provisions in past and present constitutional and international law.

The result of our research, however, is rather disappointing, as far as *explicit provisions* are concerned. Specific provisions concerning the liberty of research are written into the constitutions, among others, of the Federal Republic of Germany (art. 5 al. 3), into the Austrian Staatsgrundgesetz über die allgemeinen Rechte der Staatsbürger (art. 17 al. 1) (which is of particular interest because the Staatsgrundgesetz dates from 1867!), into some Swiss cantonal constitutions (Jura art. 8i, Solothurn art. 14, Basel-Landschaft §6 al. 2e, Uri art. 12i), into the constitutions of Greece (art. 16 al. 1), Italy (art. 33), and Portugal (art. 42). On the other side, we look in vain for such a specific liberty, for instance, in the constitutions of the United States, France, or Sweden.

In international law the situation is rather similar. Neither the Universal Declaration of Human Rights (1948), nor the European Convention on Human Rights protects the freedom of research explicitly, in contrast to the UN Covenant on economic, social, and cultural rights (1966), which provides in art. 15 al. 3:

> "The States Parties to the present Covenant undertake to respect the freedom indispensable for scientific research and creative activity."

Furthermore, the Universal Declaration as well as the Covenant mentioned above recognize the right of every man and woman to protection of the moral and material interests resulting from any scientific, literary, or artistic production of which he or she is the author (art. 27/15 al. 1).[4]

A rather puzzling situation! If research is a basic human activity, why is it not guaranteed regularly by constitutions and international human rights instruments—or at least by modern ones, which were made when scientific research had become a major—if not the major—factor "promoting" modern civilization? Does this suggest that research—or scientific research—is not as basic as is assumed? Or is the right to free scientific research deemed to be "self-evident" and undisputed, so that explicit protection seemed superfluous to various countries and international organisations?

However, our analysis of modern constitutional and international (public) law should not limit itself to explicit provisions. In some constitutional systems, basic freedoms are considered to be *implicitly guaranteed,* either within the frame of specific articles or by the "ensemble" of a country's constitutional law.

This is, for example, the case of *Switzerland.* The Swiss federal constitution requires the Federal Government to promote scientific research (art. 27sexies), but does not guarantee its freedom. As mentioned above, some (newer) cantonal constitutions do contain such provisions, as do some cantonal university laws. The Swiss Supreme Court (das Bundesgericht) has not had, up to now, an opportunity to decide whether that freedom is protected implicitly, e.g., by the (equally unwritten) freedom of expression. But the Federal authorities (Bundesrat und Bundesversammlung) consider it to be a specific, unwritten fundamental right, whereas Swiss constitutional law scholars are divided: some share that view;[5] others are opposed because they are sceptical about its "fundamentalness"[6], or at least about the "fundamentalness" of scientific research.[7] Hans Gruber's views merit our special attention because he has studied our subject (in Switzerland) with the greatest thoroughness. For him, the effort to broaden human knowledge is a perfectly essential human capacity and activity, as well as a *conditio sine qua non* of a democratic legal order, which aims at the protection of the dignity of man. However, modern research, as a highly complex cultural "institution" is, on its proper behalf, not such an essential human activity nor necessary for a modern democratic "Rechtsstaat."[8] The basic "freedom of extending knowledge" ("Erkenntnisfreiheit") itself is, for Hans Gruber, implicitly protected by various other fundamental rights (written or unwritten) as, e.g., personal freedom ("persönliche Freiheit"), freedom of expression, and of the press, etc. The distinction, as suggested by Hans Gruber, between "Erkenntnisfreiheit" and the liberty of its institutionalized form (i.e., what we usually call, in modern times, "scientific activity") seems to me to be important; it allows a refinement of our original concept of "research," which seems to be essential for an adequate legal protection.

In *US constitutional law,* the freedom of research does not seem to be considered as a specific fundamental right—usually it is not even mentioned in constitutional law treatises, nor are leading court cases to be found. But I do not doubt that American constitutionalists would accept at least some aspects of the freedom of research as constitutionally guaranteed by the First Amendment.

Even if we add to constitutions and international legal instruments containing explicit provisions those constitutional systems that are considered to protect implicitly the freedom of research and of scientific research, the situation remains unclear and puzzling. Assuming the fundamentalness of human research, why do so many such systems not give it explicit legal protection on a level with the fundamental principles of the legal order? Again, we have to ask ourselves, is research—specifically scientific research—not generally considered to be fundamental? Or is it not thought to be endangered enough to need help from a fundamental rights system? Or, even if endangered, is it beyond the reach of legal protection? These questions have to be answered both for research activities in general and for modern scientific research.

Let me try to give some personal answers to these questions— provisional, incomplete, tentative ones. What seems to me necessary in this paper is to lay a fundament upon which its proper topic—the existence, sense, and necessity of legal limits to the freedom of research—can be answered. I do not propose to do more than this.

As objects of human rights, only fundamental human activities or needs can reasonably be agreed upon. "Systems" should not be considered to be such objects themselves, but they have to be built "around them" (or constructed according to them) to make sure that the respective liberty becomes real or that the respective need is effectively satisfied. I therefore agree with Hans Gruber when he qualifies "Erkenntnisfreiheit" (freedom of extending knowledge, freedom of research) as "basic" and adds that the organizational autonomy of research is a condition for securing and promoting the researcher's freedom to extend knowledge. Thus, state legislation is not free to regulate research as it pleases. Such regulation must observe the fundamental freedoms of the *individuals* engaged in scientific research.[9] Not the autonomy of the scientific system, or of a scientific organization (such as a university, a university department, an institute, or a scientific foundation, etc.), or of the management of a specific scientific project, nor a specific university structure[10] is the object of fundamental rights, but the *freedom of the individual researcher.* This, however, means nowadays in most fields not an isolated, but a "social" activity, combined with the activities of other researchers and requiring—in most fields—the establishment and disponibility of complex institutions as well as the specific allocation of considerable financial and personal ressources.[11] And research needs to be understood in its broadest possible sense, as suggested above, comprising not only research activities, which follow established scientific (methodological) rules and covering established scientific fields or proceeding in established scientific institutions. In this broad sense only, we arrive at understanding and protecting research activities in their real "human," i.e., for human beings essential, function. These activities must be free. And since they are essential human activities, their freedom must be recognised and protected by constitutions as well as by basic international human rights instruments. Again, this fundamental right has and must have *influence on the organization and management of modern scientific research* (and of the promotion of research). Without autonomy for scientific institutions to organize these research activities and without autonomy for researchers within such institutions, that personal freedom will hardly become real. Or in the words of the German Constitutional Court: Art. 5 al. 3 of the German constitution contains a value decision ("Wertentscheidung"), based on the key importance ("Schlüsselfunktion") of free science for the development of both individual personality and of modern society. This decision not only compels the state to refrain from intrusions into the proper realm of science, but also to promote actively the idea and the reality of free science and to prevent its being undermined.[12]

The further questions asked above will be answered here very briefly. Freedom of research is, in the West, fortunately not in serious danger, certainly not by large-scale state intrusions.[13] And the "new" limit to such freedom that I am going to suggest in this paper will not change this satisfactory situation in any fundamental way. There are, of course, some doubtful limitations on other levels than that of state regulation, e.g., some ways of systematically discouraging nonorthodox topics or methods of research. But these problems are not central to my topic. It is also obviously difficult to cope with them on a legal level—which does not make them, of course, any the less important!

Legal Limits to Freedom of Research?

We are now set to tackle the problem of (legal) limitations to the freedom of research. It is true that according to traditional fundamental rights doctrine we would first have to elaborate on the precise "field" covered and of the various rights granted by the freedom of research. I prefer, however, to proceed differently and to "jump" directly to the problem of limitations, for three reasons. First, some basic remarks about the "content" of our freedom have already been made; second, our topic is precisely that of limitations imposed on freedom of research; and third, the two problems, in the last resort, coincide: "barriers" indicate how far freedom reaches. I might add that within the borders of our colloquium and of this paper, it is simply not possible to tackle all problems involved in the legal concept of freedom of research.

The present legal order contains, in every country, *a lot of general rules* directed not only at protecting but also at limiting research activities. As examples, I would like to present such limitations as enacted by my own—the Swiss—legal order; I presume that there are scarcely fundamental differences to be found, in this respect, between the Swiss and other legal systems of the Western world.[14]

Every researcher has to observe the provisions of *penal and civil codes.* Research purposes do not set one free from penal (or from civil) liability; they do not make legitimate what is to be qualified as a criminal act. For instance, research work must not use human beings under coercion and must not violate their physical or psychic integrity without their consent. On the other hand, penal and civil codes have to respect the basic freedom of research; they are not allowed to extend penal and civil liability to a point where freedom of research loses its substance. Furthermore, researchers (or their employers) have to observe—in the same way as anybody else—limitations set up by *administrative law,* e.g., by atomic energy or environmental protection or health protection codes.

Specific administrative statutes forbid *specific research methods.* For instance, the Swiss animals' protection code requires, for all experiments using animals, an official authorization that is granted if certain, legally determined conditions are fulfilled (art. 12ff.). Whoever uses animals without authorization, or against the legal rules, falls under penal provisions of the same code (which are, in fact, rather weak).

Freedom of research usually does not include the right to get any specific research project *financed,* even if that freedom requires, as the German Constitutional Court explains, state authorities to create adequate institutions and to allocate, in a general way, adequate resources. This limitation seems to be generally accepted, but, of course, it is not an immediate limitation, it does not restrain *by law* those who are eager to do research. However, *its effects* equal that of an immediate limitation, in many scientific fields at least, because in many fields interesting research work needs heavy financing, either by corporations or by the state (or by foundations). On the other hand, whenever state institutions allocate research resources, they are required, by law (i.e., by the constitutional principles of equality *and* of freedom of research) to do so by criteria as objective as possible, and this means always criteria of state science policy in a narrow sense and, by the criterion of research project quality (whatever this means; I do not think it necessary to enter into this delicate subject as well). If resources be allocated by other criteria freedom of research would in fact be hampered because certain researchers would be barred from their research on discriminatory grounds.

Further limits are specific for the institutions in which researchers do research. A researcher who is hired by a *private corporation* (or by a *private university*) is bound by the *provisions of the contract* that he has concluded with the corporation. In fixing such provisions, both the corporation and the researcher are largely but not absolutely free. Nobody is authorized by law to bind himself for good (art. 27 of the Swiss civil code) or in such a way that he is to engage in criminal activities (art. 20 of the Swiss code of obligations); and no researcher can free himself from basic responsibilities necessarily attached to any research activity (cf. below). Within these boundaries (which are difficult to determine with precision), however, the researcher may well be obliged to do his work on such fields, on such subjects, and with such intentions as prescribed by the corporation. Of course, the corporation (and particularly a private university) is free to promise by contract to respect a certain scientific autonomy—with regard either to choosing research subjects or to deciding on research methods, or finally to publishing research results. We shall return to this situation later in this paper.

If a researcher is hired by a *state university,* the situation becomes more complex because the state enters the picture—and the state, on any level, is bound in the first instance and without exception by constitutional rights.[15] But this does not mean that our researcher enjoys necessarily more freedom. In fact, he is bound in various respects:

- A university teacher (who, usually, in Switzerland as in most other Western countries, is hired as a teacher and as a researcher) has to teach and to do research work *in the field for which he has been engaged.* This seems to be self-evident; however, difficult questions may arise whenever a researcher wants to engage in interdisciplinary work—where, then, are the limits of his "realm"?

- A university teacher is in general not free to determine the proportion of his time to be spent in teaching or in research activities. He is, in general, *required to do both* (more or less at the same time), even when he expects to win a Nobel prize if he can devote all his time to research. He is also usually *bound to participate in the administration of his university.* On the other hand, he is generally free to decide what research topics he wants to tackle, in what ways he wants to do it, and what will become of his eventual results (I do not want to discuss here the delicate problems of economic valorization of research results, by taking patents, etc.; in fact, this topic would occupy us for a long time). He is even *required to use such freedom* because otherwise he would neglect his legal obligation to do research.[16] This is generally accepted and probably true, more or less, in all Western state universities. In some Swiss university laws, such freedom is guaranteed explicitly as well as by the federal research code.[17] And even where this is not the case, freedom of research, if enacted by the constitution (or by international law), certainly extends to state university teachers because, as said before, the state is bound in the first instance by its constitution and by international law.

The situation is partly different for researchers employed by *public administration agencies.* In fact, every Western state (I assume) has research institutions—in basic research as, e.g., in France, Italy, or Germany (institutes financed and controlled by the Délégation nationale à la recherche scientifique, by the Consiglio Nazionale delle Ricerche, by the Max-Planck-Gesellschaft), or in applied research (e.g., for defense, agricultural, or telecommunication purposes). For *basic research institutes,* the legal situation of researchers, with respect to the freedom of research, is, I presume, more or less the same as in state universities (further investigations would be necessary). But in *applied research centers,* researchers will usually be hired for specific activities, and they will have to accept prescriptions both with regard to research topics and to the publication of results, according to specific rules set for the various centers, and within the same limits as indicated for researchers hired by private institutions. For them, furthermore, general provisions of the state's employees code will be applicable.

These are the limits which are more or less generally accepted. They all include, in fact, uncertainties and are subject to difficult and delicate discussions. But I do not think that we should, with regard to them, enter into details. What really intrigues the Western scientific world—and the world beyond it as well and even more—is whether these limits, as listed above, are complete and "sufficient" to cope with burning problems arising out of modern science. To this topic I want to turn in the following pages.

The actual legal situation, with regard to *state university researchers,* may be summarized as follows: they are usually guaranteed, by the constitution, by law, by ordinance, or by specific engagement provisions, freedom of research; this freedom is limited to the field for which the researcher (and teacher) is engaged; it is limited, furthermore, by provisions concerning various duties of the researcher (teaching, administrative, and research duties) and, last but not least, by provisions of criminal, civil, and administrative codes forbidding or penalizing specific research methods or objects or limiting research activities in more general a way. The researcher thus remains free to decide on the topics, the methods (within the limits mentioned above), and the handling of the results of his research work. Researchers who are hired by *public administration agencies* or by *private corporations* have to accept, furthermore, orders concerning both the topics and the handling of the results of their research.

Are these limits "sufficient"? Or should further limits be added? Should state law exclude specific topics of research? Should it exclude the publication of specific results? Should it make specific research projects subject to official procedure and authorization? What should the consequences be if such provisions be neglected, e.g., if specific research activities are undertaken without authorization? The reason why these are "burning" questions nowadays is obvious; enough evidence has been presented in the other contributions to this volume.

Are there any *legal attempts to narrow the freedom of research?* As far as I know, there are in fact attempts, but hardly more—the actual legal order, as mentioned above, has almost never reacted positively to them so far. However, an interesting exception can be found in the *university code of Hessen.* §6 reads as follows, under the heading "Informationsverpflichtung":

"All members of universities, being engaged in research and teaching activities, are to consider the social consequences of scientific recognition ("Erkenntnis"). Whenever they learn of research results, particularly in their specific field, which, if made use of in an irresponsible way, could create dangers for society, for the life or the peaceful living together of men, they shall inform their faculty or a central organ of their university."[18]

This provision was brought before the German Bundesverfassungsgericht, as violating (among other articles) art. 5 al. 3 of the

German Basic Code. The court rejected the complaint with note-worthy arguments.[19] It held that the freedom of research is a constitu-tional value decision ("Wertentscheidung") among others. It cannot claim general priority. Even those fundamental freedoms that are un-conditionally guaranteed by constitutions are to be considered within the framework of responsibility towards society. Different constitu-tional freedoms and other constitutional provisions may, in specific contexts, conflict; such conflicts have to be solved by specific "balanc-ing of goods" ("Güterabwägung"). As far as freedom of research is concerned, we ought to remember that precisely scientific activities (at universities and in similar institutions) best serve state and society if they are not influenced by utilitarian or political considerations. On the other hand, such autonomy is guaranteed for scientific activities serving the well-being of individuals and of society and not isolating itself from them. Consequently, the Court held that the duty of re-searchers to consider social consequences of their research, if limited to "heavy consequences for constitutionaly guaranteed goods,"[20] was in harmony with the ensemble of the constitutional "Wertordnung," and therefore also with art. 5 al. 3. It arrived at the same result for the duty of researches to inform about serious dangers that might be created by research.[21]

The constitution of the *Swiss canton of Aargau* provides in its §14 that scientific instruction and research are free, as are artistic activities, but that scientific instruction and research have to respect the dignity of all creatures.[22]

When the *Swiss Federal Research Act* was discussed in the federal parliament, many deputies stressed the importance of scientists' re-sponsibility, but there was general agreement that it would be diffi-cult, if not impossible, to find a legal formula that would not limit too radically scientific research.[23] A similar discussion arose in the Swiss Science Council concerning the projected new *Federal Institutes of Technology Act.* Here, again, freedom of research was guaranteed. The Council, however, found, after a lively discussion and without arriv-ing at a consensus, that its "ordinary" limits were to be completed by "the responsibility of all researchers towards science and the com-munity."

The German cabinet minister for Research and Technology is-sued, in 1978, *guidelines* on in vitro fertilization. Research that does not comply with these guidelines can not be funded by any federal agency.[24]

Of particular interest for our topic are recent recommendations of the *Council of Europe's Parliamentary Assembly.* In 1982 the Assembly issued a recommendation on genetic engineering (no. 934); in 1986 another recommendation on the use of human embryos and foetuses for diagnostic, therapeutic, scientific, industrial, and commercial purposes (no. 1046); and, finally, in 1987, a recommendation on parliamentary assessment in Europe of scientific and technological choices (no. 1055). This latter recommendation is noteworthy for its clear acknowledgment of "deep rifts in public opinion" because of scientific progress and technological options.

From the German Constitutional Court's decision, we may learn an important lesson. The constitutionally guaranteed freedom of research is limited, even though the constitution does not say a word about it, by other constitutionally guaranteed freedoms or—more generally—by other constitutional "value decisions" such as the acknowledgment of the dignity of man (and of all creatures). Legislation is thus permitted and required to elaborate such limitation. Obviously, the legislator is authorized to do so, too, if the constitution itself does not even guarantee that freedom explicitly (as in the United States or Switzerland). On the other hand, limitations on freedom of research must be included in a constitution or legislative act because in a democracy limitations on any constitutional freedom are not acceptable if not elaborated in a democratic process—i.e., by parliament (and, e.g., in Switzerland, by the people themselves). What the German Constitutional Court has brought forward corresponds, in fact, with what has been generally accepted in modern fundamental rights doctrine. Fundamental rights ("Grundrechte") or human rights ("Menschenrechte") are written into constitutions and international instruments because they protect fundamental human values, against infringements that are to be feared in concrete historic situations. *No such value can be guaranteed absolutely* because other basic values that may enter into conflict with the first are to be guaranteed as well and in the same time. Thus, every "basic freedom" has its "natural" limits in other basic freedoms or interests. No such freedom is *a priori* "more basic" than others, except—in my personal view—for freedom of religion and of what we call in Switzerland the "persönliche Freiheit" (personal freedom), i.e., the right to physical, intellectual, and psychic integrity. Thus freedom of research does not stand above all other basic freedoms or interests. Even the American preferred freedoms doctrine (privileging the First Amendment freedoms in certain respects) would not, in my view, cover such a privilege.[25] The same is true of the freedom of enterprise (if and however it is guaranteed by a constitution). Thus a private corporation may not claim such a freedom as overriding any other basic freedom or value, and therefore it has to accept limitations on its activity, even on its research activity, motivated by the respect for other basic values.

Public authorities have to respect all those constitutionally acknowledged basic values, particularly all fundamental freedoms. They have to make sure that such freedoms are not destroyed by anyone; they have to protect actively—by legislation and by administrative or judicial action—those freedoms whenever and by whomever they are (or risk being) endangered.[26] In our complex civilization, public authorities certainly do not fulfill their constitutional obligations by mere abstention from infringements. They have to establish procedures and organizations for adequate protection. They even have to limit fundamental freedoms so that their enjoyment does not hamper other fundamental values. Obviously, such limitations are to be directed against those who have the power to endanger those values.

If this basic concept of bringing fundamental rights into effect is accepted (it *is* accepted in the German-speaking world, and I cannot see how it could remain unaccepted in any Western country), the question arises, in our context, as to which constitutional values could be endangered, at the end of our century, by research activities, by making use of the freedom of research.

Of course, many researchers will flatly deny that their work, that research work in general, could encroach on other persons' basic rights. However, more enlightened spirits know perfectly well that this is not only possible but has happened in various and sometimes terrible ways. Research lies at the bottom of nuclear energy installations including tremendous risks for most human and other beings. research lies at the bottom of our most sophisticated telecommunication systems, which alter not only the ways and methods but also the objects and subjects of communication. Research lies at the bottom of the most advanced genetic engineering techniques, which have already had practical results with plants and animals and which may equally be applied to human beings. Research lies at the bottom of modern sophisticated weapons, and it is furthered on a grand scale by the development, e.g., of the SDI system, which, according to Russian reactions at least, may become a new threat to the strategic balance. All this, of course, is well known. But are the sometimes disastrous applications of basic research in physics, chemistry, molecular biology, and engineering so narrowly bound to research work itself that this work and those who do it are to be held *responsible?* The existence of such a link would certainly be the reason for enacting legitimate limitations on freedom of research. In other words, the legitimacy of such limitations depends on the assumption that researchers are to be held responsible (at least partly) for the consequences to which their results may lead for basic values.

This is a fundamental ethical problem of our days, highly debated all over the world. I do not intend to summarize this discussion—which would be quite impossible—or to enter more deeply into this subject because I am not a philosopher. But, on the other hand, I have to present my personal opinion on this subject—which is by no means original, but largely influenced by thoughts brought forward by eminent philosophers. I think it useful to present my opinion in the form of six statements:

1. Research work is by no means to be considered "value free" ("wertfrei"). It may suffice here to point out that the selection of research topics (and, before, the choice of a research job in this or that institution) as well as the handling of research results is influenced by various motives, scientific and nonscientific, and certainly not only by the desire of seeking the "truth" (whatever this means in the field of science). Personal values and goals inevitably enter the picture. The researcher is not a machine inserting itself mechanically into an objective stream of scientific progress leading to the discovery of truth.

2. Modern civilization is (even beyond the fields already mentioned) largely based on the results of scientific research, and the impact of science on the further development of civilization will probably become stronger over time.

3. Human experience teaches us that research results will not only be used in beneficial ways.

4. Our civilization has come to a point where important systems fall out of balance. For the first time in human history, the future of life is endangered, in a most general way, by man himself (human life as well as the life of plants and animals). Not only is life in the biological sense endangered, but to a far greater extent, so is life in dignity. For the first time, the history of life and of culture can no longer be expected to proceed "naturally." Future history is not simply "given" any more; it depends on how man will behave, on man's willingness not to use all-destructive weapons and not to let nature be destroyed by pollution of all sorts.[27]

5. Scientists may have—and have in many situations, as Dr. Mauron's paper shows—the actual possibility to take part in the process of decisions on whether and how their research results should be "applied." And even if such possibilities are scarce, scientists are in the

same way coresponsible for what happens to their research results, as anyone is co-responsible for the effects that have been created by his activity (or passivity).

6. History teaches us that such responsibility in science cannot be left entirely to scientists themselves. Too many of them are, as mentioned already, too often inspired to choose this or that topic and to handle their research results in this or that way by motives that have nothing to do with such responsibility, e.g., by the desire to have good standing among their peers and, if possible, to obtain a Nobel prize, or by the desire for money. By this I do by no means want morally and generally to disqualify scientists—I know that I myself am not free of such motives, and I know that a scientist will often be compelled to accept a research job (e.g., in a defense project) just to earn a living. But such considerations do not alter the basic issue: all too often scientists are not willing or are not in a situation to resist research "temptations," i.e., the participation in research projects that by all standards they must consider potentially dangerous.

These six statements may be summarized as follows: man has become co-responsible for the history of life and culture. And because science is more and more the basis for human "progress," this responsibility must cover, more than anything else, the field of science. Scientists have responsibility for what they are doing and also for what will be made out of their results.[28] Of course, this latter responsibility is not entirely theirs; all those who use research results are also responsible and in the first instance. But scientists cannot leave such responsibility entirely to the users of their research. They have made the uses and misuses possible. They set the primary conditions. They may—but they must not—undertake research whose results are particularly susceptible to misuses on a grand scale. Consequently, science cannot be left to itself any longer if scientists themselves are not thoroughly willing and fit to assume and realize such responsibility. And this is, for different reasons, not at all likely—by which I do not mean that no scientist is prepared to accept such responsibility—I know many responsible (and "concerned") scientists!

But who, then, is to assume (to share) such responsibility? Should it necessarily and exclusively be the state? Should it be the whole group of scientists concerned, or a scientific institution, such as a university, or a private corporation engaged in research or in the promotion of research? But, again, the question arises: who obliges them to assume such responsibility? And, again, I think that according to experience, we cannot have simple and complete confidence in any such autonomous acceptation of responsibility. Private corporations yield to economic pressures. In a university a scientist with excellent standing will hardly be restrained, either by his colleagues or by the university administration, from activities that he is determined to engage in. And the "society of peers" has lacked, up to now, the power to make any decisions effective. This, in fact, is the problem of *guidelines elaborated by scientific academies and similar institutions.*

In Switzerland, and not only there, we come to the conclusion, then, that state action—and this means above all state legislation—directed to make the responsibility concrete and binding is unavoidable. Certainly and again, state authorities must not assume such responsibility exclusively. Rather they must cooperate with academic institutions, with corporations, with peer groups, and with the individual scientists themselves.[29] But the state must take its share of that responsibility. And state legislation must establish procedures in which such responsibility may operate.

Fundamental rights, as we have seen before, can only be limited by values of the same standing, i.e., by other basic values. And *the* basic value that is endangered today by the use of research results is human life (and the life of animals and plants). But *life in dignity* is also threatened. If creatures are brought to life by genetic engineering combining the cells of a man and of an ape (which is being discussed as a real possibility right now), then the dignity of human life is clearly violated. And not only life itself and its dignity are to be protected, but also life whose genetic caracteristics have not been artificially manipulated.

The concept of dignity has been largely discussed in philosophical, theological, and juridical literature. As a legal principle, it is *the* directive of both the construction and actions of a modern constitutional state. Again, it seems not to be necessary or even desirable to summarize those discussions; however, I want to present one statement that, I think, is generally accepted: the concept of the dignity of man means that every man and every women, as human beings and as unique individuals, have inalienable rights and duties; that he and she are "subjects" and must never be treated as objects; that as subjects they are entitled to substantial autonomy in which they are expected to act responsibly.

But "dignity" is not solely a human privilege. It is legitimate and important to attribute "dignity" also to animals and plants—not the same dignity, but a specific one. This, I have to admit, is a new concept, developed recently both in the United States and Europe, or more precisely a concept new to modern philosophical and political ideas (since the Enlightenment); we can, in fact, find aspects of this concept in older times, and even today in non-Western cultures. Dr. Beat Sitter, recently discussed the dignity of everything that has been created.[30] The dignity of animals and plants (not to speak of the dignity of landscapes etc.) is different from the dignity of man. But there is a common ground: the dignity of animals and plants is violated, as is the dignity of men, if their life is destroyed, or if an individual is intentionally exposed to heavy suffering or to life in depressing circumstances, or if it is denied "society" or the right to procreate.

In my opinion freedom of research is, then, to be limited (in a constitutional (or international) law and in research or university codes, etc.) by the *respect of life in dignity of human beings and of animals and plants, in short, of all beings.* This limitation includes *other persons' basic rights* guaranteed by the constitution,[31] e.g., no scientist might use his freedom of research to hinder other scientists to use theirs. *No human being must be "used" for research purposes without his considerate and unforced consent.* No manipulations of human germ-line are to be permitted (perhaps with some exceptions which should be circumscribed as distinctly as possible)[32] because it involves future human beings who cannot give their consent. Animals and plants cannot give their consent either; therefore scientists are not to be allowed to use them without *considerately balancing their research interests against the "interest" of the animals or plants in maintaining their life in dignity.* An elaborate procedure of balancing must be substituted here for the requirement of consent. And no intentional genetic alteration of wild animal or plant species is to be allowed.

This means that research projects are to be limited, altered, or stopped, whenever the risk of misuse of research results is considerable and the ensuing violation of dignity would be severe. Those who have to effect that limitation will have, consequently, to forecast future ways of using and misusing research results, and to estimate the risk of actual misuse. This will be difficult—the more so because one never knows what exact results may be reached in a research project. But what I propose here is a compulsory effort to estimate that risk and to evaluate possible uses and misuses. Such systematic efforts were, up to now, I guess, not undertaken frequently, in my country at least. It means that scientists will not be allowed to direct their intellectual energy and their creative force exclusively to reach scientific results, but that they must—together with other persons and institutions—think with equal intensity about possible consequences, as is required by §6 of the Hessen university code. The same duty will be imposed on scientific institutions that have to make scientific work possible or attractive by making grants, building laboratories, awarding prizes, etc. The consequence of such a concept and its realization would be that not every object that could be an interesting research topic might be admitted by such institutions as such, and not every promising research method might be sponsored or even allowed. Finally, if research work produces interesting results, the same procedure of risk evaluation should take place if they are different from the ones expected, or if the "risk context" has changed. Not all results, therefore, might be allowed to be published. What I am advocating here is science risk assessment, in analogy to technology risk assessment.

Of primary importance will obviously be legal provisions introducing *good procedures,* in which such limitation is to be realized.[33] I could imagine, in a nonexhaustive way, the following procedural rules:

- Whenever a research project requires, before being put into action, a decision from an institution (university, public administration agency, science promoting foundation, etc.) because it needs the allocation of special resources, the author(s) of the project should present, together with the usual description of the project, an evaluation of possible positive and negative consequences for Western society's basic values. This evaluation might be compared to the US "environmental impact statement procedure" (or the European "Umweltverträglichkeitsprüfung"). The evaluation presented by the project author(s) must then be judged by a person or a body of persons set up by the institution concerned. And only if that person or body of persons conclude that the possible negative consequences, if any, seem to be tolerable, may the required resources be granted—no matter how considerable the mere scientific "value" of the project may be. The main advantage of such a procedure would be, in my opinion, that researchers and institutions would both be compelled to think of possible effects; this would be exactly what the Hessen university code has imposed on the Hessen university researchers! Perhaps, in special, "hot" fields, research projects that have been authorized in such a way should be monitored by the authorizing body or by special delegates to ensure that any "dangerous" results are known in time.

  In the United States, such procedures have been established in many research institutions and even prescribed by the National Research Act of 1974 (insofar as research institutions apply for a grant or a contract under this Act for projects or programs that involve "the conduct of biomedical or behavioral research involving human subjects"; Title II §212 a). This "system" has found considerable interest in Germany.[34]

- If such a project produces results other than those that were expected, or if the social context has changed considerably since the "go ahead" for the project, the researchers concerned and the person or body of persons mentioned before should discuss whether those results should be published. I am fully aware that, in recent history, prohibiting publication is difficult to enforce and extremely problematic because, as Dr. Gruber states,[35] research results, if not published, may be used in uncontrollable ways. A prohibition of publication must thus be reserved for extraordinary situations where the risk of disastrous consequences to which the (mis)use of research results may lead is obvious and severe.

• With regard to research financed by private corporations (which amounts in Switzerland to three-quarters of all research), similar—but not identical—procedures should be discussed. Thus, corporations should be required by law to proceed themselves with the same evaluation proposed above. The delicate question is whether such evaluation should be supervised—and by whom. I could imagine a body (ethical commission or the like) set up by law and authorized to check any evaluation effectuated by any corporation in specific fields (which should be determined, as precisely as reasonably possible, by law). Of course, corporations would strongly oppose such a procedure because they would be afraid of "holes" in the commission through which research projects could find their way to competing corporations. But this problem (which must be taken seriously) should not be, I assume, entirely unsolvable. If university researchers are interested in doing research for corporations, they should at any rate submit their project to the university's "ethical commission" (or however such a body may be called). Research results obtained in fields in which the corporation's evaluation is to be supervised by the body mentioned above should be transmitted to the same body and only be allowed to be used or published if the risk of disastrous consequences is not obvious and severe.

• All researchers, whether engaged by private corporations, by state or private universities, or by public administration, should be required by law to inform the public (or special bodies, such as ethical commissions) of any special risk that they might perceive in research results already realized or to be expected, beyond the procedures proposed above. This again would correspond to the Hessen university code's provision.[36] Furthermore, I could imagine a special procedure of comprehensive risk evaluation to be undertaken by a permanent commission. This commission would thus have to consider systematically and periodically, beyond procedures concerning specific projects, if and where modern science produces or is likely to produce results that might severely endanger life in dignity. Such a procedure is being discussed now at the University of Bern.

• Every scientist should be required, when taking his final examinations, to give an oath (or the like) by which he promises to consider the possible good or bad consequences of any scientific activity he may be willing to undertake. This oath—analogous to the Hippocratic oath required from medical doctors—has been proposed by the German publicist Walter Jens.[37]

- The strongest state intrusion into research activities would be a legal provision forbidding research in specific fields altogether. Whether such a prohibition would make sense must be discussed; up to now, I have not reached a clear opinion on this. On the other hand, law should clearly determine which methods are forbidden because they encroach too heavily on fundamental rights. Such prohibitions should be controlled either by public officials or again by bodies set up specifically for such purposes.

I am aware that all such measures are difficult to make effective. However, there are a few sanctions that could be imposed on those who neglect the rules postulated above: organisations that attribute illicit grants could be censured by controlling authorities; corporations (or their managers) that become active in "forbidden fields" or use "forbidden methods" could be penalized; researchers employed by state universities or public administration agencies who violate such rules or their oaths or who neglect their duties to inform society about the results of their research would have to be reprimanded. But the success of those measures would be doubtful if researchers themselves are not prepared to assume the responsibility that, as shown above, is crucial for the survival of man and nature in "dignity." Thus, the most important effort to be undertaken will be an adequate education of prospective researchers (and of managers who will hire them).[38] Universities have therefore a special responsibility; what they omit to teach will hardly be made good later on. And in this respect, I think, universities have omitted much up to now. I very much hope that they will change their attitude, and that they will change it fast.

Notes

I want to thank very warmly my former assistant, Fürsprecherin Erika Schläppi, for her precious help.

1. Entscheidungen des Bundesverfassungsgerichts (BVerfGE) vol. 35, 79ff., 113.

2. Alexander Blankennagel, Wissenschaftsfreiheit aus der Sicht der Wissenschaftssoziologie, *Archiv des öffentlichen Rechts* 1980, 36ff., 47/48.

3. Hans Gruber, *Forschungsförderung und Erkenntnisfreiheit* (Stämpfli Bern 1986), 132ff.: "Generierung von Neuem," "exploratives Handeln."

4. Cf. also the valuable indications presented by Peter Häberle, Die Freiheit der Wissenschaften im Verfassungsstaat, *Archiv des öffentlichen Rechts* 1985, 392ff., 334ff.

5. Jörg Paul Müller, Kommentar zur schweizerischen Bundesverfassung, *Wissenschaftsfreiheit* (Stämpfli Bern etc. 1987), N. 8; Michel Rossinelli, *Les libertés non écrites* (Payot Lausanne 1987), 232.

6. Walter Haller, Die Forschungsfreiheit, in: *Festschrift für Hans Nef* (Schulthess Polygraphischer Verlag Zürich 1981), 125ff., 130.

7. Hans Gruber, *op.cit.* (note 3), 150, 175.

8. *Ibid.*, 150.

9. *Ibid.*, 181.

10. Cf. BVerfGE vol. 35, 117ff.

11. Kay Hailbronner, *Die Freiheit der Forschung und Lehre als Funktionsgrundrecht* (Joachim Heitmann Verlag Hamburg 1979), 73ff.

12. BVerfGE vol. 35, 114; cf. BVerfGE vol. 46, 367ff.

13. Cf. Hans Gruber, *op.cit.* (note 3), 354ff.

14. Cf. the comments on some doubtful limitations by Albin Eser, Der Forscher als "Täter" und "Opfer", in: *Festschrift für Karl Lackner* (Walter de Gruyter & Co. Berlin 1987), 925ff., 935ff.

15. Cf. Kay Hailbronner, *op.cit.* (note 11), 158ff.

16. *Ibid.*, 293ff.

17. Cf. Jörg Paul Müller, op.cit. (note 5, note Walter Haller, *op.cit.* (note 6), 132.

18. "Alle an Forschung und Lehre beteiligten Mitglieder und Angehörigen der Universitäten haben die gesellschaftlichen Folgen wissenschaftlicher Erkenntnis mitzubedenken. Werden ihnen Ergebnisse der Forschung, vor allem in ihrem Fachgebiet bekannt, die bei verantwortungsloser Verwendung erhebliche Gefahren für die Gesamtheit, das Leben odor das friedliche Zusammenleben der Menschen herbeiführen können, so sollen sie den zuständigen Fachbereichsrat oder ein zentrales Organ der Universität davon unterrichten."

19. Cf. BVerfGE vol. 47, 327ff.

20. *Ibid.*, 380.

21. *Ibid.*, 384. Cf. also Ralf Dreier, Forschungsbegrenzung als verfassungsrechtliches Problem, *Deutsches Verwaltungsblatt* 1980, 471ff.

22. Cf. Kurt Eichenberger, *Verfassung des Kantons Aargau*, Textausgabe mit Kommentar (Sauerländer Aarau etc. 1986), 88f.

23. Hans Gruber, *op.cit.* (note 3), 350 citing the Swiss Federal Council, in: *Bundesblatt* 1981 III, 1031.

24. Cf. Hasso Hofmann, Biotechnik, Gentherapie, Genmanipulation—Wissenschaft im rechtsfreien Raum? *Juristenzeitung* 1986, 253ff., 255f.

25. Cf. Laurence H. Tribe, American Constitutional Law, 2nd ed. (The Foundation Press, Inc. Mineola, N.Y.) 1988, 785ff.

26.   Cf. Hasso Hofmann, *op.cit.* (note 24), 255; George Turner, Grenzen der Forschungsfreiheit, *Zeitschrift für Rechtspolitik* 1986, 172ff., 175ff.

27.   Cf. Peter Saladin—Christoph A. Zenger, *Rechte künftiger Generationen* (Helbing & Lichtenhahn Basel 1988).

28.   Cf. Kay Hailbronner, *op.cit.* (note 11), 296f.

29.   Cf. Hans Gruber, *op.cit.* (note 3), 363ff.

30.   Wie lässt sich ökologische Gerechtigkeit denken? *Zeitschrift für evangelische Ethik*, 1987, 271ff.

31.   Cf. Hans Gruber, *op.cit.* (note 3), 348ff., 355; Albin Eser, *op.cit.* (note 14), 927ff.

32.   Cf. Peter Saladin, Rechtliche Aspekte de Gentechnologie in: Gentechnologie - Chance oder Bedrohung? to be published in Bern, 1989, with further indications.

33.   Cf. Albin Eser, *op.cit.* (note 14), 943ff.

34.   Cf. Reinhard Bork, *Ethik-Kommissionen in den USA,* Neue Juristische Wochenschrift 1983, 2056ff.

35.   *Op.cit.* (note 3), 363.

36.   Cf. Kay Hailbronner, *op.cit.* (note 11), 302ff.

37.   Mentioned by Kay Hailbronner, *op.cit.* (note 11), 297ff.

38.   Cf. also R. Löw, Leben aus dem Labor (C. Bertelsmann München 1985), 206.

Freedom of Research and Basic Rights

ANDREA DEGGINGER

A modern democratic constitutional state does not exist for its own sake, but for the citizens living within it. It is expected to guarantee certain fundamental rights indispensable for people and their well-being[1]. Life and life in dignity[2] count thereby among the basic values. These can be infringed in many different ways. Man's research activities are one source of potential danger.[3] Must we therefore impose a general ban on research? The practical difficulties to enforce such a stop are obvious. But even apart from them, man's curiosity, his urge to broaden his sphere of experience, which lies at the very bottom of research, may not be taken lightly. It deserves protection as a basic right not only because it is a characteristic human trait (I assume that animals do not have the capacity to search systematically for a goal set by their own free will), but also because a modern Western society vitally depends on citizens who are open to the world around them, capable of recognizing problems, of asking questions, and of moving towards solutions. A confrontation between life in dignity and the freedom of research arises inevitably. We will set out to resolve those competing interests in a manner that seeks to preserve the essential functions of each branch.

It seems necessary to state clearly what we expect of an order of protection: we want the freedom of research to be guaranteed as long as the applied methods, the acquired knowledge, or the possible misuse of results do not impair life in dignity. We must therefore ponder whether predictions about the possible positive and negative consequences of a specific research activity can be obtained and how reliable they would be. These findings should enable us to conceive a system of risk assessment. Let us then inquire into the way science works.

Man is surrounded by unknown things. They remain a permanent challenge for him. In the course of history, techniques have been gradually developed that promise to gain knowledge or at least to shed light on one dark spot or another. Thereby, it must be noted that in starting research in a new field, the goal we aim at can only be generally and globally described. At this stage, the lack of detailed knowledge does not in my opinion allow any reliable evaluation of the overall risk for life in dignity and the possible misuse of discoveries. First of all, we cannot hope to be aware of all the factors determining the outcome

241

of the project we have in mind. Even if we had identified at least the decisive parameters, could we attribute to them a realistic weight? And what will happen with the results? I suppose that any statement regarding a potential danger can merely point out scenarios and more or less arbitrarily assumed probabilities to realize them. The frame of the "mights" and "coulds" and "ifs" can hereby not be escaped. The chance of being confronted with an outcome that was never envisaged or of being immobilized by hysterical fears without due cause is obvious.

To illustrate my points, I take an example from biotechnology. In the early 1970s, molecular biologists had accumulated enough knowledge about the single gene, the entire DNA, and their functioning to make gene manipulation appear feasible. This development spread uneasiness and discomfort among the scientists concerned. The nightmare of genetically engineered man invaded scientific society. A conference of molecular biologists, held in 1975 in Asilomar, California, ordained a one-year moratorium for experiments.[4] Within that time the American National Institutes of Health elaborated an order for classifying future research projects by means of a risk scale with a corresponding set of extremely strict safety rules for the laboratory work and established the necessary administrative procedures. As researchers actually penetrated systematically into genetic engineering, they gained new and more specific knowledge that allowed them to define certain risks accurately and drop others from their considerations. On the whole, it became evident that many of the original fears lacked realistic grounds—whether because research did not turn towards the sensitive areas, because the probability of an accident could in good faith be neglected, or simply because possibilities thought to be within reach turned out to be years or even decades off. These findings resulted in a significant softening of the NIH regulations.[5]

From these observations, we have to draw an important conclusion: 'risk assessment' may serve as a tool to guide research, basic as well as applied. To do this correctly and to sustain our decisions with serious arguments, we must engage in so-called risk research. Thus, risk assessment, which has a clearly defined relation to actual situations and can therefore claim with justification to influence scientific activities, requires—generally and specifically—its own research and depends on experiments. The fact that the United States Department of Agriculture is funding risk research in agricultural biotechnology with huge amounts of money certainly supports this statement.[6]

Having shown that risk assessment requires investigation into the field of research, I will treat the two principal kinds of risk assessment—overall and specific—that have been debated up to now.

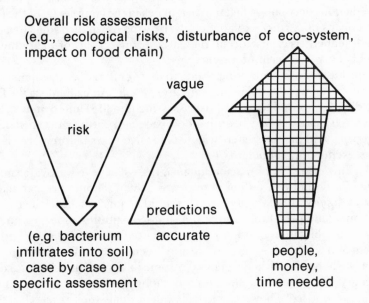

Figure 1.

An overall risk assessment looks at the experiment from a comprehensive point of view. It seeks to assess the consequences as completely as possible; the close and immediate ones as well as the remote and distant ones should be laid open. Typical questions to be answered are therefore the impact on society, on the food chain, or on the ecosystem. In specific risk assessment, the experiments are divided into groups with common characteristics, such as traditionally crossed plants, transgenic plants, or vaccine for poultry. Profound knowledge about the fields in question enables researchers to select among the theoretically unlimited number of potential hazards those that are realistically and typically to be expected. Different factors influence the grade of these risks and must be examined one after another. For example, with traditionally crossed plants, a typical danger arises from the mixing of the whole genomes, i.e., the entire genetic code, of two plants. It is then not sufficient to find out that a new potato plant produces more and bigger potatoes—the desired outcome. We must also look for unwanted results, such as toxic substances in the bulbs.[7]

Two empirically gathered items of information must be taken into account for a sound evaluation (see Figure 1):

1. The more global the risk we try to assess, the more vague our predictions become—a fact that originates in the complexity of the task and needs no further explanation. Narrowing down the radius to a few well-defined risks that occur regularly in one group of experiments yields far more accurate predictions.

2. Because of this same complexity, to do overall risk assessments, one must invest heavily in time, money, and people. An example is the first field trials exposed to overall risk assessment in the United States. The research program had been handed back and forth between federal agencies and the interested scientists for five years before permission was eventually granted.[8]

This glance at how scientific progress is achieved provides guidance for outlining a system of protecting the freedom of research and life in dignity: freedom of research should be guaranteed at the constitutional (and preferably also at the supraconstitutional) level with the inherent obligation to use it for the benefit of society and the environment and with due respect for life and life in dignity. With this conception we have established a general responsibility for the scientific community. Scientists can therefore no longer claim to operate in a value-free space. They are held by law to evaluate their research activities in the light of what is good and right for society and the environment.[9]

The constitutional guarantee of these values must be secured at juridically lower levels by laws and ordinances. We shall restrict ourselves to the precautions the legislation should take to avoid infringing these values. A necessary prerequisite for any protection is of course a concrete object to be protected. The terms "the benefit of society and the environment" and "life and life in dignity" indicate the right direction, but their content is too vague and indistinct to be protected as an entity. They may in good faith be interpreted in many different ways; what to some persons touches the core of life in dignity, for instance computers capable of recognizing human speech and transgenic animals, is to others at its outskirts. To substantiate these notions national legislatures should nominate two different types of permanent commissions. The first would be a fairly large ethics commission that should consist of research scientists from the various branches of the natural sciences and the humanities, as well as politicians, administrators, managers from institutions of higher education, representatives of public interest groups, etc. Its main activity will be the early diagnosis of potentially dangerous developments—understood in a broad sense—for life and life in dignity. It will have to consider the ever-changing content of fundamental human values, watch the great trends in research, and try to assess the global risks connected with them. A report containing these observations and ensuing recommendations should periodically be submitted to the legislature, which would then discuss the recommendations and determine what zones are to be regarded as ethically sensitive under the law, and how they must be handled: with a total ban, measures to assess and monitor potential impacts, etc. The point of reference is the article in the constitution about research proposed above. This exercise of judgment involves a comparative weighing of goods.[10] It is obvious that decisions of this kind shape the essential appearance of the state, e.g., a state that prohibits research in genetic engineering, such as Denmark. The legislature may then empower expert committees to study the problems. These boards would formulate risk research programs for specific risk assessments and would commission case by case analyses. Their work should eventually lead to new or adjusted guidelines for research and its applications in the fields concerned. Because of the dynamic nature of research, the commissions would have to continually monitor developments in each field and change the relevant guidelines accordingly.

We must remember that we are still searching for a tangible object to be protected. It is therefore essential to understand that the guidelines are intended to protect one well-defined manifestation of life in dignity. They embody precise and detailed instructions as to whether to do particular research projects at all, and if they are to be done, how research projects in "hot areas" are to be carried out. Consequently, we have acquired the object and at the same time possess the means—the guidelines—to protect it.

The legislature must make these guidelines legally binding, and the people and institutions concerned, e.g., scientists, research institutes, industries, must understand their legal responsibility to adhere to the regulations. A necessary complement to these guidelines is a set of penalties in case they are disregarded. This, of course, entails an instrument to uncover irregularities. Here I advise against anything that resembles a "science police," which is bound to be opposed by scientists. Such a measure would imply that scientists lack any sense of responsibility, although in fact the scientific community has shown itself sensitive to ethical problems. In biotechnology the already mentioned moratorium originated from the scientists' own discomfort.

They were the driving force behind the design of procedures for performing risky experiments—although admittedly for various, including economic reasons[11]. Nonetheless, scientists should participate at all levels of this process, including the enforcement of the regulations.

I therefore propose to allow the expert committees to make site visits. These visits are already common in the natural sciences. Institutions such as the National Science Foundation or the American National Institutes of Health have asked ad hoc committees of advisers to visit laboratories, usually in connection with a research proposal. These committees were dissolved as soon as they had completed the visits and reported to the institution. I propose that the state establish similar committees on a permanent basis. Their main activities would consist in setting up guidelines and overseeing both academic and industrial research groups active in "hot fields."

The composition of these bodies poses a problem. To do the work effectively, one must rely on specialists. With them, two potential dangers arise:

1. The experts might use the information they elicit during the visits. The temptation definitely exists. Groups active in basic and applied research are always competing against each other—the former more for academic distinction, the latter more for financial success. This is more acute in fields where basic researchers tend to initiate the development of practical applications of their discoveries, as, for instance, in molecular biology. But success and progress in science cannot be achieved merely by copying a neighbor's results. Moreover, the results are typically not made up of a couple of figures and letters only. In addition, the academic imperative "publish or perish" conveys a distinct picture of what is going on in international science, where something is happening and who is at the forefront of research. However, this natural survey instrument usually does not apply for scientific work in profit-making organizations where there is little or now inducement to publish the results of research.

2. Scientific and/or economic connections with the laboratories to be overseen prevent the committee from meeting obligations. There is surely no means to guarantee that only disinterested persons serve on the committees. However, there are ways to organize academic research that favor the independence of scientists. Professors who receive an important part of the means to carry out their research (finances, personnel, equipment) from a university, depend less on external funding. On the other hand, this substantial support allows

the universities to request that their professors limit their associations with industries, and make these associations known. The site visit committee itself should consist mainly of experts. But a minority should be highly respected persons who are not, or are no longer, directly involved in research and its applications, but do understand the sciences, and the president of the board should be a layman. Perhaps, this part of the group could be recruited from the larger ethics commission discussed earlier.

If research scientists are found guilty of having neglected the research guidelines, the state must punish them. The punishment should be imposed by the head of the research project for academic researchers, and by management for industrial researchers. The seriousness of the penalty to be inflicted must balance freedom of research against life in dignity and must also take into account the consequences of the researcher's failure to observe guidelines and whether humans, animals, or plants are involved. For example, if researchers are prohibited from keeping genetically engineered viruses after an experiment, their failure to comply is less serious if the site visit committee finds these viruses lying around in the lab than if it discovers that they have been released outside the lab. It was even more serious when Martin Cline implanted transformed blood cells into the bone marrow of patients, thereby disregarding the procedures established by the National Institutes of Health. Based on these considerations—freedom of research, life in dignity, precise facts—not only heavy fines, but also imprisonment should be envisaged. Any sentence must also be combined with a reduction or cut off of public grants. Scientists in public services will have to be reprimanded or dismissed. And public institutions should be prohibited from employing those researchers for a certain period of time, depending on the sentence.

To conclude, I should like to make two additional remarks. The enormous impact on society that science can potentially exert calls for state regulations. But I maintain that we should not aim to prohibit the production of knowledge. Rather, we should try to prevent its abuse. Scientific activity is ambiguous; it can lead to good and bad results. None of us would deny that we also owe important progress in our general well-being to it. . . .

Public attention is glued to biotechnology and gene manipulation—for good reasons. Several papers of the present book (including mine) merely confirm this interest. But life in dignity is not only threatened when man starts to fumble with the genetic code. Potential hazards can arise from other corners of science, e.g., from the computer or neurosciences.[17] It could be fatal if we failed to pull certain emergency brakes because of our rabbit-like fixation on gene manipulation.

Notes

1 Laurence H. Tribe, *American Constitutional Law,* 2nd edition (Mineola, New York 1988), especially the chapters about individual rights.

2 I owe the term "life in dignity" to Professor Peter Saladin's contribution to the present book. It has been formulated to indicate that the state must not only stand up for the physical survival of its citizens, but also has the duty to defend a way of life that allows people to realize their specific properties as human beings, as these properties have been elaborated by philosophers through the centuries. For brevity I shall simply speak of "life in dignity" and thereby allude both to "life" and "life in dignity".

3 Both the way of acquiring knowledge e.g., radioactive isotopes used as tracers, and the object, e.g., a toxic substance, a virus carrying a fatal disease, can be dangerous, or the results may be taken for a doubtful purpose, e.g., nuclear energy to make an atomic bomb.

4 For a comprehensive view of the recombinant DNA debate and the Asilomar moratorium, see: David A. Jackson, Stephen P. Stich (ed), *The Recombinant DNA Debate* (Prentice-Hall: Englewood Cliffs, N.J., 1979).

5 National Institutes of Health Guidelines for Research Involving Recombinant DNA Molecules, U.S. Federal Register, vol. 51, 16958–16985, May 1986.

6 See proceedings of the International Conference on Risk Assessment in Agricultural Biotechnology on the University of California, Davis Campus, July 31–August 4, 1988, in print.

7 *Ibid.,* for illustrations of these two types and for the potato example. In this case the growers did not foresee that the crossing would produce this particular class of toxins. It was discovered only when the farmers were about to harvest. The plants as well as all the potatoes had to be destroyed.

8 *Ibid.*

9 To fulfil this obligation becomes more delicate the closer we get to military research.

10 Stephen Stich, "Le Débat sur les manipulations de l'ADN," in *Ethique et Biologie. Cahiers S.T.S. Editions du CNRS* (1986), 157 ff., illustrates splendidly a case of comparative weighing of goods.

11 In the past, Ciba-Geigy has put the American Government under considerable pressure to regulate field trials for genetically altered organisms, mainly out of fear of falling behind Japanese competitors.

Ethics and the Ordinary Molecular Biologist

ALEX MAURON

Introduction

The purpose of this paper is to review some issues of ethical relevance with which a scientist working in the field of molecular genetics might get involved today. To do this from a perspective that is faithful to the concrete experiences of the laboratory scientist, I should like to try and discuss a few misunderstandings that often crop up whenever the practitioner of basic biomedical research is confronted with the challenge of ethics.

"You should worry about the ethical consequences of your work." This admonition, sometimes polite, sometimes more forceful, is one that most molecular geneticists will face sooner or later. And often enough, the scientist's initial reaction will be to reject it, resenting this outside interference with what he or she feels are the inner workings of science: "Why should I care?" will often be the initial reaction. The reasons for answering positively is what I shall discuss first; in the second part, I will review examples of ethically relevant developments of molecular genetics.

As Beat Sitter clearly showed in a recent paper,[1] this rejection of ethics is based on misconceptions about both ethics *and* science: it is too narrow a view of both. On the one hand, one is often prone to reduce science to the business of knowledge validation, the narrowly defined province of epistemology. Yet the manifold human activities denoted by the term 'science' do have many ethically relevant aspects. Choosing a research field or an experimental protocol, sitting in an ethics committee for clinical trials, shaping the editorial policies of a scholarly journal, reading grant applications as a peer reviewer, all those activities and a myriad more are also the "stuff" of biomedical science. They confront us daily with the need to choose between alternative actions, and some of these alternatives must be evaluated in the light of 'good' and 'right.'

If we now turn to ethics, we realize that under that heading we tend to gather several different things. First, there are the internal norms and rules of science: usually, they are connected directly or indirectly to the verification and validation of scientific knowledge, and include rules of proper scholarly conduct for the scientific community. Second, there is ethics in a broader sense, viz., the rational consideration of responsible human behavior: contrary to the norms mentioned so far, ethics in that sense is universal in scope, even if it can *entail* specific rules for particular activities such as biomedical research.[2]

In other words, while it is true that scientists must obey a number of rules, the utility of these rules may not belong to the sphere of ethics as defined above: some of them can be reduced to methodological rules whose purpose must be understood in the context of knowledge acquisition and validation. Others are "truly" ethical, since they relate to sets of moral norms that have a claim on general validity, at least in principle. As moral philosopher Bernard Williams puts it: "For morality, the ethical constituency is always the same: the universal constituency."[3]

All this must seem trite to philosophers, but it is worth mentioning because as scientists, we like to use terms that are ambiguous in this respect. When we speak of "the ethics of excellence," or "the ethics of knowledge" (Jacques Monod), it is not clear whether this concerns ethics at all. Along the same lines, much of the "quality control" exercised by scientists over each other is independent of ethics in the latter sense. When a researcher reviewing a grant application in the biomedical sciences says it is bad, he (usually) means that it is flawed in a methodological and/or epistemological sense. In his opinion, the proposed experiments will probably not give clear-cut answers to the questions asked, or else he thinks that these questions are not worth the bother (because they won't add anything of substance to existing knowledge). Similarly, many of the "thou shalt" and "thou shalt not" maxims that scientists must abide by are basically methodological rules, even if their breach can have "judicial" consequences. For instance, "thou shalt not fake data," not mainly because it is a naughty thing to do, but because it corrupts the existing body of knowledge. Granted, if you break the rule, you may suffer consequences of a punitive or disciplinary nature (such as losing grant support or academic tenure), but the function of this rule must be seen in the light of its epistemological implications.

All professionals hate to see outsiders meddling with their internal codes of conduct, and research scientists are no exception. But in some sense, they are right: whenever the purpose of a norm is methodological, they are justified in refusing to relinquish their control over it. What I wish to consider here is ethics as the rational and responsible judgment that scientists exercise within their professional sphere of activity in the light of some general concept of the moral experience, just as human beings in all walks of life are supposed to be responsible for their actions.[4]

"If We Don't, Others Will."

This is what the research scientist is sometimes tempted to argue at this point. Caught in the throes of fierce competition, he may well think that any misgivings he has about some developments in his line of research carry little weight against the momentum of scientific and technological development. This is closely related to the commonly held opinion that scientific-technological progress is "out of control" nowadays, driven more or less automatically by its inner logic. Scientists of a "scientistic" frame of mind and proponents of anti-science attitudes are indeed odd bedfellows in their belief in such a scientific-technological imperative! The former use it to excuse science and technology from ethical questioning, the latter to justify a blanket distrust or rejection of science.

As I shall argue later, most (but not all) ethical questions that the biomedical researcher faces are linked to more or less foreseeable practical developments that originate from his or her basic research, rather than from fundamental research itself. And when it comes to technology, I do not find much merit in the idea of a blind *fatum*, nudging us irresistibly along the path of automatic progress. The history of technology is littered with inventions that were touted as *the* solution of the future, and therefore considered inevitable, but which never came to fruition (see note 5 for an example of such stillborn technologies).[5] After all, the marketplace is the ultimate sanction of every technological novelty, and its logic need not coincide with that of the scientific-technological community. More to the point, I should like to argue that in recent times, molecular geneticists have been reasonably good at predicting the practical outcomes of their work. Indeed, they tend to be influential in the decision-making processes linked to such developments. To that extent, biomedical researchers are both free and responsible. They are not like ants working blindly in an anthill for an unscrutable purpose.

In summary, to say that for a scientist ethics does matter means that he or she agrees that not all that is doable is worth doing. Furthermore, this implies substantial moral choices that are often (not always, of course) within the reach of research scientists, at least in the field of science discussed here. This points to their important—if not exclusive—responsibility in these matters.

Ethical Problems Facing the Molecular Biologist

Most ethical challenges concerning the molecular biologist that I am aware of would fall into two classes:

- ethical concerns linked directly to the practice of basic laboratory research in this field;
- problems arising from technological developments that this research makes possible ('technological' is meant in a broad sense, including the applied science relevant to medical practice).

Direct Consequences of Basic Research.

Molecular genetics was born in the pangs of the "Great Recombinant DNA Debate," with its numerous misgivings over a problem that is basically one of laboratory safety. This, at least, is how most serious discussants view it today, after the dust has settled. Basic, sweeping challenges to recombinant DNA technology as a research tool[6] no longer come from within the scientific community, but from social activists, such as Jeremy Rifkin, who pass judgment on modern biology from a completely alien philosophical perspective. That perspective appears clearly in Rifkin's proposal for a broad prohibition of genetic engineering put before the Recombinant DNA Advisory Committee of the U.S. National Institutes of Health:

> "The crossing of species borders and the incorporation of genetic traits from one species directly into the germ-line of another species represents a fundamental assault on the principle of species integrity and violates the right of every species to exist as a separate, indentifiable creature. . . . such an intrusion violates the *telos* of each species and is to be condemned as morally reprehensible."[7]

We have here a strongly essentialist language: Rifkin hypostasizes biological species in order to apply to them a kind of natural-rights doctrine (a special kind at that, since it extends natural rights to all animal species *qua* species). This is reminiscent of the natural theology popular among Darwin's opponents in which species were real, immutable objects placed by a benevolent Providence on their proper place on the *scala naturae*.

This philosophy did not have to wait for molecular genetics to become unsustainable. The Darwinian revolution, with its radical critique of the very concept of species, its emphasis instead on the individual organism and its relation to the population, was largely fought out against biological essentialism. As analyzed in detail by Ernst Mayr (one of the major builders of the synthetic theory of evolution), an essentialist world-view makes it difficult to understand modern evolutionary biology.[8] Specifically, the fact that natural selection can be a creative force rather than a merely eliminative one becomes a great mystery when viewed in an essentialist context: it becomes hard to see natural selection as anything but a corrective mechanism that disposes of "deviations from the type." Speciation through natural selection then becomes literally unthinkable.

Nevertheless, despite the onslaught of Darwinism, essentialist thinking in biology did survive to some extent in the work of some classical geneticists. This is especially true of H. J. Muller and his school, who felt, for instance, that a precise selective value could be assigned to any allele of a given gene and that one allele had to be the best. This was contradicted by the synthetic theory pioneered by Dobzhansky, Mayr, *et al.*, especially through the concept of *balanced polymorphism*. The fact that in a state of equilibrium genetic diversity is maintained in most populations suggests that there isn't, in most cases, a "best gene." Furthermore, it is this very diversity that is fueling evolutionary change. The advent of molecular genetics fully confirmed the universality of genetic polymorphism (also in human populations) that the synthetic theorists had postulated. Today, biology is permeated by a nominalist, bottom-up approach that starts squarely with the individual living thing and has little room for essences, final causes, teleology, and orthogenetic development.

Since this anti-essentialist philosophical outlook is immanent in much of current biology, it is hardly surprising that the new opportunities provided by genetic engineering to mix genetic material from different sources came as a logical development. To most biologists, these opportunities were a natural extension of the way they were trained to think about individuals, genomes, and species. In other words, to assume that there are such things as inviolable species-barriers, whose crossing would be a frightful exemple of Faustian hubris, is simply wishful thinking. It can be grounded on nothing better than an irrational appeal to privileged intuition. Now, we may want to *establish* such barriers in certain cases, in particular between man and other animals.[9] But to do that, we have to use ethical values explicitly, rather than pretend to "read" such barriers in the state of nature, as Rifkin does.

"Essentialism, with its emphasis on discontinuity, constancy and typical values ('typology'), dominated the thinking of the western world to a degree that is still not fully appreciated by the historians of ideas."[10] It still influences many people's thinking: we have seen Rifkin's speculations about the sanctity of biological species. But ironically—if one considers Rifkin's hostility to all things manipulative in matters of life and genes—eugenics draws its inspiration from similarly essentialist sources. This is because eugenics is necessarily related to an underlying typology of genetic values: it entails a self-assured belief in "good" and "bad" genes, as we have alluded to before. We will bear this in mind when discussing the prospects for genetic manipulation in man.

A similar form of essentialism is embodied in the special treatment that the law (and such paralegal rules as are contained in the various guidelines regulating recombinant DNA) gives to any recombination process "not taking place in nature." Such experiments have often been subjected to a level of scrutiny that was no longer linked to an objective assessment of the risk associated with them. This is all the more remarkable because in all the proven serious breaches of laboratory safety that have been reported in recent years, the recombinant character of the biological material involved has never been at issue. If one considers, for instance, the deadly outbreak of smallpox that occured in 1978 at a laboratory in Birmingham,[11] or the recent case of contamination of laboratory workers with the AIDS virus at the NIH,[12] the culprit was a live, nonrecombinant pathogenic organism. This leads us to a little-appreciated aspect of recombinant DNA technology, namely, its *positive* contribution to the safety of biomedical research. To study dangerous viruses piecemeal, as it were, by cloning parts of their genome in appropriate vectors is certainly safer than experimenting with the whole, virulent organism. Those who are tempted to think that "holism" (whatever it is) is "good" and "reductionism" (whatever that is) is "bad" should take note!

Finally, I should make it clear that I am not questioning the need for guidelines or legislation. They *are* needed, and we still ought to outlaw certain experiments, such as, say, the willful construction of novel pathogenic microorganisms. My point is that these should be outlawed because of an objective appraisal of the risk and finality involved, rather than because of some arbitrary concept of "naturality." If the same nasty organism could be created by "natural" means (i.e., a series of genetic crosses) rather than "artificial" ones (*in vitro* recombination of DNA), then the experiment would be just as objectionable.

All this points to a form of naturalistic fallacy that often muddies the discussion of genetic engineering and many other issues concerning the impact of science on society. I do not think that the "naturality" of an action has any bearing on its ethical standing. Of course, many things that are done under the guise of "respecting nature" are valuable and well worth doing. Why not acknowledge that they are so for man-centered reasons (improving his safety or quality of life)?

Technological Developments.

From the perspective of the practising molecular geneticist, ethical concerns arise most often from more or less foreseeable technological developments that stem from laboratory research. "Foreseeable" is the key word of course, and one is reminded of Mark Twain's quip about prediction being hard, especially when it concerns the future. Yet it seems clear that the distance between basic science and technological application has generally diminished—and I don't just mean the time-lag between the two, but the intellectual distance as well. Certainly, in the field of molecular genetics as practised in the last five or ten years, the basic scientist has been in a good position to make educated guesses about practical possibilities opened up by his research. This is because such developments were often initiated by the basic scientist himself. Molecular geneticists have played a more active role in bringing basic research to the marketplace than was usually the case in more traditional fields of biomedicine. In fact, in the particular field of diagnostics, the path from research laboratory to the marketing of a diagnostic service or diagnostic kit is astonishingly short, especially when we consider the novel diagnostic procedures based on monoclonal antibodies or the analysis of DNA. The latter example is, of course, of special importance to molecular geneticists. One instance among many that one could quote is the study of certain highly polymorphic repetitive elements of the human genome.[13] Prof. Alec Jeffrey, who made essential contributions to this basic kind of research, also pioneered its practical application with an industrial partner by developing a novel method of genetic "fingerprinting"[14] that is revolutionizing paternity testing and other areas of forensic medicine (as well as raising new ethical and legal issues, now that this kind of evidence is also starting to appear in immigration and criminal cases).

One could list dozens of similar instances where scientific advances of the most academic kind are turned into a new technology with the discoverer himself wearing both hats: that of the basic researcher, generating new fundamental biological knowledge, and that of the applied scientist. In molecular genetics, we may soon see a situation in which the majority of highly successful scientists will in fact have this dual role. This is a satisfying development for the researcher who can personally oversee the metamorphosis of pure knowledge into useful practical technology. Yet he should not forget that the confines of his ethical responsibilities expand accordingly.[15]

Manipulating People's Genes

Manipulation of man's genetic material looms large in people's anxieties about genetic engineering. If we take human genetic manipulation to mean a *willful* and *targeted* intervention in a human being's genetic material, it is generally agreed that there are two basic kinds of situations. The first concerns interventions at the level of *somatic* cells. Certain hereditary diseases of the hematopoietic and the immune system (and possibly others) could be cured by changing the genetic defect in bone marrow stem cells (because of our experience with bone marrow transplants). First to be considered are the relatively common genetic diseases called thalassemias, the severe congenital immunodeficiencies, and also a few other extremely serious inherited conditions such as Lesch-Nyhan disease.[16] One can consider correcting the genetic defect that causes these conditions by treating the patient's bone marrow cells *in vitro,* introducing the "correct" gene by means of retroviral vectors, and transplanting the transformed cells back into the patient's bone marrow. Since the transplantation would be an auto-graft, there are no problems of tissue compatibility. There is little doubt that this will be attempted eventually. The second type of intervention is presumably what most people have in mind when they speak of genetic manipulation: the modification of genes in the germ-line of an individual, by appropriate treatment of gametes, or, more likely, of an early embryo where the germ-line cells have not yet segregated from the rest.

Going back to somatic gene therapy, it is interesting to see that it was already being talked about as an imminent development eight years ago! In 1980, Martin Cline (UCLA) made a premature attempt to cure thalassemic patients using a protocol that had no chance of success. This breach of medical ethics was duly censored, and no further attempts have been made (to my knowledge). In the intervening years, there has been much progress, both in our techniques to deliver exogenous genetic material into cells and in our appreciation of the difficult problems involved. In particular, our knowledge of oncogenes and other genes involved in tumorigenesis has progressed considerably, and we realize how crucial it is to achieve high accuracy in positioning the foreign genetic material to the correct location in the genome to avoid potential carcinogenic effects. Furthermore, our means of controlling the expression of transplanted genes are still rudimentary.

And yet, in the eight years since the Cline affair, a host of discussions and editorials have given the impression that genetic therapy of somatic cells was just around the corner. Now, even though there have recently been important breakthroughs towards that end,[17] important obstacles must still be overcome before we have a safe and effective somatic genetic therapy for any human disease (one especially vexing problem is how to insure that the grafted cells "take" in the recipient's bone marrow, rather than being progressively diluted by his cells; doing that may well entail an *additional* genetic manipulation). Finally, and for a long time, somatic gene therapy will be restricted to diseases that can be cured by transplanting cells in the bone marrow. (This may be less restrictive than it seems, however. Some experience with bone marrow transplants from healthy, histocompatible donors to alleviate lysosomal storage diseases looks promising.[18]) The first experiments involving the introduction of exogenous genetic material into human somatic cells will certainly have more modest aims, as, for instance, with the project of NIH researchers W. French Anderson and Steven Rosenberg currently under review.[19] Rosenberg has pioneered a cancer therapy involving tumor-infiltrating lymphocytes (TIL), which are obtained from tumors treated with interleukin-2.[20] The purified activated lymphocytes are then returned to the patient. To evaluate this therapy and monitor the fate of the TILs, they plan to introduce a foreign gene as a *tag* to allow tracing these cells after they are introduced into the patient's body. In this proposed experiment, the introduction of an exogenous marker gene is simply an adjunct to an existing therapy that shows some promise but would otherwise be difficult to evaluate accurately.

The pervasive feeling in the eighties that somatic gene therapy was imminent illustrates a common sociological fallacy about science that could be formulated as follows: "Scientific and technological progress is always faster than you think (*ergo* what you think doesn't matter!).'' In fact, people can be and have been overoptimistic about scientific progress, and in any event, we should never excuse scientists and science policymakers from making educated guesses about what will happen and when.

Whenever we finally see somatic gene therapy seriously tested, its ethical status seems pretty clear. Although it does represent an intervention on human DNA, it is confined to a specific population of specialized cells. These cells will die, at the latest, when their owner dies. This means that DNA is not involved in its role as the bearer of heredity, only in its function as the source of genetic information for a particular cell-type, for instance, the red blood cell. This therapy is for the sole benefit of the recipient of the graft, and all its effects will disappear with him. Therefore, it falls entirely within the confines of traditional medical ethics that emphasizes the benefit of a treatment to the individual patient. Somatic gene therapy therefore appears to pose no major ethical problems when applied to genetic defects that are otherwise lethal or severely crippling. In other words, it should be considered an acceptable procedure, once its safety and efficacy are proven within the standards that apply to any novel therapy.

The situation is entirely different when we consider manipulating the human germ-line. In this case, one would introduce a permanent change in an individual's genetic material that would be transmitted to future generations. This changes the ethical outlook completely. First, the individual finality of traditional medical ethics is replaced by a collective one. Now, to bring about a collective purpose in medicine is not, *per se,* objectionable: it underlies every public health measure, such as compulsory vaccination. The point is that public health measures necessarily translate into medical acts that are beneficial—or at least innocuous—to the individuals concerned. Furthermore, the members of the collective touched by such measures are our contemporaries, and we can go back to them to ascertain the benefit and safety of our actions. This two-way street exercise in responsibility obviously cannot exist with our descendants.

These considerations lead me to view human germ-line manipulation as unacceptable in the foreseeable future, even in the most benign case of negative eugenics: eliminating a noxious allele from an individual's germ-line. In any event, this "benign" intervention may well turn out to be the most difficult to achieve in practice. For this maneuver to retain a therapeutic aspect (as opposed to a purely eugenic one), one should be able to diagnose a severe genetic defect in a very early embryo without harming it, to correct the defect in the germ-line with all the desirable accuracy, and finally to see the embryo through complete, normal development. This will remain science fiction for a long time.

However, one type of germ-line manipulation is already widely used in animal experiments: the production of *transgenic* animals by injecting into a fertilized egg of, say, a mouse, a piece of DNA specifying some genetic trait that is absent from the recipient. When such eggs are reimplanted into a pseudo pregnant foster mother, some of them develop normally and turn out to have integrated the foreign DNA in their own genetic material. This is a useful procedure in genetic research. It allows, for instance, researchers to produce animal models for specific human diseases.[21] But in itself, transgenesis has no therapeutic purpose (and none was ever claimed for it). If we transpose it to man, it would mean to *produce* human beings with certain genetic characteristics, an instrumentalization of man that is unthinkable in any decent system of ethics.

It has been argued that the "benign" scheme that I was referring to before should not be outlawed out of hand, even if it is only a remote possibility. This was the bone of contention in a recent controversy in the pages of *Nature*. In response to Prof. David Weatherall's opinion that germ-line manipulation should not be allowed,[22] *Nature*'s editorialist objected to putting aside *a priori* a procedure that may eventually carry important benefits.[23]

However, contrary to the editorialist, I do not think that one needs somehow to hold that genomes are "sacred" (*pace* Rifkin) to feel uneasy about germ-line manipulation. As I mentioned before, such an experiment's bet on the future really takes us into *terra incognita*. In a sense, it seems that only the old-fashioned proponents of eugenics, such as H.J. Muller mentioned earlier, who thought that he could define "good" and "bad" genes in a time-independent, essentialist fashion, can really feel comfortable with such an open-ended experiment. In the face of our extreme ignorance of the long-term dynamics of the human genome and its influence on human evolution, it seems unreasonable—and not a little arrogant—to believe that we really can improve the lot of future generations in this way.

Knowing More (Too Much?) about People's Genes

As we just saw, discussions of bioethics and the new genetic technologies often center about the idea of a genetic manipulation of man. Yet there are developments, mainly in diagnostics, that are not "manipulations" in the concrete sense, but could lead to ethically problematic situations. When you use a procedure based on the analysis of DNA, you don't lay hands on the patient's genes, you generate knowledge about them. Ethics comes into the picture with some uses of this knowledge, uses that could be manipulative in a looser, yet real sense. Along similar lines, one should not forget that in most Western countries it is enormously more difficult to experiment on a 14-day human embryo than to abort a three-month foetus. With the growing criminalization of human embryo research,[24] genetic therapy of embryos (with or without genetic manipulation) is likely to remain a remote theoretical possibility. In its stead, we will see (and in fact are witnessing already) more extensive elimination of genetic defects by a combination of prenatal diagnosis and termination of affected pregnancies. In this respect, two extreme positions will be rejected by many. One is that defended by the Catholic magisterium and some religious fundamentalists, which insists that abortion is always unacceptable. This is based on the principle of the sanctity of human life (a noncontroversial proposition) combined with the oddly materialistic identification of the beginning of personhood with a contingent biological event: fertilization. This position will cut no ice with biologists who are not already committed to it for religious reasons. It also entails a passive surrender to biological fatality that is no longer acceptable to many people. The other view is represented by those who see without apprehension a massive battery of tests being applied to an embryo's genetic material, followed by selective termination of foetuses that do not pass muster according to such motley criteria as susceptibility to diabetes, or sex, or eye color. In this case, ethical blindness could lead to an alarming convergence of two hazardous tendencies: that of catering to the increasing demand by the public for scientifically guaranteed, perfect babies; and the technocratic impulse that views screening-plus-abortion as a more economic alternative to therapy and appropriate care for the handicapped. Compulsory programs of negative eugenics would then not be far away.

To help avoid this predicament, basic researchers and the clinical geneticists who apply their findings have to exercise judgment, which is not easy, given the vested interests involved on every side. On the whole, medical geneticists the world over seem conscious of these issues, and appear to agree that genetic screening with a view to terminating an affected pregnancy should be done only for defects that are unquestionably severe and crippling. Furthermore, the parents' freedom of choice should be thoroughly safeguarded at every stage.

Modern biology, with its insistence on every individual's idiosyncratic way of coping with his environment and with the limits it sets on the concept of "good" and "bad" genes (as we saw earlier), does seem of some relevance here. Still, the combined pressure of the public and the technocrats could conceivably be so strong that legislation would be necessary. Such a situation has recently developed in India, where the state of Maharastra had to legislate the use of amniocentesis because of the alarming increase in selective abortions of female fetuses.[25]

It would be wrong to view genetic screening, such as is now made possible by molecular methods, as uniquely linked to abortion. Therapy of affected persons may become increasingly feasible, either by somatic gene therapy or phenotypic correction: anatomical defects and other problems, such as hereditary spherocytosis, can often be corrected surgically. Moreover, genes often exert their effects in a complex interplay with the organism's environment, and the deleterious phenotype can sometimes be counteracted by a suitable change in that environment. The textbook case is phenylketonuria, which leads to severe mental retardation unless a phenylalanine-free diet is instituted shortly after birth. For a significant—and increasing—number of genetic diseases (e.g., hemochromatosis and hypercholesterolemia), testing is done with a view to counteracting or delaying the onset of clinical manifestations.

Furthermore, in the field of genetic screening, we will witness new developments that are not linked specifically to reproduction and pre- or perinatal medicine, but to therapeutics in general. Genetic analyses will increasingly reveal certain propensities towards specific diseases as well as many inborn reactions to drugs. It has been known for some time that specific combinations of genes within the histocompatibility complex carry a predisposition towards certain illnesses, such as diabetes or rhumatoid diseases. As the mechanisms underlying these associations between genes and disease are cleared up, we will see medicine becoming more and more *predictive.* Because of this new medical outlook, there is also renewed interest in the individual, genetically based rections to drugs. These are studied by the fledgling field of *pharmacogenetics,* which is showing outstanding promise. By testing patients for certain polymorphisms in the genes responsible for the biotransformation of drugs, chimiotherapy that is individually tailored to the patient could be devised for a number of pathologies.[26] These developments carry great hope: that of truly integrating the knowledge of our genetic background into the practice of a more personalized medicine. They also carry certain ethical problems: do we want our employer or our insurance company to know that we are at particular risk for some disease? Clearly, rules have to be established that give individuals control over their own genetic information and insure that such knowledge is only obtained for their benefit.

Conclusion

We have seen that the new medical technologies based on molecular genetics include both "genetic manipulation" and genetic diagnostics. The first of these includes procedures that are unproblematic ethically (somatic gene therapy) or still remote technically (germ-line manipulation), so that they do not deserve high priority on our agenda of ethical anxieties. The second development, namely, human genetic analysis and, more specifically, our increasing ability to read a future of health or disease in a person's genetic information, is much more troubling. How will we deal with the mass of genetic knowledge that we produce about future human beings? Or about existing ones? Genetic analysis might eventually reveal a complete profile of disease propensities for any given person. Can knowledge of such an intimate part of one's personal destiny be made compatible with human equality and freedom? More specifically, can society ensure that such knowledge does not preclude equality in medical care or in employment?[27] There lie, it seems to me, the more real and pressing ethical challenges that will be of concern to molecular geneticists in the next few years. This kind of issue is less spectacular than the ever-recurring talk of genetic manipulation. But these are the problems that will probably keep nagging us in the near future because they correspond to technical capabilities that are already with us or soon will be. They should therefore be the main focus of our ethical thinking, especially since they are not highly publicized.

In all the preceding considerations, I have taken for granted an ethic of responsibility that places great value on the ability (and the right) of scientists and technologists to make their own decisions. This, however, is not uncontroversial. It is fashionable in certain quarters to decry this ethos of science, which acknowledges that science produces power along with knowledge and views positively man's dominion over nature through this power. And yet ethics is a logical part of this ethos: this very power makes mankind (and in particular the scientific-technological community) responsible for its actions. In contrast, the ethical question has no place in certain competing concepts of science, such as the technocratic view (the belief in a scientific-technological imperative and its immanent correctness); it has no place either in the ethos of a science that is subservient to any ideology (political or otherwise). In this context, the dream of an alternative, "nicer" science, based on some brushed-up version of *Naturphilosophie,* seems a sterile illusion. This is not a purely academic point because the dream of an innocent, "soft," pristine science—one that would be forever beyond such base practices as animal experimentation and risk/benefit analysis—recurs in the media whenever ethically relevant issues of science policy are discussed. Is it not more reasonable to make do with whatever science and scientists we have, but to request that they calculate rationally the consequences of their work and exercise their responsibility accordingly?

Mankind has a positive responsibility towards the powers that it has acquired through science. It may be true that "where there's a will, there's a way." But, where there is a way, there is also a responsibility. This is the proper concern of ethics, and the ways of modern genetics are no exception.

Notes

1. B. Sitter, "Hat Ethik in der Wissenschaft nichts zu suchen?" in: B. Sitter (ed.), *Wissenschaft in der Verantwortung: Analysen und Forderungen* (Berne: Haupt, 1986).

2. One must also distinguish ethics as a bona fide effort to apply critical-rational thinking to the rights and wrongs of human conduct from the contingent moralizing that gives rise to subjective sets of moral beliefs and, more often than not, merely expresses the prejudices of a given society. The latter is something that scientists and philosophers should equally refuse to be drawn into, since they share the same commitment to critical rationality which is their common intellectual heritage. See B. Sitter, *op. cit.,* 42–43.

3. B. Williams, *Ethics and the Limits of Philosophy* (London: Fontana Press/Collins, 1985), 14.

4. I will therefore leave aside the question of whether (and in what way) the professional norms of science relate to some larger system of ethics.

5. S.C. Florman, *Blaming Technology: The Irrational Search for Scapegoats* (New York: St. Martin's Press, 1981), Chapter 2. The exemple of "fluidics," an alternative to electronic data processing that was the rage in the early sixties, is especially interesting.

6. Laboratory research is my exclusive concern here: when we discuss specific *applications* of recombinant DNA technology, for instance, those that involve the deliberate release of engineered organisms in the environment, there can be legitimate disagreements between the laboratory geneticist on one hand and the microbial ecologist or the organismal biologist who specialises in environmental issues on the other. Doing more research is the only acceptable way to resolve these differences.

7. National Institutes of Health: *Recombinant DNA Technical Bulletin,* vol. 8, number 1, (1985), 18.

8.   E. Mayr, *The Growth of Biological Thought: Diversity, Evolution and Inheritance* (Cambridge, Mass.: Belknap/Harvard, 1982).

9.   When we legislate about the man-animal barrier, we have to know exactly what we mean by crossing it! Obviously, every sane person agrees that to produce an ape-man slave race would be morally abhorrent and should be outlawed. Is it equally bad to put a human gene into a mouse? Does one make the mouse even slightly more human by doing this? Remember that a human gene in a transgenic mouse is forced to function (if at all) in a "murine" biological context. By the way, in actual research practice, the gene would often not be a "native" human gene, but a human DNA sequence in which some changes have been introduced. Now, how many nucleotide changes does it take for a human gene to lose its human essence? These are the kinds of aporias that essentialist language leads us into.

10.   E. Mayr, *op. cit.,* 38.

11.   "Smallpox: ignorance is never bliss," *Nature* (1979), 277:75.

12.   D.M. Barnes, "Aids Virus Creates Lab Risk," *Science* (1988), 239:348–349.

13.   Jeffrey, V. Wilson, and S.L. Thein, "Hypervariable 'minisatellite' regions in human DNA," *Nature* (1985), 314:67–73.

14.   P. Helminen, *et al.,* "Application of DNA "Fingerprints" to Paternity Determinations," *Lancet* (1988), I:574–576.

15.   The foregoing doesn't mean that the *conceptual* distinction between basic and applied science should be discarded. Administrators are only too prone to confuse science and technology, which regularly leads to bad science policy, as exemplified by the "war on cancer" waged in the U.S. in the early seventies: "If we can put a man on the moon, we can cure cancer." The result was a large waste of scientific and financial resources. What concerns us here is that a new relationship is being established between basic and applied science.

16.   *Thalassemia:* a group of inherited abnormalities of hemoglobin synthesis. These conditions vary greatly in severity and constitute a serious public health problem in the eastern Mediterranean and several subtropical regions.
     Severe combined immunodeficiency disorders: a family of congenital diseases characterized by a complete inability to mount an immune response. A well-studied (but rare) example is adenosine-deaminase deficiency.
     Lesch-Nyhan disease: a congenital abnormality due to a defect in the enzyme hypoxanthine-guanine phosphoribosyl transferase. Affected children are retarded and often exhibit severe neurologic signs including self-destructive behavior.

17.   See for instance: E.A. Dzierzak, T. Papayannopoulou, and R.C. Mulligan, "Lineage-specific expression of a human B-globin gene in murine bone marrow transplant recipients reconstituted with retrovirus-transduced stem cells," *Nature* (1988), 331:35–41. These authors have transduced a functional human B-globin gene in mouse hematopoietic stem cells using a retroviral vector and, by transplanting these cells, succeeded in curing mice whose bone marrow cells had been destroyed.

18.   See P.M. Hoogerbrugge, *et al.,* "Donor-derived Cells in the Central Nervous System of Twitcher Mice after Bone Marrow Transplantation," *Science* (1988), 239:1035–1038 and references therein. These authors studied the *twitcher* mouse, a model for Krabbe's disease (a lysosomal storage disease in humans). They "cured" the mice by

transplanting normal congenic bone marrow cells and showed that macrophages originating from the graft had infiltrated the central nervous system. These macrophages are presumably reversing the genetic defect *in situ* because they are enzymatically normal and can prevent the accumulation of toxic metabolites in the brain.

19. "Plans for altered lymphocyte release in humans," *Nature* (1988), 333:697.

20. Interleukin-2 is a protein that activates certain classes of T-lymphocytes. It is an essential biochemical component of the immune system.

21. Here are two exemples: 1. A transgenic mouse model for the human genetic disease osteogenesis imperfecta; A. Stacey, *et al.,* "Perinatal lethal osteogenesis imperfecta in transgenic mice bearing an engineered mutant pro-α1 (I) collagen gene," *Nature* (1988), 332:131–136. 2. Several studies in which transgenic mice are produced to analyze the involvement of various autoimmune mechanisms in type I (juvenile) diabetes; P. Parham, "Intolerable secretion in tolerant transgenic mice," *Nature* (1988), 333:500–503 and references therein.

22. D.J. Weatherall, "The slow road to gene therapy," *Nature* (1988), 331:13–14.

23. "Are germ-lines special?" *Nature* (1988), 331:100.

24. There is a *de facto* moratorium on human embryo research in the U.S. (presently under review), and legislation to outlaw it altogether is either in force or under consideration by legislative bodies in West Germany, Italy, Switzerland, and Australia, and by the Council of Europe.

25. "Move to ban sex determination," *Nature* (1988), 331:467. It is significant that the first test case should occur in India, a country that belongs to the Third World, but which is also a scientific and technological giant.

26. See for instance, J. Idle, "Pharmacogenetics: Enigmatic variations," *Nature* (1988), 331:391–392 for a short glimpse into this fast-moving area.

27. In some sense, with the present AIDS epidemic, fate has saddled us with a major, world-wide experiment in predictive medicine: a person who is shown to have antibodies to HIV has a high probability (nobody knows precisely how high) of getting AIDS eventually. How does society react to this predictive situation? This is not the place to make an international survey of societal attitudes towards HIV-positive people, but on the whole, one is not inclined to be overoptimistic. To speak only of Switzerland, there is at the present time (September, 1988) no legal protection whatsoever afforded to seropositive persons in matters of job discrimination. In fact, such discrimination is often openly practised.

Molecular Biology and the Ordinary Ethicist

REINHARD LÖW

1. Introduction

The relations between ethics and science have for various reasons become the object of discussions in recent times. For centuries, since Bacon, Galileo, or Descartes, these relations had not been problematic, since modern science was explicitly founded because of its ability to make man the lord and master of nature. Descartes in his *Discours* developed a provisional morality (provisional, until morality was based on science), and the fourth and last rule read: practice science![1] Since then, progress in science seemed to entail automatic improvements in ethics, enlargements of human freedom, and advancements in human life. However, this parallel became problematic in the last two decades, as indicated by the discussions on atomic energy, on pollution, on genetic engineering. The questions arose whether man is really allowed to do everything that he is scientifically able to, and what are the consequences when ethics and science diverge in their opinions of new faculties and techniques? One side argues that ethics has to adapt itself to the new situation; the other side demands laws against all research, the consequences of which cannot be wholly foreseen. Both sides, I believe, argue abstractly and wrongly. Both think of ethics as a phenomenon explainable by evolution, a special strategy of similar genes, and the situation in molecular biology now enables us either to command evolution ourselves towards a fantastic future, or to wipe out mankind by some little mistakes in molecular research or in its application to nature. One might be astonished that the practical demands differ so far despite the same understanding of how science and ethics are related. As a philosopher I am not surprised at all because this understanding is fundamentally wrong.[2] The right one can be found in Aristotle and in Bacon, Galileo, or Descartes as well. It says that "science" is only a highly specialized form of human acting. Human acting is always to be regarded as a matter for ethical criteria; so science, including molecular biology, is never value free or value neutral, but usually of very high value. Being

266

a matter for ethical criteria, science (molecular biology) is justifiable and normally justified. But in certain cases, e.g., high-risk techniques or the manipulation of human genes, justification is explicitly required, and this means that an ethical debate has to be held. It does not mean, however, that these cases are automatically immoral, only that they have to be carefully considered from a moral point of view.

Summing up, neither sociobiology nor any other field of science supplies ethics with moral principles; the relation between ethics and science is only an application of ethics to problematic actions and to the consequences of actions in science. Ethical discussions are not outside interferences in science; they are normal procedures in a special field of acting. Anyone is allowed on principle to take part in these discussions; but to ensure the quality of its results, one should be competent in the scientific part of the problem and, equally should understand something of ethics.

I will complete these basic considerations with comments on the "ethics of science," on ethics commissions, and on basic research. H. Mohr, a biologist at Freiburg University, introduced an "ethics of science" some years ago, which is meant to be a normative code of behavior for scientists.[3] I have criticized this concept in detail elsewhere[4] and note only two objections here. Most of the rules Mohr puts forward—intellectual honesty, precision, renunciation of dogmatism, freedom from prejudice against rivals, no faking of data, etc.—are normal ethical rules applied to the special field of science. Mohr must have had a bad experience to need to emphasize all this as being an "ethics of science." But his highest and absolute principle—"knowledge is always better than the absence of knowledge"—does not fulfill its purpose. Otherwise, the Nazi physician Mengele would have been justified in doing his experiments to find out, how much phenol has to be injected in a man's heart until the person dies. Knowledge seems here to be absolutely worse than its absence, and this is valid for all actions that are evil in themselves. The knowledge gained by such actions is unjustifiable—even when the consequences are highly desirable.

My second comment deals with ethics commissions, which are often regarded as the democratic and objective way to resolve all problematical cases. But responsibility is always an individual matter, e.g., of a physician for his patient, of a mother for her child. A commission or any group cannot be responsible; everyone could say afterwards that he had voted against the majority, and the majority can always be wrong. The rational duty of an ethics commissions is to identify and bring forward all the morally relevant arguments for a problematic case and thereby to give support to the individual scientist or physician. It would be helpful to recruit for such commissions theologians, ethicists, jurists, and probably qualified laymen. The ethics commissions I have known in Germany (e.g., concerned with in vitro fertilisation or animal experiments) have usually consisted only of scientists or physicians who on principle want the project to go forward, and also control its funding.

My third comment refers to the distinction between basic research and purpose-directed research. This is a pragmatic and often helpful distinction, but in some fields it is nonsense. A "research" nuclear reactor *is* a nuclear reactor, and "basic research" with fertilized human eggs *is* manipulation of an embryo. A famous German molecular biologist, Professor Trautner of Berlin, said during a hearing in Bonn in 1983 that a fertilized human egg is a highly complex problem of organic chemistry, and Professor Lenz of Munster added that he could see no difference in the microscope between a human and any other mammal's germ.[5] But then Professor Trautner himself is, of course, also a highly complex problem of organic chemistry, weighing approximately 200 pounds, 90 percent of which is water, the rest being nitrogen, sulphur, phosphorus, etc. The question is whether the germ and Professor Trautner have been described in their essence when we learn their chemical composition. Trautner can defend himself; the germ cannot, so it is our duty to help it. I shall treat this problem below. The other argument, "I can see no difference . . ." has the same force. Does it really mean that, if some climbers in the mountains, 2,000 feet below where I am standing, look like ants ("I can see no difference . . ."), I would be allowed to drop rocks on them? (Would my actions have the same moral quality if they really were ants?) The crucial question is not what a thing looks like or what it consists of, but rather what it *is*—what its essence is. Nevertheless, this question is often discredited as a type of essentialism. If we really were expected to avoid essentialism totally, then noone could ever say or write one sentence (one judgment) of the type "this is a . . . ," e.g., a horse, or a human being, or a desk. But I will not go more deeply into this problem—it is the old quarrel on universalia. Essentialism in the special meaning used by A. Mauron[6] refers only to living species. I, of course, cannot discuss evolutionism here,[7] but want to draw attention to three points.

First, Darwin's critique of the older concept of species was indeed radical. But why did he write of the *variation of species, changes of species, decline and death of species,* etc.? What is it that varies, changes, declines, dies? Darwin was clever enough never to tell us what he meant by the concept "species."

Second, the phenomenon of evolution is easily compatible with scholasticism, Christian theology, or *Naturphilosophie.* St. Augustine and St. Thomas Aquinas worked out a theory of double creation—horizontal-successive and vertical-simultaneous—that can easily integrate variation of species[8]; the thesis of an essential incompatibility between evolution and Christianity is mere prejudice. And as regards *Romantische Naturphilosophen,* especially Schelling, they *demanded* the variation of species as an *a priori* law of nature! This was one of the reasons why scientists in the 1830s and 1840s considered *Naturphilosophen* to be crazy. One must not be *either* evolutionist *or* fundamentalist: the history of science together with a rational philosophy of nature and science can offer a consistent mediation.[9]

Third, the problem of discontinuity in species is surely solved by the theory of evolution. But, of course, another kind of discontinuity is not at all affected by evolution: the discontinuity of individuals. Although one can surely say that one species has evolved into another one,[10] it is absurd to say that my father has evolved into me.[11]

2. The Validity of Ethical Arguments in Molecular Biology

2.1. "If we don't, others will"

I agree with A. Mauron that behind the above statement one can see the mistaken belief in blind fate, whilst on the other hand "not all that is doable is worth doing."[12] The argument must be judged on two levels. It is an apt argument (affecting job security, an international competitive position, etc.) in all cases that are morally justified (as regards weighing noncategoric goods). When the case is morally dubious, then Kant's judgment counts: the reference to others in moral problems is plebeian. Otherwise, there would be no more objection to the argument: if I don't steal his money, someone else will—so I prefer to do it myself; or: if we don't mix the genes of humans and apes, others will.[13] Philosophically speaking, this argument is immoral when the action is morally unjustified, and it is superfluous when the action is justified. Finally one can turn the argument around, i.e., a morally good action can still be a shining example. If, for instance, the German government should decide not to allow certain experiments with human embryos and cited good arguments for this restriction, then other countries would probably follow suit. But I admit that the experience with the ozone hole is not very encouraging.

2.2. "The crossing of species borders . . . violates the telos of each species and is to be condemned as morally reprehensible" (J. Rifkin[14]).

Again the statement must be judged on two levels. The argument is certainly wrong if it means that any violation of a species' telos is forbidden. We all would starve to death if the telos of an ox, of a chicken, of wild rice, of strawberries was not to be eaten by, for example, the participants of a Swiss conference on molecular biology and ethics. Against this argument St. Thomas Aquinas held that human beings in their natural needs were comparable to all other living beings and had the same right to provide for these needs. Thus taming, breeding, culturing keeping animals and plants are justified for our use, although there are moral limits (e.g., to avoid pain and torture).

But the tele of human beings—truth, morality, culture, art—are ranked higher than those of other living beings. This is also where Rifkin's argument holds: to cross the genetic borders of man, whether as mixture with other species, or as a construction of a superman, is morally not justifiable (see below).

2.3. "What nature itself does is legitimate; what we do not find in nature is to be omitted."

Against this statement A. Mauron argues that he does "not think that the naturality of an action has any bearing on its ethical standing."[15] I completely agree. If one refers to natural facticity as if it had a moral quality (a reference that often appears in discussions on abortion, on in vitro fertilisation, on ecological balances, etc.), one should imagine the following example: two human beings are killed by two falling tiles. In one case the wind blew the tile down; in the other a man threw it down on purpose. Appearing in court, this man defends himself by saying that he had only done what nature often does to eliminate annoying climbers in the mountains—rockfall. . . .

If we do not exonerate him, it is because acts of nature neither require nor can be justified. Human actions, however, do require justification insofar as they are not natural events. Applied to molecular biology, this means that a person who manipulates human genes does not act in the same way as nature: the art of *doing* it is not the *same*—

only the effects are the same. Using the facts of nature as a moral argument ignores the ethical character of human action. And this is true for the second part of the argument as well. If we omit everything that is not found in nature for moral reasons, then every traveller is a dangerous criminal: neither aeroplanes nor trains appear in nature, neither hotels nor Swiss academies of sciences. . . .

2.4. "The freedom of research and the responsibility of scientists and physicians are the guarantors against immoral actions in science."

Indeed, both freedom of research and science and the responsibility of scientists and physicians are precious and important phenomena. However, like all other precious and important things, they have limits. Freedom of scientific research ends, for example, when it conflicts with the dignity of a human being. This is, according to Kant's categorical imperative, whenever man is considered merely as a means and no longer respected as a purpose in himself. As instances of this, Kant listed slavery, killing innocents, sexual abuse, torture. In molecular biology, I would add positive eugenics, manipulation in the germ line, experiments with living embryos, interspecies research with human genetic material. If it would be possible to achieve a moral consensus on these matters, then I could not see no reason not to have strict laws against them.

The responsibility of the scientist is, of course, another good thing. But no one will deny that it is not a universal assurance against abuses in molecular biology. One look at the proceedings of the famous CIBA symposium of 1962 is sufficient evidence of this,[16] and I cannot understand resistance—of M. Eigen, for example—to legislation in these cases. Responsibility is not restricted by laws; it is reinforced by the unequivocal administration of the law. I am not sure whether to speak of a "criminalization of human embryo research"[17] does not ignore the possibility that this research really might be ethically unjustifiable.

2.5. "The cases in molecular biology that really are ethically problematic still lie in a far future."

On the one hand, I am pleased by this argument (if it is true); on the other hand, it, of course, does not excuse us from examining the ethics of these cases, especially since in almost no field of scientific research have forecasts been overtaken so quickly by developments as in molecular biology during the last two decades. And—as the following will show—I cannot understand why some biologists fear ethical debate. Almost all of their work is not only justifiable, but justified and desirable.

I especially warn against trying to avoid this debate by using two theses: that all ethical principles are relative to and explainable by history and people, and that no one is competent to tell us which principles are absolutely true or false. The first thesis is as old as philosophy itself. But it overlooks the fact that the discovery of different morals in the sixth century B.C. was occasioned by the search for the *natural right,* i.e., the standard in relation to which laws could be judged as just or unjust. If this ethical standard did not exist, it would be senseless to speak of unjust laws. And furthermore, man does not meet moral standards just because they are valid here and now. I do not starve my child to death not because this is unconventional in our civilization. On the contrary, we are confident that we could convince someone of the immorality of such an act even if it were conventional in his civilization. The first thesis does not prove the general relativity and equality of morals; it shows that different societies have had different success in approaching the standard of natural right.

The second thesis touches on the general potential for philosophical debate. However, it demands for itself alone an absolute truth: everything is relative—except this insight. I cannot discuss this problem here—it belongs in undergrade seminars in philosophy. Philosophy is a continuous discourse on so-called "last questions," e.g., questions regarding the truth, the good, the right, the sense of life, God, etc. Everyone is entitled to take part in these debates, but as is true in other fields, the participants have different qualifications—of intelligence, of knowledge, of experience. Would we accept the argument of general relativity of competence in a discussion on the beauty of a Stravinsky sonata between a nonmusical expert in acoustics and a pianist who is able to play it? Would we hold it about a hypothetical discussion on the truth of transcendental inquiries between Konrad Lorenz, who concedes he read only a little Kant and did not quite understand it, and Karl Jaspers? Philosophical competence, indeed, cannot be defined by principles that are stronger than philosophy itself. But we have hints for competence in the data of intellectual and logical training—what one reads, how one writes and discusses—and, of course, in experience as well. In ethics, Aristotle said, it is necessary to be at least 25 years old before taking part in decisions. . . . Thus, even if one has to admit that there is a problem of *Letztbegründung* (final foundation of ethical principles), it does not mean that it is impossible to rationally discuss principles, find out which are worse and which better (ethically speaking), and take decisions according to the latter.

One last word on the five arguments discussed in this section.[18] I love to read and hear counterarguments and then to fight them. I do not love to read and hear statements about the feelings one has when he reads or hears my arguments, even though the interchange of feelings in other fields is more pleasant than that of arguments.

3. Genetics and Ethics

In the introduction to this paper I argued that out of the same (but false) understanding of the relationship between ethics and science two contradictory practical consequences are drawn: to allow any research in molecular biology, or to forbid it totally. In my opinion, both sides taste of totalitarianism, which destroys ethics completely. Aristotle said that ethics begin with experience and distinctions. The distinctions for the ethical evaluation of molecular biology are evident: the first one has to be between the nonhuman and the human area, the second, which takes place within the human area includes: genetic screening, genetic therapy, germ line. I will discuss each in turn.

3.1. Nonhuman Area

Research and technical application in the nonhuman field of molecular biology, especially genetic engineering, is in my ethical view almost always a problem of weighing noncategorical goods *(Güterabwägungen)*. Although the economic and medical advantages achieved by genetic changes and new constructions of micro-organisms and useful plants are to be considered carefully in respect of problems of security (e.g., the production of highly pathogenic agents—for plants, animals, humans), of problems of a possible genetic erosion, of problems of a possible underestimation and nonfunding of interesting alternatives, etc. I think these problems can be solved, and thus the weighing of the goods will usually favor the molecular biologist's side (although the principle *in dubio contra experimentum* (in doubtful cases no experiments) should be valid). In genetic engineering with animals, the animals' emotionality (feeling pain and fear) must be considered. To construct an animal in a way that prevents them from leading a proper life (macrosomia, hypertrophy of organs, or parts only wanted for human purposes) might violate the rights that animals' subjectivity give them.[19]

3.2. Human Area

For an adequate ethical treatment of the relations between molecular biology and human life one has to distinguish three cases.

3.2.1. Genetic screening.   Genetic screening of human beings seems to be the least ethically problematic. It can help adults who are stricken with an anomaly or a severe defect to plan their lives (and their children's lives as well) in a better way. Nevertheless, this genetic screening of adults is subject to three conditions: voluntariness, confidentiality for the physician, and protection against the abuse of data. Otherwise, genetic inequalities might lead to great injustice (at work, for insurance).

Genetic screening of unborn human beings allows an early diagnosis of certain hereditary diseases. But as long as there is no effective method of curing these diseases, this usually leads to killing the embryo. A side-effect of this screening is finding out the sex of the child. The—ethically unjustifiable—consequence is a high number of abortions, especially in India and the United States, because the embryo is the wrong sex. Another serious side-effect might be a change in how we regard the existing handicapped. Should they have been aborted? Of course, they would prefer to be healthy rather than handicapped if you ask them. But the right question must be whether they preferred to live than to having been killed as embryos. The moral niveau of a society can be measured in its treatment of the unborn, the weak, the ill; the intensification of genetic screening must not lead to a loss of respect for human life.[20]

3.2.2. Genetic therapy (somatic).   Somatic gene-therapy is not an unusual intervention in the personal life of an existing human being, and is therefore not a radically new problem for ethics. I agree with Mauron that it has to be seen in analogy to organ transplants, although the ethical debate over this technique has not yet ended.[21] The ethical legitimacy of experiments that aim at a successful somatic gene therapy have to be thoroughly studied, so that the welfare of human beings, considered only as objects for experimentation, is not sacrificed to achieve medical success in the future.

3.3.3. Germ-line therapy.   Genetic therapy in the human germ line, i.e., the manipulation of human genes in the narrow sense, is in my opinion ethically not subject to a comparing and weighing of goods because the respect due to the dignity of a human person cannot be compared to commercial, economic, medical goods. There are many clever arguments about when a something starts to be a human being: the loss of the omnipotence of cells; the nidation; the beginning of cerebral activities; the third, fifth, or sixth month of gravidity; the birth of the child; the first self-breathing of the child; the cooptation and adoption by the father or society, etc. But I believe that the only ethical conclusion is related to the only undoubtable criterion of whether man is man: his biological belonging to the human race. Man acknowledges the fertilized egg as a germ, out of which a free man shall come forth equal to himself. Every human enters human society as a created and born, not a produced and chosen member. He seizes his rights without owing them to anybody. If there is genetic manipulation in the germ line, even for medical purposes, then an existing person is not cured— his identity is manipulated. This process involves no improvement in medical science; it manipulates its fundamental law. Such an intervention, in which research is inseparable from manipulation, is not to be justified ethically. I would like to strengthen Mauron's argument[22] that this extends to more then one individual: the genetic know-how of our time could lead to an increasing power over coming generations, and that means, from their point of view, to the absolute domination of the dead over the living. It would, moreover, be absolutely irreversible. Surely, genomes are not "sacred,"[23] but human beings are, and if we deny some part of this "sacredness" to genomes, human beings will loose their rights as quickly as their genomes. Why then should I not apply to patent "my DNA," whose world-wide producer I am, so that my children are *mine* again in the Roman strict sense? If dignity, freedom, human rights are to be conceived of as "fundamental," I gladly declare my "fundamental" approach to ethics, which differs in no way from the "Declaration of Human Rights" in 1789, from the Rütli-Schwur in Switzerland 1291, or the German Grundgesetz of 1949. They are not pluralistic; they are simply human, and they are tolerant. But tolerance is not the highest ethical principle, but is a simple part of natural law.[24]

4. Conclusion

It was not by accident that I chose the title of this essay to be so close to that of A. Mauron. I especially liked his modest way of speaking of the "ordinary molecular biologist" because I myself cannot see anything especially noble, magnificent, or mysterions in my discipline philosophy (I also finished a Ph. D. in chemistry in Munich 1977). I understand philosophy the way Aristotle did: rational argument to come as close as possible to what we all call truth. Thus, everyone who reflects on and gives reasons for the truth of a perception, the morality of an action, the beauty of a product of nature or art is a philosopher.

There is only one restriction: philosophy, too, has different niveaus. One needs erudition and competence to discuss the construction of bridges, horse races, discuss throwing, and molecular biology. Socrates said that everyone thought it completely impossible to have similar expertise in rearing children or in philosophy. Reading books on these subjects is not only useless, but usually dangerous. The adoption of these ironical words of Socrates is found in popular books by authors such as R. Dawkins, E. O. Wilson, F. Capra, R. Riedl, H. von Ditfurth, and many others. This is not the place to construct a counterposition; but I must emphasize that philosophy, and especially ethics, is really concerned directly with men and their actions, while bridges, horses, discuss throwing and molecular biology have a more indirect relation to the problem of how to lead a reasonable and happy life. To help us find the true and the good, philosophers should descend from their metaphysical clouds or leave their extremely analytical abstractions to face facts, and scientists should think about the limits of the objectivity of their facts and what is meant by a reasonable relationship between science and "ordinary life." Then discussions and conferences would be *interdisciplinary,* rather than *multidisciplinary.* This conference, thanks to Beat Sitter, has been a good start at this doing just that.

Notes

1. Cf. R. Spaemann, "Praktische Gewissheit. Descartes' provisorische Moral," in R. S. Spaemann (ed.), *Zur Kritik der politischen Utopie* (Stuttgart: Klett, 1977), 41–56.

2. Cf. R. Löw, *Leben aus dem Labor. Gentechnologie und Verantwortung, Biologie und Moral* (München: Bertelsmann, 1985), 17–109.

3. H. Mohr, "The Ethics of Science," in F. M. Wuketits (ed.), *Concepts and Approaches in Evolutionary Epistemology* (Dordrecht/Boston: Reidel, 1984), 185–208; H. Mohr, *Natur und Moral* (Darmstadt: Wiss. Buchgesellschaft, 1987).

4. R. Löw, "Zum Verhältnis von Naturwissenschaft und Ethik," in *Scheidewege* 16 (1986/1987), 30–45.

5. P. Lange (ed.), *Ethische und rechtliche Probleme der Anwendung zellbiologischer und gentechnischer Methoden am Menschen* (München: Schweitzer, 1984).

6. A. Mauron, "Ethics and the Ordinary Molecular Biologist," in William R. Shea and Beat Sitter (eds.), *Scientists and Their Responsibility* (Nantucket, Mass.: Science History Publications, 1989).

7. Cf. Löw, op.cit., and R. Löw, "Evolutionismus in naturphilosophischer Kritik," in *Communio* 17 (1988), 263–272.

8. Cf. R. Löw, "Zur Interpretation evolutionärer Entwicklungren bei Augustinus und Thomas von Aquin," in R. Spaemann (ed.), *Evolutionismus und Christentum* (Weinheim: ACTA HUMANIORA, 1986), 7–28.

9. Cf. R. Spaemann and R. Löw, *Die Frage "Wozu?" Geschichte und Wiederentdeckung des teleologischen Denkens* (München: Piper,[2] 1985).

10. With logical restrictions; cf. R. Löw, "Die Entstehung des Neuen in der Natur," in P. Koslowski (ed.), *Evolution und Freiheit* (Stuttgart: Hirzel, 1984), 54–74.

11. "Reproduction"; even more strikingly the German verb "sich fortpflanzen" suggests that it is I, who reproduces myself. In fact during this act someone comes into existence who is himself an individual—is a "sich."

12. Mauron, op.cit.

13. This is not such a far-fetched example: the scientists who participated in the famous CIBA Symposium in London in 1962 demanded this kind of research to produce a new mixed race for, e.g., work in mines, outer space, and on one-man torpedoes, and a well-known Italian physician repeated this demand in 1987. Cf. F. Wagner, *Menschenzüchtung* (München: Beck, 1969).

14. Quoted by Mauron, op.cit.

15. Ibid.

16. See above note 13, and cf. Löw, *Leben aus dem Labor*, 185–189.

17. Mauron, op.cit.

18. In addition to the five arguments I discussed in part 2 of this paper, one can find criticism of a further ten arguments "pro and contra molecular genetics" in Löw, *Leben aus dem Labor*, 139–152.

19. The whole subject of section 3.1. is extensively discussed in *ibid.*, 157–172.

20. *Ibid.*, 173–181, and Löw, "Die vorgeburtliche Diagnose konsequent weitergedacht," in H. Krautkrämer (ed.), *Ethische Fragen an die modernen Naturwissenschaften* (München: Schweitzer, 1987), 31–37.

21. Cf. R. Löw, "Die moralische Dimension von Organtransplantationen," in *SCHEIDEWEGE* 17 (1987–1988), 16–48 (prize-winning essay of the Lentamendi Forns Foundation, Barcelona 1985).

22. Mauron, op.cit.

23. *Ibid.*

24. The material in section 3.2.3 is extensively discussed (including the new human reproduction techniques) in Löw, *Leben ans dem Labor*, 183–200.

Models of Medicine:
From a Biomechanical to a
Biopsychosocial View

HANNES PAULI

It is often said that scientific and technological development in medicine has blurred the natural boundaries of human life. This is evidenced by a widening gap between the biological and the perceived circumstances of life and death and between the physical and the functional boundaries of the body. Even the definition and the perception of parenthood have become flexible. While formerly a woman and a man having had sexual relations leading to a successful pregnancy outcome unquestionably were considered to be parents, this concept may be changed through prenatal and extrasomatic techniques. Parenthood, under these circumstances, may be defined on genetic, gestational, or social grounds. Formerly there were no problems to perceiving delivery as the beginning of life. The feasibility of prenatal procedures raises questions about where to set this point—at the time of fecundation, nidation, cellular division, or differentiation of organs? Techniques of terminal and intensive care have also complicated the definition of death. Should medical (a certain degree of invalidity, to have or not have a beating heart), biologic (the presence of metabolic transactions between cells), physical (rigidity of the dead body), or neurological (such as a flat tracing in the electroencephalogram) phenomena be accepted as criteria? Are transplants, endo- or exoprostheses to be placed within or without the boundaries of the body? Whatever answers are given to these questions, the circumstances of life and death have become conditioned by science and technology.

Many medical "practitioners" and "patients" accept their roles of administering and tolerating this alienation from earlier basic views on life. One might add that practitioners frequently give this administration a moral or even a priestly attitude by considering science and technology as omnipotent powers.

An alternative vision considers the patient as an agent responsible for, or even determining, his or her own health, who consults a practitioner for selected domains of medical competence. The practitioner in this perspective reinforces the self-support, the autonomy of the patient, by taking a personal view of health on a nonscientific level seriously. Science and technology are then admitted as instruments when they serve as a means towards the final goal of the patient's personal health. Thus, the heteronomy formerly produced by the domination of an abstract and generalized concept of health (whether dictated by scientific fundamentalism or defined by an external agency, like the World Health Organization) is diminished.

Against the background of this critical view of the scientific and technological dominance of life and death and with a perspective concerned with its reorientation, some analyses of the biomedical (the term biomechanical will be used) model will be presented here. An alternative biopsychosocial model of medicine will be presented, as the expression of a generalized change in scientific paradigms in our time applied to the field of health. Emphasis will be put on the difficulty of reversing the basic trends in the present powerful system of administering medical care simply by redefining the roles of those concerned. Within science in general the domain of health care stands out by its human and appealing characteristics. One should not think of altering the main features of the accepted view too lightly. Without modifying basic concepts of the medical sciences early in the future physician's socialization, there is little hope for role changes.

The arguments against or for a fundamental change in the current medical model are well known. On one hand, is the history of unquestionable and fascinating accomplishments resulting from past medical research and development. On the other, is the view that the main decrease of morbidity and mortality in the so-called developed part of the world has to do with an increase in the resources of a more general nature, especially in nutrition (McKeown 1976). Furthermore, it may be added that these medical resources are to a limited extent only efficient in what is left of health problems and human suffering. Finally, it is pointed out that the cost-benefit ratio of health-care delivery is soaring to uncontrollable heights. In Switzerland the amount of 1.3 billion Swiss Francs spent on health care in 1960 has risen to 6.8 billion (at the 1960 currency value) in 1987, while the population has increased by less than 20 percent, and the overall status of health cannot be considered to have changed significantly, which suggests that this relationship has attained the area of "fringe benefits."

1. The Biomechanical Model

The new facets of human existence described above and the economic issues mentioned are closely related to the existing biomechanical model of medicine. The present helplessness in the face of some of these facets indicates the gap between what can be done in the medical enterprise on one side and what human nature can cope with on the other. It is therefore appropriate to recall some of the features of the current model.

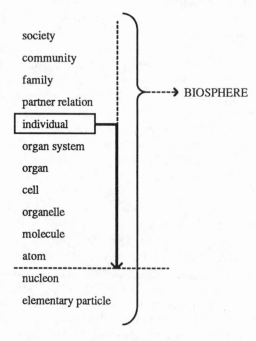

Figure 1.

In Figure 1, human life science is defined by levels of different integration according to the general systems theory. On the basis of what nowadays is considered to be the components of matter, the hierarchy of levels extends "upwards" in the sense of increasing integration. In turn, the whole spectrum relates with the biosphere, in which human society is contained. The traditional developmental axis of biomedicine or biomechanics is characterized by the thick arrow in Figure 1. It points towards *analysis* within the context of a *single individual.* The mental strategy is the dissection of structures into their components. Each analytic step "downwards" leads to a multiplication of the categories on the lower level. Scientists think and talk within the confines of these categories. Although complexity increases on the way "up," it is unlimited "downwards," as far as the components of the single organism are concerned. The consequence is that new phenomena have to be described incessantly by new terms—by new terms that will hardly be understood in the adjacent subcategory, in the adjacent subspeciality. Consequently, researchers are concerned with objects, the significance of which on a human existential level is unknown to them.

Fascination with this biomechanical model has been explained by the fact that medicine has become effective in the sense of cure and repair. This assumption is not supported by history, as documented by the following description of a physician:

> "Originally concerned with natural sciences, physicians initiated the gospel that all that exists must be explained by man. For him (the doctor) natural sciences, therefore, were the light in this world, the key to everything. From this lofty point he looked down on all those below him, fumbling in the dark and believing in things, which they could neither see nor dissect. . . ."

This description was written 150 years ago (Gotthelf 1982), when the natural sciences had added nothing to the feasibility of medical intervention. The main fascinating feature of the biomechanical model seems to be its practically inexhaustible explanatory power. In other words, the principle of splitting a given biological (in this case medical) phenomenon into its components continues to provide new insights. The idea of man being a machine that consists of separable parts is obviously in keeping with our technical culture. The conceptual tools of intervention at the level of circumscribed locations of the organism have been refined since Gotthelf wrote the above sentences. Leaving aside the question of what benefit has thus been attained at what cost, the *social* significance of this state of affairs must be considered. The analytical division of the constantly growing enterprise of medical research guarantees the maintenance of ownership and power within the ever-increasing number of units that are represented by subjects and specialities and within which research goes on. One should not neglect the fact that this enormous research undertaking has long ceased to produce just scientific insight. We all know that it must also guarantee the physical and mental survival of the ever-increasing number of those working in it. An ongoing socialization of future and present researchers in the reductionistic and dualistic mode of thinking prevailing in our educational institutions will in turn continue to reinforce their multicompartmentalized structure, thanks to positive feedback. Thus, avenues of success in the medical sciences point in this analytical direction. The canonizing agency of today's science, the Nobel Prize Committee, keeps on confirming it. Great medical scientists are predominantly selected among molecular biologists. Is this, then, the whole truth of the medical enterprise? When one looks at the bulk of existing medical structures, it seems to be the case.

Nevertheless, alternative developments propagated by minorities should be considered. These minorities consist of both individuals professionally involved in medicine and "outsiders" concerned with medicine. They propose a systemic rather than an analytic model of *medical science and science basic to medicine.* They do so in context with an historical and newly emerging *philosophy of medicine.*

2. A Philosophical Critique

During most of its several thousand years of historical evolution, the central thrust of medicine has, of course, not been biomechanical. Both Hippocrates and Galen had elaborated concepts of health that stressed the balance of individual, healthy life styles and the options and constraints of man's environment, resulting in the Hygieia concept. Asclepius, the god of "practicing" and healing, found his biomedical "hard-core" representatives only three centuries ago in the works of Descartes and Newton, which were the roots of a mind-body dualism and the machine concept of the human organism. Despite the considerable scientific crop produced by these concepts, a sense of crisis is developing today. More and more people are painfully aware that modern medicine, which boils down to somatic medicine for the body without a soul and to psychotherapeutic medicine (based on psychological concepts including psychoanalysis) of a soul without a body, does not cover the whole range of the etiological factors that today endanger human health.

Even before the shortcomings of a biomechanical model of medicine had become widely criticized in the United States (Engel 1977; Foss, et al. 1987), alternative lines of medical thought were being followed elsewhere. A Western European tradition of medical philosophy serves as an example. The term "Anthropological Medicine"—not to be confounded with the American term "Medical Anthropology"—denominates an orientation based on various philosophical trends in the 1920s. In the medical tradition of Germany, the members of the "Heidelberg School" with Victor von Weizsäcker (1950) as their central figure were its main representatives. To them disease is an expression of human fate leaving an essentially incurable trace, rather than a defect of a machine to be repaired. Likewise, the physician's role is to accompany and support and not to dominate. The work of the Swiss physician and philosopher Medard Boss (1975) moves anthropological medicine even further from a natural-science oriented concept. According to him such a concept, even when supplemented by psychology and sociology, results in an extremely distorted picture of man. For Boss—the "Daseinsanalytiker"—man can only be understood in the context of his own personal world.

3. Systemic Views of the Medical Sciences

A distinction between a scientific and a philosophical domain is arbitrary. Both are intimately interrelated. Indeed, the new advances in biology and medicine seem to be approaching philosophy again, as was the case before the biomechanical thrust induced by the heralds of enlightenment and especially of the germ theory. Once more, the demarcation between medicine and other domains of culture is apparently receding.

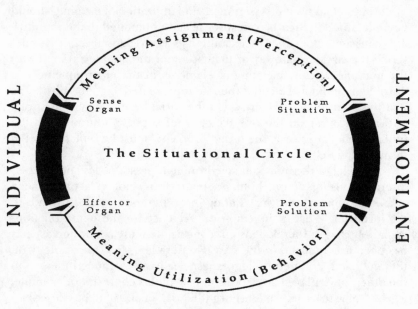

Figure 2.

The description of a tradition will serve as an example for others concerned with the development of science. This tradition was initiated by the biologist Jakob von Uexküll (1957). Early in this century, he described the intimate connection between the living organism and its environment, determined by the nature of its sensory and motor organs. Thus, the concept of a system of the "subjective universe" embracing the organism coping with it was developed. One line branching off from this development is a systems-oriented concept of biology, including the concept of autopoiesis represented by L. von Bertalanffy (1968), I. Prigogine (1976), E. Jantsch (1979), and H. Maturana and F. Varela (1987), to name a few prominent representatives of a vast and heterogeneous field. Parallel to this, a medical research concept was developed by the physician Thure von Uexküll, the son of the ecological biologist. The latter had described the circular process of interaction between a living organism and its environment by means of a "functional circle" that represents the concept of a negative feedback circular system. Thure von Uexküll (1986) has extended this concept in the form of the "situational circle" (Figure 2) that represents the circular pathway by which the individual perceives items in his environment to which he assigns meaning. The utilization of this meaning will then result in activity at the effector end of the individual system. Assignment and utilization of meaning should be understood in their broadest sense and not limited to the cognitive and conscious domain. For example, at the somatic level, it can describe the circular pathway of the coping of the immune system with the immunologically meaningful elements in the environment. The "problem" in Figure 2 could then be represented, e.g., by substances that threaten cellular integrity. On the social level, it may consist of a critical life event on the one hand, or of social gratification on the other. In the latter case, the term "problem" must be replaced by the term "resource."

A model of the individual environment presupposes and stresses interrelationships among human somatic or psychological phenomena and environmental factors. Among those the social domain stands in the forefront. What is the empirical evidence for these interrelationships? Much well-founded insight concerning these connected aspects has been accumulated in the past two decades. Medical sociology on the one hand, and neurosciences, especially neuroendocrinology, on the other, have played an important role in this context. For example, a group of researchers in Marburg (Siegrist, et al. 1988) has described and analyzed an important environmental element of this society, namely, the situation at the place of work. In retrospective studies, they were able to identify circumstances of stress with a high incidence of myocardial infarction. These circumstances can be characterized as having limited or no control over one's work situation combined with long-lasting, high-level performance demands. In a prospective study, similar stress situations could be correlated with blood lipid levels indicating a high risk of myocardial infarction. In considering the diagram of the situational circle (Figure 2), this type of situation at work can be interpreted as having a double point of attack. On the perceiving side, the work situation is stressful and threatening. On the effector side, the utilization of this perception is impeded, since the individual cannot control his work. The development of disease can thus be interpreted in terms of impairment of the circular flow of information in this circle. Among the many studies of the pathways between social stress and somatic processes at the basis of chronic diseases, the work of the sociophysiologist James Henry (1977), describing the two axes over which social experiences are mediated, is of interest. In a situation of stress that is perceived as potentially controllable by the individual, one finds activation of the hypophyseal-adrenomedullary axis with its known quality of increasing mobility and aggression (defence orientation). Situations with obvious loss of control, on the other hand, were accompanied by activation of the hypothalamic-hypophyseal-adrenocortical axis accompanied by a tendency towards a "conservation-withdrawal reaction" (Engel 1962). Thus, the well-known sympathico-parasympathicotrope model of vegetative regulation conceived on the basis of animal experiments by Walter Hess (1948) in Zurich more than 40 years ago has been meaningfully extended to the human context by the integration of bio- and social sciences.

A systems view of the medical sciences on the basis of concepts in systems theory and semiotics can now be summarized graphically in Figure 3. The individual-environment system can be conceived of as projected on four levels: physical, biotic, psychic, and social. From the "lower" (physical) to the "upper" (social) levels of the individual, new qualities emerge that cannot be described by language used at lower levels. However, the vectors upward and downward, as indicated in Figure 3, might be inverted. Social conditions and processes—especially the mother-child relationship—lead to emerging psychic and somatic (biotic) attributes. Thus, the processes between levels of different integration are of a cyclic nature. The interaction between the individual and his environment along the pathways of the situational circle (Figure 2) at each of these levels can be described by the relevant scientific languages (those, respectively, of physics/chemistry, technology, biology, psychology, and sociology).

A coping process in the presence of a health problem (right side of Figure 3) takes place on the psychic or social level. For example, social circumstances prevail in the case of an unconscious patient. A professional or nonprofessional group then takes over the role of the "individual." The health problem and the coping process will be accompanied by changes on the individual's somatic (biotic), psychic, and social level. In the case of a patient-physician encounter, both partners are confronted with upward and downward developments connecting the three levels of Figure 3.

4. Three Consequences

In view of these interrelationships and developments, consequences must be drawn from which goals can be derived for up-to-date medical researchers, practitioners, students, and educators.

Consequence 1: Health as an Object of Medical Research

The model of Figures 2 and 3 complements the biomechanical model in one fundamental respect. The biomechanical view, on the basis of its linear cause-effect-oriented explanation of phenomena stresses *pathogenesis:* The main stream of inquiry of the medical sciences is centered around the mechanisms by which damage is established. Thus, the question of *how health is to be maintained or "made"* is removed from the medical researcher's view and consequently also from the medical practitioner's. The central importance of factors and risks *endangering* health has become paradigmatically evident in the context of infectious diseases after the discovery of pathogenic microorganisms. Infectious diseases seemed to (and to a certain extent actually did) offer an ideal basis for a successful application of a medical strategy based on pathogenesis. As opposed to this, the model of the "situational circle" deals with the integration of the individual into his environment and with the *maintenance* of his health, at least to the same extent as it does with the avoidance and repair of pathogenic factors and outcomes. In this respect Thure von Uexküll's (1986) view approaches the *"salutogenetic" model* of the medical sociologist Aaron Antonovsky (1987), which was developed on the basis of scientific evidence of nonspecific "general resistance resources." It explains the

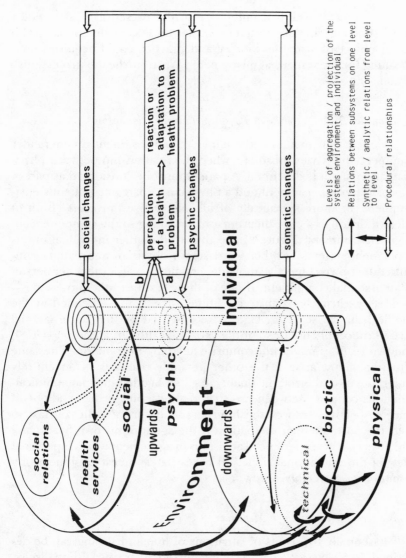

Figure 3.

phenomenon of health maintenance in the presence of a generally health-endangering environment. Under these considerations, health as an object of scientific inquiry and practice could acquire a new meaning for the somewhat misnomered Western "health professions" (Pauli 1988a).

Consequence 2: A Bidirectional Physician-Patient-Relationship

Concepts of an interactive, individual-environment system render a subject-object view obsolete, when the relationship between physician and patient is described. A patient must be considered as part of a physician's environment and a physician as part of a patient's environment, or more specifically of his "subjective universe." Both of these individuals assign their personal meaning to the components of their environment (Figure 2) and thus to the other individual in this bipersonal system. In other words, both physician and patient construct their own respective individual reality of which the other person is an essential component. If one of these realities—the physician's—consists exclusively of abstract entities such as those defined by the medical-clinical sciences, e.g., as represented by the "International Classification of Diseases" of the World Health Organization (1978), the two realities might not comprise anything in common. The same situation might arise if the other person's reality is of an entirely different cultural or ethnic quality, e.g., embedded in a metaphysical-religious context. Between two such realities, only orders and obedience respectively can establish a therapeutic process. In contrast to this, the postulate that the patient is the agent of his own health and the physician his experienced advisor is in agreement with a bipersonal view of the "situational circle." It necessitates the establishment of a common *communicative reality.*

Consequence 3: Learning in Medicine

Essentially two types of situations of human learning can be described. In *Situation A* a baby is being nursed. Ever since Freud discovered the significance of these early events on later life, this situation has been investigated thoroughly. Moreover, this type of situation can be analyzed on the basis of the situational circle (Figure 2). The suckling's situation can be described as follows: the mother is essentially the environment of the suckling. Her breast will be the answer to the suckling's problem—to appease his hunger, provided he assigns an adequate meaning to this breast, and provided he utilizes this meaning accordingly by activating his motor organs to grasp and suck. If the mother understands and supports this assignment and utilization of meaning, she and the suckling have attained a common individual reality. Many people hesitate to consider this circular flow of psychoperceptive, cognitive, and psychomotor events as a *learning process*.

Strangely, we have less difficulty in recognizing learning in *Situation B:* a school child memorizes and imitates the alphabet as later a medical student memorizes the Krebs cycle of glucose metabolism enabling him or her to reproduce it in a biochemistry examination. A child of preschool age will continue to learn the way the suckling does. This learning will include essential things in his life—from personal hygiene, to expressing his love or manifesting his distance to others, to riding a bicycle. This remains so until the child is taken over by the educational system (or even earlier by academically oriented parents impatient to start their offspring on a glorious educational career). Thus, in the educational institutions, starting at the primary and continuing into the higher level, one is brutally pushed from learning things when they are needed for solving ones problems, to sequential learning. We are sequentially being shifted from one artificial domain, which we call *subject* or discipline, to another. In contemporary medicine, in agreement with the analytic trend described above, most central or "basic" disciplines are located at abstract morphological, microscopic, or physicochemical levels. The sequence of learning is then "bottom up" (Barrows 1985), starting with abstract issues and only then by necessity moving to practical and "vocational" ones.

The relatively few learners and educators familiar with problem-based learning usually confirm its superiority over subject-based or systematic learning. They regard the baby as being a more efficient learner than the scholar. This is especially the case in clinical medical education where the problem is constantly at one's disposal (the patient and his problems, including both those he is aware of and those he is not). The relevance and usefulness of this didactic setting is well documented (Barrows 1980). Why, then, does subject-oriented learning continue to be dominant over problem-oriented learning? The irrationality of not utilizing this approach must stand for more than just ignorance or skepticism. The thesis presented here is that a certain mode of *learning* is intimately related to a certain way of *seeing the world* and a certain mode of *thinking*. The two contrasting modes in medicine have been described above under the terms of biomechanical and biopsychosocial model respectively. An integrating mode of thinking,

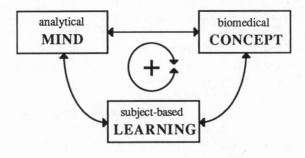

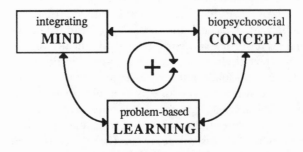

Figures 4a and 4b.

an *integrating mind,* correlates with a *biopsychosocial concept of medicine* (Uexküll, et al. 1988). This is in contrast with a *biomechanical concept. Problem-based learning* as described here (Situation A) contrasts with *subject-based learning* (Situation B). The kind of thinking which goes along with subject-based learning has been termed *analytical.* These entities can be interrelated as represented in Figures 4a and 4b. These mind-concept-learning loops are characterized by positive feedback. Problem-based learning has been successfully introduced into medical education, and the circular reinforcement described in Figure 4b has been confirmed (Kaufman 1985), as has the one described in Figure 4a, concerning traditional systems of medical education. At the interpersonal level, the teacher-learner relationship can be regarded as analogous to the physician-patient relationship. From an input-output model, one can conceive of a transition to a situational circle (see Figure 2) in which both participants attain a common individual reality. Problem-based learning must therefore be viewed on a more fundamental level than as a mere educational tool. It is an integral part of a world view that aims at reintegrating man as a biopsychosocial entity in his environment (Pauli 1988b).

5. Consequence of Consequences: Is Medicine an Ecological Discipline?

The assumption of a positive feedback maintaining the two mind-concept learning modes represented in Figures 4a and 4b is in agreement with Thomas Kuhn's (1970) description of "normal science." Scientific communities carefully define and demarcate the nature and extent of their scientific concepts. The forbiddance of going beyond these boundaries defines and delimits, by necessity, the mode of thinking within them. Figure 1 served to explain the trend of the analytical in-depth ("downward") development of the biomechanical scientific model. On the atomic level, however, this development comes to an abrupt stop. In the subatomic area, aspects emerge that seriously interfere with the work above. Such aspects are derived from quantum mechanics and irreversible thermodynamics among others.

Physicists have accepted this interference and have redefined their scientific models and concepts. The representatives of biomechanics cling to the basic views of nineteenth-century physics. In fact, they maintain a *scientific materialism*. It boils down to an ideology that implies that all phenomena, including those on the level of psychology and sociology, will ultimately be explained by characteristics applicable to *matter* and by functional principles applicable to *machines*. According to this view, the concept of matter is based on assumptions that were proven to be *wrong* by modern physics (Foss, et al. 1987).

By returning to the basic assumption of two modes linking thinking, concepts, and learning, it has now become clear why the biomechanical concept has to be supported by analytic methods and subject orientation. It is an expression of a world view, of an ideology that treats man as a machine amenable to repair. This is not a notion of evil people, of inhumane physicians, but the structure of perception and cognition, setoff by the Enlightenment. It is also a method of maintaining a sense of intellectual security. It enables the mind to be surrounded by elements with which it is familiar, to implant it in its "native country," and to protect it from sights that might be frightening. By this, however, medical science—not necessarily medical practice—has lost one of its central conceptions: the conception of man as an indivisible entity, indivisible as to his matter and indivisible as to his integration into his environment. The reacquisition of this scientific approach may be considered the most important progress in the health sciences in this century. Foss and Rothenberg (1987) call this the second medical revolution, after the historical first, biomechanical one.

Thus, one is left with a new prescription for the reintegration of what has been taken apart during a glorious but ultimately not fully enlightening period of the natural sciences. This prescription, however, thanks to its positive feedback loop nature (Figure 4b), also results in an ideology. All we can do is accept in all modesty that human views, including scientific ones, must be considered as ideologies. Nevertheless, the new prescription has overcome some of the "anomalies" of the old "paradigm"—as Kuhn (1970) calls them. Among these anomalies, *dualism* stands in the forefront, dualism between body and mind, the individual and his environment, theory and practice, subject and object (Uexküll, et al. 1986).

There is some debate over whether a biopsychosocial model of medicine may be considered a paradigm (Engel 1977; Foss, et al. 1987) as defined by Kuhn. As a consequence, the question arises whether medicine is a discipline or rather a "field with an external social need as raison d'être"—again as formulated by Kuhn. It has been suggested that a new paradigmatic view of medicine has entered a stage of realization with the rise of an interdisciplinary instead of a multidisciplinary (Piaget 1972) approach to medicine as proposed by the exponents of an integrated view of "general practice" or "family medicine" (McWhinney 1978). Other representatives of the same field have taken the opposite position, stressing the need for nonspecialized practitioners to apply multiple paradigms applicable to a multitude of disciplines (Ruane 1988; Phillips 1988). The scope of this review does not allow a thorough discussion of all questions requiring an analysis on the level of science theory, thereby answering semantic questions concerning paradigms, disciplines, and specialties. There can be no doubt, however, that since Kuhn's definition of the term paradigm, the biopsychosocial model, as described here, has offered a unifying concept applicable, in a systemic and semiotic context, to *all* fields of medicine that deal with human beings in the environment relevant to their health (i.e., the "clinical" fields). Whatever terminology is chosen for this unifying concept, it should not preclude the use of "paradigms" that are attributed to traditional "disciplines" adding up to the biomechanical model, such as biochemistry, physiology, or pharmacology. "Unity" in this context is not attained by a classification of content or methods (as in the examples of the disciplines mentioned), but rather by a perspective that allows the description of a system consisting of the individual and its environment with its intrinsic semiotic connecting pathways (see Figure 3).

Can medicine be considered an ecologic discipline? In this volume Kristin Shrader-Frechette correlates ecologic arguments with what she calls the "balance presupposition" and the "wholism presupposition." While a balance presupposition is certainly compatible with a concept of health within a framework of an individual-environment-system as presented here, a wholism presupposition is not. As Beat Sitter argues in this book, to aim at a "balance of nature" on the level of health would involve the transgression of the boundaries of rational practice or research. It is not surprising that metaphysic and esoteric views are usually included in the term "wholistic medicine." In medicine one is thus restricted to dealing with states of balance in concrete ecosystemic situations. On the other hand, the goals of medical science within an individual-environment context cannot be restricted to the well-being of the individual patient.

6. In Lieu of a Summary: Freedom and Responsibility in Medicine

New aspects become apparent to medical practitioners and researchers upon reviewing the spectrum ranging from a biomechanical to a biopsychosocial model. They are called upon to choose between what is familiar and established and what is new, uncertain, and difficult. An ecologic view will force professionals, who during a heroic biomechanical aera were considered to be "quick doers," to engage in reflections and "second opinions." The context serving as a basis for the medical enterprise is widened. For example, the application of antibiotics shortly after their discovery was considered to be a simple matching of a pathogenic germ with a substance—tolerated by the patient's organism—that specifically inhibited the growth of or killed this particular germ. Today, one has to consider the emergence of resistant strains of the microorganism, fundamental changes of the whole microbiologic environment, toxic and immunological reactions of the patient's humoral and cellular systems. Life-saving procedures, such as artificial respiration and cardioversion, were considered to be exclusively technical interventions 20 years ago. Today we know that the psychosocial stress that the patient undergoes while he is in a highly technicalized and alienating environment could in the long run wipe out the decrease in mortality and morbidity attained by the interventions in the acute phase of the disease. Furthermore, results that prolong a life of questionable quality have to be deliberated. There are many examples in which there is a need to think in broad as well as narrow terms. The difficulty seems to lie in the question *how far* the considerations have to reach, i.e., what suprasystems have to be included in starting from a given subsystem. However, this question about breadth can be designated as artificial in the sense of being the outcome of the development of academic subjects and disciplines referred to in section one. Everyday thinking on the basis of "Situation A" as described in section four crosses disciplinary borders. It *is* "ecologic," provided that the one who thinks has an ecologic, interdisciplinary view. If medicine is dealing with everyday situations of individuals as suggested by the biopsychosocial model, it must acquire such an everyday perspective. Thinking should be as broad as needed to solve a given problem. Transition from a biomechanical to a biopsychosocial model means widening the limits of the medical problem from the skin of an individual to the confines of the biopsychosocial model (Figure 3). This does not mean that medical intervention or medical research should not be reductionistic or specialistic if, based on ecologic and interdisciplinary knowledge, the solution of a given problem does not require a broader approach. A broken forearm might call for a purely technical approach, but it might also call for much more than that, for it might severely disrupt the patient's life. The effect of a multilevel approach, where indicated by the problem situation, can be expected to be superior to the sum of the effects of the isolated approaches due to interactive potentiation (Foss, et al. 1987).

As a matter of course, medical ethics are considered to be anthropocentric. In the framework of a biomechanical model, such a statement is incontestable. Is this also the case in the context of a biopsychosocial model? While a medical view is always, by definition, primarily anthropocentric, a scrutiny of today's medical problems reveals this does not exclude an ecocentric approach. Nutrition as one of the most important determinants of health and disease can serve as an example. In the industrialized world, an excess of intake of calories, certain lipid substances, and refined carbohydrates is among the most important factors of ill health (mostly due to impairment of the cardiovascular system), while in the developing regions, excess mortality and morbidity (manifested by impairment of growth and development and low resistance to infectious diseases) is due to insufficient intake of calories and of essential food components. Interventions concerning human health on the one hand and the global ecosystem on the other would be highly analogous. They would comprise, among others, restoring the balances of food transportation (with emphasis on reducing the caloric transport from southern to northern regions of the world) and promoting domestic food production, by shifting resources from industry to agriculture, from large to smaller farms, from capital-intensive to labour-intensive activities. Other areas with concurring medical, anthropocentric, and general ecologic priorities are those of population density and of physical activity versus transportation of persons and goods by technological (energy consuming) means. These examples were not meant to suggest that medical practice and research should turn to matters of international policy; they should rather demonstrate an ecologic framework reaching to a global level, within which medical measures can and should be reflected.

Such a broad view of the medical enterprise will, of course, provoke and intensify opposition by those who have reason to criticize medical professional dominance (Freidson 1970) and the "medicalization" of our lives. The general charges against "ecocraty" or "environmental fascism" cannot be discussed here. There can be no doubt, however, that an ecologic widening of a medical perspective will necessitate an adjustment of political and professional competences and power. Among other considerations, it should be repeated in this context that the role of the medical profession will have to change from a position of dominance and power to one of advisory expertise as specified in section four.

The transition in medicine from an engineering, biomechanical approach to a cybernetic, biopsychosocial one, thus raises many questions concerning the freedom of development of professional practice and scientific research, which have remained dormant during a progress-oriented thrust in this field. The definition and assumption of new responsibilities stand in the forefront, as is the case in other fields discussed in this volume by Bruno Messerli. Medicine is but one of the most compelling examples.

References

Antonovsky, Aaron. *Unraveling the Mystery of Health. How People Manage Stress and Stay Well.* San Francisco: Jossey-Bass Inc., 1987.

Barrows, Howard S., and Robyn M. Tamblyn. *Problem-Based Learning. An Approach to Medical Education.* New York: Springer, 1980.

Barrows, Howard S. *How to Design a Problem-Based Curriculum for the Preclinical Years.* New York: Springer, 1985.

Bertalanffy, Ludwig von. *General System Theory. Foundations, Development, Applications.* Revised Edition. New York: George Braziller, 1968.

Boss, Medard. *Grundriss der Medizin und der Psychologie.* Bern, Stuttgart, Wien: Verlag Hans Huber, 1975.

Engel, George L. *Psychological Development in Health and Disease.* Philadelphia: W.B. Saunders, 1962.

Engel, George, L. "The Need for a New Medical Model: A Challenge for Biomedicine," *Science,* 196:129–136 (1977).

Foss, L, and K. Rothenberg. *The Second Medical Revolution. From Biomedicine to Infomedicine.* Boston, London: New Science Library, Shambhala, 1987.

Freidson, Eliot. *Professional Dominance: The Social Structure of Medical Care.* New York: Atherton Press, 1970.

Gotthelf, Jeremias. *Anne Bäbi Jowäger.* Zürich: Verlag Eugen Rentsch, 1982.

Henry, J.P. and P. Stephens. *Stress, Health and the Social Environment.* New York: Springer, 1977.

Hess, W.R. *Die funktionelle Organisation des vegetativen Nervensystems.* Basel: Schwabe & Co. AG, 1948.

Jantsch, Erich. *Die Selbstorganisation des Universums. Vom Urknall zum menschlichen Geist.* München: Deutscher Taschenbuch Verlag, 1982.

Kaufman, Arthur. *Implementing Problem-Based Medical Education.* New York: Springer, 1985.

Kuhn, Thomas S. *The Structure of Scientific Revolutions.* Second Edition, Enlarged. Chicago: The University of Chicago Press, 1970.

Maturana, Humberto und Francisco Varela. *Der Baum der Erkenntnis. Die biologischen Wurzeln des menschlichen Erkennens.* Bern, München, Wien: Scherz Verlag, 1987.

McKeown, Thomas. *The Role of Medicine. Dream, Mirage, or Nemesis?* London: The Nuffield Provincial Hospitals Trust, 1976.

McWhinney, Ian R. "Family Medicine as a Science," *The Journal of Family Practice,* 7:53–58, (No. 1, 1978).

Pauli, Hannes G. "Von der Bekämpfung der Krankheit zur Erhaltung der Gesundheit—Paradigmenwechsel?" in *Sich gesund fühlen im Jahre 2000. Der Arzt, sein Patient und die Krankheit; die Technologie, das Team und das System,* Hrsg. W. Schüffel. Berlin, Heidelberg: Springer, 1988a, pp. 34–41.

Pauli, Hannes G. "Der Paradigmenwechsel in der Medizin und die ärztliche Ausbildung," in *Arzt 2000: Perspektiven und Probleme einer Reform der Medizinerausbildung/1. Bad Boller Konsultation,* Hrsg. J. Mohr und Ch. Schubert. Berlin, Heidelberg: Springer, 1988b, pp. 59–68.

Phillips, Theodore J. "Disciplines, Specialties, and Paradigms," *The Journal of Family Practice,* 27:139–141 (No. 2, 1988).

Piaget, Jean. "L'Epistémologie des Relations Interdisciplinaires," in *Interdisciplinarité. Problèmes d'Enseignement et de Recherche dans les Universités,* ed. Centre pour la Recherche et l'Innovation dans l'Enseignement. Paris: Organisation de Coopération et de Développement Economiques, 1972, pp. 131–144.

Prigogine, Ilya. "Order through Fluctuation: Self-Organization and Social System," in *Human Systems in Transition,* ed. by Erich Jantsch and Conrad H. Waddington. Reading, London and Amsterdam: Addison-Wesley, 1976.

Ruane, Thomas J. "Paradigms Lost: A Central Dilemma for Academic Family Practice," *The Journal of Family Practice,* 27:133–135 (No. 2, 1988).

Siegrist, Johannes, et al. "Atherogenic risk in men suffering from occupational stress," *Atherosclerosis* 69:211 (1988).

Uexküll, Jakob von, and G. Kriszat. "A Stroll Through the Words of Animals and Men: A Picture Book of Invisible Worlds," in *Instinctive Behavior,* ed. by C.H. Schiller and K.S. Lashley. New York: National University Press, 1957.

Uexküll, Thure von, and H.G. Pauli. "The Mind-Body Problem in Medicine," *Advances, Advancement of Health,* 3:158–174 (No. 4, 1986).

Uexküll, Thure von, und H.G. Pauli. "Das Allgemeine in der Medizin. Integrierendes ärztliches Denken, ärztliche Wissenschaft und Ausbildung." *Meducs* 2 pp.11–19 (1) 1989.

Weizsäcker, Viktor von. *Diesseits und Jenseits der Medizin.* Stuttgart: Koehler, 1950.

World Health Organization. *International Classification of Diseases.* 1975 Revision. Geneva: World Health Organization, 1978.

Moral Obligation in Biological Research:
A Theological Perspective

FRANZ FURGER

"We must come to see ourselves no longer as participants in natural history, but as responsible for its nurture through appropriate care," writes Robert Colwell. I fully agree with him because our dealings with nature have acquired a new dimension or a new quality in the last few years. Technological possibilities are no longer the only criteria for action. Value free research in splendid isolation from the rest of the world has become a dangerous illusion.

This feeling of responsibility among scientists is new, fairly general, but still vague. A closer investigation of its roots may clarify ethical obligations, where, at present, we find only general feelings.

I. A New Moral Feeling

Human history was determined for ages by the threats and dangers of nature. Nature was obviously stronger than man. His life was characterized by the tension between forces of nature and its domination by man. But man, whose life was long threatened by nature, has himself become a threat to nature. In a long and slow process, mankind has reached the point at which men realize that they are on the way to destroying nature and with it the foundation of life. At the end of this historical process, human life is even more in danger than at the beginning.

But this dangerous future is not a kind of blind fate or a dialectically determined evolution. Rather it is the result of our own decisions and deeds. Technological evolution gives us the means to dominate nature, but also to create culture. Whether we use this increasing freedom to destroy nature or to live in harmony with it is our own decision. Since we remain part of nature despite all our technological progress, we must seek harmony with it. Man's freedom is not just an arbitrary caprice; it is a duty and a challenge. Being free, man is also responsible. The less he is constrained by natural forces, the more he is obliged to be a promotor and not a destroyer of nature. Responsibility belongs to mankind itself; it is not the "heteronomous" prescription of an external authority, but part of man's own being.

II. What Are the Presuppositions?

This general acceptance of an ethical responsibility among scientists remains rooted in vague ethical arguments. It is not sufficiently grounded in critical discussion, and is therefore probably not strong enough to resist various vested interests. Scientists and philosophers must therefore ask the following question: What presuppositions are at least implicitly accepted, when a scientist speaks about responsibility and does not thereby mean a mere sentimental feeling, but real moral obligation?

One way of answering this question is to refer directly to a religious faith, namely, to the belief that God, as the creator of the universe, is asking man as his creature to be responsible for nature. This would be a theologically founded ecology, or a moral theology of the good use of creation.

In a secular society, however, the debate has to rest on presuppositions accepted by scientists who may not have a religious faith. It thus seems to me important to emphasize that there can be no ethical argument without general prereligious presuppositions. We accept in any ethical statement that man is somehow free to make his own decisions, that he is always more than the mere result of psychological needs and cybernetic steering. Second, and more important, we agree that human existence is not without meaning, that it is more than just a casual product of a blind evolution.

Contrary to the views of some modern philosophers, we accept that human existence makes sense, i.e., we believe that our life in this world has value despite the daily experiences of death, suffering, etc. Without this "philosophical faith"—as Karl Jaspers (1883–1969) called it—without the acceptance of sense and goals in human existence, ethical question would be meaningless. "Responsibility" would become an empty word. A purely "rational" affirmation of the existence of beings would deteriorate into a naturalistic fallacy or into scientism or a narrow kind of rationalism. Therefore, it is important to note this point clearly from the beginning: before even raising the ethical question of responsibility, the scientist has already, at least implicitly, accepted that human existence in this world makes sense. He has already made an "act of faith."

In this context I use the word "sense" to mean that something is worthy to exist, that it would be a shame to destroy it. It has a value for me, for mankind, and perhaps even in itself. It is therefore impossible to raise the ethical question in a value-free, objective, scientific way.

The acceptance of such a "philosophical faith" is not mere sentiment. When we try to avoid an ethic based on pragmatic behaviorism or cultural positivism, we need this fundamental insight. It follows that responsibility has to be considered on the level of scientific investigation. The preservation of the rich diversity of species is, for instance, a necessity for scientific research and the use of biological technologies. That means that the preservation of species is an ethical value. But this ethical view remains anthropocentric. It is not absolute, but stands in competition with other anthropocentric values. Nevertheless, it is a value that has to be taken into consideration in any further decision.

But with regard to the recent experiences of environmental destruction, it is reasonable to doubt the effectiveness of this anthropocentric view: values that are important only because of their relation to man are not sufficiently founded to serve as a base of moral obligation and easily get lost when facing vested interests. It makes sense to raise the more general question: Can we accept that every living being has its own and specific intrinsic value?

Most scientists say, yes. Such a conviction is, of course, useful and may even be sufficient to motivate initiatives to preserve biological life from destruction. But we have to probe deeper; if man belongs to nature and if this relation is in itself a real value, then every attempt to destroy a part of nature is also a loss of value which calls for justification. Albert Schweitzer (1875–1965) showed at the beginning of this century that we are responsible for every life we destroy; but since not every life (as individuals and as species) is of the same value, there are different degrees of responsibility leading to different moral obligations. These have to be discussed in a concrete bioethical content.

When biologists speak of "appropriate care," I fully agree with them, but I would add that every animal is then necessarily supposed to have a "right" to this kind of care. Where the concepts of "right" or "value" are not, of course, univocal, but analogous. That means it is predicated in different ways for different living beings. Therefore, the right to appropriate care is also not absolute. It is different for different animals, related to the different levels of life. The capacity for feeling pain and irreplaceability are then possible criteria for an approximate determination of the degree of care that is ethically asked for, but they are not the basis for the obligation of care itself. These are exterior criteria and it is a matter of prudence to infer *in dubio semper pro animali.* The reason for the attribution of such "rights" to animals has to be rooted more deeply in the intrinsic value of all living beings, and finally in nature itself or in the universe as such.

As man cannot exist without a constitutive relation to nature, and as we agree that this relation makes sense (by the affirmation that it is better to maintain than to destroy), man's self-respect also implies the respect of nature. Therefore, we can conclude that bioethics has firstly and pragmatically to insist on the protection of mankind from the evil effects of gene-manipulation, the overexploitation of natural resources, and the irresponsible destruction of animals. But it has also to insist on respect for all species because they not only have a value for man, but are also a value in themselves.

There may still be some anthropocentrism in this argument, but the values themselves are not anthropocentric at all. Nature itself, all living things, and all species have their proper values, including their relations to mankind. Respect for nature is necessary for the healthy existence of mankind itself, but the reason for the ethical obligation to preserve it lies in its own value of a being.

III. A Theological Outlook

But this fundamental postulate of sense as the minimum presupposition for the possibility of a methodologically coherent judgment of ethical obligation is still formal and vague. This acceptance of a fundamental value is truly an act of philosophical faith. But this faith remains somehow open so long as the sense or value of limited (and even mortal) beings has no absolute foundation. As Kant already pointed out, an ethically categorical respect of values refers necessarily to an absolute value, i.e., a categorical imperative postulates the existence of God.

Philosophical ethics can go no further. But as a religious believer the philosopher himself may refer his "philosophical faith," to his religion. He may view his ethical insight in the light of his religious viewpoint and its truth. As a Christian theologian, I see the sense of relating values in nature to God as the creator and conserver of the universe and its order. Nature and man are not just thrown into existence by blind fate, but are called into existence by God's love. Man as God's "own image" (Gen 1, 26) is entitled to use and shape the world according to his needs, but while respecting its inherent structures.

Man must therefore act responsibly. For although man is certainly free to use and shape the world, he must not pretend to be its creator.

He therefore has to respect its values, and has to answer for the use he makes of it. Responsibility in a Christian understanding means just that. It gives an absolute but personal basis to what men in general and ecologically interested scientists in particular feel in their moral obligation. Thus, the religious and especially the Christian understanding of ethical obligations does not change these obligations' concept, but understands it in the light of faith, which opens to the faithful a new and deeper way of conceiving of their own existence in nature. Thus, moral obligations acquire a more personal concern, which should lead Christians to be more sensitive to ecology and have respect for nature as a whole. It would also bring them to work closer with their fellow men.

Robots for Noah's Ark:
Ethical Implications of Building Robots

CHRISTOF W. BURCKHARDT

Introduction

Since world war II and the atomic bomb the ethical situation of science and technology and their mutual relation have changed. The idea of freedom of science has to be revised. The distinction between fundamental and applied science makes no sense from the point of view of ethics, and there is little difference between the creative engineer and the scientist concerning their responsibility towards humanity. Technology and science are closely interconnected.

In the present paper, I raise the difficult questions about which technical and scientific activities are to be restrained and which promoted. I shall also consider who should have the right to give and modify the rules that govern engineers and scientists: how should decisions be enforced? I shall also look briefly at time scales, or time constants as engineers usually call the duration of the impact of a specific action. Conflicts arise between decisions entailing different time constants. In ethical questions the answer will often depend on the time scale considered by the person making the judgment. I am an engineer with limited ability for handling general problems, but I will try to illustrate some ethical questions in relation to my own field which is robotics. In conclusion I show that humanity is becoming a planet-covering organism.

Two Difficult Questions

Which Scientific and Technical Domains Have to Be Restrained, and Which Promoted?

Experts have predicted that at the current rate of consumption of natural resources, it will no longer be possible at some point in the next century to feed humanity, especially if the population increases at the current rate. There are two different reactions to this problem:

303

Either you say that all means have to be mobilised to reduce the birth rate of the world population. It has been said many times that to ensure a decent life to the plant population, the number of people on the planet must decrease.

Or you say birth control is not ethical, or not feasible, and everything has to be done to reduce consumption of natural resources per capita by other means. This is to say that we have to reduce our living standards, e.g., that we have to reduce energy consumption. This concerns food, heating, and, in the first instance, transportation.

In this connection some say that it is a luxury to have animals other than humans on our planet, at least for food production. To guarantee food to the highest number of human beings, only plants are needed, and special care should be devoted to plant growing on a minimum surface and with a minimum of solar energy.

Apart from lack of food, other dangers also arise from the irresponsible application of new technologies: ecologists remind us of the fragility of the biosphere. Currently, the newspapers write about two problems that endanger our planet:

The *destruction of the ozone layer* by the abusive use of fluoric hydrocarbons. Spray cans, refrigerators and industrial solvents are the main culprits. There is now some worldwide action toward restricting fluoric hydrocarbons.

The *warming-up of the whole planet* due to the CO_2 layer produced by our irresponsible burning of fossil fuel. Scientists predict that the climate of the Earth will change. The melting of the glaciers will accelerate in the coming years, and the sea level will rise.

There is also the well-known and often described danger of *nuclear war*, with the possibility of a very long winter for the whole planet. A persistent cloud of dust may cover our planet after a few nuclear explosions, similar to the cloud that covered our planet after it had been hit by an extraterrestrial object. An event of that type is now considered to have caused the extinction of the dinosaurs 70 million years ago and to a lesser extent to have been the reason for the big flood that pushed Noah to build his Ark some 10,000 years ago. As a consequence of this danger, should all research on nuclear physics be banned? On the other hand, if we want to maintain our standard of living and avoid burning more fossil fuel to reduce the CO_2 content of the planet's atmosphere, we have to develop nuclear energy as the main source for our industrial activities.

Biogenic engineering is another of the potentially dangerous technologies on the horizon. Should research in this field be banned because of the danger of abuses or accidents, or should its potential be used to fight another urgent problem in all developed countries; the explosion of costs for medical care. Should gene inspection of unborn children help to reduce the burden to society of the handicapped?

To Whom or to Which Organisation Should the Right Be Granted to Dictate and Modify Rules That Govern Engineers and Scientists, and How Should the Decisions Be Enforced?

There are different bodies that try to deal with ethical questions of this type:

Governments. How does one avoid hegemony and militarism? In our Western democracies, time constants for the decisions of politicians are at the best a few years, given by the duration of legislation periods, which is much too short for ethical scientific problems. In a country where the members of parliament have to be elected every four years, the politician wants the results of his actions to show up before election time.

Political parties. In this case, too, the time constants are too short for ethical scientific decisions. Political parties need immediate results to remain credible.

Multinational companies could take ethical scientific decisions, but they are profit-guided and have little ethics of conduct. In Western countries the bulk of scientific and technological research is done or financed by big companies. Should they not be encouraged to develop scientific ethics? By whom?

The churches and other religious associations. Unfortunately, all religions have many nonrational elements. Many religious ideas are not accessible to reasoning. Therefore, it is not astonishing that the churches do not have the scientific expertise to make the kind of decisions we expect from them.

Scientific associations could be efficient in taking reasonable ethical decisions, but they lack the power to enforce them. However, they are certainly the best means to form the ethical consciousness of scientists and engineers. Like universities and *ad hoc* groups, they can discuss complex problems and stimulate individuals to take ethical decisions, but they have no powerful means to interfere with unethical individuals and groups, such as governments producing nuclear arms.

International organisations could theoretically enforce ethical behavior on scientists and engineers. But this is still a utopian idea, as the example of the BIT (*Bureau International du Travail*—the International Labour Organisation), which fixes maximum working hours for workers that some member countries simply ignore, demonstrates.

Finally, the complexity and dynamic nature of the ethics of science and technology imply the need for a team of highly intelligent and responsible persons, well qualified to work on the problems involved: something like the *Club of Rome* (COR). It is undeniable that the COR has carried on an extremely valuable work in publishing "Limits to growth" and other studies. The main merit of the COR is that it uses a language understandable to scientists and engineers, and even when some of its work is oversimplified, the COR makes a permanent effort to update its findings. Furthermore, the members of COR are always open to discussion. Modelling and building scenarios are the best means to discuss the possible comes of a complex situation.

Motivation to Develop Robots

This section is an effort to highlight some of the ethical aspects of robotics as seen by a researcher in that field. These aspects may be of general value and thus applicable to researchers in other branches of technology.

What Are Robots and What Might They Be in the Future?

An industrial robot is an autonomous programmable handling machine used in industrial production. There were about 200,000 of them worldwide in 1989. The reasons to install them are both humanitarian—to replace workers doing dangerous and monotonous work—and economic. As can be seen from the above figure, the ratio of robots to human workers is insignificant today, but if the number of installed industrial robots doubles every three or four years, as it has in the past two decades, the situation will change: in about 15 years, robots would become a tenth of one percent of the working population of our planet. Furthermore, with future technological progress, robots will find applications outside factories, for instance, in public services (e.g., cleaning, security, garbage collection, mail service) and in agriculture (e.g., fruit collection, sheep shearing). In Japan a lot of research is devoted to using robots for health care of the elderly and the disabled. Eventually, robots will compete with all manual professions, and with the development of artificial intelligence, robots will also compete for almost all human professional activities.

Social Implication for the Future

The active population working in agriculture in the industrialized world is approximately five percent, whereas the proportion in industry is around 20 percent. By expanding automation in the form of more computers and industrial robots, the latter percentage will gradually decrease to about five percent in 10 to 20 years. Handicraft and manual skills in industry will be replaced by fewer technicians and engineers. What will become of skilled and unskilled manual labour? In the short term, this will undoubtedly lead to unemployment and youth unrest. To ensure a smoother transition from adolescence to the working population, coming generations of young people will have to learn more and spend more years in training. Is this desirable? With fierce competition for places in colleges and for jobs, do we risk higher rates of juvenile delinquency? And if so, does the development and installation of robots have to be curtailed? This reasoning may be applied to all technical progress.

The *social arguments* speak strongly against robots and in particular against their *uncontrolled application*. There are ethical arguments for not developing them or at least not using them to replace human workers. When should such a decision be taken and by whom? Here again this is a complex situation involving different time constants, which should be discussed in groups. Models based on different alternatives should be made.

One answer to the social argument lies in the enhanced development of leisure activities in combination with a new and adequate distribution of industrial income and wealth throughout the entire planet. This sounds utopian, and there is much for concern and debate.

Personal Pleasure

Most human activities have numerous motivations. The main reason for developing industrial robots was the pleasure of *homo ludens* who wishes to create some intelligent toy and have the magician's pleasure of controlling a machine that unquestioningly carries out his every command and does all the hard work without the intervention of the operator.

Often a professional activity based on a profound wish is implanted by education and lasts for a person's whole professional life, which may be about 30 years. Any essential change has to be made by educating further generations. Here the influence of a directive organisation is difficult and in most cases inefficient. It takes a long time to educate people until they become efficient on a large scale.

The Humanitarian Aspect

An industrial robot is developed to replace a human in a production process, especially for dangerous and monotonous activities. In the manufacture of motorcars: spotwelding, arcwelding and spraypainting, activities that are adverse to workers' health, are nowadays carried out almost entirely by industrial robots. Nevertheless, many workers still perform tasks that jeopardize their physical and mental health; tasks that could be performed by robots. Herein lies a most important incentive to develop more robots to encompass a wider variety of applications. The idea of replacing workers performing production chain tasks ("factory slave") is ethically rewarding.

The Economic Drive

In factories, workers are also replaced by industrial robots for economic reasons: a robot may be more viable, since its rate of production is often greater for a given financial outlay. Today robots are frequently used in manufacturing processes to improve the quality of the manufactured product. They are generally accepted as a means to improve industrial productivity because of their greater speed and reliability.

Worldwide competition is becoming more intense in the race to promote high-quality products at a low price and in large quantities. Countries of the Far East produce consumer products (motorcars, cameras, home electronics, etc.) for less than the Western countries. Industrialists generally agree that only flexible automation with its key figure—the industrial robot—will be able to solve the problems Western industry faces. Engineers are therefore obliged to concentrate on increasing the productivity of our industries, which, in turn, means developing and installing industrial robots.

Policy, based on world economics, can change in a very short time. For example, the energy crisis of 1973 and the stock market crash in 1987 put a break to the expansion of robotics. The time constant of decisions based on world economics can be estimated to about five years.

The Future of Robotics

Robots, like computers, are powerful tools that increase the possibilities and power of their human creators. Laboratory work has started to extend the applications of robots into scientific fields, such as medicine and biology. Robots will be used in surgery, and first results of this use have already been published. More and more robots will perform delicate operations beyond the capacities of the human being. Robots do not spread dust and germs, and their movements can be controlled perfectly. They do not tire and can stand up to environmental conditions that we can not endure—extremes in temperature and radiation, for example.

In the future a robot will be considered as a programmable scientific tool. It will move from technology to science. For the scientific applications of robots, the time constants concerning their impact on humanity become very long as for other scientific work.

The Link between Robots and Noah

Noah was a master of the technology of his time: he knew how to build ships. He also knew of the dangers of floods. This combination of technical know-how and foresight enabled him to escape disaster and ensure the survival of his own kind and of many species of animals.

The scenarios of disasters that endanger our survival are numerous and easy to imagine: from the spreading of an uncontrollable disease through global nuclear war to the collision of our planet with another celestial body. Only the correct mastering of science and technology will enable the human race to survive. In this respect one may consider robotics, like space technology and many other technologies, as the tools that will build our Ark and see us through, like Noah of old.

Conclusion

The present development of humanity can be compared to the development of multicellular plants and animals, when the large majority of living cells alive still are monocellular beings. The development of multicellular beings is a long process that needs the invention of intracellular communication of many types, by chemical means through hormones, by electrical means through nerve cells. Humanity has had a long history of developing communication: the invention of language, of writing, the Gutenberg revolution, the telephone, radio, television, and now computers. Communications between individuals are developing progressively, and the slow movement of humanity towards becoming a global organism is accelerating through progress in communication technology.

Ethical questions concerning science and technology, such as the future problem of robotics, are of a concern for such global organism. The question of how such an organism should work is as important as the problems it has to treat. Which is the best body to deal with ethical questions of the type that interest us? It should comprise a group of intelligent and highly competent people; it should have a democratic base; and it should have the means to enforce its decisions and resist those who do not conform to those decisions.

Ethics and the Interaction Among Technology, Culture, and Political Systems

Introduction

As an engineer concerned for decades with research and the management of research in the electrical industry, I base my considerations on the following assumptions. Both basic and applied research are involved in the creation of technologies. The speculative phase of science that takes place in the laboratory, generally speaking, requires fundamentally different ethical attitudes from those involved in the application of products or processes for public use.

How do Technologies Evolve?

The idea that technologies are the result of basic and applied science is debatable. The industrial evolution was started by the steam engine. The main condition for realizing such a machine was the availability of high-quality cast iron. The initial motivation of such metallurgical science was the century-old quest for better guns. In turn the steam engine and its derived products, such as the railway, gave added impulse to metallurgy and steel making. The steam engine (Papin 1707, Watt 1780) was the result of the interaction among crude ideas on the use of steam, crude knowledge about metallurgy, and the vision of independent moving force in nature, unlike man, horses, water, or wind. Basic science (first principle of thermodynamics, Carnot 1820–1830) came later. As far as aircrafts are concerned, experiments (Ader 1890, Wright 1903) were long well ahead of aerodynamic science (Mach, 1838–1916). For other technologies, the sequence has been different. In electrical machinery (Gramme 1871, Siemens 1888), scientific knowledge of electrodynamic laws (Ampère 1775–1830) came first.

Looking at these and numerous other examples of technological history, it can be said that the vision of a new product is the key element at the start of a chain of steps leading to fully developed technologies, such as the automobile, the aircraft, or the computer. The other elements of such developments are the knowledge of natural laws (often in crude form) and the existence of suitable materials. After the initial steps, the new technology is shaped in the interplay with its user. Depending on the match of the product with the need of users, the product is successful or not. After the initial success, the evolution has to be seen as a continuous feedback among user experience, improved scientific know-how, and better materials. The evolution of a technical product is similar to the evolution of a biologic species: it is the successive refinement of individual parts within a certain basic framework even when a general redesign would seem to have a better potential (the lungs of the dolphin should have been replaced by branchia). Trying to assess the role of the user, we can consider what happened in the last 40 years. In this period all major technological developments (except the Russian share in astronautics) have taken place in countries with democratic political systems and with market-oriented economic systems. Technology is the expression of human needs.

How Different Are Human Needs?

The identity of technology and human needs holds for the Western industrialized countries (including Japan). A small segment of the population in these countries rejects responsibility for the present state of technological development. Without going into this "internal" aspect, we accept that this attitude has helped focus our attention on real problems concerning the sustainability of technologies.

In terms of responsibility, it is important to think about the homogeneity of technology with respect to the different civilizations. Note the extraordinary similarity between the technological path of Japan and that of the West (meaning Europe and North America), despite widely different cultures. Countries that apply Marxist political and economic ideas develop identical technologies, sometimes with a time lag, and sometimes for the benefit of a more limited group of their population.

If we look at the less developed countries, the picture concerning technology or rather the acceptance of individual technical products is at first sight more difficult to assess. But look at their enthusiasm for walkmen, television, cars, and air transportation!

Is Technology a Threat to Cultures?

If we assume the responsibility of scientists for the evolution of technologies, we have to consider if the demand in the third world should be discouraged or limited, for instance by conditions attached to development aid.

Western industrialization has, to a certain degree, leveled not only the fauna and flora but also cultural diversity. It is therefore understandable that zoos with exotic animals are welcome. They reveal an intrinsic desire for a wholistic understanding of nature. This same desire for diversity is at the root of geographical or ethnic interest: to a certain extent every tourist welcomes different political or esthetical systems, and when he finds that the natives crave walkmen and motorcars, he is disappointed. While in colonial days, the European nations imposed their own culture and religion on their subject populations, today we support whatever aspect of life in the third world we consider original. Not without reason, the citizens of these countries reject this interference with their right to self-determination as a new form of imperialism.

Technology interacts with culture. Cultures that have lost their dynamism may disappear; others will receive a new impulse. The technological challenge to cultures is part of modern life. To call for restrictions of technological evolution for cultural reasons is to lack faith in human beings. Technology has to be made a free choice for any community. It is gratifying to see the similarity of technology, or the desire for such, around the world, because it shows that human nature is similar everywhere.

The historical failure of either religious or political systems to penetrate and unify the whole world should not be a reason to despair of the potential for human understanding. Despite restrictions in the transfer and use of technologies, the underlying idea of satisfying common human needs creates a true urge for peaceful development.

Modelling of Economic and Technological Development.

The Club of Rome has shown that our present way of life (which can be termed industrialized and which most economists consider an expanding system) is not sustainable. The exponentially rising consumption of raw material, and energy will lead to a collapse. Hitherto, science and industry have ascertained the safety aspects of their work.

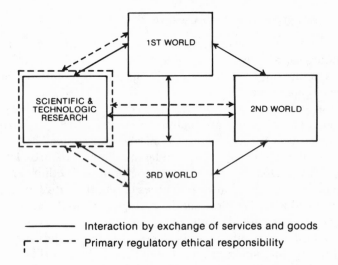

Figure 1: Ethical regulation of world evolution at the source of science and technology input

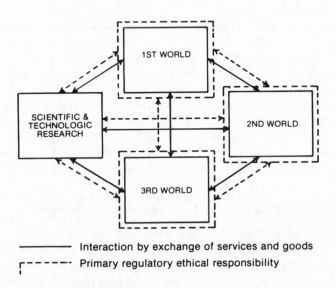

Figure 2: Ethical regulation of world evolution by political society entities, support function of science and technology.

This approach has been successfull. There are three major areas where we will confront problems: the genetic future of *man himself;* the effects of technology on the *bio-sphere;* and the problems of the actual and potential resources of the *planet earth.*

I offer a few personal comments on these problems. Our present system has not been created solely by science and technology. The unsatisfactory aspects of present conditions could be controlled by political decisions without new scientific input, but with a loss of human freedom and welfare.

Figures 1 and 2 show two possible ways in which the scientific world can interact with the three worlds often used as subsystems. These crude diagrams illustrate that while science and technology are common to all, the world of human society has to be divided, even as a first approximation. The figures also show two basically different ways of applying a certain amount of ethically induced control on the world's evolution.

Should Regulatory Concepts Apply to Knowledge or to Behavior?

The problems that the new technologies generate in human genetics, in biotechnology, and in ecology have led to the demand for control of science and technology. Two approaches to regulation seem possible. First, all sensitive research areas could be restricted to block relevant research and therefore new potentially harmful knowledge. This presupposes an *ethics of knowledge* (Figure 1). Second, all risk-carrying applications of science to man, the biosphere, or space could be scrutinized. Relevant guidelines, rules, or laws would be enacted to safeguard human values. This would be based on an *ethics of use* (Figure 2).

Limiting knowledge (i.e. not opening Pandora's box) looks at first like an efficient answer. Such an approach would be feasible under two conditions: a reasonably uniform concept of value priorities, and a reasonably clear link between knowledge and specific use. Concerning value priorities we have to acknowledge that the survival of a nation, a culture, or a race often takes precedence over peace. Knowledge can lead to therapeutic improvement or to irresponsible experimentation. Knowledge in these and many other cases is clearly ambivalent. At different times in history, knowledge was censored along allegedly ethical guidelines. In the longer term, these attempts failed.

If we consider the other approach, the ethics of use, the situation is fortunately much better. In many instances the interference of technology with human values can clearly be identified. The next step of finding guidelines remains empirical, despite theoretical contributions from science, art, and religion. This empirical way will probably continue in the future. It is not fortuitous that many theories of modern evolution of nature are based on a mixture of mathematical probability, experiments in survival, and the laws of thermodynamics. While it is probably not possible to find an ethical foundation for the regulation of research, I believe that the regulation of behavior regarding technological application is possible.

Special Considerations Concerning Information Technologies.

I now consider information technologies (IT), namely, telecommunications, storage (memories, data banks), and information processing (computers). Building political communities beyond the level of tribes was (and still is) based on available facilities for message transmission. IT have always been an object of regulation by national authorities. Depending on political maturity, freedom of speech has been accepted in IT insofar as the state telecommunication system allows private messages and guarantees their privacy. IT and their regulation have therefore a strong impact on the political and cultural life of a nation.

Since thousands of years the basic concerns are over freedom of expression, the right of access, and privacy. These are largely matters of managerial and legal skills. The engineer can reduce cost through deregulation and standardization. Deregulation will lead to better performance while standardization will ensure compatibility of equipment for direct access. These aspects have genuine ethical implications.

Ethical choices regarding the use of technology will influence research. For instance, it would be absurd to regulate automotive research to prevent cars that can go more than 130 kilometers an hour from being built. On the other hand, speed limits are an important factor in determining automotive research.

Conclusion

The evolution of technology is closely linked to political and cultural systems it is representative of human needs in as much as such systems include democratic principles and a market oriented economy. The complexity of the interaction of technology with social, political, and cultural systems, and the dynamics of the evolution itself make it difficult to assess the long-term effects of technological change. The world cannot be guided by regulated scientific and technological input. This input plays an important part, but the real guidance comes from the political and economical level in a system comprising a hierarchy of subsystems with different degrees of dependance.

Scientific research, in its basic and applied forms, owes its present vitality to its highly developed organization. But in its essence, it is the playground or interface of subconscious dreams, scientific hypotheses, and experimental proof. Research certainly has to be a safe and contained procedure, but to submit this process to the inquisition of ethical committees at the national or institutional level would result in third-rate science and deprive the community of increased and better knowledge.

In contrast to the necessary freedom of research an ethical civilization calls for a conscious regulatory activity in the application or use of science and technology. Scientists must be involved in formulating acceptable standards. Within science and society as a whole, a continuing debate over ethics must be encouraged.

Bibliography

Meadows, L.D., *The Limits of Growth* (Universe Books, 1972).

Monod, J., *Le hasard et la nécessité* (Paris: Editions du Seuil, 1973).

Riedl, R., *Strategie der Genesis* (München Zürich: R. Piper GmbH & Co. KG, ²1984).

The World Commission on Environement and Development (UNO), *Our Common Future* (Oxford/New York: Oxford University Press, 1987).

Roth, A.W., "The Choice of a Technology for the Future of the Human Race," *International Journal of Technology Management*, 1987, Vol. 2, No. 3/4, 329–335.

Freedom and Responsibility in an Information-Oriented Society

HIROSHI INOSE

1. Introduction

Remarkable progress in information technology has brought a revolutionary expansion in our ability to collect, transmit, process, store, and retrieve information. As a result, our societal activities have become increasingly dependent on information. The information-oriented society thus formed has both benefits and problems.

Information technology has integrated activities that in the past were often functionally or geographically separate. This has permitted sophisticated functions to be performed more efficiently and has allowed geographical separation of individual activities that are part of a single, unified project. However, societal activities that are closely knit by information technology may be vulnerable to misuse of, or accidental or intentional leaking of personal information, which infringes on privacy. Such activities are also vulnerable to destruction of data, to errors introduced in data, and to breakdowns or malfunctions of information systems. Further, effective integration may not be possible if technological standards do not permit adequate interfacing.

Information technology can help change the present industrial structure of mass production and consumption into a structure that consumes less materials and energy and produces fewer, but greater-value-added products. Further, the productivity and working conditions of traditional industrial sectors can be improved by the use of information technology. However, changes in the industrial structure can lead to a loss of jobs in traditional areas and a shortage of workers in emerging industrial sectors that include software production. Evaluation of software products as well as societal receptivity of software workers may also present problems.

Information technology promises to improve such societal infrastructures as medical care and transportation, making it possible to provide these services efficiently and at less cost. However, in such areas, the same information technology may endanger human life if it

318

does not work reliably. It may also infringe on privacy if security measures are inadequate.

Information technology permits the integration of various information services that have been provided separately. Such integration, known as the convergence of service modes, can provide users with diversified information more effectively at less cost. But, if we are to take full advantage of the convergence of service modes, regulatory policies must be changed. Moreover, appropriate measures are needed to avoid concentration of control over a number of media and to alleviate uneven distribution of information resources among countries and districts.

Information technology can provide a powerful tool for understanding and preserving the human cultural heritage and for enhancing the cultural creativity of mankind. Information technology can help a community learn about the cultures of other communities, and can enrich its culture by selectively introducing elements from foreign cultures. However, communities can lose their cultural identity and be overwhelmed by outside influences if their own endogenous cultural strength is weak.

Market forces have played and will continue to play a major role in promoting and bringing into use the capabilities of information technology for the betterment of human life. However, in some areas market forces are weak or do not function properly. Maintaining integrity of information, insuring security and reliability of information service, standardizing hardware and software, enhancing education and training for the smooth shift of the work force from declining to emerging industrial sectors, restructuring regulation of information services, alleviating regional differences in information resources and preserving identities of different cultures, are typical examples of measures that our society as a whole, including public sectors, should take full responsibility for to insure maximum possible freedom in utilizing the benefits brought about by the information technology.

2. Integrity, Privacy, Security, and Reliability

Information comes to us from diverse sources, even when it is supplied through a single information network. It has become extremely difficult for the users, who are increasingly information dependent, to know the source of information. Therefore, information providers should expend considerable care in gathering and handling of data to maintain the integrity and authenticity of information. Full documentation of sources and methods is essential. Only authorized persons should be allowed to enter important data into databases, to change data, or to process its use by others, and these persons and their activities must be recorded. An audit trail must be provided through which entries into and changes in databases and all steps in processing can be traced.

When information concerns the background, knowledge, or activities of individuals, integrity includes privacy and confidentiality. If information gathered is of a private, proprietary, or confidential nature, the disclosure might damage an individual or might be financially injurious to an organization. Insofar as possible, such information should be gathered only for compelling reasons, should be kept only as long as necessary, and should be guarded diligently against ill use.

To make such protection effective, the security and reliability of data files and computers should be maintained at the highest level possible. Technologies for enhancing the security and reliability of information systems have an important role in this respect. Authorization of access to data files should also be placed under strict administrative control. Technological and organizational means will need to be strengthened, since "computer crime" is growing. Reliability is a major concern not only for personal data files, but also for all the information systems that are so deeply involved in almost all aspects of society. Any malfunction or outage of information systems may endanger human life or health, cause serious destruction of industrial plants or the environment, or result in great financial loss. Although the reliability of information systems is already extremely high, every effort must be expended to enhance reliability even further. The government should play a leading role in establishing and enhancing liability coverage and backup safeguards, in concert with the activities in private sectors, because no system can be made absolutely failure free.

3. Standardization[1]

Standardization of the hardware and software of information technology is extremely important because telephone sets, terminals, transmission lines, and switching centers are always connected in networks, and, increasingly, computers and databases are connected to such networks. To permit maximum freedom in transmitting and receiving information between these network components, interfaces should be agreed upon, clearly defined, and made as simple as possible.

Standardization is difficult for a number of reasons. First, the pace of innovation in information technology is very fast. A standard set too early may jeopardize future innovation; set too late, it may never become operational. Second, standardization is required to cover both hardware and software, that is, computer programs and the like. A large amount of software at each switching center has to be standardized to attain economy of scale and ease of maintenance. To permit communication between terminals and computers, a software standard known as a communication protocol has to be implemented. Generally, to operate and interconnect equipment that has higher intelligence, more software has to be standardized. Third, new products tend to have diversified specifications, since they are designed by competing private industries. This makes it particularly difficult to establish a single standard in such areas as computers, terminals, and video packages, where market forces are powerful and new technologies are continually emerging. Fourth, conflicts of interest may occur between countries or groups of countries in trying to establish a single standard. For instance, three standards—namely, NTSC, PAL, and SECAM—exist for color television broadcasting. This necessitates complicated interfaces for format conversion when an exchange of programs is required. For the digital hierarchy for multiplexing digital signals, three standards exist, which may require costly interfaces for future interconnection. But settling on a single standard would benefit some more than others, so there are problems of fairness and politics in addition to the technical side of these issues.

Standardization in information technology requires collaboration and compromise between all the responsible bodies, namely, governments, common carriers, and industries. It also requires a thorough understanding of the state of the art, as well as a far-reaching insight into the future by all the participants, including those from academia and those who represent users. It is encouraging that despite two world wars and other international conflicts in the past, the standardization activities of the world have continued and are even accelerating in recent years. Standardization may be one of the few areas of international activity in which countries, industries, and individuals of diversified backgrounds and interests can think and act constructively and cooperatively for the good of humanity.

4. Shift of Work Force

Whenever structural changes in industry have occurred, workers in traditional industrial sectors have become obsolete and have lost their jobs, while newly emerging industrial sectors have suffered from a shortage of workers. A change to an information-oriented industrial structure can be no exception. Skilled workers, such as those doing routine machining jobs in industrial plants, may lose their jobs because of the increasing use of process-control computers and industrial robots. General office workers without special talents may also lose their jobs because of the rapid penetration of word processors and other office automation equipment. Changes in distribution channels may cost jobs in various areas, for example, food production and distribution. On the other hand, enormous job opportunities will be created in software production, since much new software is needed to improve productivity in traditional industrial areas and to support knowledge-dependent products and services. No matter how extensive machine support in this effort is, this software is ultimately written by human beings, and the need is immense. Education and training, which allow a smooth shift of the labor force from decaying to emerging areas, are crucial for such a change in industrial structure. Governments, industries, and educators must provide educational opportunities that permit maximum mobility of the labor force to adopt to the change.

Another question arises: Can developing countries adopt such structural changes in their industries, or can such changes in developed countries benefit developing countries? Clearly developing countries need information technology to develop their natural resources and enhance the productivity of their agriculture and industries. Moreover, in view of the enormous amount of software needed for the informatization of industries, software production has to be shared on an international basis. In particular, programs for specific applications have to be produced locally to meet end users' needs, which differ in many respects among differing societies. Developing countries, where wages are relatively low and job opportunities for educated people are insufficient, may have an advantage over developed countries, where wages are high and people are not motivated to promote the structural changes in industry. In fact, many newly industrialized countries have been active and successful in software production.[2]

Implications of information technology for industrial structure, if correctly understood, may hasten the arrival of the developing countries among the ranks of the developed. Indeed, if the developed countries do not correctly perceive the technical possibilities, they may join the ranks of the underdeveloped.

5. Evaluation of Software

The computerized information industry is on the brink of turning from a capital-intensive manufacturing industry to a labor-intensive service industry. Hardware costs for information systems are decreasing drastically because of progress in microelectronics technology. Software costs, on the other hand, are increasing steeply because of diversification and sophistication in hardware use and rising wages. No efficient way of automatically producing and testing software is yet known. If these trends continue, software cost may exceed 90 percent of the total cost of an information system before the end of the century.

The computerized information industry is an unprecedented type of industry because it was born a highly capital-intensive industry and will mature into a labor-intensive industry, though the labor required is knowledge intensive. This may present an interesting subject of study for economists. However, nothing has yet been written on the evolutionary mechanism of the information industry.[3]

Labor intensiveness presents many problems. Some of these are labor issues, which has been described in the previous section. Another problem is the evaluation of software products. As software cost is becoming the major cost of information systems, the evaluation of software and its costs will become as significant for producers as for users. Can we evaluate a software product by simply counting the number of program steps? Definitely not, because inexperienced programmers write software with more steps than experienced programmers do. If software is paid for in terms of program steps, software houses may employ inexperienced programmers to reduce wages and increase their income. In general, clever programmers will make more money as owners or part owners of small software houses, than they will as employees of large organizations. Yet, evaluation of the skills of experienced and inexperienced programmers is difficult.

Simple services provided by doormen and porters can be rightly rewarded by paying tips. Sophisticated services provided by information-oriented professionals are too complicated and expensive to allow any simple and just system of payment.

Software workers are skilled specialists (known as white-collar workers) and the present society has never had any experience in accommodating a large number of skilled specialists. Can a software worker in an on-line banking center perform well as a branch manager of that bank if he is promoted? Probably not. A university graduate employed by a bank may not want to work on software even if he is interested in it. Computer users should reconsider their organizational structures to ensure the status of their software workers.

Moreover, automation may transfer a worker from manipulating simple machines to merely monitoring complex machines. The worker may be bored, if everything is normal, or frustrated and confused if something goes wrong because the malfunctioning machines may prove too complex to control properly. He may lose the feeling of accomplishment and become unhappy in dealing with these new, not-too-friendly machines. There should be a conservation law for the feeling of accomplishment, so that there would be other new things for the worker to do that would be at least as rewarding as the old activities. Computer-aided crafts manufacture, in which each individual can communicate interactively with a computer in realizing his or her creativity, may be the solution in the future.[4]

6. Regulation and Centralized Control

The convergence of service modes brings economy of scale and provides a variety of information in various forms through a variety of media. The high cost of information collection, processing, and creation in the forms of databases and audio and video programs can be shared by users of a number of media. More smaller-scale communities of interests can be served by providing the specific information they need. However, the convergence of service modes presents some problems.

One such problems is regulation, since the convergence is dismantling barriers between traditionally regulated and unregulated services. For instance, data communication or on-line processing is a result of convergence between telecommunication, which is regulated, and information processing, which is unregulated. If a user of a data communication system instructs the computer to process information and forward the results to another user, it may seem to be an extension of information processing. If, on the other hand, a user instructs the computer merely to store information and forward it without any processing to another user, it may seem to be an extension of telecommunications known as message switching.

Here questions arise as to whether an information-processing firm that provides message switching should be regulated or whether a common carrier that is a regulated monopoly can enter the information-processing business in which firms are unregulated and competing. This is one of many examples that make it difficult for policy makers to keep abreast of the rapid progress of information technology. Unless the policy makers have foresight and wisdom, the merit of the convergence of service modes will be totally lost.[5]

Another problem is the danger of centralized control of various media. A conglomerate that owns newspaper companies, book and journal publication companies, radio and television stations, and computerized information vendors could use its information resources very efficiently, take advantage of the complementary characteristics of various media, and provide information to match its customers' needs at low cost. However, the conglomerate might also use its influence to control public opinion by providing biased information through a variety of media. Such multiple control of media might have a significant influence if the conglomerate had a nationwide network of operation and few major competitors who held different views. Clearly the worst case is that in which the conglomerate is part of a totalitarian government and is given a complete monopoly. It is the responsibility of governments to restore regulatory measures, so as to take full advantage of the convergence of service modes while ensuring freedom of expressing different views.

7. Information Resources

Still another problem arises because information resources are unevenly distributed on the earth. The success of information services that take advantage of the convergence of service modes depends almost solely on the quantity and quality of the information they can provide. However, it is not easy to collect, accumulate, update, and distribute information. Hence, the supply of news reports in the world is largely in the hands of five major news agencies, AFP, AP, Reuters, Tass, and UPI. The majority of databases for bibliographical retrieval and other purposes are in the United States. In general, we find more information resources in developed countries than in developing countries and more in large metropolitan districts than in remote rural districts. This brings about differences in the ease of access to information resources in countries and districts.

If the convergence of service modes is left solely in the hands of market forces, more information will be collected and distributed in developed countries and in large metropolitan districts, rendering them even more information rich, and the rest of the countries and districts even more information poor. It is the responsibility of governments and other parties concerned to strengthen information resources in developing countries and remote rural districts to alleviate existing differences.

8. Cultural Issues

Information technology has already been useful and will be even more so to humans in learning about the cultures of different communities. However, exposure to different cultures brings both advantages and disadvantages. It helps one community understand the cultures of others, and by selectively borrowing from them, a community will be able to enhance its own culture. If, on the other hand, a community is exposed to a powerful culture and absorbs it without discrimination, the cultural identity of that community will be lost. This is particularly true when a remote rural community is suddenly exposed to an advanced civilization. Because of the conveniences it provides, an advanced civilization may quickly overwhelm the rural community and destroy its traditional culture.

In the past, we have seen many instances in which an advanced civilization was successfully adapted by other communities and flourished through the endogenous efforts of such communities. However, we have also seen instances in which the introduction of advanced civilization merely caused chaos or complete loss of identity. Thus, an effort should be made to strengthen the endogenous culture of individuals and communities and to maximize the profit and minimize the loss due to such interaction.

9. Concluding Remarks

What has been described is only a small part of many issues relative to the freedom and responsibility in a society that is increasingly becoming information oriented. Among other issues, perhaps the most significant is the rapid growth of many diverse communities of interest that have largely been fostered by the rapid growth of communication and transportation networks. These range from small ones that serve narrow scientific or cultural interests to large ones, such as today's nongovernmental organizations. Members of these communities of interest understand the problems within their specific range of interest better than anyone else and therefore can find solutions better than anyone else. Communities of interest form an enormous number of invisible nets that span the world, and each individual belongs to several of them.

Through overlapping memberships in a variety of communities of interest, an essential network of interconnection has come into being. These invisible nets are networks of mutual interest, understanding, and problem-solving ability. They have solved and will be able to solve a host of problems so numerous and diverse that governments and intergovernmental organizations could not begin to address them all.

It is the responsibility of our society not to interfere with the growth of communities of interest within a country and across national boundaries, for the strengthening of these communities not only helps citizens of all countries to solve particular problems, but, more importantly, works towards greater world stability by allowing people to identify and solve common problems across national boundaries. Thus, the strengthening of these linking communities of interest allows for a gradual and constructive reorganization of world communities based on cooperation and mutual help. These positive and integrative forces engender world stability on a deeper level than diplomatic bargaining or a mere balance of military forces. Given the perilous situation of the world today, world stability should be a foremost concern of every government, and all governments should thus promote communities of interest.

When Prometheus stole fire from heaven and gave it to mankind, Zeus sent Pandora to earth with her box of evils. Since then, human beings have used fire to improve their lives. However, the evils that escaped from Pandora's box have crept into the human mind and have led to the abuse of that tool, fire, to devastate civilization. Like fire— and all other technologies—information technology is a tool. It is a powerful tool; the extent to which it is used to help or harm humanity is up to human beings themselves.

In the past, possibilities of abusing technology were often overlooked. Technologists and social scientists tend to look for the potential for use rather than abuse, and social scientists and humanists have found it difficult to understand the implications of technology in general. The public has been reluctant to admit that the human mind can be infected by the evils that crept out of Pandora's box. Technology assessment is an important step toward clarifying the situation.

Through the joint efforts of technologists and sociologists, technology assessment analyzes all the conceivable positive and negative impacts of a technology and provides alternatives to alleviate the negative impacts. Unfortunately, however, technology assessment does not always provide reasonable alternatives because the options that alleviate negative impacts of a technology sometimes diminish its positive impacts. Nevertheless, our society must identify the positive and negative impacts of a technology together with its alternatives and also encourage people to think sensibly and make reasonable choices. Through public participation of this sort, people may be provided with the opportunity of understanding a technology and constructing their own ethical standards or means for avoiding its abuse.

Reference

Inose, H. and J. R. Pierce, *Information Technology and Civilization* (W. H. Freeman, 1984).

Notes

1. By standardization, the author does not mean the standardization of information or language. While it may be necessary to standardize the format of information for the convenience of information handling, standardization of the content of information is hazardous for the freedom of expression, and should therefore be avoided. Standardization of language may also be hazardous if it diminishes local languages and dialects because human cultural heritage is predominantly based on the richness of local languages and dialects. Because languages change spontaneously and are highly imprecise, they develop over time. This is another reason to deplore the excess standardization of languages, which would impair this development.

2. In the United States an unusually large proportion of talented software engineers are Americans of Chinese descent. This may be attributed among other things, to the combination of Chinese talent and American education, and may indicate that with appropriate education not only mainland China, but also Hong Kong, Taiwan, Singapore, and other countries or regions in East Asia with a large Chinese population may have enormous potentialities in software production. Software production, which is labor and knowledge intensive, is an appropriate high technology for East Asia where education is highly esteemed in accordance with Confucian tradition, but job opportunities for educated people are insufficient. Similar arguments may also apply to India and other newly industrializing economies.

3. Another paradox may be observed in our information age: computers are getting quickly becoming obsolete because of technological innovation and fierce competition, while human beings are not if appropriate education is provided. Computers are much faster in information processing than human beings, but are much less able to recognize, associate, learn, and create than humans. Nevertheless, while people are investing heavily in building "more intelligent" computers, they tend to feel, especially in the developing part of the word, that new borns are a nuisance rather than a gift. Continuing efforts to dispel poverty and hunger are therefore necessary, and the highest priority should be given to education.

4.   Automation applied to services also causes problems. Users of modern automatic telephone systems are obliged to remember and dial correctly 10 digits or more to get connected. They may feel nostalgic for the good old days when operators of manual switch boards attentively helped them even if they could not exactly remember the numbers they needed. Similarly, passengers at modern train stations are obliged to make sure how much they have to pay and push the right button to buy their tickets. In the old days, someone at the counter gave passengers their tickets and change when told their destinations. These are only a few of many examples in which automation helps service providers but not users. It is necessary to provide user-friendly interface for automated services by taking full advantage of the newest information technology, including artificial intelligence.

5.   As a citizen of Japan where telecommunication service has been largely deregulated and the ensuing competition has been lowering tariffs and improving user interface, the author is generally in favor of deregulation. However, in most countries with the exception of the United States and Britain, deregulation has been much slower, and monopoly in basic telecommunication service is still considered essential. There seems to be no unique and immediate solution to this issue, considering the social and economic difference of various countries. Nevertheless, service providers are obliged to bring as much benefit as they can to their users. Thus, deregulation seems to be an inevitable solution for taking full advantage of the convergence of service mode.

The Information-Oriented Society
and the "Limits of Growth"

BRUNO MESSERLI

Introduction

Eighty-seven million people were added to the world's population in 1987, the largest per-annum increase in recorded history, and virtually all of it occurred in the poorest countries of the world. The "median" age of the world's five billion inhabitants is 23 years. More than 800 million new jobs must be generated in the next decade just to accommodate people already born. Twenty-one developing world cities will have 10 million or more people by the year 2000. The earth's forests are shrinking, its deserts expanding, and its soils eroding, all at record rates. Each year thousands of plant and animal species disappear; the ozone layer may be thinning; and the temperature of the earth appears to be rising, posing a threat of unknown dimensions to virtually all the life support systems on which humanity depends (Fornos, 1988; Brown and Flavin, 1988).

Perhaps it is unfair to ask if a future information-oriented society will be able to solve these crucial global problems or at least produce some contributions to the solution of some of them. But if we accept that the information-oriented society is the society of the future, then we are obliged to raise these fundamental questions and to examine society's capability and competence to answer them. Or should we assume that some of these global problems could even be reinforced and intensified by a too exclusively information-oriented society? The jobless millions, the no longer manageable cities, the increasing economical and technological gap between the developed and developing world are only some of the key factors that might relate to a highly concentrated communication society.

In this sense we can agree that the information-oriented society has both benefits and problems (Inose, 1988). But we must examine the advantages and especially the disadvantages closely in the light of our future global problems. Moreover, we can no longer view our world only from the perspective of a highly technological society that, as a minority, uses the nonrenewable resources of a majority. We need

330

a new and higher orientation: freedom and responsibility cannot be restricted to one part of humanity. Information and communication are tools, not aims for our future global development.

Integrity, Privacy, Security and Responsibility Need More Regulation and More Control

Taking two sections of Inose's paper (1988) together, we can see the close relationship between increasing information and increasing control. If we want to guarantee the integrity, privacy, security, and reliability of all the data coming from diverse sources and concerning both general human ranges of operation and the private sphere, we shall need an ever growing density of regulations. We see this in our daily life in the discussions about new laws, with the permit problem in our data centers, or with the observance of secrecy at different levels of our political and social life. Therefore, it is extremely interesting to notice in Inose's paper how many times we need regulation, a dictating authority, a political decision, etc. to guarantee the functioning of this so-called information-oriented society. The following sentences from his paper give us an idea of this thinking:

—"Access to data files should be placed under strict administrative control."

—"Government should play a leading role in establishing and enhancing liability coverage and backup safeguards."

—"Unless policy makers have foresight and wisdom, the merit of the convergence of service modes will be totally lost."

—"It is the responsibility of governments to restructure regulatory measures so as to take full advantage of the convergence of service modes while ensuring freedom of expressing different views."

I am afraid that we shall have to pay for this new freedom with a lot of lost freedom. What politician or government will be responsible for guaranteeing all this integrity, privacy, security, and reliability? Switzerland is not Japan, and Japan is not the Third World (Muheim 1987).

But more important than the doubts about the realization of all the necessary regulations is the question of freedom and responsibility. Because we all know that not all partners and interest groups in a future information-oriented society will be obliged to assume a common responsibility, we shall have to pay a price. And this price is more legislation, more centralization, more bureaucracy, and more concentrated political power. For me these are unacceptable elements of a future development toward more responsibility on the individual and social level because we urgently need reinforced responsibility for a better and long-term oriented management of our personal environment and our limited resources. I agree that we need a better information system, and I accept also that communication technology will soon bring us new instruments and new possibilities. But we need careful planning to assure the balance between input and output, and we need still more an overall promotion of responsibility to keep our freedom.

Standardization, Media, and Cultural Issues

"Standardization is perhaps one of very few areas of international activity in which countries, industries and individuals of diversified backgrounds and interests can think and act constructively and cooperatively for the good of humanity" (Inose, 1988). Certainly this development has—after the worldwide conflicts that have characterized our century—an extremely positive side. But we are obliged to look always at both sides, the positive and the negative. The complexity of our world includes enormous amounts of information, and with today's technology, the flood of information is increasing so rapidly that we can no longer manage it. We have to reduce it; we need order and often simplification. Conscious human thinking is slow and can handle only a small bit of information at a time. Therefore, storage capacity and the availability of information are powerful instruments that can be used with good or bad effect on human development. I am not so sure if a worldwide media network will be aware of its responsibility. With my long experience in Third World countries, I see the enormous and uncontrollable influence of the technologically most advanced cultures. I agree that we need in future a worldwide exchange of information to manage global problems. I agree also that we need a more pluralistic view in scientific, economic, and cultural thinking, but I disagree with a development of uniformity of mankind through the power of the technologically advanced societies and their media. Just as our civilization every year destroys thousands of plant and animal species, we shall also destroy a lot of cultures whose richness is not in the field of technology. To avoid this danger, we should have well-defined aims for the worldwide application and mobilization of information and communication, e.g., for more solidarity in the management and use of resources, for monitoring the changing global environment, for fair intercultural exchange, for education and dissemination of knowledge, etc., but never for the profit of a powerful economy or technology. How can we realize these ideas in a totally

standardized information-oriented society? The only answer must be
that information is a tool and not an aim, that we need very clear
objectives for the use of a sophisticated information system, and that
we have to develop a strong commitment primarily to responsibility
and only secondarily to technology.

I am afraid of another development. Today we can observe that
human relations decrease when technical possibilities of communication increase. Is it only a question of time until our learning processes
can adjust to this phenomenon (Baitinger, 1987)? I have not yet arrived at an answer, but it is a tragedy that a doubling of the time for
consuming information in the last 15 years has led to a lower standard
of information (Noelle-Neumann, 1988). This means that we need a
quantity and quality of information great enough so that we can still
assess its sources, transfer it to our specific conditions, and form our
own opinion. It is our responsibility to fight against manipulation
through the power of information and to keep our freedom for a better
management of responsible information. The development of pure
technology-oriented information is insufficient, irresponsible, and
harmful to the cultural diversity of our world.

Shift of Work, Hardware, Software, and Developing Countries

In the developed or industrialized countries about 55 percent to
75 percent of the working population can be found in the tertiary
sector. This means that information is a dominant factor. But also in
the secondary sector about 50 percent are occupied in processing and
marketing, in documentation and construction, etc. where information
is an important component. Is it true that working time at the beginning of the next century will be reduced to 30 hours per week? Although the average life span is longer, in the year 2030 we shall work
only 44,000 hours (Bechtler, 1988). I do not want to discuss the probability of these scenarios nor their consequences for life style, mobility,
and recreation, or for cultural and political activities, etc. I simply want
to point out the illusion that developing countries could follow such
a dynamic change of our economic and technically-oriented society.
How can a population, consisting of more than 80 percent self-suffi-
cient farmers, doubling every 25–30 years, working with a low-level
input, having to struggle for existence, even dream of such a development? It is absolutely impossible for these societies to follow developments, when hardware must be imported and when the cost of software is becoming the major cost of information systems (Inose, 1988).

Africa in particular has remained standing with its back to its own hinterland and government leaders have often not yet realized the potential of the domestic economy and society (A. M. Babu, et al., 1987). At the moment we see a development toward more independent thinking, which can be seen in the revitalization of native culture and history, but also of native languages, even for scientific purposes at university levels (Hountondji, 1988). These societies need the development of new and independent thinking and a new social and political consciousness before they can be integrated into a worldwide communication network.

With all these problems and trends in mind, I believe that the dynamic change to a global information-oriented society will create an even stronger state of dependence for the developing world and a bigger gap between the industrialized and nonindustrialized countries. The increasing gradients between centers and peripheries on the national and international level will bring us new economic and political tensions and conflicts. We need something else and something more than only information and communication.

New Objectives and Responsibilities for the Development of Information Systems

Though we are very critical of expanding communication technology, we also use it with success and try to follow its dynamic developments with the greatest interest. Especially in resource management, new methods and new technologies are offered.

Figure 1 (Messerli 1988) shows in the lower part an example from an African country—the Simen mountains in Ethiopia. The ecosystem is differentiated in three subsystems: nature, land use, and man. In the subsystem "nature" we find the interconnected components, such as the abiotic elements of climate, water, soil, relief, geology, natural hazards, and the biotic elements vegetation and fauna. The subsystem "man" contains economic activity, social and demographic characteristics, the political structure, and the cultural background with all its traditional and normative elements. In the middle we have the subsystem "land use." It reflects both the natural suitability and man's activity. If this intervention is ecologically adapted, we have a positive interaction. If this impact is not adapted and results in overuse or misuse, then we disturb or even destroy the natural system, which has a negative effect on the land use potential, and from there to the socioeconomic system of man. In this complex interactive system, we

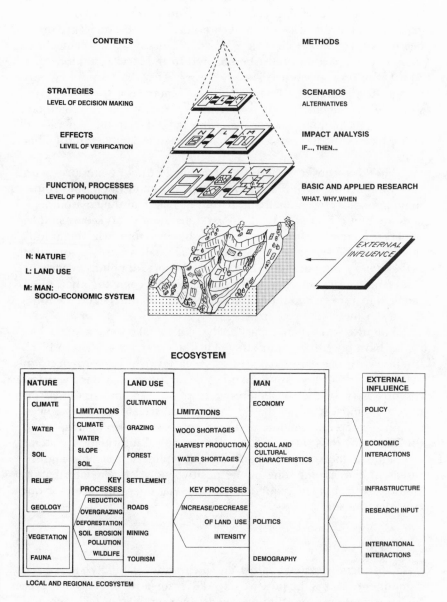

Figure 1: Key processes and limitations in a regionally limited ecosystem of a Third World country and the generalized assessment of a man—environment system

can define certain key processes and some important limitations. Of course, we can never limit a local or regional area so strictly (e.g., a village, a valley, a district, etc) that external influences, such as political decisions, economic interactions, resource use, etc., affect it. Also, such a system can and must be adapted to the local conditions of a Third World or an industrialized country. This short summary only shows the number of variables and their interactions in today's resource management. Therefore, we need better information methodology and technology. If we transfer this basic data in the generalized upper part of the figure, we see what we need today for careful planning.

The lowest level is the understanding of the ongoing processes and the functioning of the system. What, why, and when does something happen between man and nature or man and the environment, and how is it reflected in the land use subsystem? This seems simple, but I recommend strongly that everyone begin to think why things look the way they do where he or she is living. This takes a lot of knowledge and understanding of nature and natural history, of political decisions and economic activities, etc. All these data must come together, often reduced to a so-called "minimum data need," to understand the functioning of the whole system.

The next level is an impact analysis: if we take some action, then it may have one result or another. Finally, we arrive at the top level, where we can develop strategies or scenarios, which allows decision making based on alternatives, in other words, decision making with full responsibility for the consequences. If we want to analyze the effects of certain impacts and to develop substantial scenarios, then we need a sophisticated information methodology that can also be adapted to the Third World's infrastructure. Geographical information systems are fantastic tools for inter- and multidisciplinary basic and applied research. This is only one of the positive sides of new information systems; we could cite many others. But what does this mean for our considerations?

"Limits of Growth"

Information systems allow an integration of highly specialized components; this is the positive effect. The negative effect is that ever higher scientific specialization needs an ever higher technological communication system. How can we control this process? Do we need more responsibility in the development of science or in the development of information technologies? Both are needed. We must be fully aware that more doubts about development of science and technology are turning up. Are we taking into account the risks that are produced by the constantly working motor of competition? Are new innovations only the result of economic forces and processes? Is the motivation of these processes only to raise the standard of living of an industrialized society? Do we really believe that new technologies will improve our quality of life? Who is responsible for the whole if everyone is only competent for a small part? How can we keep our freedom if we live in a densely regulated society, dependent on a flood of disordered information?

There are many questions and no answers. But we have to discuss new answers, new responsibilities, and new ethical guidelines. They must come from society as a whole and include local, national, and international institutions and organizations.

Moreover, we have to take into consideration the crucial problem of a divided world. Figure 2 shows the estimated expenses for basic needs, especially for food. From the fifteenth to the eighteenth centuries, the average population of today's industrialized countries had to spend 80 to 90 percent of their daily working time or energy on survival, especially on providing the food they needed to live. Some small fluctuations were caused by the decrease or increase of population, climatic oscillations, availability of land, etc. The most important change was the so-called agricultural revolution, which was the result of a long cultural history until the Enlightenment, which laid the foundation for scientific and economic societies. Stall-feeding, fertilizer, clover (nitrogen fixing), new products, such as potatoes, etc. are only some key components of this agricultural transformation. Food production increased rapidly, paving the way for the beginning of the industrial revolution. The increasing population could thus be supported, and today we spend only 10 to 20 percent of our daily working time or salary for our daily food. Without going into more detail, we can recognize in this figure the practical outcome of the philosophical and cultural development of the last three centuries.

In comparison, the curve of the poorest developing countries, e.g., in Africa, is very different. Having no written documents, we can reconstruct the daily "price" for providing the daily food only on the basis of the first European descriptions. It was also between 80 to 90 percent, and in this situation the developing countries were confronted immediately with a rapidly increasing population: the result of this unprepared development was the hunger for new land in marginal

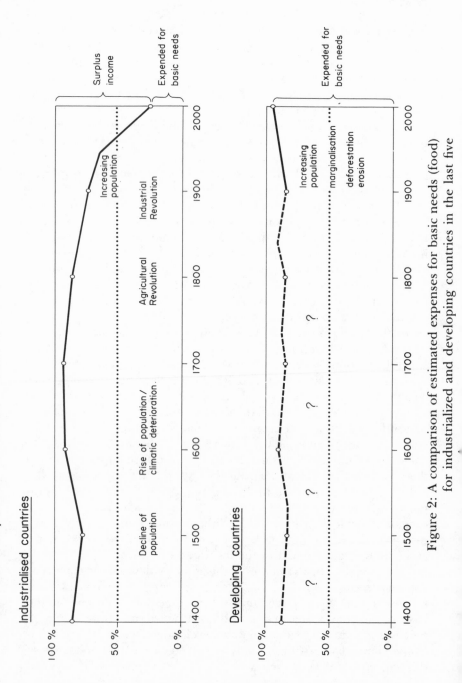

Figure 2: A comparison of estimated expenses for basic needs (food) for industrialized and developing countries in the last five

areas and, as a consequence, deforestation, erosion, decreasing poten-
tiality, partial famine, etc.

This simplified figure clearly shows us that the link between new
technologies and human needs is a crucial problem. Some parts of our
world need something besides a communication technology. Of
course, education by information is very important for these populations, but in a totally different way than for the industrialized countries.
We cannot improve the quality of life around the world with the same
methods and the same Western style of thinking. We have to take into
consideration the diversity of our world. We need a better and decen-
tralized form of communication for better adapted information. Limits
of growth are necessary: the concentration of information is a mistake
and will reinforce the gulf between the rich and the poor world! The
uniform information society is not the proper goal for our future, for
a rich cultural heritage, or for differentiated and ecologically adapted
resource management.

The scientific community must go ahead with new thinking and
new responsibility, but it needs the carrying capacity of the whole
society. We all have to learn that the environment and the resources
of our earth will not adapt to humanity, but that humanity has to adapt
to earth's environment and resources. If we do not begin to learn this
by our own free will now, we shall have to learn it painfully by force
either in our own or in the next generation.

Conclusions

Thesis 1

Information and communication are tools and not aims for our
future global development. Therefore our society has to be primarily
responsibility-oriented, not information-oriented. We can no longer
look on our world from the perspective of a highly technological society
that, as a minority, uses the nonrenewable resources of the majority.

Thesis 2

More information is closely related to more regulation. An information-oriented society will need more legislation, more centralization, and more bureaucracy. This development could lead to a loss of
responsibility at a time when we need more responsibility to manage
local, national, and global problems.

Thesis 3

It is an illusion to believe that we can create new responsibility
through an increasing flood of laws. Increasing governmental activity

is accompanied by decreasing governmental authority. This could be a key problem in a too exclusively information-oriented society.

Thesis 4

The worldwide standardization of information leads to a global cultural uniformity through the domination and power of the technologically and economically most advanced societies and their media. Therefore, we must have clear objectives for the use of standardized and sophisticated information systems: we need more commitment to responsibility than to technology.

Thesis 5

Human relations decrease when technological communications increase. We need a rationality of men and not of machines to solve the increasing problems of our world. But we also need well-adapted information and communications for better vocational training and education, especially for the countries of the Third World.

Thesis 6

The dynamic change in the developed world to an information-oriented society will create even a stronger dependence of the developing world and a wider gulf between the industrialized and nonindustrialized countries.

Thesis 7

The increasing gradients between centers and peripheries on the national and on the international level will bring us new economic and political tensions and conflicts. We need more decentralisation of information and more responsibility for local natural and cultural conditions.

Thesis 8

New information systems are excellent tools for interdisciplinary and multidisciplinary work. But an ever more highly developed scientific specialization demands an ever more highly developed form of technological communication. This process has a cumulative character and could soon become uncontrollable. Limits of growth are necessary.

Thesis 9

Economic competition is the leading factor that produces innovations. New technologies are often the result of economic forces and pressures and not of reasonable and responsible thinking and acting. Thus, more and more doubts about the development of science and technology are turning up. We have to discuss the limits of growth and its relations to freedom to keep our freedom and to understand our responsibility for future development.

References

Baru A. M. 1987. *The State and the Crisis in Africa. In Search of a Second Liberation.* Development dialogue No. 2: 5–29.

Baitinger Urs G. 1987. *Mikroelektronik und Informationstechnik—Das Mittel und die Mitteilung.* Alexander von Humboldt Stiftung. A.v.H.-Magazin Nr. 50: 15–24.

Bechtler Thomas W. 1988. *Die Herausforderung der Flexibilisierung. Wandel der Arbeit in der Dienstleistungsgesellschaft.* NZZ Nr. 134, 11./12. Juni: 25.

Brown L. and Flavin C. 1988. *The State of the World Today.* Development Forum Vol. 2: 1.

Fornos W. 1988. *Population Perspectives.* The Population Institute, USA. Development Forum Vol. 2: 17.

Gaudin M. Th. 1986: *Prospective scientifique et prévision du risque technologique.* Schweiz. Wissenschaftsrat. Wissenschaftspolitik. Beiheft 33: 66–79.

Hountondji Paulin J. 1988. *L'appropriation collective du savoir: Tâches nouvelles pour une politique scientifique.* Genève-Afrique Vol. XXVI, No 1: 49–66.

Inose Hiroshi 1988. *Freedom and Responsibility in Information-Oriented Society.* (In this publication)

Messerli Bruno, et al. 1988. *African Mountains and Highlands. Introduction and Resolutions.* Mountain Research and Development. Vol. 8, No. 2/3: 93–100.

Muheim Franz. 1987. *Welche Politik angesichts der neuen Anforderungen? Die Antwort eines Politikers.* Colloque: La Suisse face aux nouvelles Technologies de l'Information. Genève: 1–15. (Unpublished)

Noelle-Neumann Elisabeth. 1988. *Der Leser von morgen und die Verantwortung der Zeitung.* Vortrag. Schweiz. Verband der Zeitungs- und Zeitschriftenverleger, 18.9.1987, Basel. Telex I/88: 20–25.

Ruh Hans. 1986. *Freiheit und Begrenzung für den Zugriff zum Leben.* Schweiz. Wissenschaftsrat. Wissenschaftspolitik. Beiheft 33: 20–33.

Signer Rolf. 1987. *Von Schwierigkeiten im Umgang mit Informationen—Befunde und Maximen.* Dokumente und Information zur Schweiz. Orts-, Regional- und Landesplanung DISP Nr. 89/90: 23–30.

Sitter Beat. 1987. *Konstruktive und destruktive Wechselwirkungen zwischen Wissenschaft und Ethik.* Vortrag, gehalten vor der Swiss Metra am 13./14. März 1987, Bern. (Unpublished manuscript, 37 pp.)

Index of Names

343